Neuropsychology

To Francis Patrick Bowler

Neuropsychology

A clinical approach

Kevin W. Walsh B.A., M.B.B.S., M.Sc.

Senior Lecturer Department of Psychology, University of Melbourne. Honorary Psychologist, Austin Hospital Melbourne

CHURCHILL LIVINGSTONE
EDINBURGH LONDON AND NEW YORK 1978

CHURCHILL LIVINGSTONE
Medical Division of Longman Group Limited

Distributed in the United States of America by Churchill Livingstone Inc.,
19 West 44th Street, New York, N.Y. 10036 and by
associated companies, branches and representatives throughout
the world.

First Edition 1978
  Reprinted 1978
  Reprinted 1980

ISBN 0 443 01569 4 (Cased)
ISBN 0 443 01570 8 (Limp)

Library of Congress Cataloging in Publication Data

Walsh, Kevin W
  Neuropsychology.

  Bibliography: p. 332
  Includes index.
  1. Neuropsychology.   I. Title.   DNLM: 1. Neurophysiology. 2. Psychophysiology. WL102 W225n
QP360.W34   616.8'04'7   77–1451

Printed in Singapore by
Kyodo-Shing Loong Printing Industries Pte Ltd

Preface

The principal aim of this book is to provide an introduction to neuropsychology which brings together a good deal of the findings, particularly of the past decade, from diverse sources in psychology and the neurological sciences. The accent is on clinical and experimental findings in studies of human subjects with little or no reference to findings from animal experimentation. The material is presented in such a way as to be understandable to those who come to the subject with little or no formal background in biology.

Clinical neuropsychology appears to have at least two roles at the present time (1) in developing further psychology's help in early diagonosis of the nature and location of lesions disrupting brain function; (2) extending our understanding of the psychological processes themselves and thus provide understanding of how the patient's functions are disrupted by his lesion. Though the text has a 'localizationist' structure, this is used solely to further the appreciation of the complex results of lesions in different locations.

The selection of topics is wide though no attempt has been made to make the coverage exhaustive. As usual the selection of topics reflects the writer's bias but it is hoped that a range of major areas has been adequately represented. Equal emphasis is placed on clinical and experimental research approaches and much of the material has been presented in the author's courses and seminars and covers the most commonly encountered problems of the clinic and the most frequently raised questions in the classroom. The introduction of practical courses in neuroanatomy has been of great value in developing a neuropsychological approach in our clinical trainees. For this reason a traditional treatment of neuroanatomy is presented as a background to the study of neuropsychology. Numerous illustrations have been used to try to engender a conception of the nervous system as a three-dimensional set of structures connected through fibre pathways and thus prevent the student from becoming fixated on the cerebral cortex when thinking about psychological function. This should make it easier to understand that a small, strategically placed lesion, for example, may lead to a greater disconnection of brain structures than a very much larger lesion in another area.

The anatomy necessary for understanding *specific* topics in later chapters is laid down in this outline, e.g.
1. the section on the blood supply shows the areas irrigated by the main arteries. This knowledge helps to explain why narrowing of the middle cerebral artery gives rise to a pattern of deficits which partakes of features of lesions of several lobar divisions since the area supplied by the artery cuts across the artificial lobar boundaries;

2. distinctive differences between the effects of lesions of the superolateral as against the basomedial cortex of the frontal lobes is understandable in terms of the different sets of structure with which each is connected;

3. an understanding of the distribution of fibres which cross the midline to join homologous areas of the cortex on the other side of the brain is basic to the understanding of the important work on the 'split-brain' subjects.

Chapter 3 is an endeavour to provide an account in simple terms of neurological conditions which are most likely to be encountered by the neuropsychologist, together with some relevant terminology of the neurosciences, and sufficient details of the commonly used special diagnostic procedures for the student to understand the literature, and for the beginning clinical psychologist to communicate more effectively with his medical colleagues. One has only to place oneself in the position of the naive reader confronted with one of the journals in the neurological sciences to appreciate the need for an acquaintance with this material. The need for a section on elements of neurology has been shown by questions posed by students and psychologists in discussion of case material and journal articles.

Chapters 4 to 8 deal with recent findings in human neuropsychology and are mainly concerned with the questions of localization and lateral specialization of function. In these chapters, examples of a variety of clinical and experimental procedures for tackling neuropsychological problems are cited in detail.

Chapter 9 is concerned with the methodological issues surrounding the assessment of neuropsychological impairment. Many of these are far from resolved and need careful consideration both in training and research. The chapter concludes with further treatment of major clinical topics and some illustrative case histories. No attempt is made to deal exhaustively with the practical methods of assessment as this will be dealt with elsewhere.

It is hoped that the diverse groups who are interested in brain-behaviour relationships in their professions (psychologists, medical students and practitioners, occupational therapists, speech therapists, and others) may gain something from a basic text which brings together recent knowledge of man's higher cortical functions and their assessment by psychological procedures, presented in a manner which can be understood without requiring too much training in academic psychology. It could also form the basis of courses to be integrated with traditional courses in psychology at the intermediate and later years of such programmes.

The author is very much aware of his indebtedness to the numerous texts and articles on the subject and gratefully acknowledges this.

Melbourne, 1977   KWW

Acknowledgements

The author has made every effort to trace the ownership of all copyrighted materials and to acknowledge their use. Regret is expressed for any omission or errors if these have occurred.

Grateful acknowledgement is made to the following authors, publishers and others for their permission to reproduce copyrighted materials. Acknowledgement of permission to reproduce a number of illustrations is given separately with the figure captions. In the case of illustrations from other sources from whom no reply has been received, normal citation is used. The majority of illustrations are the author's own work.

Academic Press and the author for quotations from Dr Kinsbourne's chapter in J.L. MCGAUGH (Ed.), *Psychobiology*, 1971.

American Academy of Neurology and the authors for Table 8.3 from SMITH, A. and SUGAR, O. *Neurology*, 1975, **25**, 813.

Annual Reviews Incorporated for quotation from H.L. TEUBER, *Annual Review of Psychology*, 1955.

Dr David Bowsher and Blackwell Scientific Publications for a quotation from BOWSHER, D. *Introduction to Neuroanatomy*, 1970.

Ciba Foundation and Churchill Livingstone for quotations from MAGOUN in the Ciba Foundation Symposium: *The Neurological Basis of Behaviour*, 1958.

Paul Elek Limited for quotations from J. LEVY in S.J. DIMOND and J.G. BEAUMONT (Eds.), *Hemisphere Function in the Human Brain*, 1974.

Journal of Neurosurgery and the authors for Table 6 from BRAUCH, C. MILNER, B., and RASMUSSEN, T. *Journal of Neurosurgery*, 1964, **21**, 399.

Oxford University Press for a quotation from GESCHWIND in *Brain*, 1965, **88**, further material from the journal *Brain*.

The Regents of the University of California for quotations from E. CLARKE and C.D. O'MALLEY. *The Human Brain and Spinal Cord*, University of California Press, 1968., and a quotation from E.C. CARTERETTE (Ed.), *Brain Function: Speech Language and Communication*, University of California Press, 1966.

University of Chicago Press for quotations from J.H. BREASTED. *The Edwin Smith Surgical Papyrus*, 1930.

Dr Denis Williams and Elsevier/North-Holland Biomedical Press for two case descriptions from P.J. VINKEN and G.W. BRUYN, (Eds.) *Handbook of Clinical Neurology*, Volume 2, 1969.

Personal Acknowledgements

The writer of a textbook is indebted to a large number of people. I would like to thank all those research workers whose work I have described and whose ideas I have so freely borrowed and I trust that I have done justice to their work.

The text was written with the encouragement of two Chairmen of the University of Melbourne, Department of Psychology, Professor Alastair Heron and Professor Gordon Stanley. Professor Austin Doyle of the Austin Hospital, Melbourne provided the opportunities for clinical practice in neuropsychology which form the background of the book.

In the preparation of the manuscript, I was ably assisted by Sandra Carter, Edna Lenny, and Sandra Licquorice, and the technical assistance with photography was given by Geoffrey De Jonge and Maxwell Rademacher.

In an interdisciplinary area such as neuropsychology, it is impossible to proceed without constant help from colleagues in a variety of professions. In this case may I thank all those psychologists, neurologists, and neurosurgeons who gave so willingly of their time to help the author clarify his material. I am conscious of a deep debt of gratitude to that most penetrating and helpful critic Dr Peter F. Bladin whose intellectual stimulation and encouragement through the long period of gestation and the painful process of parturition, enabled the work to be brought to the light of day.

Finally my graduate assistants Maureen Molloy, Mary Kotzmann and Carole Burton together with other senior students provided the maintenance of motivation when application might otherwise have flagged.

Kevin Walsh

Contents

1. History of Neuropsychology

Ancient civilization

The earliest written information we possess on localization of function in the brain is contained in the Edwin Smith Surgical Papyrus. The copy acquired by Smith in Luxor in 1862 is thought to date from the seventeenth century B.C., while orthographic and other evidence would place its origin some thousand years earlier, somewhere between 2500 and 3000 B.C. It contains the earliest known anatomical, physiological and pathological descriptions and has been described as the earliest known scientific document.

The papyrus contains reports of some 48 cases of observations and description of treatment of actual cases many of them suffering from traumatic lesions of various parts of the body including many injuries to the head and neck. Translation of the papyrus was undertaken in 1920 and the detailed examination of the text and commentary was published by Breasted in 1930. It is in this papyrus that a word for brain appears for the first time. The papyrus 'opens the door on cortical localization of function with its description of injuries to the brain' (Gibson, 1962).

The material of the papyrus may be divided into two parts namely the original text and the explanatory comments which have been added at a later date to expand and clarify the text. That these glosses which appear on the back (verso) of the manuscript are of a much later date, is witnessed by their explanation of terms in the text which had, by the time of our extant copy, apparently become obsolete.

Of the 48 cases the first eight deal directly with injuries to the head and brain. Though some of the injuries may have been sustained in civilian occupations, it is more than likely that many of them, as well as wounds described in other parts of the body, were sustained in war. If so, this would be the earliest recording of the contribution of the study of war wounds to the study of brain-behaviour relationships, a source which has been of paramount importance in more recent times.

The following cases serve to illustrate the careful observations made by the ancient medical practitioner. The direct quotations are from Breasted (1930). Thirteen cases of most interest to the neurological scientist have been reprinted in Wilkins (1965).

1. The examination of case four reads in part—

If thou examinest a man having a gaping wound in his head, penetrating to the bone, (and) splitting his skull, thou shouldst palpate his wound. Shouldst thou find something disturbing therein under thy fingers, (and) he shudders exceedingly. . .

The shuddering which occurred upon the surgeon's palpation may refer to convulsive movements produced by pressure upon the exposed brain. It is reminiscent of the extraordinary case described by Gibson(1962).

2. Case six described a skull fracture with rupture of the coverings of the brain.

If thou examinest a man having a gaping wound in his head, penetrating to the bone, smashing his skull, (and) rendering open the brain of his skull, thou shouldst palpate his wound. Shouldst thou find that smash which is in his skull (like) those corrugations which form in molten copper, (and) something therein throbbing (and) fluttering under thy fingers, like the weak place of an infant's crown before it becomes whole—when it has happened there is no throbbing (and) fluttering under thy fingers until the brain of his (the patient's) skull is rent open—(and) he discharges blood from his nostrils, (and) he suffers with stiffness in his neck, (conclusion in diagnosis).

The commentator has written two glosses in clarification:

Gloss A

As for: 'Smashing his skull, (and) rendering open the brain of his skull,' (it means) the smash is large, opening to the interior of his skull, (to) the membrane enveloping his brain, so that it breaks open his fluid in the interior of his head.

Gloss B

As for: 'Those corrugations which form on molten copper,' it means copper which the coppersmith pours off (rejects) before it is forced into the mould, because of something foreign upon it like wrinkle.

Here is a clear description of the meninges and an awareness of the cerebrospinal fluid which bathes the brain, together with a picturesque but apt description of the appearance of the brain's convolutions.

3. In a further example (case eight) we are introduced to statements which obviously relate brain injury to disordered function, that is, the earliest recorded findings in neurophysiology or functional neurology.

If thou examinest a man having a smash of his skull, under the skin of his head, while there is nothing at all upon it, thou shouldst palpate his wound. Shouldst thou find that there is a swelling protruding on the outside of that smash which is in his skull, while his eye is askew because of it, on the side of him having that injury which is in his skull; (and) he walks shuffling with his sole, on the side of him having the injury which is in his skull. . .

The ancient Egyptian has noted that injury to the brain may affect other parts of the body, here the eye and the lower limb. The shuffling of the foot presumably refers to the weakness of one side of the body produced by damage to the motor pathways from their origin in the cortex of the brain, what would now be termed hemiparesis. The manuscript had been written so long before that the commentator had to explain the obsolete word for shuffle. The physician who wrote the manuscript also appears to have been aware that the effects of brain injury varied according to the side of the brain receiving the injury. Breasted notes that the physician has reported weakness of the limb on the same side as the head injury and suggests that the physician may have been misled by a *contre-coup* effect. If so, this could be the first of innumerable occasions in the history of neurology where an incorrect inference has been made on the basis of accurate observation through lack of sufficient information. The *contre-coup* effect refers to the fact that trauma to the head may produce injury to the brain either beneath the site of external injury (*coup*) or to an area of brain opposite to the external injury (*contre-coup*). Examples are depicted in Figure 3.14. Since damage to the motor region of the brain produces weakness or paralysis of the opposite side of the body a contre-coup injury may give the appearance of weakness on the same side as the scalp or skull wound.

Apart from these examples of effects resulting from brain injury the papyrus also describes several effects of spinal injury, e.g., seminal emission, urinary incontinence and quadriplegia as a result of injury to the cervical portion of the spine. However, there appears to be no evidence that the author considered the brain and spinal cord to be part of a single system.

Turning from Egypt to the other ancient cradle of civilization in the Tigris and Euphrates valleys we find evidence that medical and surgical practice was well organized and legally regulated in this region in the latter part of the third millennium B.C. However, information from this civilization was recorded on fragile clay tablets which have largely perished and even the few surviving fragments from a much later period provide us with no evidence of knowledge of brain-behaviour relationships possessed by these great peoples. It is unfortunate that no surgical treatise, if such existed, has survived from ancient Assyria and Babylon to compare with the Egyptian papyri.

Craniotomy

No history of the brain and behaviour, no matter how brief, would be complete without reference to the neurosurgical procedure of craniotomy or surgical opening of the skull. This serious and difficult surgical intervention was carried out with extraordinary frequency from late Paleolithic and Neolothic times and has continued without interruption down to the present century. Whether such procedures also included operation upon the brain itself is open to conjecture. Some of the interventions show associated skull fractures but many do not. It is likely that only a relatively small proportion of operations was undertaken for traumatic injury.

The widespread use of craniotomy is evidenced by the discovery of prehistoric trepanned skulls from Europe (Italy, France, Austria, Germany, the Netherlands, England), Africa (Algeria, Rhodesia), South America (Peru, Bolivia, Colombia), North America and numerous islands of the South Pacific region.

In some places such operations continued in their primitive form into the twentieth century. Apparently no skulls showing prehistoric trepanation have been reported from China, Vietnam or India (Gurdjian, 1973).

Early instruments were made of obsidian or stone while, with the development of later civilizations, metallic instruments of iron and bronze were employed. Hundreds of examples of trepanation have been reported from the Peruvian civilizations beginning with the Paracas Culture around 3000 B.C. and extending up to the end of the Inca civilization in the sixteenth century A.D. In their examination of these pre-Columbian craniotomies Graña, Rocca and Graña (1954) have provided us with illustrations of (1) operations in every part of the human skull; (2) operative openings of different shapes, circular, oval, rectangular, triangular, and irregular; (3) sets of craniotomy instruments from different eras which include chisels, osteotomes, scalpels, and retractors as well as bandages and tourniquets.

That many patients successfully survived such major cranial surgery is amply attested by skull specimens which show more than one surgical opening and having evidence (such as the bony changes around the opening) of different dates of operation in the same individual's lifetime. As many as five separate craniotomies have been discovered in a single specimen.

In 1953 Graña and his colleagues successfully employed a set of these ancient instruments for the relief of a subdural haematoma (a large clot of blood pres-

Fig. 1.1 Ancient Peruvian tumi

sing on the brain) in a patient who had suffered a head injury resulting in aphasia and right hemiplegia.

An elegant example from the Peruvian collection of instruments is shown in Figure 1.1. Known as a tumi, it depicts on its handle an operation on a patient where the surgeon is employing a similar instrument.

One can only speculate about the reasons for many of these early operations. Gurdjian lists as possible indications for operation headaches, the releasing of demons from the cranial space and for certain religious and mystical exercises. . .' also 'the fact that some of the openings in the skull have been repaired with silver alloy suggests surgical treatment for the possible skull wound caused in battle.' (Gurdjian, 1973, p.3).

How much evidence regarding brain functions was brought to light by these ancient operations is lost to us because of the absence of a written language among these various early peoples.

Classical Greece

The most frequently referred to writer from this period is Hippocrates. As Clarke and O'Malley (1968) point out, the Hippocratic writings were clearly the product of a group of physicians between the latter part of the fifth century B.C. and the middle of the fourth century B.C. These physicians probably had little familiarity with the human brain because of the aversion for dissection of the human body which existed in Greece at that time; but they did open the skulls of certain animals. Despite this lack of anatomical knowledge they considered that the brain was the seat of the soul or of mental functions and offered comments which showed that they had made very careful observation of their patients. Many would agree with McHenry (1969) that the Hippocratic tract *On the Sacred Disease* contains antiquity's best discussion of the brain and demonstrates the care with which a number of epileptic patients were studied. Another of the Hippocratic writers observed that damage to one hemisphere of the brain produced spasms or convulsions on the other side of the body though little was made of this observation and it appears to have been forgotten in the period which followed. Hippocrates also 'warned against prodding blindly at a wound of the temporal area of the skull lest paralysis of the contralateral side should ensure' (Gibson, 1969, p.5).

The ventricular localization hypothesis

This theory of localization of function postulated that the mental processes or faculties of the mind were located in the ventricular chambers of the brain. The cavities were conceived of as cells, the lateral ventricles forming the first cell, the third ventricle the second cell, while the fourth ventricle made up the third cell. Hence this doctrine is often termed the Cell Doctrine of brain function.

In its almost fully developed form the ventricular doctrine was first put forward by the Church Fathers Nemesius and Saint Augustine around the turn of the fourth century A.D. and it was to remain very much the same for well over one thousand years, that is, well into the beginning of the Renaissance. Outlines of the doctrine together with excellent pictorial representations are given in Magoun (1958) and Clarke and Dewhurst (1972).

The ventricular theory had its roots in a number of earlier ideas particularly those of Aristotle and Galen. Aristotle had discussed the separate sense modalities and their contribution to perception. To account for the unity of sense experience he proposed a mechanism of integration which he called the common sense or *sensus communis*. Aristotelian psychology divided mental activity into a number of faculties of thought and judgment, e.g., imagination, fantasy, cogitation, estimation, attention and memory. These faculties were to become allotted to the ventricular chambers in the Cell Doctrine. Even as early as 300 B.C. Herophilus of Alexandria had localized the soul in the fourth ventricle.

Galen, in the second century A.D. contributed his theory of the psychic pneuma or gas and, though he himself did not propound the ventricular theory he contributed to it in no small way. The reverence with which the writings of the 'prince of physicians' were held in the centuries which followed helped to set the doctrine in a form which was to remain unchanged for the next millenium. Unfortunately, Galen's followers were to copy his ideas slavishly without developing further his knowledge of the brain's anatomy and his careful and detailed observations of behavioural change. As Gibson (1969) has it, Galen's 'brand of orthodoxy overcame medical science for a thousand years so that it required a Leonardo and a Vesalius to overcome it.'

With the intellectual ascendancy of the Arabic speaking peoples around the eighth century all the important Greek medical works were translated into Arabic and preserved in this way for some five hundred years until retranslated, this time into Latin, where they formed the basis of medical science at the beginning of the Renaissance and, indeed, long after. The anatomy of the great Arabian medical writers, Avicenna, Hali Abbas, and Rhazes around the tenth century depended to a great extent on translations of Galen.

Galen had incorporated into his system the knowledge of the anatomy of the ventricles already present in Alexandrian medicine. He described the ventricles in detail and, though he laid the foundation for the final form which the Cell Doctrine was to take, did not himself do more than hint at the association of the ventricles with intellectual functions preferring to locate the faculties in the brain substance itself.

Magoun (1958) gives the following concise account of Galen's theory of the 'psychic gas'.

Nutritive material passed from the alimentary canal through the portal vein to the liver, where natural spirits were formed. These ebbed and flowed in the veins, taking origin from the liver, to convey nutriment to all parts of the body. A portion of these natural spirits passed across the septum, from the right to the left side of the heart, and joined with material drawn from the lungs to form the vital spirits. These ebbed and flowed to all parts of the body through the arteries, taking origin from the heart, to provide heat and other vital requirements. A part of these vital spirits passed to the base of the brain, to be distilled there in a marvellous vascular net, the rete mirabile, and to mix with air inspired into the cerebral ventricles through the porous cranial base, for, at this time, the pulsing of the brain in the opened cranium was conceived as an active process, much like that of thoracic respiration. As a consequence, animal spirits were formed, and 'animal', in this use, was derived from the Latin 'anima' and Greek 'psyche', meaning soulful, and was not animal in any lowly sense. This psychic pneuma, stored in the brain ventricles, passed by the pores of the nerves to the peripheral organs of sense and to the muscles, to subserve sensory and motor functions. Its equivalently important role in managing central functions of the brain was effected either within the ventricles themselves or in the immediately bordering substance of their walls.

Sherrington pointed out how the movement of the brain which is a passive or transmitted pulsation misled Galen and his followers by apparently supporting their notion of the ventricular system as pumping the fluid to different parts of the body. Sherrington supposed that Galen had not only seen it in the scalp of the young child before the vault closes but that he had observed it often after trauma since Galen had written that 'war and the gladiatorial games were the greatest school of surgery,' (Sherrington, 1951).

It was as cells to contain the animal spirits that the ventricular chambers took on their great significance. A number of writers have pointed out that, of course, the ventricular cavities are the most striking features on gross dissection of the untreated brain. Sherrington comments 'It is interesting to speculate how much this concentration on meninges and ventricular cavities, an obsession that was to dominate thought about the brain for nearly two thousand years, was due to the simple fact that, unless fixed and hardened, the brain resembles an amorphous gruel, of which one of the few distinguishing features is that it possesses cavities.'

After Galen there was no significant development of anatomical knowledge for many centuries and Galen's influence can be most clearly seen in the slavish copying by those who followed of the *rete mirabile* a network of blood vessels at the base of the brain. This network which appears in ungulates such as the pig and the ox is not found in man and those who followed Galen's findings for so long were apparently unaware that, although the master had knowledge of the human brain and that of the Barbary ape, his neuroanatomical descriptions were mainly derived from the ox. This also explains how his descriptions of the ventricles seem erroneous for man while they are highly accurate for the ox.

Two early Sixteenth Century woodcuts serve to illustrate the Cell Doctrine. Because of its clarity, Figure 1.2 has been reproduced very frequently. It is from an encyclopedia produced by the Carthusian monk, Gregor Reisch about 1504. It shows the senses of smell, taste, sight, and hearing connected to the *sensus communis* at the front of the first chamber. This chamber is the seat of fantasy and imagination, the second of cogitation and estimation and the third memory. There is also a possible depiction of part of the cerebral convolutions. The label *vermis* or worm would seem to refer to the choroid plexus which passes through the opening which connects the lateral ventricle (first cell) with the third ventricle (second cell) (see Fig. 1.3).

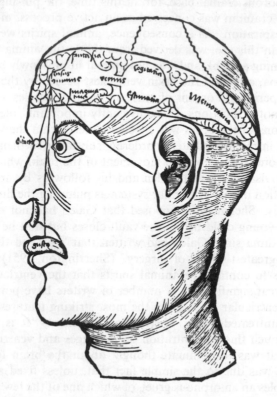

Fig 1.2 Cell doctrine. Gregor Reisch (1504)

The second illustration is noteworthy for its reproduction of the *rete mirabile* at this late date. It is taken from Magnus Hundt, 1501 (Fig. 1.4) and illustrates not only the Cell Doctrine but also the cranial nerves according to Galen's classification together with the skull sutures and the different layers of the scalp. Magoun (1958) gives us a liberal interpretation of the Cell Doctrine.

'On passing to the brighter functional aspects of these early views, they first proposed that incoming information from a peripheral receptor was conveyed to a sensory portion of the brain, where it could be interrelated with other afferent data. Activity was thence transmitted to a more central integrative region, equivalently accessible to internal impressions related to sense and to general memory. Last, activity was capable of involving a motor portion of the brain, so as to initiate movement or behaviour. The sequential ordering of these Aristotelian faculties from the front to the back of the brain conveyed an implication that central neural function normally proceeded through such successive stages. Such conceptualization is not excessively different from that reached by Sherrington in his founding studies of modern neurophysiology nor from that which confronts us continually today.'

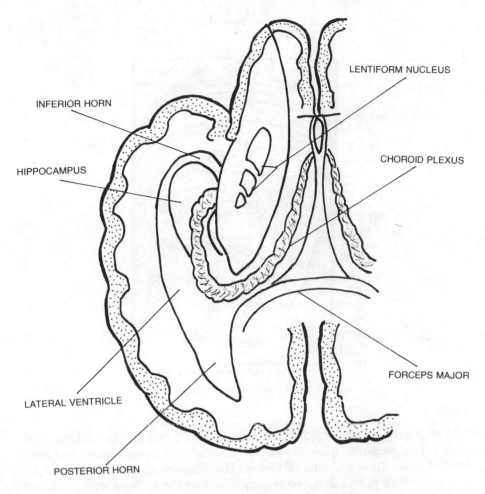

Fig. 1.3 Worm like appearance of the choroid plexus

This interpretation may be overgenerous but the crudity of depiction should not be taken as the only measure of the state of development of ideas. In reviewing such ideas from antiquity Woolam (1958) warns of the danger of imputing too much knowledge to our predecessors. 'The great scientific names of the ancient world, Aristotle, Democritus, Galen and Hippocrates have received so much tribute, that it is easy to fall into the belief that all our modern scientific belief already existed in embryo as it were in the ancient world. . . Hippocrates described how a blow on the head could produce paralysis on the opposite side of the body. It is not too difficult to fall into the trap of reading backwards from our knowledge of the anatomy of the brain and see in this statement the first reference to the crossing of the pyramidal tracts. The study of the knowledge of the anatomy of the brain displayed in the Hippocratic Corpus proves a salutary corrective to this view.'

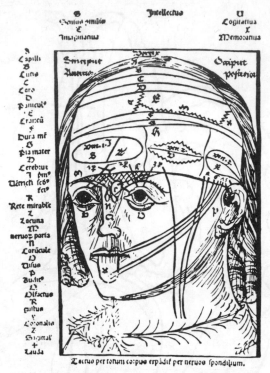

Fig. 1.4 Cell doctrine. Magnus Hundt (1501)

Vesalius

With Andreas Vesalius (1514–1564) came the era in which careful scientific observations began to triumph over the dogmatic statements which had been handed down from the time of Galen. His anatomical masterpiece, the *De humani corporis fabrica* and its companion volume the *Epitome* were published at Basle in 1543. This work has been called the embodiment of the spirit of the Renaissance and many have considered it the most influential factor in establishing the modern era of observation and research.

Vesalius was a pupil of Sylvius (1478–1555) who was known as a great follower of Galen. Vesalius was instructed in the ventricular hypothesis and recounts how he and his fellow students were shown the illustration from Gregor Reisch's *Margarita philosophica* (Fig. 1.2) which they had to copy as an adjunct to their lectures on the functions of the ventricular chambers. The teaching of the time is well preserved in the following extract which records what Vesalius learned at the University of Louvain.

'Indeed, those men believed that the first or anterior, which was said to look towards the forehead, was called the ventricle of the sensus communis because the nerves of five senses are carried from it to their instruments, and odors, colors, tastes, sounds, and tactile qualities are brought into this ventricle by the aid of those nerves. Therefore, the chief use of this ventricle was considered to be that of receiving the objects of the five senses, which we usually call the common senses, and transmitting them to the second ventricle, joined by a passage to the first so that the second might be able to imagine, reason, and cogitate about those objects; hence cogitation or reasoning was assigned to the latter ventricle. The third ventricle (our fourth) was consecrated to memory, into which the second desired that all things sufficiently reasoned about those objects be sent and suitably deposited' (Clarke and O'Malley, 1968, p.468).

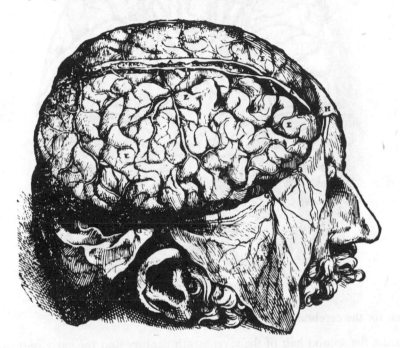

Fig. 1.5 Brain anatomy. Vesalius

The detail of Vesalius' anatomy (Figs. 1.5 and 1.6) is in sharp contrast to the crudity of the earlier sixteenth century woodcuts. However, despite their artistic excellence and their dependence upon actual observation of anatomical specimens, the influence of his early Galenical teaching can be seen in the perpetuation of errors which cannot have been present in dissections. Though later commentators have stressed his anti-Galenism and though he was attacked by his contemporaries for his departure from their slavish following of the Galenical teachings, Vesalius himself was at pains to point out his respect for the greatness of the 'prince of physicians and preceptor of all'. What he would not condone was an indiscriminate acceptance of every one of Galen's teachings. His greatness lay in using the observational method to confirm earlier postulations and to note where the observations were at variance with accepted dogma.

Unfortunately, this sudden increase in the knowledge of structural neuroanatomy was not paralleled by an increase in knowledge of the brain's functions and this discrepancy between anatomy and physiology continued well into the twentieth century.

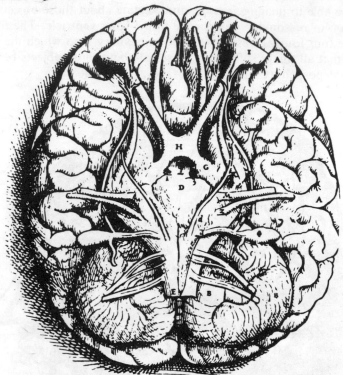

Fig. 1.6 Brain anatomy. Vesalius

Search for the cerebral organ

During the second half of the seventeenth century and the early part of the eighteenth a number of separate investigators attempted to find the one part of the brain that was the seat of the mind or soul. The essential feature of these attempts is the fact that they were based on speculation not on clinical observation or experimentation. The most well-known of the theories was that of Descartes who, in selecting the pineal gland as the seat of the soul argued that it was so strategically situated with regard to the ventricular chambers that it could influence and be influenced by the flow of the spirits between them —'a certain very small gland situated in the middle of its (the brain's) substance and so suspended above the channel by which the spirits in its anterior cavities have communication with those of the posterior, that the slightest movements which take place in it can greatly alter the course of these spirits; and reciprocally that the least changes which occur to the course of the spirits can greatly alter the movements of this gland' (From Clarke and O'Malley, 1968, p.471).

Descartes reasoned that since our experience of the world is unitary despite the multiple organs of sense, each of which is double, there must be some place where these separate sense impressions could come together 'before they reach the soul'. 'It can easily be conceived how these images or other impressions could unite in this gland through the mediation of the spirits that fill the cavities of the brain. There is no other place in the body where they could be thus united unless it be in this gland' (op. cit. p.472).

Other writers thought that this cerebral organ or organ of the soul might be represented by such structures as the corpus striatum (Willis), the white matter (Vieussens), or the corpus callosum (Lancisi). The fact that many were preoccupied with the search for a single vital structure does not mean that excellent observations and inferences were not made during the seventeenth and eighteenth centures. However they were greatly overshadowed by the search, and the clues to the nature of brain organization found in such fine examples as those cited by Gibson (1962) seem to have been overlooked when interest in the problem of localization blossomed some two centuries later.

Faculty psychology and discrete lozalization

In the period which followed, the notion of the unity of conscious experience gave way to the 'faculty psychology' which divided mental processes into a number of separate, specialized abilities and this was to precipitate the search for the neural substrate of such faculties or powers of the mind. In founding the system which came to be known as phrenology, Gall leaned heavily on the lists of faculties provided by the Scottish philosophers Tomas Reid (1710–1796) and Dugald Stewart (1753–1828). Gall's was not the only attempt to relate separate mental functions to discrete parts of the brain but it was certainly the most influential, its influence persisting for a century. For all its drawbacks phrenology proved a more fertile notion than the earlier search for 'the single organ'.

Gall taught his new doctrine in Vienna from 1796 on, and was soon joined by Spurzheim who in fact coined the term 'phrenology' and was to develop a moralizing version of Gall's ideas which was to become as keenly supported as it was contested. The essence of this movement is simply stated. The brain is composed of a number of separate organs each of which controls a separate innate faculty, i.e., there are as many cerebral organs for mental processes as there as faculties. The location of the faculties according to Spurzheim is shown in Figure 1.7.

The development of the cerebral organs led to prominences in the individual's skull so that by the process of 'cranioscopy' or palpation of the prominences the practitioner of phrenology could divine the nature of the person's propensities.

Gall stressed the role of the cortex in which he located his faculty organs. This was an advance since the cortex had been considered relatively unimportant up to this stage. Gall made a number of important discoveries in neuroanatomy but these have been greatly overshadowed by his speculative physiology. When one reads the original work one is struck by the extraordinary lack of evidence given in support of what seem today strange and sweeping claims. Nevertheless it certainly stimulated the scientific thought of the period. Boring (1929) called it 'an instance of a theory which, while essentially wrong, was just enough right to further scientific thought.' Although not providing proof it established the belief in many minds that the localizationist position was a tenable one.

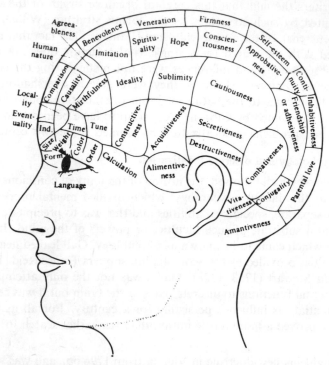

Fig. 1.7 A phrenological map (Figure 19.1 p318, *The Science of Mental Life*, 2nd edn., courtesy of Harper & Row) G.A. Miller and R. Buckout (1973) Psychology.

The most powerful and influential opponent of phrenology was Flourens (1794–1867). He is commonly credited with beginning the movement that resulted in the holistic theory of brain function which held that mental functions are not dependent upon particular parts of the brain but, rather, that it functions as a whole.

Flourens experimented mainly with birds and demonstrated that animals may recover after ablations of part of their central nervous systems and that the same recovery takes place irrespective of the site of the ablation. This work anticipated the notion of equipotentiality, the ability of other parts of the brain to take over the functions of damaged neural tissue. Flourens stated quite clearly that he did not believe that the nervous system was a homogeneous mass but he did believe that it operated in a concerted, integrated fashion unlike the theory of discrete localization.

Lesion studies of the nineteenth century

During the long controversy between the supporters of Gall on the one hand and those of Flourens on the other, what one writer refers to as the controversy between the skull palpators and the bird brain ablators, numerous clinicians were making valuable observations on brain-behaviour relationships. Unfortunately even the more important of these were not seen in their true light because of their association in people's minds with one or other side of the controversy, e.g., Bouillaud in 1825 pointed out the frequent association of loss of language with lesions of the anterior or frontal lobes but clouded the contribution by stating that this could be taken to support Gall's contention that the faculty of language lay in this region. It was quite some time later that Broca was to publish his well known dictum. Even when Dax read a paper in 1836 clearly relating the left half of the brain with aphasia it remained unpublished until his son brought it forward 25 years later. A number of factors may have conspired to bring about this delay, not the least of which may have been Dax's political unpopularity in the region at the time he delivered his paper. It is clear that Dax understood the specific role of the left hemisphere in the production of aphasia since he searched for cases of right handed aphasics with right hemisphere lesions but was unable to find one such case.

Broca and the localization of speech

Broca's role in this history of functional localization is a particularly complex one which has been discussed in many places. Joynt's (1964) paper provides a brief but clear outline of the main contentions. Broca himself made no claim for priority in the discovery of the relation between the frontal region and language disturbance. He acknowledged more than once the contributions of Bouillaud. His sustained and systematic observations did however greatly advance the cause of the localization of function in the brain.

In 1861 Broca exhibited the brain of his patient 'Tan' who had died only the day before and who had in life lost the power of speech so that the only word which he was able to utter was 'Tan'. The lesion lay in the posterior part of the left frontal lobe. Later in 1861 Broca exhibited a similar case which confirmed his notion that the lesion in cases of aphasia was situated in the frontal lobes of the brain. At this stage, like the cautious observer he was, Broca posed the question as to whether a more exact localization was possible, leaving the question open for further investigation.

'It is a much more doubtful question to know if the faculty of articulate speech is dependent upon the whole anterior lobe or particularly upon one of its convolutions; in other words, to know if the localization of cerebral faculties happens by faculty and by convolution, or only by groups of faculties or by groups of convolutions. Further observations must be collected with the object of solving this question. It is necessary for this purpose to indicate exactly the name and place of the diseased convolutions and, if the lesion is very extensive, to seek, wherever possible by anatomical examination, the place or rather the convolution where the disease appears to have begun' (Clarke and O'Malley, 1968, pp.496-497).

However he did consider that even his first observations were more consistent with the system of localization by brain convolutions than the phrenological notion that he termed the 'system of bumps'. Even with the further accumulation of cases over the next two years he was still restrained in his statements. 'Here are 8 cases where the lesion is situated in the posterior portion of the third frontal convolution... and, a most remarkable thing, in all of these patients the lesion is on the left side. I do not dare to make a conclusion and I await new findings.' (Benton, 1965). At this time Broca also speculated on the possibility of localizing other functions than speech. Finally, in 1885 Broca published his famous dictum which was to become such a landmark in the history of brain function—'Nous parlons avec l'hémisphère gauche.'

Broca's work stimulated a good deal of clinical research into the anatomical basis of language and numerous workers published findings in his support and soon others began to report observations which supported the view of localization in other areas of functioning.

Broca himself noted, with other workers, that exceptions to the location of language in the left hemisphere appeared to occur in left-handed individuals and from such observations began the notion that a crossed relationship existed between hand preference and hemispheric dominance for language, a notion that has bedevilled us ever since and one that is only now beginning to be clarified (See Ch. 8).

Wernicke and the beginning of modern neuropsychology

In 1874, several years after Broca's demonstration of the importance of the left posterior frontal region for spoken language Wernicke described a case where a lesion of the left superior temporal gyrus caused difficulty in the comprehension of speech. The addition of this finding to that of Broca meant that at least two separate functions could be affected by lesions in two separate locations. This could not fail to reinforce the ideas of those leaning towards a theory of localization and the search for similar 'centres' for other mental functions was greatly stimulated.

Wernicke's place in the history of brain function has been overlooked by most writers. Even the comprehensive and thoroughly documented work of Clarke and O'Malley does not mention him while other writers see him as merely subscribing to the notion that the 'discovery of a lesion in a particular area of the brain in an individual with a concomitant definite type of disturbance (signifies) that the area containing the lesion is in the "centre" for the function that had been impaired. .' (Luria, 1966, p.12).

Geschwind (1966, 1967) considers that Wernicke's contribution was very much greater, pointing out that his paper on receptive aphasia provided a potentially productive theoretical approach which made possible scientific method in the study of aphasia. 'On the basis of this theory it was possible to predict the existence of syndromes not previously seen and to devise experimental means of testing hypotheses' (Geschwind, 1966, p.4).

'Wernicke's reasoning was simple. He applied Meynert's teaching on the fiber tracts of the brain to the problem of aphasia. The phrenologists, he argued, had been wrong in their attempt to localize such complex mental attributes as magnanimity or filial love; what was actually localizable were much simpler perceptual and motor functions. All the complex array of human intellectual attributes must somehow be woven from these threads of different texture. The cortex could at its simplest provide two means of achieving this higher integration, it could store sensory traces in cells for long periods of time and, by means of association fiber tracts, it could link together different parts of the system.' (op. cit. p.5).

Subsequent workers such as Lichtheim (1885) and Dejerine (1892) used this method both to predict and explain specific defects of psychological processes with localized brain lesions. Geschwind summarizes Wernicke's position in the following way.

'Wernicke was one of the first to see clearly the importance of the connections between different parts of the brain in the building up of complex activities. He rejected both of the approaches to the nervous system which even today are often presented as the only possible ones. On the one hand, he opposed the doctrine of the equipotentiality of the brain; on the other, he rejected the phrenological view which regarded the brain as a mosaic of innumerable distinct centers. He asserted that complex activities were learned by means of the connections between a small number of functional regions which dealt with the primary motor and sensory activities. Although this third view dominated research on the neurological basis of behaviour for a period of nearly 50 years, it has been omitted almost entirely from the discussions of the higher functions in recent times'. (Geschwind, 1967, p.103).

Wernicke's point of view has been fully developed in Geschwind's logical analysis and development of the notion of 'the disconnexion syndrome' described later in this chapter (Geschwind, 1965a,b,c).

The cortical map makers

From the era of Broca and Wernicke until well into the twentieth century there were numerous reports of the discovery of similar localized centres in the cortex so that maps of the brain surface with functional labels attached to different areas appeared frequently in the literature. The cortical cartographers were aided by the widespread acceptance of associationism in the new science of psychology which was beginning to assert its independence. They were also in tune with the discoveries on the finer anatomical detail of the cortex and its physiology. The diagrams of the cortical map makers began to relate these latter findings such as the location of primary sensory and motor functions (mainly derived from ablation and stimulation experiments in animals) to the human brain and to add possible sites for higher mental processes many of which were as speculative as the assignment of functions to particular areas by the phrenologists.

Cytoarchitecture and myeloarchitecture

. Cytoarchitectonics refers to the study of the architecture of cells or the disposition of cells and their type and density in the layers of the cortex. This study was dependent on the discovery of methods for fixing and staining the nerve tissues so that adequate examination of cell population could be made.

Soon after the early development of these techniques of neurohistology by Ramon y Cajal and others it became apparent that the composition of the cortex was not everywhere the same and the discovery that the cortex could be subdivided into differently composed areas invited the possible inference that differences in structure might mean difference in function. Again the relationship between morphology and function could be demostrated for the sensory and motor areas of the cortex which left the tantalizing possibility that the same might hold for higher functions. Though few such relationships have been found to date this story is not yet concluded.

The corresponding study of the fibre structure of the brain is known as myeloarchitectonics and Flechsig (1849–1929) had quite early related the time of development of the myelin covering of fibres to the development of different areas of the cortex. This suggested that the neural bases of higher functions might lie in cortical-subcortical systems rather than being restricted largely or wholly to the cerebral cortex.

The first major work in the new field by Campbell (1905) *Histological Studies on the Localization of Cerebral Function* shows in its title the avowed aim of the author to correlate function with histological structure. His map divided the cortex into some 20 regions. Shortly after, Brodmann (1909) produced his map with the separate zones now numbering around 50. This map has been widely reproduced and referred to ever since (see Fig. 7.3). Still other workers increased the number of subdivisions until 200 or more separate areas were differentiated in some systems. Milner comments: 'The difference between many adjacent regions in these later maps were so small as to be imperceptible to all but the anatomists who first described them. This problem was pointed out by Lashley and Clark (1946), who found only a few regions of the cortex that they could recognize from anatomical sections alone *if they did not know beforehand what part of the cortex the sections had come from.*' (Milner, 1970, p.109).

The earliest subdivision of the cortex related large areas of the brain's surface to the name of the overlying bones and this division into frontal, temporal, parietal and occipital lobes remains with us today. It has been stressed very often that these are artificial abstractions. However, 'as far as the psychologist is concerned the acid test of (any) such subdivisions is whether or not they can be shown to mean anything behaviorally. Does a lesion of an anatomically or physiologically defined area produce a more isolated and clear cut behavioral disturbance than a lesion that ignores such boundaries?' (Milner, 1970, p.112). A century of lesion studies has demonstrated that these abstractions, the 'lobes' of the brain, are still more useful at this stage in discussing brain-behaviour relationships than those based on the finer subdivisions of cytoarchitecture.

Modern neuropsychology

The past two decades have seen and accelerated growth in the new or re-awakened science called neuropsychology as lines of evidence converge from the parent disciplines of neurological medicine and psychology and as the special methods of each are modified for use in the new field. As with other areas where scientific endeavours overlap, new conceptions and formulations arise which not only advance the new science but also provide useful stimulation for the progenitors. The two principal aspects of clinical neuropsychology are clearly outlined by Luria one of its ablest practitioners and developer of an influential theory whose principal features are outlined below—'The study has two objectives. First by pinpointing the brain lesions responsible for specific behavior disorders we hope to develop a means of early diagnosis and precise location of brain injuries. . . Second, neuropsychological investigation should provide us with a factor analysis that will lead to better understanding of the components of complex psychological functions for which the operations of the different parts of the brain are responsible.' (Luria, 1970, p.66).

This twofold nature of neuropsychology means that by utilizing appropriate tools and concepts to examine brain-behaviour relationships we may be in a position to further our knowledge of the nature of the psychological processes themselves. Neuropsychology has already given us greater insight into some of the processes of perception, memory, learning, problem solving and adaptation. The sophisticated techniques and methodology of modern psychology have also allowed a more detailed analysis of higher nervous disorders than was previously possible.

Leaving aside the psychological measures themselves since they are dealt with in some detail in Chapter 9 there seem to be a number of concepts developed only in recent years which are proving very fruitful. Among these the following four are chosen as they provide a basis for what follows:- (1) the adoption of the syndrome concept as against the unproductive 'unitary' concept of brain damage; (2) a re-evaluation of the concept of 'function' and the development of the concept of functional systems as the neural substrates of psychological processes; (3) the use of 'double dissociation' of function to strengthen the certainty with which statements may be made concerning the relation between anatomical lesion and behavioural disturbance, and (4) the development of the notion of the 'disconnexion syndrome' to explain neuropsychological findings and to predict others.

Though these notions are interrelated with each other and with other ideas in the field they will be outlined separately.

Neuropsychological syndromes

The general failure of psychological tests to provide suitable measures of 'brain damage' was one of the key factors in moving neuropsychologists in the direction of describing the effects of cerebral malfunction in terms of syndromes. Those with a background in medicine and neurology are already familiar with the utility of the syndrome as a conceptual tool in everyday practice. More and more psychologists have moved in the direction of syndrome analysis at least in clinical diagnostic practice. Piercy (1959) and McFie (1960) favour this approach—'a patient's performance should be described not so much in terms of extent of deviation from statistical normality as in terms of extent of approximation to an established syndrome or abnormality.' (McFie,

1960). The use of psychological test methods in the appraisal of the patient's preserved abilities as well as deficits has helped to clarify the definition of some syndromes and is already beginning to describe new ones. The syndrome concept has allowed the more realistic use of psychological test procedures aimed at gauging patterns of impairment on appropriately selected measures. In discussing the objections to the syndrome method in clinical research as opposed to practice Kinsbourne (1971) reminds us that the association between the constellation of signs and symptoms which we term a syndrome and the presence of a disease, is a probabilistic not an invariant one. 'Partial syndromes abound, and it is often not clear how many ingredients have to be present to justify the diagnosis. This is particularly true since not all ingredients of a syndrome are of equal importance, their relative valuation being unformulated outcome of the interaction of medical instruction and clinical experience, and thus a somewhat individual process.' (Kinsbourne, 1971, p.290). On the research front he points out that correlative studies between lesion and syndrome need to employ valid experimental designs and that appropriate statistical .procedures such as cluster analysis should prove useful in the validation of clinical syndromes. 'Pending validation by appropriate testing, the clinically observed 'syndrome' represents an educated guess at a relationship which has value in generating hypotheses and experimentation.' (op. cit. p.291). One of the major tasks of present day neuropsychology is to increase the degree of confidence with which such probabilistic statements can be made.

Closely related to the interpretation of signs and symptoms as a syndrome is the medical concept of differential diagnosis. This means the awareness that similar constellations may be seen in several different diseases or disorders. Ignorance of some of the possibilities will result in a proportion of incorrect diagnoses. This may occur in two directions. Either the pattern of signs and symptoms may be ascribed to the wrong cause or the pattern may not be recognised as a result of a particular disease, or both. The seriousness of the error will depend on the implications for prognosis and treatment.

One of the principal advantages of the differential diagnostic approach is that it allows hypotheses to be set up both to confirm the presence of one disorder and to disconfirm the possibility of others. This approach using psychological tests is exemplified with clinical case examinations in the final chapter. Unfortunately in neuropsychology there are fewer pathognomonic signs than there are in medicine. The term pathognomonic refers to a sign or symptom which is specifically characteristic of a particular disease. Most symptoms and signs in neuropsychology have multiple significance.

The syndrome approach is close to the distinction made in recent years between monothetic and polythetic classification in biological taxonomy. 'The ruling idea of monothetic groups is that they are formed by rigid and successive logical divisions so that the possession of a unique set of features is both sufficient and necessary for membership in the group thus defined'. (Sokal and Sneath, 1963, p.13). With regard to the description and classification of brain damage such a system is not applicable in the light of present knowledge. On the other hand the notion of 'polytypic' (Beckner, 1959) or polythetic groups is very much of value since no single attribute or set of signs and symptoms defines the group. A polythetic classification would place together in one group of syndrome all those cases which share a sufficient number of common characteristics. However, 'no single feature is either essential to group membership or is sufficient to make an organism a member of the group.' (Sokal and Sneath, 1963, p.14). The first major attempt to apply a taxonomic key approach to the problem of assessment of brain lesions is that of Russell, Neuringer and Goldstein (1970) described in Chapter 9.

The description of syndromes in neuropsychology is of the polythetic type and is of undoubted value in the preliminary allotment of a patient to a diagnostic category which may then be checked further in the process of differential diagnosis.

Functional systems

The idea of a functional system as the neurological underpinning of a complex psychological function has been developed over a long period by Luria and is clearly outlined in his recent textbook (Luria, 1973b). At the outset he draws attention to the fact that the term 'function' may be used in at least two principal ways. Firstly one may describe the function of particular cells or organs, e.g., one of the functions of the liver is to produce bile, the function of the islet cells of Langerhans is to produce insulin. This usage is readily understood. On the other hand, the term function is widely used to describe more complex processes involving the integrated participation of a number of tissues and organs in a functional process, e.g., the function of digestion, circulation, and respiration. Such organizations are termed systems and though the final result such as the absorption of nourishment, or the provision of oxygen to the tissues remains constant, the way in which the system performs the function varies considerably according to a wide variety of factors. 'The presence of a constant (invariant) task, performed by variable (variative) mechanisms, bringing the process to a constant (invariant) result, is one of the basic features distinguishing the work of every functional system.' (Luria, 1973, p.28).

The systemic approach has a second advantage which proves useful in topical diagnosis. While it is true that damage in any part of a functional system may lead to disruption of a psychological process it is also true that damage to different parts of a system will impress a different character on the complex of symptoms and signs which result from the damage. Thus it is of paramount importance to establish not only that there is an alteration in a particular psychological function following a brain lesion but also what qualitative features this loss of function has. It was principally for this reason that psychological tests, particularly some of the more widely used psychometric measures proved of such little value in diagnosis since they did not allow this difference in the quality of performance to be brought out or psychologists were too impressed with the scores or level of performance to see the significance of qualitative changes. Indeed workers like Goldstein were roundly attacked because of their lack of norms, standardization and other features of the epitome of psychological assessment, the intelligence test. This overgeneralization is easy to make with hindsight and it is true, particularly of the British clinical psychologists that they quite early realized the shortcomings of dependence upon test scores alone. Shapiro (1951) expressed it pithily when he commented 'the test scores do not communicate the responses in full.'

The notion of functional systems is a marked advance on the notion of strict localization of function in discrete areas of the cortex. The functional system has as its anatomical basis a number of cortical and subcortical areas working in concert through the action of fibre pathways and it is for this reason that a working knowledge of the gross anatomy of the brain will be indispensable for the neuropsychologist. This becomes apparent in the understanding provided by the disconnexion model discussed below.

Double dissociation of function

This concept was put forward by Teuber (1955, 1959) and has been widely accepted and quoted by other workers. In discussing whether certain visual discrimination difficulties described after temporal lobe ablations in animals were specific to those particular areas Teuber commented:

To demonstrate specificity of the deficit for visual discrimination we need to do more than show that discrimination in some other modality, e.g., somesthesis, is unimpaired. Such simple dissociation might indicate merely that visual discrimination is more vulnerable to temporal lesions than tactile discrimination. This would be a case of hierarchy of function rather than separate localization. What is needed for conclusive proof is 'double dissociation,' i.e., evidence that tactile discrimination can be disturbed by some other lesion without loss on visual tasks and to a degree comparable in severity to the supposedly visual deficit after temporal lesions. (Teuber, 1955, p.283).

A more general statement appeared a few years later in discussion of Teuber's findings in his extensive studies of human subjects with wounds to the brain. '. .double dissociation requires that symptom A appear in lesions in one structure but not with those in another, and the symptom B appear with lesions of the other but not of the one. Whenever such dissociation is lacking, specificity in the effects of lesions has not been demonstrated.' (Teuber, 1959, p.187).

Numerous examples of double dissociation of function appear in the later chapters. The concept has proved extremely useful but care must be exercised in transposing the word 'symptom' in the above quotation to mean the patient's performance on a psychological test. Kinsbourne has discussed the application of the concept to *groups* of individuals with damage in different parts of the brain.

If a patient group with damage centered at location A is superior to one damaged at B in respect to task P, but inferior in task Q, a double dissociation obtains between these groups. This permits the inference of at least one difference between the two groups specific to location of damage, for P may be a nonspecific task, relating, say, to general intelligence or some other variable in which the groups are imperfectly matched. But then it must be admitted that function Q must have been selectively impaired by a lesion at location A; since the inferiority in performing Q cannot be accounted for by failure of matching on the other task. The search for double dissociation is a valid means towards progress in neuropsychology. (Kinsbourne, 1971, p.295).

This author warns that the converse situation, namely the failure to find dissociations, should not lead us to conclude that specific relationships do not exist between performance on specific tasks and particular anatomical sites or structures since performance on a particular task may be affected by a number of factors. The recognition of the multiple determinants of the performance on many psychological tests should lead to the design of more 'discrete' tasks which are tied to single factors which might then be studied for their association with or dissociation from particular brain structures.

With the double dissociation paradigm Weiskrantz (1968) points out that 'the maximum information is conveyed when two treatments are alike in all but one critical aspect (e.g., for brain lesions—same mass, same damage to meninges, but different in locus) and that the two tasks similarly are alike in all but one critical aspect (e.g., same training procedure, same cue-response contingencies, but difference in sensory modality). This is simply to restate the essence of analytical control procedures, and the double dissociation paradigm is simply a way of combining two control procedures into a single pattern. But there are also great risks of reifying a dissociation between tests into a dissociation between functions and arguing that the affected function has been isolated by a single instance of dissociation.'

Finally, the principle of double dissociation is intimately associated with the syndrome analysis as proposed by Luria and others. 'The initial hypothesis in this line of work is the assumption that in the presence of a given local lesion which directly causes the loss of some factor, *all functional systems which include this factor suffer, while, at the same time, all functional systems which do not include the disturbed factor are preserved*' (Luria, 1973b, pp. 13-14). As one of numerous examples he points to the different effects of damage in the left temporal region in man as opposed to the effects of damage in the parieto-occipital region. Temporal damage leads to disturbance of acoustic analysis of that class of acoustic stimulation which we term phonemes and this leads to disturbance of any function which depends to any marked extent on this analysis and the greater the dependence of any function on the analysis of phonemes the greater will be the secondary disturbance of the function, e.g., repeating what another person has said or writing to dictation will be markedly affected. On the other hand functions such as spatial perception which do not depend to any extent on phonemic analysis will be unaffected. Conversely, parieto-occipital damage will spare all those functions dependent upon phonemic analysis but disrupt all functions which have a dependence on spatial orientation.

Since naturally occuring lesions are liable on most occasions to affect portions of functional systems which are geographically adjacent the establishment of two or more 'double dissociations' will render the location of the causative lesion more and more certain. In other words the establishment of one dissociation may suggest application of appropriate test in the form of a 'crucial experiment' in single cases.

The disconnexion syndrome

The notion of the disconnexion syndrome dates back to the classical neurologists of the latter half of the nineteenth century. With their conception of specialized sets of cells disposed over the cerebral cortex and the emerging knowledge of the fibre pathways connecting the various parts of the cortex with nearby and distant structures, a distinction arose between 'cortical' and 'conduction' syndromes. Wernicke, for example, knowing the effects of damage to the motor speech area and the quite different effects of damage to the sensory speech area which he himself described, was able to predict what would result if these areas were disconnected or isolated from each other. Though his anatomical assumptions about the pathways involved were not correct the value of the conception of disconnexion was validated by the discovery of the so-called 'conduction aphasia'. (See Ch. 3).

The late nineteenth century and the early years of the present century produced a number of findings consistent with the disconnexion theory particularly those of Liepmann whose analysis of apraxia was in terms of disruption of connexions. He was also aware that 'disconnexion' symptoms or syndromes could be brought about by interrupting connexions between the hemispheres, interhemispheric or callosal disconnexion, (Liepmann and Mass, 1907) as well by interrupting connexions between different parts of the same hemisphere.

However, the disconnexion theory for all its factual support gradually lost ground in the first three decades of the present century under the impact of holistic theories espoused by such neurologists as Head, Marie and von Monakow. When Akelaitis and his group published their findings on sectioning of the corpus callosum for the relief of epilepsy in the early nineteen forties the apparent absence of any of the predicted interhemispheric disconnexion effects in their patients seemed to sound the death knell of the disconnexion theory (Akeliatis, 1940, 1941a,b,c; 1942a,b; 1943; 1944; Akelaitis, Risteen, Herren and Van Wagenen, 1941; 1942; 1943; Smith and Akelaitis, 1942). It was only much later that it became obvious that the negative findings were due to lack of appropriate techniques for eliciting disconnexion signs. Another ten years was to pass before the elegant experimentation of Myers and Sperry (1953) in monkeys demonstrated convincingly that such callosal effects do in fact occur and the 'split-brain' techniques which they developed were soon applied to the small number of commissurotomy operations being performed on human subjects for the relief of epilepsy. The detailed findings of these hemisphere disconnexion operations and their contribution to our understanding of the asymmetry of function in the two halves of the human brain are discussed in Chapter 9.

The split-brain work in animals also stimulated Geschwind and his colleagues both to re-examine the older clinical literature and to reassess their patients with disturbances of the higher functions. They were soon to find excellent examples (Geschwind, 1962; Geschwind and Kaplan, 1962; Howes, 1962).

The following brief summary is condensed from the extensive treatment by Geschwind (1965b, 1965c).

1. disconnexion syndromes are those produced by lesions of association pathways (see Ch. 2);

2. these pathways may be within the same hemisphere (intra hemispheric) or between the two hemispheres (interhemispheric or commissural);

3. following 'Flechsig's principle' primary receptor areas of the cortex have neocortical connections only with adjacent 'association' areas;

4. the association areas on the other hand receive information i.e., have connexions with several other cortical areas and send their outgoing connexions to other areas at a distance;

5. Flechsig's principle also applies to linkages between the two hemispheres. There are no direct connexions between the primary receptor areas of one side and the primary receptor areas of the other, only commissural connexions between 'association' cortex. The effects of such an anatomical arrangement are summarized by Geschwind:

These anatomical facts imply that a large lesion of the association areas around a primary sensory area will act to disconnect it from other parts of the neocortex. Thus, a "disconnexion lesion" will be a large lesion either of association cortex or of the white matter leading from this association cortex. The specification of the association areas as way-stations between different parts of neocortex is certainly too narrow, but it is at least not incorrect. This view, as we shall see, simplifies considerably the analysis of effects of lesions of these regions. Since a primary sensory region has no callosal connexions, a lesion of association cortex may serve both to disconnect such an area from other regions in the same hemisphere and also to act in effect as a lesion of the callosal pathway from this primary sensory area. (Geschwind, 1965b, pp.244-245).

This notion of a disconnexion syndrome has been expressed in several ways in recent years depending upon the theoretical background of the author and is closely related to the notion of a functional system, a concept which is widely used in electronics and other sciences where the 'systems approach' has proved useful in pinpointing the site of lesions or faults in the system.

The brain may be considered as a communication network, incorporating multiple information transmitting channels which lead to and from decision points. A limitation of function, namely the impairment or abolition of the ability to make particular decisions, may result from damage to the decision point and from interruption of input to or output from that point. Those points of the system which are most closely aggregated in cerebral space will be most vulnerable to selective inactivation by focal cerebral injury. The extreme example is the corpus callosum, division of which reliably induces a pure disconnection syndrome (Geschwind and Kaplan, 1962; Myers, 1956) without damage to decision points in either hemisphere . . . .The *neurons that constitute a decision point are widely diffused over the cerebral cortex. But their distinctive function depends on their mode of linkage rather than on physical features of individual neurons, and this is not necessarily reflected in morphological differentiation. (Kinsbourne, 1971, p.287) (emphasis added)*

The remainder of the present text is devoted to an exposition of the anatomical, neurological and psychological facts necessary to a fruitful implementation of these principal concepts.

2. Basic Anatomy of the Brain

Anatomical terms of direction and relationship

Because some readers may be unfamiliar with anatomy while still wishing to gain a basic knowledge of the structure of the nervous system, it will be worthwhile to explain a few commonly used terms. In particular, one of the difficulties which students of anatomy encounter is in learning the manner in which the various structures are disposed in relation to each other. When, as is too often the case, students learning neuropsychology have little or no opportunity to attend demonstrations of dissection of the brain, it is of paramount importance to be clear about the terms which follow. Some confusion is also likely to arise in reading different texts unless equivalent terms are explained.

In lower animals the head-to-tail direction has been described by the Latin-derived terms *rostral* and *caudal* and the belly-to-back direction by the terms *ventral* and *dorsal*. These axes are often at right angles to each other. However, in man, the nose and belly point in the same direction so that the terms anterior and posterior may substitute for rostral and caudal while the terms *superior*

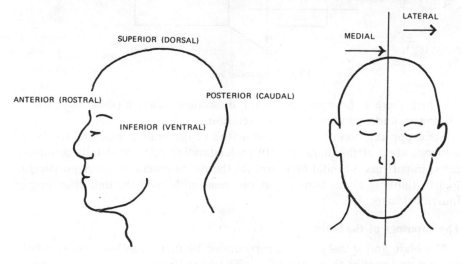

Fig. 2.1 Terms of relationship in neuroanatomy

and *inferior* stand for dorsal and ventral. Sometimes when speaking of the inferior aspect of the brain one also uses the term base or *basal* aspect. A third set of directional terms relates to whether the structures are near the mid-line—*medial*—or away from it—*lateral* (Fig. 2.1).

The terms proximal and distal are used to refer to the portion of the structure near to or away from its origin, e.g. the proximal part of an artery is near its origin, the proximal part of a nerve is near the brain or spinal cord. Finally, an appreciation of the relative position of structures within the nervous system can be gained from studying series of sections cut through the brain after it has been hardened. There are three principal planes of reference: (1) *Coronal* or *frontal* sections are parallel to a vertical plane through both ears; (2) *Sagittal* or *longitudinal* sections are at right angle to the coronal plane in a vertical direction. A median or midline sagittal section would divide the brain into its two hemispheres; (3) *Horizontal* sections are at right angles to the other two (Fig. 2.2).

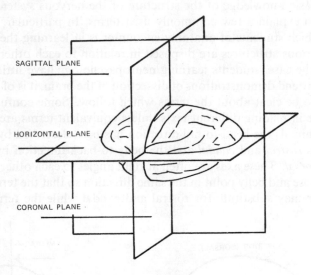

SAGITTAL PLANE

HORIZONTAL PLANE

CORONAL PLANE

Fig. 2.2 Planes of reference

Where there is no opportunity for dissection, brain models may help in gaining an understanding of spatial relations.

Some appreciation of the basic structure of the brain is essential for (a) an understanding of the literature, (b) understanding relevant details communicated in patients' hospital files, and (c) the development of the neuropsychologist's thinking about brain-behaviour relationships in the understanding of individual cases.

The coverings of the brain

The brain and spinal cord are surrounded by three membranes which both support and protect these structures. These are the *dura mater, the arachnoid mater, and the pia mater.*

Dura mater

The tough outermost layer, called the *dura mater*, is closely attached to the inner surface of the skull and also provides several partitions which divide the skull cavity into relatively separate compartments. Since these partitions are anchored to the skull, they help to prevent the very soft and fragile brain tissue from excessive movement which would result in tearing of the brain substance whenever the head was suddenly accelerated, decelerated, or rapidly rotated. Even this protection breaks down when such movements are very violent.

The two major partitions of the *dura mater* are the *falx cerebri* and the *tentorium cerebelli* (Fig. 2.3).

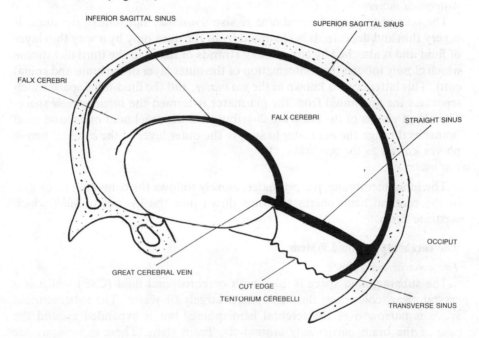

Fig. 2.3 Partitions of the dura mater

The *falx cerebri* provides a partition between the two major divisions of the cerebrum, the left and right cerebral hemispheres. It is a vertical partition, shaped like a sickle with its narrow end attached to the base of the skull anteriorly. Its upper edge is attached to the vault of the skull in the midline while its lower edge arches over the upper edge of the *corpus callosum* to join on to the other major partition, the *tentorium cerebrelli*, just posterior to the splenium (Fig. 2.12) of the corpus callosum. The falx cerebri becomes deeper as it sweeps backwards.

The *tentorium cerebelli* is a sharply arched or tent-like structure which is attached to the falx cerebri above, while the lower edge of the tent is attached to the periphery of the posterior skull depression which houses the *cerebellum*. Thus the tentorium serves to separate the posterior part of the cerebral hemispheres (the occipital lobes) above from the cerebellum below. The tentorium and falx cerebri are stretched taut while the free margins of the front of the tentorium provide an opening through which the mesencephalon or mid-brain passes.

In the outer layer of the dura mater are embedded arteries which are termed meningeal arteries though their main purpose is to provide blood supply for the bones of the skull as well as the relatively avascular dura mater. The dura also forms the walls of the large channels or sinuses which drain the venous blood from the brain. The narrow space between the dura and arachnoid mater is termed the *subdural space*.

Arachnoid mater

The second meningeal membrane is also avascular but, unlike the dura, it is very thin and delicate. It is separated from the dura only by a very thin layer of fluid and is attached by cobweb-like strands of tissue to the third membrane which closely follows the conformation of the outer layer of the brain and spinal cord. This latter layer is known as the *pia mater*, and the fluid-filled space which separates the arachnoid from the pia mater is termed the *subarachnoid space*. The blood vessels of the brain are distributed in the arachnoid mater and send branches through the pia mater to supply the outer layer of the cerebral hemispheres known as the cerebral cortex.

Pia mater

The inner membrane, the pia mater, closely follows the convolutions or *gyri* of the cerebral hemispheres and dips down into the fissures or *sulci* which separate them.

The cerebrospinal fluid system

The subarachnoid space

The subarachnoid space is filled with cerebrospinal fluid (CSF) which is a crystal clear, colourless, fluid composed largely of water. The subarachnoid space is narrow over the cerebral hemispheres but is expanded around the base of the brain particularly around the brain stem. These expansions are known as cisterns and the *cerebellomedullary cistern* is important for our understanding of this fluid system since it is here that the subarachnoid space communicates with the ventricular cavities within the brain. The cerebrospinal fluid acts as a buffer to protect the brain and spinal cord. It also helps to provide a constant pressure within the bony cavity under normal conditions. The numerous other functions of the cerebrospinal fluid are beyond the scope of the present outline. An idea of the complexity of this system and its functions can be gained from Davson (1967).

Ventricular cavities

There are four ventricular cavities within the brain. These are continuous with each other and the central canal at the upper end of the spinal cord. Each cerebral hemisphere contains a *lateral ventricle*. Each of these communicates with the midline *third ventricle* which in turn communicates with the *fourth ventricle* (Fig. 2.4).

The lateral ventricles are cavities with an arch-like or C-chaped contour

which conforms to the general shape of the brain. They are filled with cerebrospinal fluid and may be divided into five parts: (1) the anterior (frontal)
horn, (2) the body, (3) the collateral trigone, (4) the inferior (temporal) horn,
and (5) the posterior (occipital) horn.

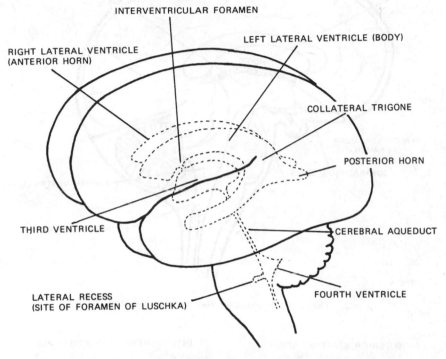

Fig. 2.4 Outline of ventricles projected onto lateral view of the brain

Each lateral ventricle opens by means of an *interventricular foramen* into
the third ventricle which is situated in the midline.

The frontal horns are anterior to the interventricular foramina ending in
the substance of the frontal lobe.

The body extends posteriorly from the foramina to the region of the splenium
of the corpus callosum. It is narrow and slightly arched in form.

At the posterior end of the body there is a widening into the region termed
the collateral trigone which is confluent also with the posterior horn, which
extends into the occipital lobe, and with the inferior horn, which turns downwards into the substance of the temporal lobe.

Since we will have cause to mention conditions which may impair brain
functions as a result of alteration in the CSF system, it will be of value to outline
in a gross way the characteristics of the circulation of this fluid. Figure 2.5
provides a schematic diagram of the main anatomical features while Figure
2.6 sketches the fluid dynamics.

The cerebrospinal fluid is largely produced by the *choroid plexuses of the
lateral ventricles* which are paired cavities, one in each cerebral hemisphere

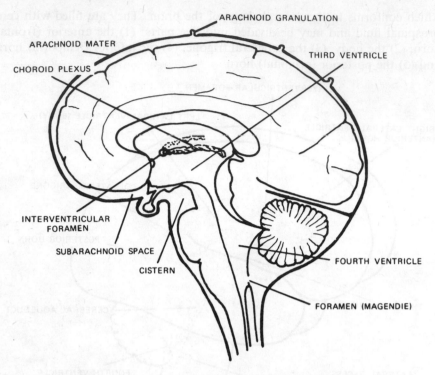

Fig. 2.5 The subarachnoid space and cerebrospinal fluid system

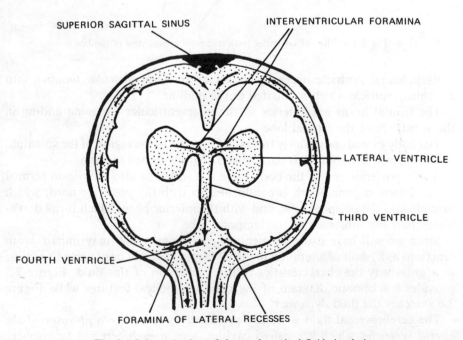

Fig. 2.6 Schematic view of the cerebrospinal fluid circulation

(Fig. 2.4). These lateral ventricles are connected to a single narrow midline cavity by two short channels or openings known as the *interventricular foramina* (passages). From this third ventricle the cerebrospinal fluid passes by way of the cerebral aqueduct into the fourth ventricle which has one median aperture and two lateral apertures through which the CSF passes into the subarachnoid space to bathe the whole of the brain and spinal cord.

Finally, the circulation is completed by the drainage of the fluid into the venous system via the *arachnoid granulations*. In the region of the great venous channel termed the *superior sagittal sinus*, the closely related membranes the pia and the arachnoid, send prolongations through openings in the dural wall of the venous channel and these permeable granulations allow the fluid to drain into the blood stream (Fig. 2.7).

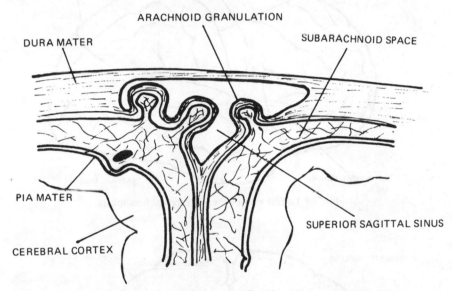

Fig. 2.7 Drainage of the cerebrospinal fluid into the venous system

The cerebrospinal fluid is produced by the plexuses of blood vessels principally in the lateral ventricles and, to a lesser extent, elsewhere. Two main theories have been put forward for its production: (1) a process of filtration or dialysis or (2) a process of secretion. Whatever the mechanism some 600 or 700 ml may be produced each day and need to be passed into the blood circulation. Such disposal may be prevented by a failure of the fluid to be filtered away or by an obstruction in such sites as the interventricular foramina, the aqueduct, or the apertures in the roof of the fourth ventricle. These obstructions may lead to local or general ventricular dilation with increased intracranial pressure and wasting of the surrounding brain tissue. This condition, known as *hydrocephalus*, may occur in the young infant or in the adult and lead to severe cerebral impairment if some surgical method is not employed to restore a free circulation to the cerebrospinal fluid. In adults an insidious onset of dementia may signal the presence of often unsuspected acquired hydrocephalus.

Gross topography of the brain

The brain has three major divisions, the cerebral hemispheres, the brain stem, and the cerebellum. Our main concern will be with the cerebral hemispheres and, to a lesser extent with the midbrain. Description of the cerebellum will be omitted since it is little concerned with man's higher functions. The cerebellum is concerned primarily with motor coordination and the control of muscle tone and equilibrium.

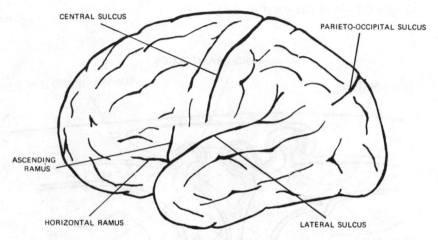

Fig. 2.8 Lateral view of the left cerebral hemisphere

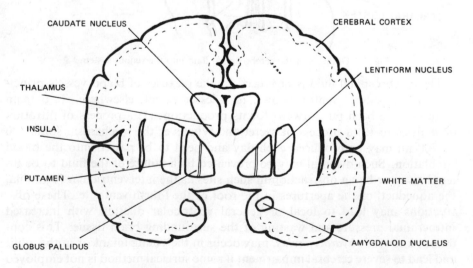

Fig. 2.9 Coronal section of the hemispheres

The cerebral hemispheres

The paired hemispheres appear to be mirror images of each other. They are covered by a convoluted layer of grey matter, the *cerebral cortex* (Fig. 2.8) which covers the internal white matter and deeply placed collections of grey matter or neuronal masses collectively known as the *basal ganglia*. The grey matter represents nerve cell collections while the white matter represents cell fibres which unite the various regions of the brain with each other (Fig. 2.9).

The two hemispheres are separated by the *longitudinal fissure* which completely separates them in the anterior (frontal) and posterior (occipital) regions (Fig. 2.10). The falx cerebri forms a partition between the two sides. In the central region the two hemispheres are united by a thick band of white matter, the *corpus callosum* which is the chief functional link between them.

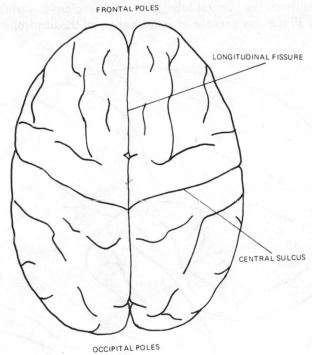

Fig. 2.10 Superior view of the hemispheres

Superolateral surface. Each cerebral hemisphere has three surfaces, the large convex superolateral surface, the flattened medial surface in contact with the falx, and the inferior surface which lies on the floor of the anterior and middle cranial depressions (fossae) in front and on the tentorium cerebelli behind.

The convoluted portions of the cerebral cortex are known as *gyri*. They are separated from each other by fissures or *sulci*. Some of these sulci and gyri are relatively constant features of most human brains and form the basis for describing the general external topography of the brain. On the lateral surface three prominent sulci are used as a basis for dividing each hemisphere into five major areas or lobes. A sixth lobe, the limbic lobe, will be described separately. The three sulci are (1) the lateral sulcus, (2) the central sulcus, and (3) the parieto-occipital sulcus.

The *lateral sulcus* is a very deep division between the frontal and temporal lobes anteriorly and portions of the parietal and temporal lobes posteriorly. Towards the anterior end two small branches (rami), the *anterior horizontal ramus* and the *anterior ascending ramus* run for about 2 cm into the lower part of the frontal lobe while the terminal *ascending ramus* extends into the inferior part of the parietal lobe.

Buried within the lateral sulcus is a cortical area known as the *insula*. This can only be seen when the lips of the fissure are drawn apart (Fig. 2.11).

The *central sulcus* is less easy to find. It runs from the superior margin of the hemisphere downward and forward towards the lateral sulcus separating the frontal from the parietal lobe. The central sulcus is variable in form and runs only a little way over the superior border of the hemisphere to the medial surface.

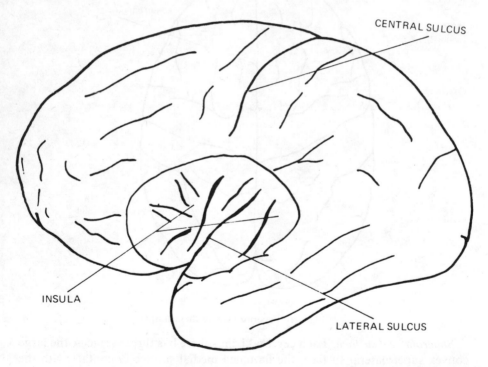

Fig. 2.11 The insula (temporal lobe retracted)

The *parieto-occipital sulcus* is a fairly constant deep sulcus which cuts into the superior border of the hemisphere some 5 cm anterior to the occipital pole and runs on the medial surface in an anterior and inferior direction to intersect the well marked *calcarine sulcus* about midway along its length.

Lobar divisions. The arbitrary boundaries of the lobar divisions are shown with respect to the major sulci in Fig. 2.12.

The *frontal lobe* is that part of the hemisphere above the lateral sulcus and in front of the central sulcus.

The *parietal lobe* is bounded in front by the central sulcus and below by the lateral sulcus before it turns upwards to the line which forms the posterior boundary of the lobe. This line runs from the point where the parieto-occipital sulcus crosses the superior border of the hemisphere to a small notch (pre-occipital notch) some 4 cm in front of the occipital pole.

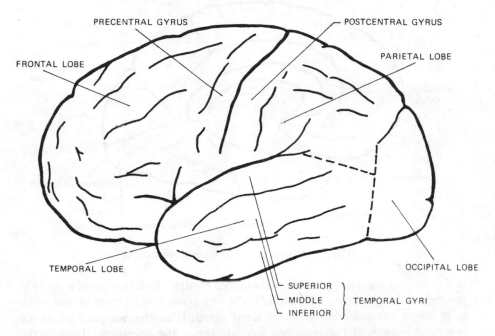

Fig. 2.12 Lobar divisions of the hemispheres (lateral aspect)

The *occipital lobe* lies posterior to the vertical boundary line on the convex surface and, on the medial aspect, to the parieto-occipital sulcus and a line joining the junction of the parieto-occipital sulcus with the preoccipital notch.

The *temporal lobe* is bounded by the lateral sulcus and the artificial line of demarcation described above.

Further details of the frontal, temporal, parietal and occipital lobes are described in the separate chapters devoted to each lobe.

Apart from the major divisions into lobes, certain gross features of the external topography of the brain may be described on the three surfaces of the hemispheres, the superolateral, medial, and inferior surfaces.

The superolateral surface is divided into more or less constant gyri as depicted in Figure 2.12.

Medial surface. The medial surfaces of the hemispheres are seen after cutting through the corpus callosum which joins them (Fig. 2.13). The corpus callosum is some 8 cm in length. The anterior curved portion is known as the *genu* of the corpus callosum and this tapers posteriorly and inferiorly as the *rostrum*. The corpus callosum ends posteriorly in a blunt enlargement termed the *splenium* which lies over the pineal body and the midbrain. The corpus callosum is separated on its upper surface from the *cingulate gyrus* by the *callosal sulcus*. Posteriorly this gyrus curves around the splenium of the corpus callosum to enter the temporal lobe as the *parahippocampal gyrus*.

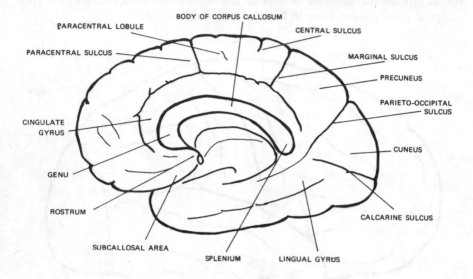

Fig. 2.13 Medial view of the right hemisphere

Above the cingulate gyrus is a well marked fissure which runs from a position just below the genu (*the sub-callosal area*) to a point just in front of and vertically above the splenium where it turns upwards as the *marginal sulcus* (or marginal branch of the cingulate sulcus), above the splenium. Usually the cingulate sulcus gives off a prominent branch, the *paracentral sulcus* which crossed the upper medial border of the hemisphere vertically above the middle part of the body of the corpus callosum. The area between the paracentral sulcus and the marginal sulcus is the *paracentral lobule*. The lobule is divided by the small part of the central fissure which just reaches the upper medial surface of the hemisphere so that the paracentral lobule contains the extension over on to the medial surface of the *precentral* and *postcentral* gyri. The area between the marginal sulcus and the parieto-occupital sulcus is the *precuneus*. This is the extension medially of the superior *parietal lobule*. The *calcarine sulcus* runs forward from the occipital pole to divide the occipital lobe the cuneus above and the lingual gyrus below.

Inferior surface. The inferior surface of the hemisphere consists of two parts (Fig. 2.14). The smaller anterior portion is the inferior or orbital surface of the frontal lobe while the larger posterior portion represents the inferior surfaces of the temporal and occipital lobes.

The orbital surface of the frontal lobe has a deep straight sulcus the *olfactory*

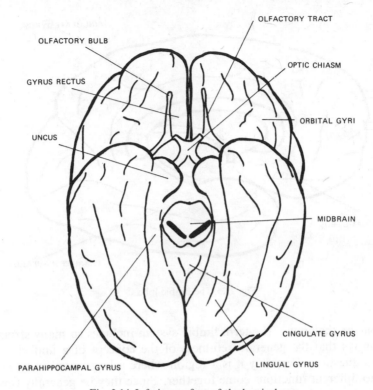

Fig. 2.14 Inferior surface of the hemispheres

sulcus with the *olfactory bulb* and *tract* lying on it. Medial to this sulcus lies the *gyrus rectus* while lateral to it lie the *orbital gyri*.

The inferior surface of the occipital lobe and the posterior part of the temporal lobe lie on the tentorium cerebelli while the anterior portion of the temporal lobe lies in a depression in the skull, the *middle cranial fossa*. The gyri in this posterior portion are the *lingual gyrus* medially, the *parahippocampal gyrus* and *uncus*, and the *occipitotemporal gyri* laterally.

The limbic lobe and limbic system

On the medial surface of each cerebral hemisphere there is a ring of structures which surrounds the anterior (rostral) part of the brain stem and the commissures uniting the hemispheres. The major portion of the limbic lobe is made up of the *cingulate gyrus* above and the *parahippocampal gyrus* below. (Fig. 2.15). It also includes the smaller *subcallosal gyrus* and the *hippocampal formation* and *dentate gyrus*.

The term *limbic system* refers to a much more extensive complex of structures which includes not only the structures of the limbic lobe but also the temporal pole, anterior portion of the insula, posterior orbital surface of the frontal lobe and a number of subcortical nuclei. These subcortical nuclei include thalamic, hypothalamic, septal, and amygdaloid nuclei, and there is also evidence of a close relationship with the midbrain reticular formation and the reticular

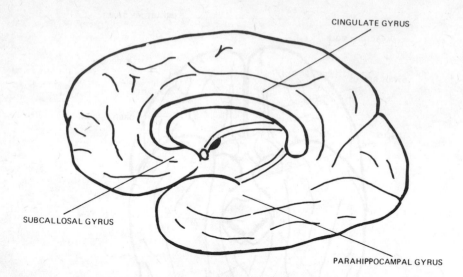

Fig. 2.15 The limbic lobe

nucleus of the thalamus. The term limbic system includes so many structures and pathways that the general usefulness of the concept of a unified system is open to question. Certainly it is a region where a large number of circuits relating to different functions come together. Since they lie generally towards the middle axis of the brain mass we will later refer to them as axial or mesial structures (Fig. 2.16).

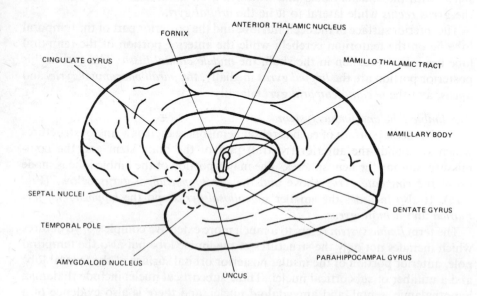

Fig. 2.16 The limbic system

As early as 1937 Papez defined a recurrent or 'closed' part of the system, now known as the 'circuit of Papez' as the substratum for controlling emotions and emotional expressions. The Papez circuit forms the following linkage: hippo-campus-fornix-mamillary bodies-thalamus-cingulate cortex-hippocampus. A good deal of evidence has also accumulated in recent years to associate lesions of the hippocampal-fornix-mamillary body connections with a disorder of memory of the type known as the Korsakoff amnesic syndrome. The importance of the limbic system in emotional experience and expression has also been demonstrated by bilateral removal of the limbic structures in the temporal lobe, amygdaloid nucleus, hippocampus, and parahippocampal gyrus as well as the temporal neocortex overlying these structures.

The hippocampal system

The *hippocampal system* (Fig. 2.17) is one of the more primitive parts of the cerebrum and has an extremely simple three-layered cortex, the *archipallium*. The hippocampal system is made up of the *parahippocampal gyrus* and *uncus*, the *hippocampal formation, dentate gyrus, gyrus fasciolus, indusium griseum, fimbria* and *fornix*. These structures form a pair of arches extending from the region of the interventricular foramina to the tip of the inferior horn of the lateral ventricle (Fig. 2.16, 2.17). The *parahippocampal gyrus* and *uncus* have

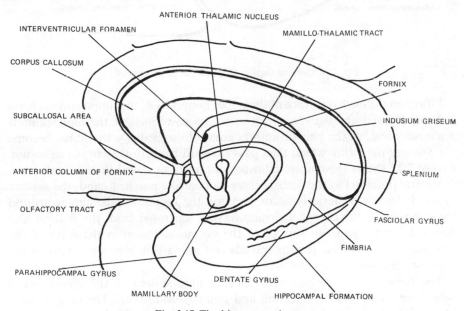

Fig. 2.17 The hippocampal system

been seen on the inferior surface of the brain towards the midline. The *hippo-campus* is a slightly curved elevation in the floor of the inferior (temporal) horn of the ventricle. Its broader anterior end is just posterolateral to the uncus and the hippocampus diminishes rapidly as it moves posteriorly. The structure of the hippocampus and its relation to neighbouring structures can be further appreciated in a transverse or coronal section through the temporal lobe (Fig. 2.18).

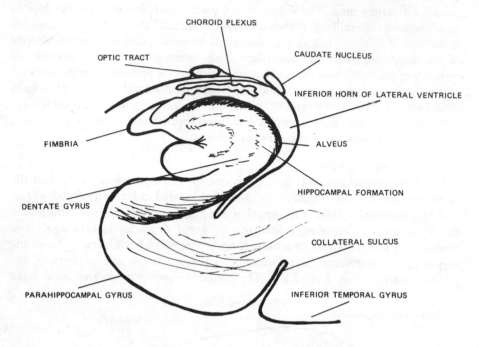

Fig. 2.18 Coronal section through the hippocampus

Fibres on the medial surface of the upper convexity of the hippocampus form a flattened band, the *fimbria*, which increases posteriorly as the hippocampus diminishes and, as the pair of fimbria curve dorsomedially the fibres become the *crura of the fornix* which then pass forward beneath the corpus callosum. Figure 2.19 shows the corpus callosum cut away to reveal these structures.

Ventral (inferior) to the fimbria there is a narrow notched band, the *dentate gyrus*. It lessens posteriorly accompanying the hippocampus, curves around the splenium of the corpus callosum having separated from the fimbria and passes on to the superior surface of the corpus callosum in the form of the delicate *fasciolar gyrus*. It then spreads out into a thin grey sheet termed the *indusium griseum* or *supracallocal gyrus*.

The *fornix* forms the principal efferent fibre system of the hippocampal formation. It has both projection and commissural fibres. The commissural fibres of the fornix (*hippocampal commissure*) are described below. As the crura of the fornix come together under the ventral surface of the corpus callosum they form the *body of the fornix* which travels forward to the rostral margin of the thalamus where they separate again into bundles forming the *anterior columns of the fornix*. The bundles again diverge from each other, arch in front of the *interventricular foramina* and posterior to the *anterior commissure* and incline slightly posteriorly to terminate in the *mamillary bodies*.

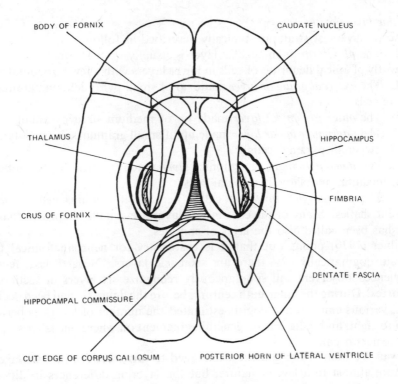

BODY OF FORNIX

CAUDATE NUCLEUS

THALAMUS

HIPPOCAMPUS

FIMBRIA

CRUS OF FORNIX

DENTATE FASCIA

HIPPOCAMPAL COMMISSURE

CUT EDGE OF CORPUS CALLOSUM

POSTERIOR HORN OF LATERAL VENTRICLE

Fig. 2.19 Overlying tissue removed to show hippocampus and fornix.

The cerebral cortex

The cerebral cortex is the most recently elaborated structure in the central nervous system. It is only in the mammal that it takes on special significance and it reaches its greatest size relative to other structures in man.

The notion of architectonics was mentioned in Chapter 1. Though the cellular arrangement of the cortex varies in different areas of the brain, it is customary to describe a sample of 'modal' or 'typical' cortex made up of six layers. This six layered pattern distinguishes the *neocortex* or new cortex from the *paleocortex* which predominates in lower animals and is largely concerned in them with olfaction. Though a certain amount of more primitively structured cortex has been preserved in man, it has become displaced to deeper parts of the brain where it is almost completely covered by the neocortex which comprises the major part of the cerebral cortex in man. The stages of development of the different types of cortex from primitive animal to man is well described by Romer (1955). The paleocortical structures, because of their earlier assocation with smell, are sometimes termed collectively the *rhinencephalon* or nose brain. In man, as in other higher mammals, the functions of these structures have little to do with olfaction. They might best be described as being made up of (a) olfactory components and (2) the limbic components described elsewhere.

Cellular layers of the cortex

The six layers or strata are typically described as follows:

I. The *plexiform* or molecular layer is usually quite distinct; It is made up mostly of apical dendrites of cells in lower layers with a few horizontal cells:

II. The *external granular layer* made up of small pyramidal and granule or stellate cells:

III. The *outer pyramidal layer* made up of medium sized pyramidal cells:

IV. The *internal granular layer* made up of small granule cells (stellate cells) and a few small pyramid cells:

V. The *inner pyramidal* (ganglionic) *layer* made up of a large number of large, medium, and short pyramidal cells:

VI. The *polymorphic layer*, so called because it contains cells of many different shapes. Many of the cells in this layer are spindle shaped so that the layer has been called also the layer of spindles.

Milner (1970) points out that it is customary for neuroanatomical texts to state dogmatically that there are six basic layers...Nevertheless, few inexperienced observers will spontaneously recognize six layers in sections of the cortex. During the nineteenth century, before the figure six had been decided upon, various eminent histologists estimated the number of layers as between five and eight, and there was no general agreement on where one layer stopped and the next began.

It was Brodmann who somehow managed to raise the idea of a six-layered structure almost to a law of nature, but the layering differences in different regions of the cortex are so great that his idea can be sustained only by subdividing layers in some places or making arbitrary distinctions where in fact there is a gradual and smooth transition (Milner, 1970, p.113).

Certain areas of the cortex, such as the precentral region of the frontal lobe, show very poor development of the granular layers II and IV and are called agranular. The 'typical' six layers are more characteristic of the post-central lobes, i.e., the parietal, temporal, and occipital lobes.

Within and between the layers of the cortex there are complex sets of connections between nerve cells. These connections are beyond the scope of this chapter and work in clinical neuropsychology at the moment is more concerned with connections made by the fibres of cortical cells which leave the cortex and travel short or long distances to link cortical areas together.

Functional areas of the cortex

Functional areas of the cortex have been defined in a number of ways including the study of electrical potentials evoked in the cortex on the presentation of different stimuli and the stimulation of the exposed cortex in conscious human subjects undergoing neurosurgery (Ch. 5). The *motor area* is situated in the precentral gyrus and the *sensory area* in the post-central gyrus, both having somatotopic representation. The *visual area* is situated in the cortex of the occipital lobe on either side of the calcarine sulcus mainly on the medial and partly on the superolateral aspect of the hemisphere. The *auditory area* is situated in the *transverse gyri of Heschl* and is largely concealed in the depth of the temporal cortex in the lateral fissure just extending on to the lateral surface of the hemisphere (Fig. 5.5). The remainder of the post-central cortex of the parietal, temporal, and occipital lobes is concerned with the integration and elaboration of incoming sensory information.

Cortical zones Luria (1973b) has divided the whole area of the brain behind the central sulcus into three types of cortical region. He describes how disruption of these different functional types of cortex, known as cortical zones, may confer characteristic properties on the deficits observed. The following brief description scarcely does credit to the elegance of the conception nor the great value which this system has for the understanding of the individual case and for its usefulness in gaining a deeper appreciation of the psychological processes themselves. The principal features of Luria's system have been sketched in Chapter 1. Here a brief relation will be made to the cortical structure itself.

The *primary zones* of Luria are what are commonly termed primary projection areas. They possess high modal specificity, i.e., each particular area responds to highly differentiated properties of visual, auditory, or bodily sense information. They are also topologically arranged so that specific aspects of the stimulus are located systematically in order in the cortex, e.g., sense information from different parts of the body projects to particular sensory cortical areas, specific tones project to specific areas of the auditory cortex, and specific parts of the visual field to specific areas of the visual cortex. These primary zones consist 'mainly of neurons of afferent layer IV' of the cortex and their specificity and topological organization may be of considerable help in neurological diagnosis.

Each primary zone is made up largely of cells which respond only to a specific sense modality but also possess a few cells which respond to other modes of stimulation and may be concerned with the property of maintaining an optimal state of arousal or alertness in the cortex, or what Luria terms 'cortical tone'. Cortical tone is regulated by the reticular formation of the brain stem. Information on cortical arousal may be found in textbooks of physiology and physiological psychology.

The *secondary zones* are the areas adjacent to the primary projection areas where the modality specific information becomes integrated into meaningful wholes. In a general sense the primary zones may be said to be concerned with sensation while the secondary zones are concerned with perception or gnosis. In the secondary zones 'afferent layer IV yields its dominant position to layers II and III of cells, whose degree of modal specificity is lower and whose composition includes many more associative neurons with short axons, enabling incoming excitation to be combined into the necessary functional patterns, and they thus subserve a synthetic function' (Luria, 1973, pp.68-69). Disruptions of these secondary zones will give rise to gnostic or perceptual disorders restricted to a perceptual modality, e.g., auditory or visual or tactile agnosia.

The *tertiary zones* serve to integrate information across sense modalities. They lie at the borders of the parietal (somato-sensory), temporal (auditory), and occipital (visual) secondary zones. In these *zones of overlapping* of the P-T-O association area modal specificity disappears. The tertiary cortex is typified by a predominance of cells from the upper cortical layers and this type of cortex is seen only in man. These are the last portions of the brain to mature in ontogenetic development, not reaching full development until around seven years of age. Disruption of the tertiary zones gives rise to disorders which transcend any single modality and hence may be thought of as *supramodal* in character (see Ch. 6).

Luria's concept of the post-central cortical territory (or retrofrontal cortex) is thus a hierarchical one which moves from regions of high modal specificity to those which are supramodal.

The nature and connections of the frontal cortex are dealt with in Chapter 4.

The brain stem

The brain stem is divided into four parts, the medulla oblongata, pons, mesencephalon or midbrain, and the diencephalon. It is an extension upwards of the spinal cord. The brain stem contains nuclei and nerve circuits which control important bodily functions such as respiration, cardiovascular function and gastrointestinal function. It also contains the nuclei for the cranial nerves concerned with the special senses.

In the intact brain the lateral and posterior surfaces of the brain stem are hidden by the cerebral hemispheres and cerebellum but, on the anterior surface, parts of the inferior surface on floor of the hypothalamus (part of the diencephalon), midbrain, pons, and medulla can all be seen (Fig. 2.20).

The uppermost portion of the brain stem, the *diencephalon*, is surrounded

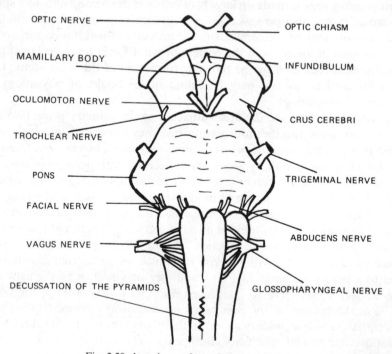

OPTIC NERVE

OPTIC CHIASM

MAMILLARY BODY

INFUNDIBULUM

OCULOMOTOR NERVE

CRUS CEREBRI

TROCHLEAR NERVE

PONS

TRIGEMINAL NERVE

FACIAL NERVE

VAGUS NERVE

ABDUCENS NERVE

DECUSSATION OF THE PYRAMIDS

GLOSSOPHARYNGEAL NERVE

Fig. 2.20 Anterior surface of the brain stem

by the hemispheres on all sides except for a small region between the mamillary bodies and optic chiasma. The diencephalon is one of the most complex regions of the central nervous system and any real understanding of its structure requires detailed study. It extends from the region of the interventricular foramen to the posterior commissure above and is continuous with the midbrain (mesencephalon) below (Fig. 2.21). The superior surface of the diencephalon

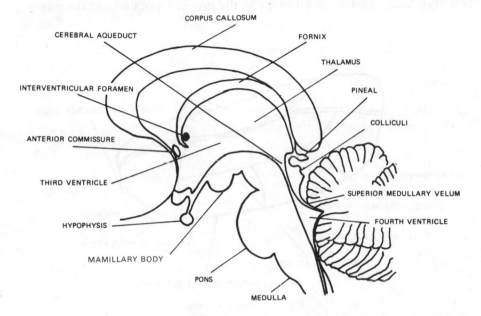

Fig. 2.21 Mid-Sagittal section of the brain stem

forms part of the floor of the body of the lateral ventricle. The internal capsule and optic tract form its lateral boundary. The floor includes the following structures on the inferior surface of the brain: mamillary bodies, infundibulum, neurohypophysis, and the optic chiasma. Anteriorly it pases into the basal olfactory area of the anterior perforated substance and posteriorly is continuous with the posterior perforated substance of the midbrain. The diencephalon encloses the third ventricle. Its principal components are the epithalamus, the thalamus and metathalamus, the hypothalamus, and the subthalamus.

The *epithalamus* contains a number of structures which can be recognized macroscopically in particular the *pineal gland* and the *posterior commissure*. The pineal gland begins to calcify from early adult life so that it forms at times a useful midline marker in radiographs and its deviation may indicate a space-occupying lesion within the skull cavity.

The *thalamus* is an oblique mass of grey matter on either side of the midline at the rostral end of the brain stem. It is separated on the medial aspect of the hemisphere from the hypothalamus by an indistinct groove called the *hypothalamic sulcus.*

These paired nuclear masses are separated by the third ventricle. The somewhat more pointed end of the ovoid forms the posterior wall of the interventricular foramen. The more rounded blunt end of the ovoid projects over the midbrain and is termed the *pulvinar*.

The thalami have been divided into a number of nuclei whose classification and nomenclature varies somewhat from one authority to another. Some classifications include more than twenty nuclei but a simpler division is used here (Fig. 2.22). This is related below to the projection of fibres to the cortex.

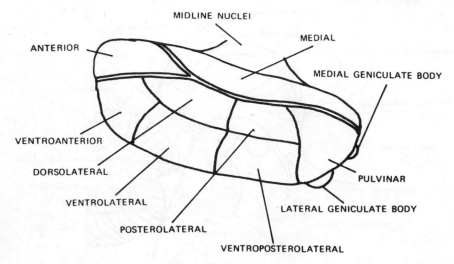

Fig. 2.22 Thalamic nuclei

The thalamic nuclear complex lies between the interventricular foramen and the posterior commissure and extends laterally from the third ventricle to the posterior limb of the internal capsule (Fig. 2.30). Sometimes the medial surfaces of the thalami are joined across the midline of the third ventricle by a mass of grey matter termed the *interthalamic adhesion* or *massa intermedia*. Though it crosses the midline it is certainly not to be considered as a commissure.

Apart from its role in projecting sensory information, the thalamus also plays a part in controlling the electrical activity of the cortex and helps in the integration of motor functions by providing relays through which the cerebellum and parts of the basal ganglia can influence the motor cortex.

The *metathalamus* is the collective name for the medial and lateral geniculate bodies which lie underneath the pulvinar (Fig. 2.22). From the *medial geniculate body* fibres of the acoustic radiation pass to the auditory area in the temporal lobe while the *lateral geniculate body* gives rise to the optic radiation.

The *hypothalamus* forms the inferior and lateral walls of the third ventricle. The hypothalamus is divided into medial and lateral groups of nuclei by fibres of the fornix which terminate in the mamillary bodies. These nuclei are concerned with a wide range of functions, e.g., emotion, sleep, temperature regulation, hunger, and thirst.

The *subthalamus* is a small transitional region lateral to the hypothalamus and ventral to the thalamus. It contains a large lens-shaped discrete nucleus (subthalamic nucleus) on the inner aspect of the internal capsule.

Midbrain. The *midbrain* is the smallest part of the major divisions of the brain and the least differentiated. It passes through the opening in the tentorium cerebelli and it is traversed by the narrow cerebral aqueduct which joins the third and fourth ventricles (Fig. 2.21). The thinner part posterior to the aqueduct is known as the *tectum* of the midbrain and is made up of the *superior* and *inferior colliculi* (Fig. 2.23). The superior colliculus is concerned with eye movements

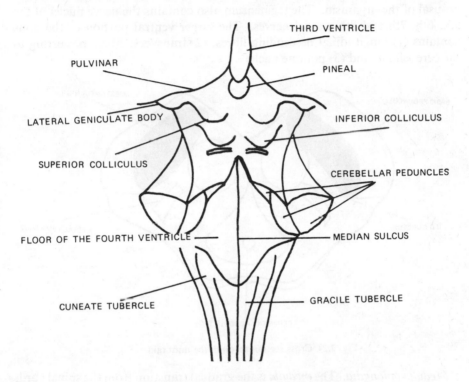

Fig. 2.23 Posterior aspect of the brain stem

and reflexes while the inferior colliculus receives auditory impulses which it relays to the auditory cortex of the temporal lobes. The thicker portion of the midbrain anterior to the aqueduct is made of two lateral masses, the *cerebral peduncles* (Fig. 2.24). In turn each cerebral peduncle is divided into an anterior and a posterior portion by a broad, deeply pigmented band of grey matter, the *substantia nigra*. The anterior portion, the *basis pendunculi (crus cerebri)* contains collections of fibres originating in the cerebral cortex which pass through the internal capsule. These fibres pass to the lower brain stem, pons, and spinal cord. The two trunks of the cerebral peduncles converge form the undersurface of the hemispheres and are close together as they enter the pons. The deep triangular area thus formed is the *interpeduncular fossa*.

The substantia nigra, which is the largest single nuclear mass in the midbrain, has connections with the basal ganglia and the thalamus and is thought to subserve motor function.

Pons. The *pons* is well delimited as a mass of fibres arching transversely around the anterior aspect of the brain stem and is separated from the cerebellum posteriorly by the fourth ventricle. The pons is divided into a large anterior part and a smaller posterior part of *tegmentum.* The tegmental portion contains a central core of nerve cells and fibres with an open structure known as the *reticular formation.* This reticular formation is continuous into the midbrain above and the medulla below and is concerned with the state of alertness or arousal of the organism. The tegmentum also contains the nerve nuclei of the 5th, 6th, 7th and 8th cranial nerves. The larger ventral portion of the pons contains (1) longitudinal descending fibres, (2) transverse fibres projecting to the cerebellum, and (3) pontine nuclei.

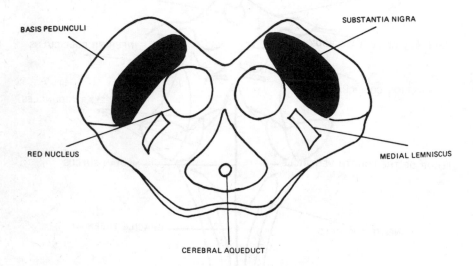

BASIS PEDUNCULI

SUBSTANTIA NIGRA

RED NUCLEUS

MEDIAL LEMNISCUS

CEREBRAL AQUEDUCT

Fig. 2.24 Cross section through the midbrain

Medulla oblongata. The *medulla* is the gradual transtion from the spinal cord, expanding in a conical fashion to the lower border of the pons. The transition from spinal cord to medulla is a gradual one and shows a number of features: (1) The midline anterior fissure of the spinal cord disappears; (2) The *decussation of the pyramids* or decussation of the cortico-spinal tracts takes place. Here bundles of fibres interdigitate as they cross the midline anteriorly carrying impulses for motor control of one half of the body from the contralateral cerebral cortex; (3) Posteriorly the gracile and cuneate tubercles appear; (4) The spinal nerves give way to the cranial nerves; (5) The fourth ventricle appears.

As the medulla continues upwards the fourth ventricle widens on the posterior aspect, the inferior cerebellar peduncle becomes more prominent, the eminence of the olivary complex appears dorsolaterally, and the medullary pyramids medially. The fourth ventricle is a shallow, rhomboid shaped depression overlying both the pons and medulla posteriorly. One point of the rhombus continues superiorly into the cerebral aqueduct while the inferior point extends into the central canal of the upper cervical spinal cord. The roof is formed by the cerebellum and the *superior* and *inferior medullary vela*. The superior medullary velum forms the roof of the pontine part of the ventricle while the inferior medullary velum forms the roof of the medullary part. At its widest part the fourth ventricle develops two tubular recesses which curve laterally over the inferior cerebellar peduncles. There is an opening in each recess, the lateral apertures (foramina of Luschka). The third or median aperture (Magendie) is found at the lowest point of the roof. It is through these three apertures that cerebrospinal fluid escapes into the subarachnoid space (Fig. 2.4).

The internal structure of the hemispheres

The principal structures within the hemispheres are (1) the white matter, (2) the basal ganglia, and (3) the lateral ventricles.

The white matter

The white matter or medullary substance is made up of millions of fibre processes or axons of nerve cells. The white colour is conferred by the myelin sheaths which coat the fibres and act as an insulating layer around the fibre as it transmits nerve impulses from one spot to another. The fibres may be divided into three categories. (1) The *association* or *intracerebral fibres* which connect various regions within one hemisphere. These may join areas which are close together or the fibres may be very long. (2) Intercerebral or *commissural fibres* unite homologous or equivalent areas or structures in the two hemispheres. (3) *Projection fibres* that convey impulses from deeper structures to the cortex or from the cortex to deeper structures. These deeper structures include the thalamus, hypothalamus, brain stem, cerebellum and spinal cord. An understanding of the pathways linking the various parts of the brain is of paramount importance in understanding one of the central concepts in neuropsychology, that of the disconnection syndrome, i.e., many symptoms and signs can best be understood as the result of a break in the normal connections between brain areas or systems. It is possible only to outline the major sets of connections here. Those interested in a more thoroughgoing treatment may consult references such as Kreig (1963) and Wright (1959).

Association fibres. (1) Association fibres may be divided into short fibre groups and long association groups. The short fibres lie beneath the cortex and arch around the bottom of the sulci to join adjacent convolutions or gyri. The long fibres lie more deeply and may be gathered into rather indefinite bundles or tracts which connect the different lobes. A number of the tracts are sufficiently circumscribed to warrant description (Fig. 2.25 and 2.26).

The *superior longitudinal fasciculus* courses backward from the frontal lobe to the occipital lobe and this tract sends some fibres to the posterior part of the temporal lobe. Fibres at the bottom of this fasciculus sweep around the region of the insula connecting the superior and middle frontal gyri with parts of the temporal lobe. These fibres, known as the *arcuate fasciculus,* are important for an anatomical understanding of the aphasias.

The *inferior longitudinal fasciculus* runs from the occipital to the temporal poles.

The *uncinate fasciculus* connects the anterior and inferior parts of the frontal lobe with parts of the temporal lobe by a bundle which is fan shaped at either end and drawn together in a compact bundle as it arches sharply around the stem of the lateral sulcus.

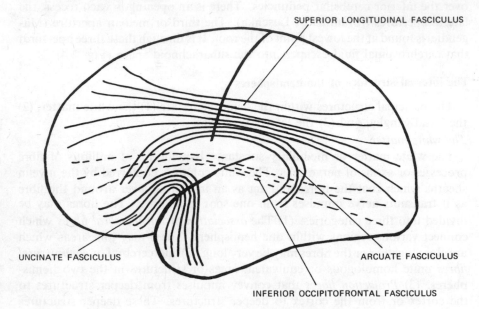

Fig. 2.25 Association tracts. Lateral view

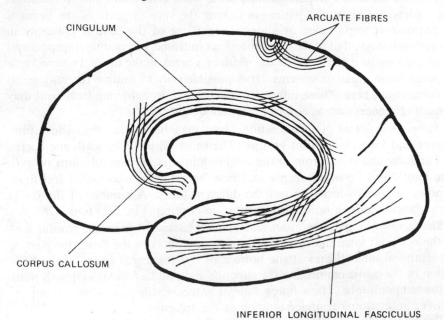

Fig. 2.26 Association tracts. Medial view.

On the medial aspect the principal association tract is the *cingulum* which lies within the cingulate gyrus. Like the cingulate gyrus the cingulum runs an arched course over the corpus callosum beginning below the rostrum and terminating in the uncus. The cingulum contains fibres of different length and it connects regions of the frontal and parietal lobes with parahippocampal and adjacent temporal regions. The tract is much reduced in the parahippocampal gyrus and uncus.

Commissural fibres. Interhemispheric fibre systems have three wellmarked commissures, namely the corpus callosum, the anterior commissure, and the hippocampal commissure or commissure of the fornix.

The *corpus callosum* is the largest mass of connecting fibres in the nervous system. It joins corresponding areas in the neocortex in the two hemispheres. Fibres enter it from practically every part of the cortex (Fig. 2.27). The degree of development of the corpus callosum in animal species is proportional to the degree of development of the neocortex itself, hence its prominence in the human brain. The major named portions of the corpus callosum, i.e., the rostrum, genu, body, and splenium have already been mentioned (Fig. 2.13).

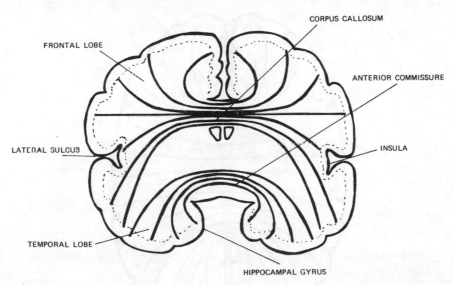

Fig. 2.27 Coronal section showing the two major commissures

Sunderland (1940) described the distribution of the fibres in the corpus callosum of the macaque. The distribution can be considered essentially similar in man. Fibres from the frontal lobes occupy the genu and the anterior third of the body. Other frontal fibres, together with fibres from the parietal and temporal area, occupy the middle third of the body. The posterior third of the body contains fibres from the parietal, temporal, and occipital lobes, those from the parietal regions being more numerous. The splenium is given over to fibres from the occipital regions.

Partial transections of the corpus callosum in man have confirmed that the posterior portion is principally concerned with the transmission of visual information while the central portion transmits somatosensory information (Ettlinger, 1965; Myers, 1961; Sperry, 1965). In 1953 Hoff put forward the interesting hypothesis that the different portions of the corpus callosum had different roles. The posterior parts were thought to integrate information, the anterior portions to separate functions, e.g. the independent functions of the two hands, while the middle parts of the corpus callosum were thought to allow 'for joint or independent activities of the hemispheres, as need for joint or independent operations may arise' (Gloning and Hoff, 1969, p.36).

The effects of commissure section or commissurotomy are detailed in Chapter 8.

Callosal fibres from the frontal and occipital poles and the medial aspects of these lobes take curved pathways known as the *anterior* and *posterior forceps*. (Fig. 2.28). Where the fibres cross the floor of the interhemispheric fissure they form the roof of the lateral ventricles.

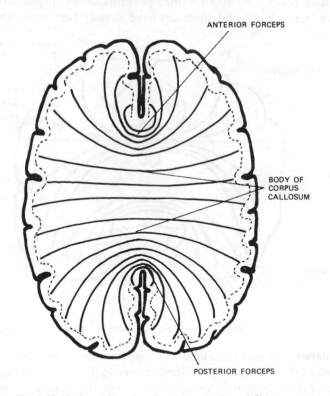

Fig. 2.28 Horizontal section showing commissural fibres

The *anterior commissure* is a rounded compact bundle of fibres which crosses the midline just anterior to the anterior column of the fornix and just below the interventricular foramen. Its shape has been likened to bicycle handlebars (Carpenter, 1972). Its main part connects regions of the inferior and middle temporal gyri while a smaller portion interconnects olfactory regions on the two sides (Fig. 2.27).

The *hippocampal commissure* is composed of transverse fibres which join the posterior columns of the fornix. Fibres arising in the hippocampus pass into the posterior columns of the fornix which sweep around the splenium of the corpus callosum approaching each other as they pass forward to join in the body of the fornix. The transverse fibres of the hippocampal commissure become shorter as the columns converge and the appearance of this portion gave rise to the name psalterium because of the resemblance to an ancient stringed instrument. (Fig. 2.19 and 2.29).

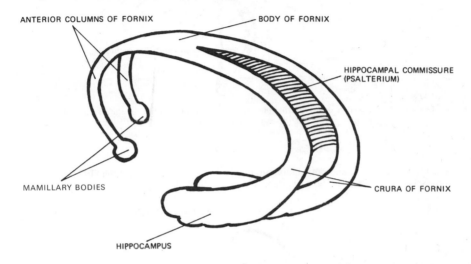

Fig. 2.29 Hippocampal commissure (psalterium)

Projection fibres. The projection fibres are of two types, afferent and efferent. Afferent fibres convey impulses to the cortex while efferent fibres carry impulses away from it. The projection fibres are arranged as a radiating mass, the *corona radiata* that coverges towards the brain stem (Fig. 2.30). Near the upper part of the brain stem the fibres are arranged in a narrow area between medial and lateral nuclear colections and are known as the *internal capsule*. The *caudate nucleus* and *thalamus* flank the capsule on the medial side while the *putamen* and *globus pallidus* flank it laterally (Fig. 2.31). A horizontal section through the brain shows the internal capsule has an anterior limb and a posterior limb.

The most posterior portion of the posterior limb of the internal capsule contains fibres of the *optic radiation* travelling from the lateral geniculate body to the calcarine sulcus in the occipital lobe.

The afferent fibres in the internal capsule arise mainly from the thalamus and project to nearly all areas of the cortex. Efferent fibres arise from various parts of the cortex. Among these are the important motor pathways which innervate the musculature of the opposite side of the body and whose disruption gives rise to contralateral paralysis since the fibres cross the midline lower down in the decussation of the pyramids.

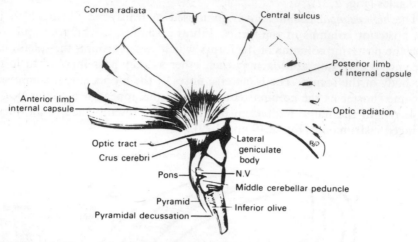

Drawing of a dissection demonstrating the continuity and relationships of the corona radiata, the internal capsule and the crus cerebri.

Fig. 2.30 Corona radiata and optic radiation. Figure 2.8, p. 21, M.B. Carpenter (1972) *Core text of Neuroanatomy*. (Courtesy of the author and Williams and Wilkins.)

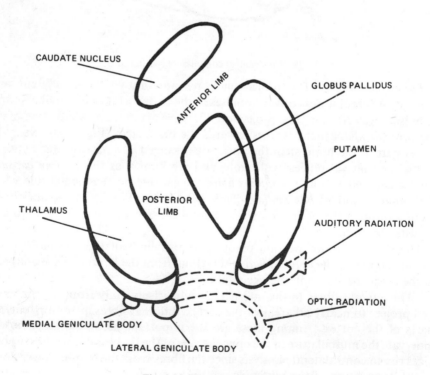

Fig. 2.31 The internal capsule

One of the ways of understanding the projection fibres is to consider how specific thalamic nuclei project upon the cortex. Bowsher (1970) points out that 'with the exception of certain areas in the temporal lobe, the whole neo-cortex and the corpus striatum receive specific fibres from the thalamus' (p.125). Schematic views of the thalamus and its constituent nuclei were shown above (Fig. 2.22) while the projecting zones of specific thalami are shown in Fig. 2.32 and 2.33.

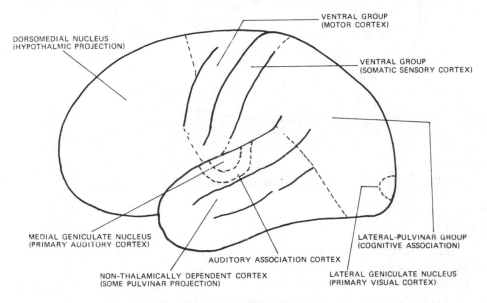

Fig. 2.32 Projection of thalamic nuclei. Lateral view.

'Thus the whole telecephalon (cerebral hemisphere) except some of the neocortex of the temporal lobe, can be regarded as an umbrella cover, whose hub is the thalamus and the spokes of which are the specific thalamo-telencephalic projections. . .It can be seen from this that the true definition of a functional cortical area depends not upon the fortuitous folding of its surface into sulci and gyri, nor upon its cytoarchitecture (though this is related), but upon its specific projection from a particular thalamic nucleus. For example, the primary somatosensory cortex (roughly defined as the post-central gyrus) is, in precise terms, only and entirely that area of cortex which receives its specific projections from the ventroposterior nucleus of the thalamus' (Bowsher, 1970, p.125).

The basal ganglia

The basal ganglia are subcortical nuclear masses. The principal structures are the *putamen*, the *globus pallidus*, the *caudate nucleus*, and the *amygdaloid complex*. The putamen and globus pallidus are sometimes referred to collectively as the lentiform nucleus.

Putamen. The putamen is the largest and most lateral part of the basal ganglia and its anterior portion is continuous with the head of the caudate

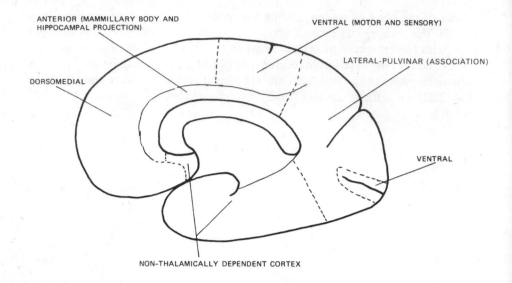

ANTERIOR (MAMMILLARY BODY AND
HIPPOCAMPAL PROJECTION)

VENTRAL (MOTOR AND SENSORY)

LATERAL-PULVINAR (ASSOCIATION)

DORSOMEDIAL

VENTRAL

NON-THALAMICALLY DEPENDENT CORTEX

Fig. 2.33 Projection of thalamic nuclei. Medial view

nucleus (Fig. 2.34).

Globus pallidus. The globus pallidus forms the medial portion of the lentiform nucleus. It consists of two separate sections and is paler in colour than the putamen, hence its name. The medial border of the globus pallidus is formed largely by fibres from the posterior limb of the internal capsule.

Caudate nucleus. The caudate nucleus is a long, arched mass of grey matter which is closely related throughout its length of the lateral ventricle. Its enlarged anterior part is termed the head of the caudate nucleus and this portion protrudes into the anterior horn of the lateral ventricle. The body and tail of the caudate nucleus lie dorsolateral to the thalamus near the lateral wall of the lateral ventricle. The tail of the nucleus follows the same curvature as the inferior horn (or temporal) of the lateral ventricle and enters the temporal lobe to terminate in the region of the amygdaloid complex (Fig. 2.34).

Amygdaloid complex. The amygdaloid complex is a mass of grey matter in the dorsomedial part of the temporal lobe. It is dorsal to the hippocampal formation and in front of the tip of the anterior horn of the lateral ventricle.

Blood supply of the brain

Since the central nervous system is one of the most metabolically active tissues in the body it requires a rich supply of oxygen. Some estimates put the nervous system's utilization of oxygen as high as one fifth of that of the whole body. If there is serious diminution in blood supply to nervous tissue for even a relatively short period, there is tissue death or necrosis. The importance of understanding the rudiments of the circulation can be seen when it is realized that impairment of blood supply is the most common cause of lesions in the

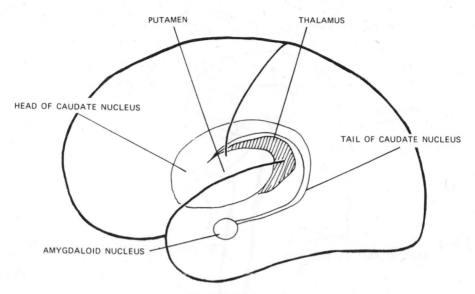

PUTAMEN   THALAMUS

HEAD OF CAUDATE NUCLEUS

TAIL OF CAUDATE NUCLEUS

AMYGDALOID NUCLEUS

Fig. 2.34 Basal ganglia

central nervous system.

Apart from the physiology of the cerebral circulation, it is important to understand the distribution of the blood via the various branches, since regional interruption to the blood supply is often associated with characteristic neuropsychological signs and symptoms, and a careful examination of the higher functions in such cases may allow inferences to be made about the nature and location of vascular blockages, insufficiencies, haemorrhages or the like. As yet, insufficient investigation has been given by neuropsychologists to this field.

The bloods supply to the brain comes from two pairs of arterial trunks, (i) the internal carotid arteries and (ii) the vertebral arteries (Fig. 2.35).

Internal carotid arterial system

The *internal carotid artery* enters the skull and, after making several sharp curves which form the *carotid siphon*, ascends lateral to the optic chiasm and breaks up into its major branches—the smaller anterior cerebral artery, and the larger middle cerebral artery. The latter is often considered as the direct continuation of the internal carotid artery. On its way to this major bifurcation, the internal carotid artery sends off three important branches, one anterior and two posterior. The anterior branch is the *ophthalmic artery* which passes forward through the opening in the optic orbit to supply the eye. The two posterior branches are the *anterior choroidal artery* and the *posterior communicating artery* (Fig. 2.36).

The *anterior choroidal artery* is usually of small calibre and passes backward across the optic tract and then laterally toward the anteromedial portion of the temporal lobe. The artery enters the inferior or temporal horn of the lateral ventricle where it supplies the choroid plexus. As well as the choroid plexus

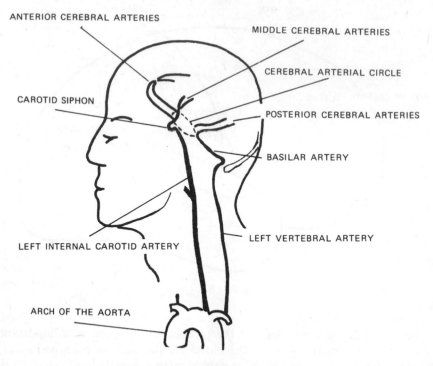

ANTERIOR CEREBRAL ARTERIES

MIDDLE CEREBRAL ARTERIES

CEREBRAL ARTERIAL CIRCLE

CAROTID SIPHON

POSTERIOR CEREBRAL ARTERIES

BASILAR ARTERY

LEFT VERTEBRAL ARTERY

LEFT INTERNAL CAROTID ARTERY

ARCH OF THE AORTA

Fig. 2.35 The two arterial supply systems

the anterior choroidal artery supplies the hippocampal formation and other deeply placed structures such as parts of the amygdaloid complex, caudate nucleus, thalamus, globus pallidus and internal capsule. As mentioned later, recent evidence has strongly implicated this hippocampus in the process of memory and for this reason a knowledge of the blood supply of this region becomes relevant to the neuropsychologist.

The *posterior communicating arteries* run backward to become joined to the proximal portions of the posterior cerebral arteries.

Anterior cerebral artery. The anterior cerebral artery (Fig. 2.37) passes dorsal to the optic nerve and approaches the anterior cerebral artery of the other side and is soon joined to it by the *anterior communicating artery*. The artery then enters the fissure between the two hemispheres, curves upward over the anterior portion (genu) of the corpus callosum and courses backwards on the medial surface of the cerebral hemisphere on the superior surface of the corpus callosum. It has a number of named branches: (1) orbital branches which supply the orbital lobes, (2) the frontopolar artery which supplies medial parts of the frontal lobe and extends on to the convexity of the hemisphere, (3) the callosomarginal artery which supplies the paracentral lobule and parts of the cingulate gyrus, (4) the pericallosal artery lies along the dorsal surface of the corpus callosum which it supplies *en route* to provide branches to the medial surface of the parietal lobe (e.g. the posterior parietal). The anterior cerebral artery also supplies the anterior columns of the fornix.

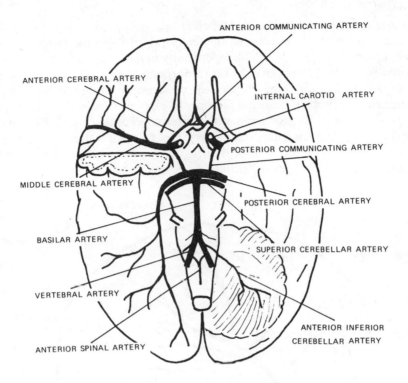

ANTERIOR COMMUNICATING ARTERY

ANTERIOR CEREBRAL ARTERY

INTERNAL CAROTID ARTERY

POSTERIOR COMMUNICATING ARTERY

MIDDLE CEREBRAL ARTERY

POSTERIOR CEREBRAL ARTERY

BASILAR ARTERY

SUPERIOR CEREBELLAR ARTERY

VERTEBRAL ARTERY

ANTERIOR SPINAL ARTERY

ANTERIOR INFERIOR
CEREBELLAR ARTERY

Fig. 2.36 Arteries at the base of the brain

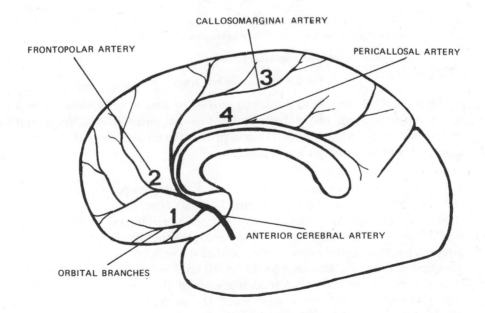

CALLOSOMARGINAL ARTERY

FRONTOPOLAR ARTERY

PERICALLOSAL ARTERY

ANTERIOR CEREBRAL ARTERY

ORBITAL BRANCHES

Fig. 2.37 Anterior cerebral artery

Middle cerebral artery. The middle cerebral artery passes laterally to enter the lateral cerebral fissure between the temporal lobe and the insula. It often breaks up into two stems which lie superficially in the lateral fissure (Fig. 2.38). The middle cerebral artery gives by far the largest supply to the cerebral hemispheres, accounting for some 75 per cent or more of the blood going to the hemispheres. It supplies branches not only to extensive areas of the cortex but also to the internal nuclear masses and internal capsule (Fig. 2.39). One of these branches, the lenticulostriate artery has been known as 'the artery of cerebral haemorrhage' because of the frequency with which it is involved in spontaneous haemorrhages or 'strokes'.

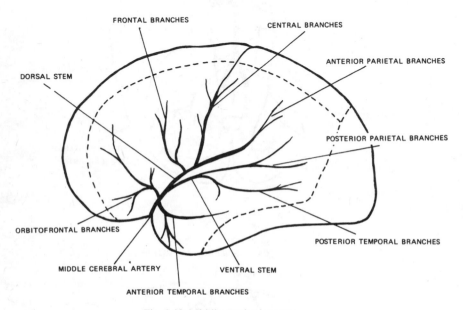

Fig. 2.38 Middle cerebral artery

The cortical branches from the dorsal portion or stem of the middle cerebral artery supply the area above the lateral fissure, i.e., orbitofrontal, precentral and anterior parts, while the ventral stem provides anterior temporal, posterior temporal, and posterior parietal branches.

Vertebral arterial system

The *vertebral arteries* enter the skull through the large opening, the *foramen magnum* through which the spinal cord becomes continuous with the brain stem. The two vertebral arteries rise along the anterolateral surfaces of the medulla and unite in the midline at the lower edge of the pons to form the basilar artery. Thus this major supply is often termed the vertebrobasilar system. The vertebral arteries give branches to the spinal cord before their entry into the cranial cavity while the intracranial branches of the vertebrobasilar system supply the spinal cord, brain stem (medulla, pons, midbrain), cerebellum, posterior diencephalon, and towards the termination of the system, the basilar artery bifurcates to form the two posterior arteries which supply parts of the

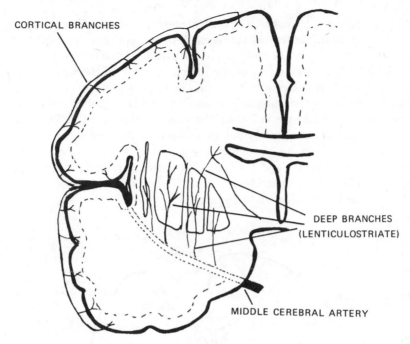

Fig. 2.39 Middle cerebral artery—lenticulostriate branches

temporal and occipital lobes of the cerebral hemispheres.

The *posterior cerebral arteries* pass around the lateral aspect of the midbrain and then pass dorsal to the tentorium cerebelli on to the inferior and medial surfaces of the temporal and occipital lobes (Fig. 2.40). The posterior cerebral

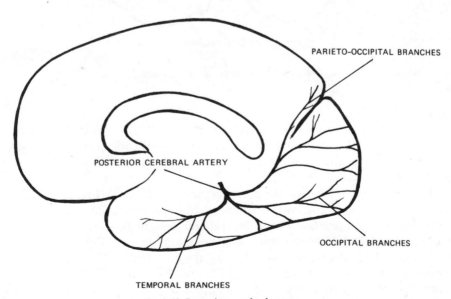

Fig. 2.40 Posterior cerebral artery

artery has three main branches: (1) the anterior temporal which supplies all the inferior surface of the temporal lobe with the exception of a small area of the tip which is supplied by the middle cerebral artery, (2) the posterior temporal which supplies the posterior part of the inferior surface of the temporal lobe, and (3) the largest or occipital which runs in the calcarine fissure and gives branches which supply the whole of the medial and a large portion of the other surfaces of the occipital lobe including the visual cortex (see Ch. 7).

As the posterior cerebral artery passes around the cerebral peduncle it supplies adjacent structures and provides the *posterior choroidal branch* which supplies the choriod plexus and the larger, posterior part of the hippocampus that is not supplied by the anterior choroidal. The arterial supply of the deeper structures of the brain is shown in Figure 2.41.

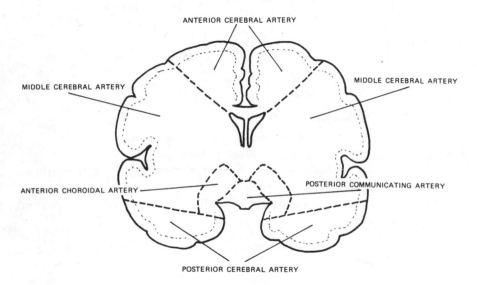

Fig. 2.41 Blood supply to deep structures

Venous drainage

The venous drainage is effected by three sets of vessels: (1) the superficial veins which drain the lateral and inferior surfaces of the hemispheres, (Fig. 2.42), (2) the deep veins which drain the whole of the internal area of the brain, and (3) the venous sinuses.

The deep veins converge on the great cerebral vein (Galen) (Fig. 2.43) which is a short wide vein just below the splenium of the corpus callosum. It runs a short course to the junction of the sagittal and straight sinuses.

The various cerebral veins empty into the venous sinuses (Fig. 2.44). These are channels formed between two layers of the dura mater. They converge at the *confluence of sinuses* in the region of the occipital bone and the bulk of the venous blood finally enters the large *internal jugular vein* though a small amount is drained through other channels.

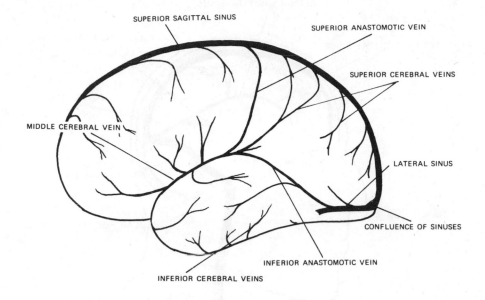

Fig. 2.42 Superficial cerebral veins

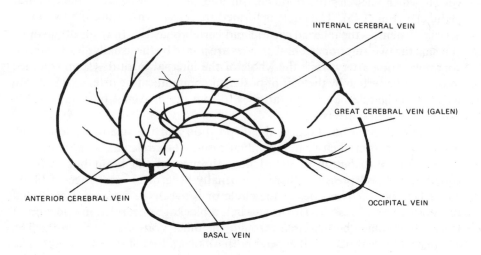

Fig. 2.43 Deep cerebral veins

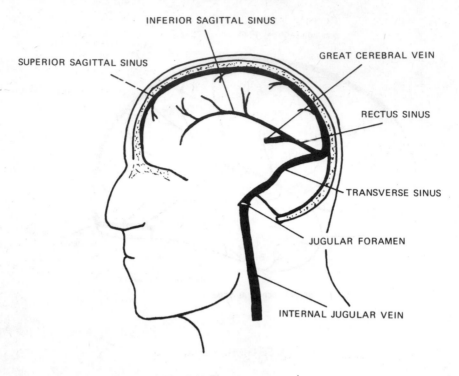

INFERIOR SAGITTAL SINUS

GREAT CEREBRAL VEIN

SUPERIOR SAGITTAL SINUS

RECTUS SINUS

TRANSVERSE SINUS

JUGULAR FORAMEN

INTERNAL JUGULAR VEIN

Fig. 2.44 The great venous sinuses

The cerebral arterial circle

The cerebral arterial circle (Circle of Willis) is a ring of connecting blood vessels which encircles the optic chiasm and the region between the cerebral peduncles (Fig. 2.45). The circle is formed by vessels which link the two great arterial systems—the internal carotid and vertebrobasilar. In front of the optic chiasma the two anterior cerebral arteries are joined by the usually short anterior communicating artery while the whole of the internal carotid system is joined to the basilar system by the pair of posterior communicating arteries which run back from the internal carotid arteries to join the proximal portions of each posterior cerebral artery.

There are variations both in the disposition and the size of vessels which enter into the arterial circle in individual cases. The circle has been thought to equalize the distribution of blood flow throughout the brain but, with an equality of blood pressure, there is normally little or no exchange of blood either between the two sides of the circle or between the internal carotid and posterior cerebral vessels. However when a blockage occurs at any portion of the circle this may be bypassed through the other portions of the circle. The adequacy of this process will depend both on the calibre of the vessel occluded, the size and nature of the alternative circulation, and the rapidity or otherwise of the occlusion. Such 'alternative' pathways are known as *anastomoses*. They are defined by Zulch (1971) as 'intercommunications of a network character in one or between two or more functionally separate systems, allowing the possibility of draining blood from them. An auxiliary supply may result, usually after widening of the channel, and flow may result in any direction' (p.107). Thus the slow narrowing which occurs due to the thickening of an artery (arteriosclerosis) may allow an anastomotic circulation to develop while a rapid occlusion by an embolus may not.

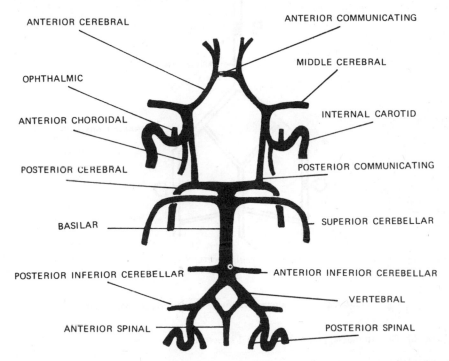

Fig. 2.45 The cerebral arterial circle (Circle of Willis)

Figure 2.46 provides a schematic representation of several possibilities of alternative supply with blockages in the vertebrobasilar system. Alternative routes for the flow of blood may be worked out for the points of occlusion indicated. For example, blockage of the right posterior cerebral artery at A will deprive the right occipital and basal temporal regions of their blood supply. Blockage at B will cause a loss of supply to the territory of both posterior cerebral arteries. Occlusion at such a 'bottleneck' will have serious consequences. On the other hand, even where both vertebral arteries are occluded (C and D) the effects may not be nearly so pronounced since an alternative supply may reach the brain via the patent branches which connect the anterior spinal artery with the vertebral arteries.

This oversimplified version of the supply pattern of the cerebral circulation can be expanded by the more extensive treatment by Zulch (1971); Kaplan and Ford (1966) and others. The arterial supply of the principal structures may be summarized as in Table 2.1.

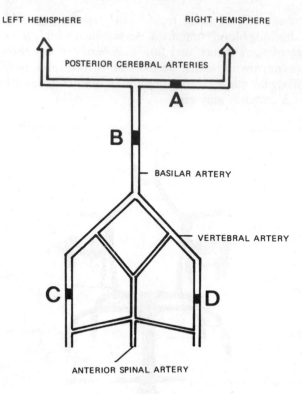

LEFT HEMISPHERE   RIGHT HEMISPHERE

POSTERIOR CEREBRAL ARTERIES

A

B

BASILAR ARTERY

VERTEBRAL ARTERY

C   D

ANTERIOR SPINAL ARTERY

Fig. 2.46 Occlusions and alternative routes in the vertebro-basilar circulation

Table 2.1 The arterial supply of the principal structures

Frontal lobe
    Lateral surface — middle cerebral artery
    Medial surface — anterior cerebral artery
    Inferior surface — middle and anterior cerebral arteries
Temporal lobe
    Lateral surface — middle cerebral artery
    Medial surface — middle cerebral, posterior cerebral, anterior choroidal, and posterior
                            communicating arteries
    Inferior surface — posterior cerebral artery
Parietal lobe
    Lateral surface — middle cerebral artery
    Medial surface — anterior cerebral artery
    Occipital lobe
    All surfaces — posterior cerebral artery
Corpus Callosum — anterior cerebral artery
Hippocampus — anterior choroidal artery, posterior choroidal branches of posterior cerebral
                        artery
Fornix
  Anterior columns — anterior cerebral artery
    Body and crura — posterior choroid branches of posterior cerebral artery
Mamillary bodies — posterior cerebral and posterior communicating arteries

3. Elements of Neurology

The neuropsychologist is most often a psychologist by primary training. Whether he is engaged in research or acting as a consultant concerning the patient's higher cortical functions, he brings to his collaboration with other workers in the neurosciences a rather different background. Tallent (1963), points out that 'the psychologist and his associates are members of considerably different cultures'. These cultural differences may bring fresh information and orientations which will prove helpful but they also create barriers in understanding and communication. The present chapter is aimed at providing the psychologist with the barest background to neurology including some of its terms and methodology, so that he may begin to understand, albeit in a very rudimentary fashion, the majority of neurological conditions he is likely to encounter in the literature and in practice. Absorption of some of the medical culture along with a sensible expression of his own is likely to prove mutually rewarding. Perhaps the greatest contribution in any cultural interchange is an understanding of the other culture's language.

The selection of topics is biased in the direction of the issues which have concerned neurology and neuropsychology in common in recent years. Standard textbooks of neurology will provide a means of expanding the psychologist's understanding of the field. A comprehensive source of information is the recent *Handbook of Neurology*, especially Volumes 2, 3 and 4 (Vinken and Bruyn, 1969).

Methods of investigation

Clinical investigation

Neurological examination consists firstly of the taking of a detailed history from the patient and, often of paramount importance, from those around him. Much valuable information about the types of neuropsychological tests to employ may be gained from a perusal of the patient's neurological case notes though, regrettably, many patients are still referred to the psychologist with a request 'for psychometric testing'. Where the anamnesis is insufficiently detailed., e.g. in questions relating to the patient's higher cortical functions, the psychologist should develop a routine of careful questioning.

A clinical neurological examination in itself is often an extensive, careful record of the patient's sensation, reflexes, movement, and muscle tone, and clinical neuropsychologists will need to familiarize themselves with the details of the neurological examination and with the traditional interpretation of neurological symptoms and signs. A standard text such as that of Alpers and Mancall (1971), forms a useful desk reference at all times.

Disturbances of integrative cerebral functions and the terminology in common use are described below.

Neurology has developed special methods in the investigation of disorders of the nervous system and a neuropsychologist will be better equipped to assist in the solution of neurological problems if he understands them. The remainder of the book is concerned with the most recently developed method namely neuropsychological investigation, which is aimed at obtaining information on the changes in specifically human functions which occur with lesions in the nervous system so that this information may be added to the methods already in use for the diagnosis of the nature and location of the lesions. 'In this respect neuropsychology is merely the most complex and newest chapter of neurology, and without this chapter, modern clinical neurology will be unable to exist and develop'. (Luria, 1973b)

Radiological investigation

The principal methods of radiological investigation are arteriography and encephalography. Together with other similar procedures they are termed contrast methods since they rely on the introduction of substances which alter the density of the structures studied to the passage of X-rays.

Arteriography. This is the technique for outlining the circulation by injecting a radio-opaque fluid directly into the blood stream. The term cerebral angiography is used to refer to the radiological investigation of both the arterial and venous channels of the brain and is often used interchangeably with the term arteriography.

The radio-opaque material may be injected directly into the artery beneath the site of puncturing the skin (the percutaneous method), or it may be introduced by a long thin tube termed a catheter which is passed along an artery until it reaches the vessel into which the material is to be injected. This technique

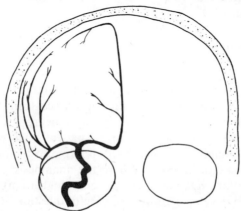

Fig. 3.1 Branches of the internal carotid circulation as seen in an arteriogram

is becoming increasingly popular, particularly as the catheter may be left *in situ* for periods as long as an hour and repeated injections made at intervals. The catheter method may also be used for the injection of other substances such as sodium amytal for the purpose of studying the effects of temporary deprivation or ablation of function of one cerebral hemisphere or a large portion of it. This procedure is described in Chapter 5.

As the radio-opaque material is swept through the cerebral circulation, serial X-ray photographs are taken in rapid succession and the procedure is repeated with X-rays taken in a plane at right angles to the first set so that a complete visualisation of the circulation in its various phases can be effected.

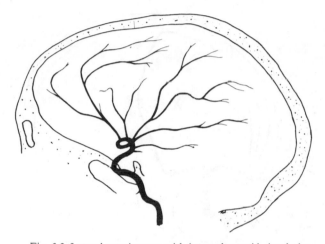

Fig. 3.2 Lateral arteriogram with internal carotid circulation.

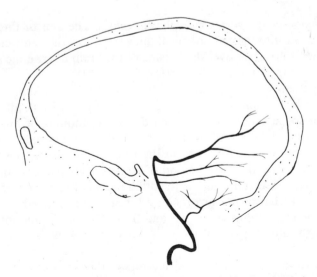

Fig. 3.3 Lateral arteriogram showing the vertebrobasilar circulation

Two principal techniques are carotid arteriography and vertebral arterio-graphy. In the first procedure the internal carotid artery and its branches (the anterior and middle cerebral arteries and their radicals) are demonstrated. (Figs. 3.1 and 3.2). In the second, the vertebral, basilar and posterior cerebral arteries are filled (Fig. 3.3).

Angiography is of particular value in the investigation of structural abnor-malities of the blood vessels themselves, e.g. stenosis or narrowing of one or more vessels, or an intracranial aneurysm or angioma.

On the other hand, alteration in the shape and position of vessels may indicate the presence of a space occupying lesion such as a cerebral tumour (Fig. 3.4).

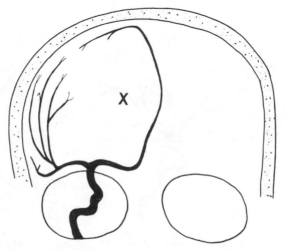

Fig. 3.4 Displacement of the anterior cerebral artery by a tumour

Air encephalography (pneumoencephalography). The aim of this procedure is to introduce air into the cerebrospinal fluid to outline the ventricular system, and sometimes, to pass air over the outside of the brain to examine for possible atrophy or wasting of the cerebral cortex.

With the patient sitting upright, a needle is introduced into the space between two vertebrae in the lumbar region so that the tip of the needle enters the subarachnoid space below the spinal cord. Small amounts of fluid are with-drawn and replaced by air which rises in the fluid and is made to enter the ventricular system via the foramina in the fourth ventricle by positioning the head and body. After the introduction of some twenty-five cm^3 of air, X-ray photographs are taken and, because the differences in opacity of air to the rays is much less than that of the surrounding brain, the entrapped air appears as a dark shadow in the films (Figs. 3.5 and 3.6). The small amount of air can be manipulated into all parts of the ventricular system by careful positioning of the head.

The localization of lesions such as tumours of the cerebral hemispheres can be inferred from signs of displacement and distortion of the lateral, third and

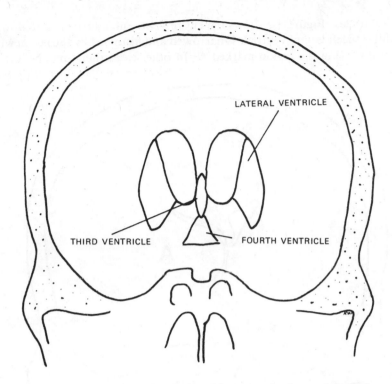

Fig. 3.5 Antero-posterior view of the ventricles as seen in air encephalography

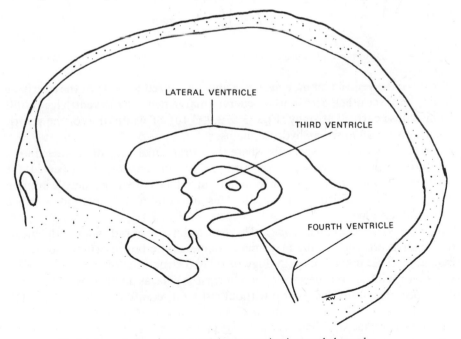

Fig 3.6 Lateral view of the ventricles as seen in air encephalography

fourth ventricles. Figure 3.7 shows the entire ventricular system shifted to the right while the left lateral ventricle is narrowed and distorted by the lesion which is assumed to lie in the region marked A. In other cases there may be dilation

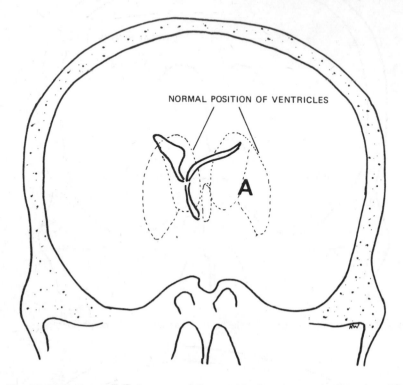

NORMAL POSITION OF VENTRICLES

A

Fig. 3.7 Distortion and displacement of the ventricles by a tumour in the region of A

of part of the ventricular system suggesting a localized wasting of the overlying brain while on other occasions a general enlargement of the ventricles results from diffuse cortical atrophy (Figs. 3.8, 3.9, 3.10). This dilation of the ventricular system is known as hydrocephalus.

On some occasions, especially where the intracranial pressure is raised, or a blockage of the canal between the third and fourth ventricles is suspected, the air used to outline the ventricular system is introduced through a needle inserted through a hole drilled in the skull. This direct puncture method is called ventriculography.

Computerized axial tomography. This new technique of radiological diagnosis has made it possible for the first time to demonstrate both normal and pathological cerebral tissue and pathology of related structures such as the cerebral ventricles without the necessity for contrast media as in the procedures just described. The procedure is also without risk or discomfort to the patient. The method consists basically of the use of a computer to recover information, particularly about soft tissues, which was previously lost because of the insensitivity of earlier methods of recording radiographic images. In line with earlier forms of tomography the computerized axial tomogram depicts the condition of a thin slice or plane through the head in a roughly horizontal position, several cuts being made at different levels. Technical aspects of the procedure together with a survey of some 300 cases with illustrations are given in New, *et al.* (1974).

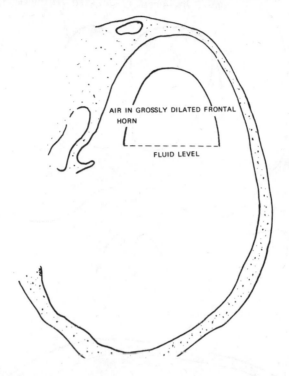

AIR IN GROSSLY DILATED FRONTAL HORN

FLUID LEVEL

Fig. 3.8 With the brow up air is shown in dilated ventricles

Evidence of the great value of this procedure is accumulating very rapidly and already in centres where such equipment is available has already greatly lessened the incidence of pneumoencephalography and to a lesser extent radionuclide brain scanning. The procedure is of inestimable value in more accurately localizing brain lesions of all kinds including the sites of vascular lesions and the extent of damage to cerebral tissue in closed head injury, conditions less clearly localized by other procedures.

The great value of computerized axial tomography to neuropsychology will be in providing a more accurate delineation of neurological lesions against which correlations with behavioural indices can be made more meaningfully.

Electrical investigation: Recording

One of the most widely used investigative techniques in neurology is electroencephalography. This is the technique of recording the electrical activity of the brain through the skull by means of electrodes placed on the scalp. The potential differences between two points on the skull produced by brain activity are very small and have to be amplified many times before they can be used to drive a recording device such as a pen recorder.

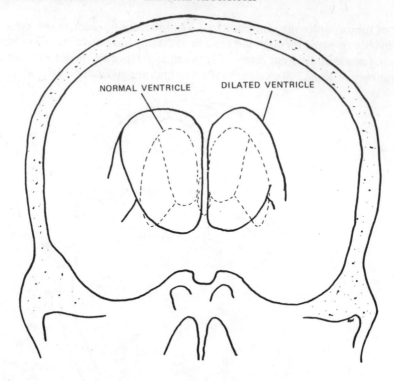

Fig. 3.9 Gross enlargement superimposed on normal pattern

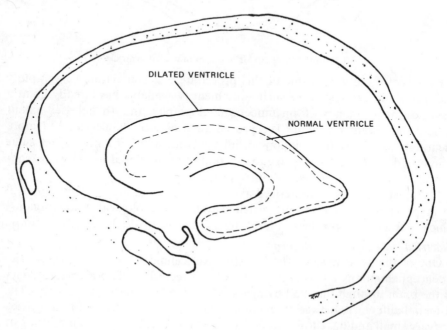

Fig. 3.10 Lateral view of enlarged ventricle associated with wasting of overlying brain tissue

The scalp electrodes are usually placed in a standard pattern (Fig. 3.11) and the activity between any pair of electrodes recorded as a single channel of which there are usually about eight. The various areas being analysed at any one time

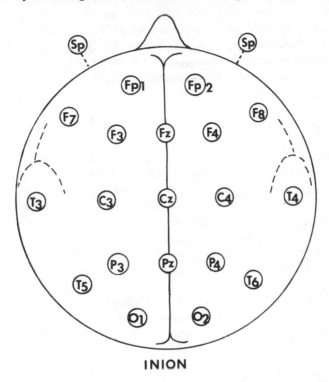

Fig. 3.11 Electrode placement in electroencephalogram

may be varied by switching the outputs between pairs of electrodes, e.g. in one period of examination eight channels might be devoted to the potential differences between Fp2-F8; F8-T4; F4-T6; T6-O2; and the corresponding areas on the left side of the head. In a subsequent 'run' differences might be examined in the transverse direction, e.g. T3-C3; C3-Cz; Cz-C4; C4-T4; and other areas. In this way a thorough coverage of the brain can be achieved and the activity of the various areas compared.

For some time after the invention of the electroencephalograph it was hoped by many that it would provide the tool to unlock many of the brain's secrets. The study of the relation between the EEG and higher mental functions has been singularly disappointing though increasing sophistication in recording and analysing equipment, including computer analysis, may yet prove of value. However, the technique is often valuable in neurological diagnosis. It is a safe and relatively simple procedure routinely used in most larger hospitals.

The EEG is of particular value in the investigation of epilepsy. Here abnormal electrical activity may be recorded in the period between the patient's clinical seizures—the interictal period. The observed abnormalities may be apparent in many of the channels or may be restricted to a clearly defined focus such as over one temporal lobe.

Unfortunately, any one EEG record taken from an epileptic patient may prove to be normal and serial recordings often need to be taken. Latent abnormalities may be brought out by using various activation procedures which may be effective in evoking the epileptic discharges so that they appear on the record, though the patient may not have any clinical manifestations. Commonly used activation techniques are: (1) recording during sleep; (2) overbreathing for two or three minutes (3) photic stimulation in the form of repetitive light flashes; and (4) adminstration of drugs.

The EEG is also of diagnostic value in the *localization* of organic lesions of the brain such as cerebral tumours, abscess, or infarction (see below) but is of much less value in determining the *nature* of the pathological process. It should be borne in mind also that, while positive findings in the EEG are of diagnostic significance, in most cases negative findings do not rule out the presence of even major pathology since in some proven pathological lesions EEG recordings sometimes appear entirely normal. The more superficial the lesion the more reliable is the localization.

Sometimes when the brain is exposed at operation, recordings are made from the surface of the cortex (corticogram) or even from the deeper part of the brain (depth electrogram).

Like evidence from other specialized diagnostic procedures the findings at electroencephalography must be examined in the light of the patient's history and clinical examination. Further details on the use of the EEG are to be found in such standard texts as Brazier (1968).

Electrical stimulation

. Electrical stimulation of nerve tissues is historically older than electrical recording techniques and in many respects, is complementary to it. The value of both techniques has increased with the advance in sophistication of electronic equipment.

Modern electronic stimulators permit investigators to control such parameters of stimulation as the frequency, duration, shape, and intensity of the pulses used.

Parallel with the development of electronics, advances in local anaesthesia and neurosurgical techniques have allowed the effects of brain stimulation to be explored in conscious human subjects. Extensive experience of brain stimulation such as that of Penfield and his colleagues, has provided an excellent opportunity to correlate stimulation effects with clinical signs and symptomatology (Penfield, 1958; Penfield and Jasper, 1954; Penfield and Perot, 1963; Penfield and Rasmussen, 1950; Penfield and Roberts, 1959). Examples of such findings are reported in later chapters.

Radioisotopic encephalography (Brain scan)

This method differs fundamentally from the methods outlined above. While both arteriography and pneumoencephalography are visual methods, the nature and the location of the lesion must be inferred from the displacement and distortion of structures such as blood vessels or the cerebral ventricles. In the brain scan the affected area can be more directly visualized. Though again, caution must be used since all lesions do not necessarily appear in the brain scan. If forms only one part of the investigative procedure.

A radioisotopic compound such as technetium 99 (T 99) is given by injection into one of the veins and travels through the vascular system to all parts of the body including the brain. Areas of increased focal uptake of the radioisotope, termed a positive brain scan, may be obtained with a number of pathological conditions such as cerebral tumours, abscesses, and vascular disorders. Certain

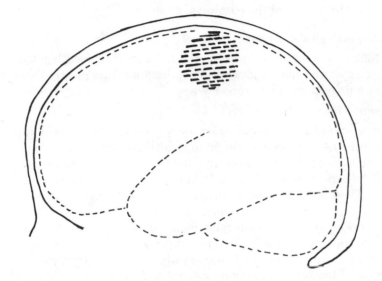

Fig. 3.12 Lateral view showing focal uptake of radioisotope in meningioma

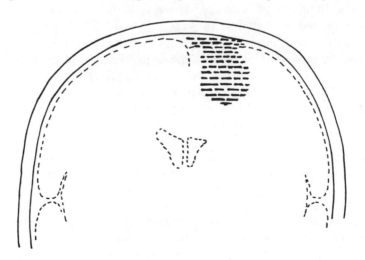

Fig. 3.13 Antero-posterior view of brain scan of meningioma

tumours, particularly meningiomas stand out particularly well in brain scans. (Figs 3.12, 3.13)

Neuropsychologists should find such depictions of great value since they provide the most direct evidence of the site and extent of lesions and allow more secure inferences to be made about the type of disconnection which can then be related to the patient's behavioural deficits. In some respects they are likely to be of more value than post-mortem findings since, on the relatively rare occasions where the psychologist has such information, it is usually presented to him in verbal terms which he may find difficult to visualize in relation to the areas of the brain and the pathways involved.

Common neurological disorders

The following conditions are those which are most frequently mentioned in the chapters which follow and which have been most frequently the object of neuropsychological studies in recent years.

Cerebral trauma

The functions of the brain can be seriously disturbed by physical injury. The effects of penetrating wounds of the brain resulting from high velocity projectiles such as bullets and shrapnel fragments have been studied intensively in large series of military cases, some of which have been followed up for one or more decades. These studies have contributed greatly to our understanding of neurology and, in more recent times, of neuropsychology. It is unfortunate that the drawings of such lesions often pictured as a small dot on a map of the brian, tend to leave the reader with the impression that one is dealing with a small circumscribed lesion which affects only the cortex at the point of entry. The nature of the fibre connections severed and the effect of the shock wave produced in the very soft brain mass by the penetrating missile are seldom known with any degree of accuracy. These wounds are, of course, relatively uncommon in studies of civilian subjects.

On the other hand, closed head injuries constitute an increasing problem as the result of motor car accidents. The term 'closed head injuries' refers to the fact that the brain may be severely injured even though the skull is not penetrated. Closed head injuries may produce a wide range of symptoms depending upon the severity of the injury. Surviving patients may show little or no impairment of higher cortical functions with minor injuries or a gross deterioration of intellect and personality with more severe damage.

Concussion. Prominent among the symptoms of head injury is impairment of consciousness. In a simple concussion there may be only a brief clouding of consciousness or a temporary loss. This temporary loss of consciousness is probably due to injury to the brain stem reticular formation. The patient cannot remember the incident causing the concussion and has a loss of memory for events just preceding it. The length of this *retrograde amnesia* is related to the severity of the injury. There may also be a period of memory loss for the period after the injury which is also related to the severity of the injury and is termed anterograde or post-traumatic amnesia. These memory disorders have been discussed recently in detail by Barbizet (1970) and others, and are outlined later in this chapter.

A recent study by Lynch and Yarnell (1973) has demonstrated that concussion may lead to a period of delayed forgetting. Concussed athletes interviewed shortly after the injury were shown to have good recall for events just before the injury but when questioned a short period later (3 to 20 minutes) were unable to recall the same pre-injury events.

When loss of consciousness is prolonged it is probable that the patient has sustained a more severe injury, but there is no hard and fast rule which might distinguish between concussion, from which patients usually recover in a few days or less, and the more severe conditions.

Contusion. In closed head injuries the brain may be bruised or torn in the region of impact or in places far removed from the point of impact. Also, in injuries where the skull has been fractured and the underlying brain lacerated, it is important to remember that there may also be considerable injury to other parts of the brain distant from the obvious site of external injury. These injuries are often on the side of the brain away from the site of impact and are termed *contrecoup* injuries. They are bought about by the brain, which is capable of moving relative to the skull, striking the inner table of the bones of the skull as the head is suddenly decelerated after the initial blow (Fig. 3.14).

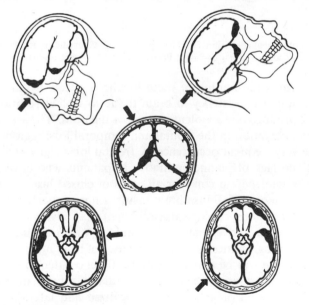

Fig. 3.14 Mechanism of cerebal contusion. Fig. 137, p. 292. C.B. Courville (1945), *Pathology of the Nervous System,* 2nd. edn. Courtesy of Pacific Press Publications Association).

An understanding of the mechanism of cerebral contusion is important for neuropsychology and it helps to explain why some patients after head injuries have psychological deficits which suggest damage to localized areas distant from the obvious lesions. The marked tendency for the bruising and laceration to affect the basal portions of the frontal lobes and much of the temporal lobes has been demonstrated in clinical cases by Courville (1942, 1945) who discusses the mechanism of production of craniocerebral injuries (Fig. 3.15). Holburn

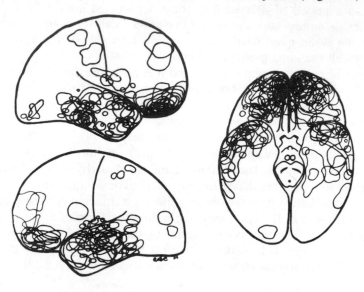

Fig. 3.15 Sites of cerebal contusion. (Fig. 138, p. 293. C.B. Courville (1945), Pathology of the Neurous System, 2nd edn. Courtesy of Pacific Press Publications Association).

(1943) confirmed the finding of these localized effects by subjecting gelatine moulds of similar consistency to brain tissue to violent rotational stress such as might be produced by a violent motion of the head. These stresses produced extreme fragmentation in the frontal and temporal lobe regions. This helps to explain the very frequent occurrence of 'frontal lobe' signs such as uninhibited behaviour and lack of planned initiative in patients who have sustained head injuries. The tendency to consider all cases of closed head injury as suffering only from the effects of diffuse brain insult is not supported by such evidence and careful neurolopsychological assessment may give valuable information about the location and extent of the damage which should prove useful in rehabilitation programmes. While many cases of head injury will have features in common, there will be many essential differences due to the different locus of lesion. The information that has accumulated rapidly in neuropsychology in recent years based on the study of localized and lateralized cases should prove of value in the future assessment, and hence management, of head injury patients.

Smith, E. (1974) in a study of long-term effects of severe closed head injuries provided further evidence for the *contrecoup* effect. In particular, impact on the right side of the cranium tended to produce much greater deficits than impact on the left presumably due to 'dominant' hemisphere damage. The right sided impact cases showed greater deficits on non-verbal as well as verbal skills.

Over recent years there has been a marked increase in a type of severe injury termed the exploded temporal pole. This injury is the result of high speed head-on motor vehicle collisions. The injury is often bilateral and usually results in significant residual memory impairment.

The repeated concussion and contusion which occurs in many boxers often results in deterioration of memory and intellect. One of the earliest signs that all is not well is a falling off in the ability to learn new material and this is apparent on psychological testing long before the obvious clinical signs of deterioration appear. Routine serial testing might help considerably in the early prevention of the *punchdrunk syndrome* which, in the past, has often progressed to a severe degree of dementia.

Traumatic haemorrhage. While small haemorrhages may occur in virtually any part of the brain after any form of head injury, more extensive haemorrhages occur from the laceration of blood vessels inside the skull, e.g., a fracture of the skull may tear the middle meningeal artery which, by bleeding under considerable pressure into the space outside the covering of the brain, greatly compresses the cerebral hemisphere and later the basal portions of the brain. This *extradural* haematoma is a neurosurgical emergency and has little relevance for neuropsychology.

On the other hand, bleeding from blood vessels beneath the *dura mater*, produces a *subdural haematoma*, which may be less dramatic and, in elderly patients, may follow an injury so trivial that the patient does not even recall

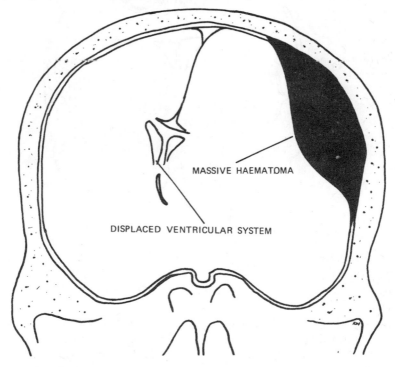

MASSIVE HAEMATOMA

DISPLACED VENTRICULAR SYSTEM

Fig. 3.16 Massive subdural haematoma with ventricular shift

it (Fig. 3.16). This condition may produce changes which develop over days or even weeks after injury often simulating the picture of senile dementia with loss of concentration, episodes of confusion, and memory loss.

Tumours

The word tumour has been used somewhat generally to refer to any abnormal swelling in the tissues of the body. When referring to brain tumours or cerebral tumours the term usually means a *neoplasm* or new growth. Such a neoplasm has been defined as a 'mass of cells. . .resembling those normally present in the body, but arranged atypically, which grow at the expense and independently of the organism without subserving any useful purpose therein' (Handfield-Jones and Porritt, 1949, p.86).

These neoplasms in the brain may be benign or malignant. Benign neoplasms most frequently grow from the coverings of the brain. These coverings are termed *meninges* and tumours arising from them, *meningiomas*. Such benign tumours may grow slowly and attain a large size before they cause symptoms from their pressure effect on the brain or they may be symptomless and only be discovered at autopsy. They can be successfully removed in their entirety as they do not invade the brain substance (Fig. 3.17).

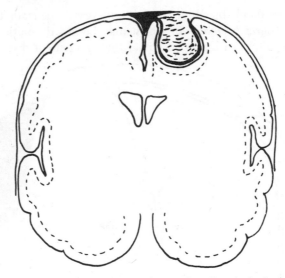

Fig. 3.17 Meningioma compressing but not invading the brain tissue

Unfortunately, benign tumours are much less frequent than the malignant type which invade the tissue of the brain. The latter can rarely be removed fully by surgery because of the extent to which they infiltrate the surrounding tissue (Fig. 3.18).

Most malignant brain tumours arise from the glial cells or fibres themselves and are termed *primary neoplasms*. The most common type, the *glioma*, which accounts for some forty percent of adult brain tumours is also the most malignant. A smaller proportion of brain tumours are called *secondary neoplasms* since they multiply from cells of malignant tumours in other parts of the body. These cells of origin of cerebral secondary neoplasms have become detached from their parent tumours and carried by the blood stream to lodge in the brain to begin independent growth there. Tumours of the lung or breast often give rise to such *metastatic* or secondary tumours.

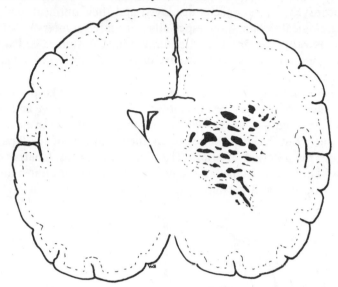

Fig. 3.18 Malignant tumour invading cerebral tissue

Sometimes conditions that are not neoplastic may give rise to very similar signs and symptoms, e.g. an abscess in the brain. Though these may be diagnosed from signs which signal the presence of infection their nature may not be discovered until an exploratory operation is carried out. For this reason tumours, abscesses, and other mechanically similar conditions are given the title of 'space occupying lesions'.

It can be seen from this short description that tumours within the skull may produce a multitude of symptoms which depend on their nature, location, and growth of the lesion. While most space occupying lesions will produce a set of general symptoms, each particular case will have specific features which depend on the interruption of connections between different parts of the brain. Thus, a small lesion in a strategic situation may have disastrous early effects because it interferes with vital centres or cuts a large number of interconnections between different areas of the brain while a large lesion in another area may be almost silent for a relatively long period.

It is this failure to take into account the nature and location of cerebral lesions which defeated many of the earlier attempts to draw conclusions from psychological studies of heterogeneous populations of 'brain-damaged' people.

Vascular disorders

Disorders of the blood vessels and of the blood supply to the brain are extremely common. They produce a bewildering variety of symptoms. Though these disorders are frequently seen in later life, they are by no means restricted to this age group and may be seen in relatively young adults. Neuropsychological examination may prove very difficult in this group of patients and a wide variety of techniques may have to be employed to clarify the exact nature of the neuropsychological deficits displayed and their implications. A careful neuropsychological examination, especially if repeated at intervals, often proves of value in assessing prognosis and guiding rehabilitation. The two principal categories of cerebral vascular disorder are *spontaneous intracranial haemorrhage* and *cerebral ischaemia*.

Spontaneous intracranial haemorrhage. Bleeding may take place within the brain substance itself. This is termed *intracerebral haemorrhage* and is responsible for the very common 'stroke' which is often associated with elevation of the blood pressure (Fig. 3.19). It is most often due to rupture of small pathological dilations on the internal arteries. These are known as Charcot-Bouchard aneurysms. Though spontaneous haemorrhage may occur almost anywhere in the brain, it occurs with greater frequency in some areas than others, e.g. in

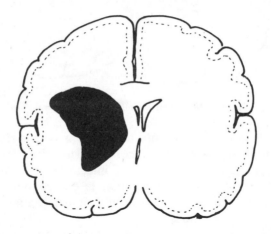

Fig. 3.19 Intracerebral haemorrhage disrupting the white matter

the branches of the lenticulostriate artery. This set of vessels, which themselves are branches of the middle cerebral artery has been called 'the artery of cerebral haemorrhage'. Here the bleeding damages the brain tissue in the area and the effects are in keeping with the extent of the haemorrhage. Since the pathways which serve the opposite side of the body pass through this region, one of the major signs of a haemorrhage from the lenticulostriate artery is the commonly observed paralysis on the opposite side of the body. At the same time there may be disorders of higher mental function when the haemorrhage disconnects various cortical areas.

Primary intracranial haemorrhages vary a good deal in their severity, and the residual disability in those who survive such episodes varies from relatively slight impairment to profound loss of function. The common disruption of language functions which occurs when the lesion is in the left hemisphere is discussed below.

The second major class of intracranial haemorrhage is termed, somewhat loosely, *subarachnoid haemorrhage*. The term subarachnoid signifies under the arachnoid mater, the extremely thin covering of the brain and its blood vessels. In at least half such cases there is damage to brain tissue as well as the irritative and pressure effects of the bleeding. While such cases are important neurologically, they seldom pose problems to which the neuropsychologist can make a contribution.

Cerebral ischaemia. The word ischaemia means a reduction in blood supply to a local region due to mechanical obstruction. This obstruction may affect vessels of any size and, if the blood supply to any part of the brain is reduced below a critical level, the tissue served by this vessel will die unless it can receive an alternative blood supply from a collateral source. The death of portion of the brain substance from this vascular cause is termed a *cerebral infarct*. The blockage may be sudden when for example, a clot travelling from elsewhere becomes lodged in a cerebral artery and leads to its obstruction, or primary clotting may take place in one of the cerebral arteries due to narrowing brought about by arterial disease and the consequent slowing of the circulation.

The symptoms produced by cerebral infarction will depend on a number of factors such as the rapidity of the occlusion and the size and location of the vessel involved. Narrowing of arterial vessels is referred to as *stenosis* and is of increasing importance since it is now possible by means of vascular surgery to re-establish an efficient circulation by clearing accumulated plaque from the lumen of the artery, an operation known as *endarterectomy*. Neuropsychological examination forms a useful method in assessing the degree of restoration of function after such operations. Only one such neuropsychological study has appeared to date. Goldstein, Kleinknecht and Gallo (1970) describe changes in the direction of improved performace on the Reitan battery of neurological tests (Reitan, 1966b) and other measures including standard intelligence tests as well as improvement in motor function. This demonstration of at least a partial restoration of function after *endarterectomy* is of significance since studies using solely clinical neurological assessment have led to the opinion that the operation was purely prophylactic rather than restorative.

Arterial stenosis often leads to temporary loss of function in the brain especially if it is accompanied by transient falls in blood pressure which deprive portions of the brain of an adequate blood supply for short periods of time but which are not severe enough to produce a massive death of nerve cells. In such cases the condition may be referred to as recurrent cerebral ischaemia and this is commonly associated with the narrowing of the two major systems of cerebral blood vessels, namely the internal-carotid artery system and the vertebro-basilar artery system or their branches.

Stenosis of the arterial system can be demonstrated by arteriography, though, where vertebrobasilar insufficiency is diagnosed clinically, the performance of arteriography carries serious risks. The review by Silverman, Bergman and Bender (1961) shows that vertebral angiography in these cases may produce transient blindness, memory changes, and other serious complications.

Numerous clinical syndromes have been referred to the insufficiency or thrombosis (that is, clotting) in separate branches of the cerebral circulation. As pointed out in Chapter 2, the final result of arterial occlusion whether partial or total will depend not only on the distribution of the blood vessels, which may vary from individual to individual, but also of the availability of anastomotic connections which may moderate the effects of occlusion particularly if

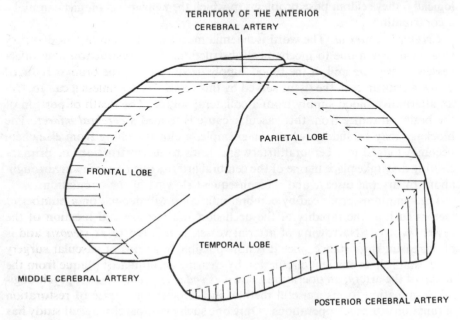

Fig. 3.20 Territory of supply of the major cerebral arteries

this is slow in its development. Occlusion of a particular vessel will give rise to a set of changes the nature of which will depend on the area supplied by the vessel concerned. Figure 3.20 shows the territory on the convexity of the hemispheres served by the three main cerebral arteries. A stenosis of the middle cerebral artery will give symptoms referable to the frontal, temporal, and parietal lobes.

Convulsive disorders

The multiplicity of disorders which have convulsions as a prominent or frequent symptom is well illustrated in the recent publications of the Marseilles group (Gastaut and Broughton, 1972).

The term epilepsy means essentially a sudden disruption of the patient's senses and, because it manifests itself in a great variety of ways, it is difficult to define more clearly in a short space. The problem is aggravated by the vast array of terms which have been used to define the same or very similar conditions. Because many of the older terms are still in use, they will be employed in this section, though the classification suggested by Gastaut (1970, 1972) is strongly recommended. The EEG characteristics must be considered always in close conjunction with the clinical manifestation. The following outline owes much to Gastaut's (1970) fine summary. Several main groups of seizures are recognised in this classification:

1. Generalized seizures with no features referable to a localized anatomical or functional system. Probably the most commonly used term is *centrecephalic epilepsy* on the assumption that their origin is deep in the centre of the brain, and the excitation is projected symmetrically to both hemispheres (Fig. 3.21). There is usually loss or impairment of consciousness and the major convulsions of the musculature which so many associate with epilepsy may or many not be present. The convulsions when present are caused by the spread of excitation over the motor areas. The term *grand mal* seizure has been in vogue for a long period to describe this frequently observed variety of generalized major seizure.

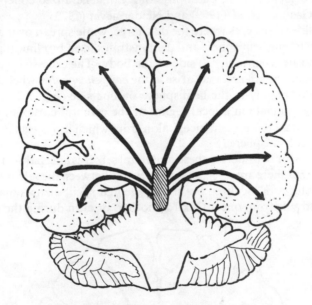

Fig. 3.21 Schematic representation of the spread of excitation from the centre of the brain

The difficulty rises when one realizes that while there may be no demonstrable cause of these major attacks in some individuals, particularly the younger age groups, the proportion of patients who have an organic cause such as a cerebral tumour or vascular disease increases greatly in middle age.

The EEG features in these generalized seizures irrespective of their clinical form are bilateral, symmetrical, markedly synchronous discharges from the very inception of the seizure. Apart from the *grand mal* seizures, generalized epilepsy may be demonstrated in a number of other forms such as pure tonic or pure clonic seizures, or it may appear as *absences*. These absences often take the form of an abrupt loss of mental functions for from five to fifteen seconds. The patient's ongoing activity is interrupted and he is unresponsive for this short period. The patient will then resume his previous activity where he left off and will have retrograde amnesia for the event. These absences have generally been called *petit mal* episodes.

While the present brief outline is described in terms of the popularly approved centrecephalic theory there is growing evidence that the initial site of origin for generalized epilepsy may lie in 'higher' structures such as the frontal lobes, at least in some cases. This position on the pathogenesis of generalized seizures has been supported by studies in man, particularly depth electrographic studies. In recent times the discovery of an animal model has been found in Papio papio the Senegalese baboon. This animal provides a partial model since it has only some of the characteristics found in generalized epilepsy in human subjects. It shows both photosensitivity and spontaneous generalized seizures. The electrical discharges in this animal appear initially in the frontal lobe and are maximal there, only spreading later to more deeply placed structures.

The recent evidence on the pathophysiology of generalized epilepsy has been surveyed by Gastaut, *et. al.* (1969) and Neidermeyer (1972).

2.   Unilateral seizures where the discharge, while spread over a wide area, is restricted to one hemisphere and demonstrates itself by clinical phenomena on the opposite (*contralateral*) side of the body. The excessive neuronal discharge causing the seizure, may arise in the *centrencephalon* whence it spreads exclusively or mainly to the hemisphere on one side (Fig. 3.22), or the discharge may originate in a local region of the cerebral cortex of one hemisphere and spread to the centrencephalon from which it projects in turn to the whole of that hemisphere (Fig. 3.23).

The reason for considering these unilateral seizures as separate from partial seizures, is that there are no signs in the periods between the seizures of clinical or EEG features of localized brain damage and such seizures may alternate from side to side from one attack to another, or even during the course of a

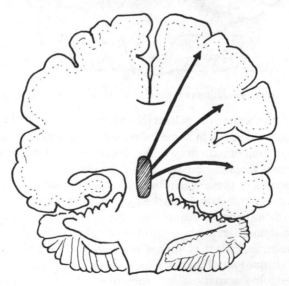

Fig. 3.22 Unilateral spread from the centrencephalon

single attack. As with generalized seizures unilateral seizures have been classified into a number of subtypes according to the symptomatology.

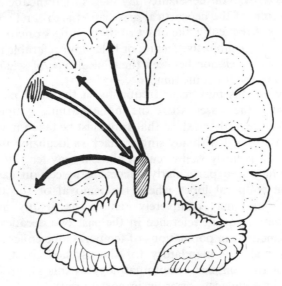

Fig. 3.23 Unilateral seizures resulting from a cortical focus

3.   Partial seizures, often termed *focal epilepsy* or *local epilepsy*, are of particular interest to modern neuropsychology with its emphasis on the study of the location of functional systems within the brain. For this reason, numerous psychological studies of the higher functions in patients with partial epilepsy have been carried out, and a number of them are reported in later chapters. Gastaut's system classifies the partial seizures according to the functions of the areas effected, with major divisions into: (a) simple partial seizures consisting of sensory, motor, and autonomic symptoms and signs, and (b) complex partial seizures producing symptoms disruptive of man's higher cortical functions.

Simple partial seizures. 1. Motor symptoms may take many forms and point to the localization mainly in portions of the region in front of the central or *rolandic fissure* though the focal abnormality may lie in the temporal or parietal region, e.g. when *dysphasia* is bought about by the epileptic or ictal discharge.

2.   Sensory symptoms may take the form of any of the sense modalities, i.e. somotosensory phenomena or sensations referable to the special senses of vision, audition, and olfaction in particular. There may be a fine line between the designation of a symptom as a simple sensory seizure, a sensory illusion or even a sensory hallucination but a careful examination may be of value in localization. Patients differ a good deal in their ability to describe their symptoms and carefully phrased questions will help.

3.   Symptoms of autonomic disturbance. These rarely occur without other symptoms.

Complex partial seizures. Since these seizures present so frequently with symptoms of disruption of higher mental functions, they have become of increasing interest to neuropsychologists.

Certain characteristics of the seizure may suggest that the focus of abnormal excitation lies in one of the neocortical association areas and so may be used as localizing signs. Frequently, the onset of the seizures or *aura* as it is usually called, is signalled by a subjective feeling or behaviour referable to a particular area and tables of the relation between the clinical type of seizure and localization have been in use for some time.

Though many attacks may recur frequently in the same manner in some patients, there are other cases where the initial warning symptoms or auras vary from one seizure to the next, so that care must be taken in using the signs and symptoms associated with any single attack as localizing indications.

Where the lesion is fairly well circumscribed, it may lend itself to surgical removal. This has been particularly successful in certain cases of lesions restricted to the temporal lobes where the removal of the temporal lobe (temporal lobectomy) may completely remove or greatly ameliorate the condition. The very frequent reference in the past two decades to studies of various higher functions in populations of temporal lobe epileptics before and after lobectomy makes it mandatory for the psychologist to have a clear understanding of the complex symptomatology of this group of seizures of which temporal lobe epilepsy forms an important part.

The portions of the cortex which may be involved in complex partial seizures are the frontal, temporal and parietal neo-cortex, and the sub-cortical structures associated with them. The clinical features which distinguish the sub groups mentioned below are often present in the same patient, either in the one attack or at different times and may be accompanied by impaired consciousness which may obscure the picture. The main types can be grouped as follows:

1. Cases where impairment of consciousness is the principal or even the sole symptom.

2. Psychomotor attacks where the principal symptoms are confusion and automatic behaviour. Confusional automatisms may be merely a 'mechanical' prolongation of the behaviour in which the patient was engaged at the onset of the attack, or the automatisms may represent new behaviour beginning during the attack. Many forms of automatisms have been given descriptive labels, e.g. *ambulatory automatisms* in which the patient may carry out coordinated movements of some complexity during the attack and for a varying time after the seizure, *verbal automatisms*, *gestural automatisms*, and the like.

3. Seizures with sensory illusions or hallucinations. The nature of these seizures varies with the region of cortex which is the site of discharge. Where the primary projection areas of the cortex are mainly affected, the phenomena are simpler sensory experiences or alteration of the perception of present stimuli, while excitation of the secondary association areas which surround the relevant primary projection cortex appears to give rise to integrated perceptual experiences which, since they occur in the absence of appropriate stimuli in the environment, have earned the title hallucinations.

Once again, a careful examination of the patient's experience may point to the affected area. The illusions may be related to a specific sense modality, i.e. visual, auditory, olfactory, somaesthetic illusions, or, when the discharge affects the borderland between the parietal, temporal and occipital areas, compound illusions may result.

A special form of alteration in sense experience occurs with some temporal lobe seizures so that present experience is interpreted in a manner quite different from usual. New situations or objects may be perceived as having been seen or heard before (déjà-vu, déjà entendu) or familiar ones as not having been experienced before (jamais-vu, jamais-entendu).

An early description of an olfactory hallucination associated with a temporal lobe lesion was given by Hughlings Jackson (1890). The following account was provided by the patient and her sister.

The patient was a cook. In the paroxysm the first thing was tremor of the hands and arms; she saw a little black woman who was always very actively engaged in cooking; the spectre did not speak. The patient had a very horrible smell (so-called 'subjective sensation' of smell) which she could not describe. . .She had a feeling as if she was shut up in a box with a limited quantity of air. . .She would stand with her eyes fixed. . .and then say, 'What a horrible smell!''. The patient did not, so her sister reported, lose consciousness, but remembered everything that happened during the attack; she turned of a leaden colour. The patient told us that she passed her urine in the seizures. There was no struggling, and the tongue was not bitten. She never believed the spectre to be a real person. After leaving her kitchen work she had paroxysms with the smell sensation but no spectre.

At autopsy a tumour 'the size of a tangerine orange' was found occupying the anterior portion of the temporal lobe.

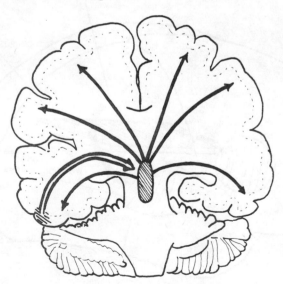

Fig. 3.24 Temporal lobe focus giving rise to a generalized seizure

4.   Some partial seizures may produce sudden alteration in the emotional state usually in the form of fear.

5.   Disturbances of memory and thought processes may occur during temporal lobe seizures.

Finally, it is common for simple symptomatology to be followed by the more complex or there may be an admixture of both. Temporal lobe epilepsy is discussed in more detail in Chapter 5.

Partial seizures may at times progress to generalized seizures. (Fig. 3.24).

Disruption of higher cortical functions

The following section presents an outline of the disorders of higher mental functions which have formed the focus of the bulk of recent neuropsychological studies in man. They are reviewed here in general terms only, each topic being dealt with in greater detail in the remainder of the text.

Aphasia

The term aphasia refers to an impairment in the reception or manipulation or expression of the symbolic content of language due to organic brain damage. Such definitions normally exclude perceptual, learning and memory difficulties and purely sensory or motor deficits unless they specifically involve language symbols.

Speech difficulties due to interference with the peripheral speech mechanisms, larynx, pharynx, and tongue are termed *dysarthria*.

In general, the various forms of aphasia develop as a result of lesions in the so-called dominant hemisphere.

The importance of aphasia lies in its great localizing value in diagnosis and

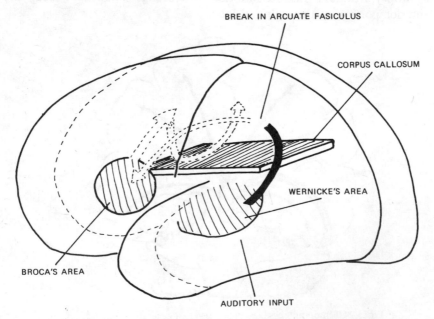

Fig. 3.25 Conduction aphasia due to a lesion disrupting the arcuate fasciculus

no neuropsychological examination is complete without a careful examination of the patient's language functions. More recently, and perhaps more correctly, the term *dysphasia* has been used to denote any disorder, however mild, of the patient's normal symbolic function.

Aphasic disturbances have usually been classified under two principal headings:

(i) Expressive or motor aphasia, and

(ii) Receptive or sensory aphasia.

Expressive aphasia or Broca's aphasia generally results from a lesion in the posterior part of the inferior frontal convolution (Fig. 3.25) though cases have been reported where complete removal of Broca's area has led to only transient dysphasia. The disability may vary from a complete loss of speech to a mild deficit in which the patient's sole difficulty may be in finding the appropriate word. Where the difficulty is great, the patient may become extremely distressed and the examination of the aphasic patient is never an easy task. With the less severe disability, the patient's language may be characterized by a restriction in the range of his vocabulary, and he may use words repetitively with long pauses between words or phrases.

The dramatic quality of certain symptoms in individual patients has led some authors to give a variety of different descriptive labels to a large number of aphasias. More systematic study in recent decades has emphasised the fact that aphasia may show itself in various guises but that pure forms of any of the many aphasias described in the earlier literature are extremely rare, and some may be a function of the author's abstracting an entity and giving it a name. This is not to imply that a careful detailed analysis of the language disturbance should not be carried out, rather that we should not continue to multiply labels which have little or no implications for the nature or location of lesions which produce the disabilities or the types of treatment that might be employed to assist patients with these difficulties.

Since it is true only in the broad sense that in expressive aphasia understanding of language through the auditory and visual modalities is retained, it follows that careful examination will often demonstrate that such patients will have difficulty in understanding language as well as expressing it.

Patients with expressive aphasia often have difficulty with grammatical construction and tend to use sentences of very simple structure with a predominance of nouns and verbs and a paucity of adjectives and adverbs which gives their speech a telegraphic style. This disorder is referred to as agrammatism.

It has been commonly believed that in persons who have learned more than one language, the more recently acquired patterns of speech are more readily disturbed than speech in their native tongue. While this may occur on some occasions it is usually true that in aphasia all the patient's languages are equally impaired. This misconception rests in many cases on the examiner's own lack of fluency in the other language so that he fails to recognize the extent of the deficit. The use of an intelligent interpreter in doubtful cases is essential since the alterations of language may be of a subtle nature and thus may not be evident in simple conversation.

The expressive difficulty may also extend to written language where the expressive aphasic patient will show the same difficulty he shows in verbal expression. On rare occasions this *dysgraphia* has been described in cases with no obvious difficulties of verbal expression. The second frontal gyrus has been implicated in some of these cases (Aimard, *et. al.*, 1975).

Sensory aphasia. (receptive aphasia) generally results from a lesion in the region of Wernicke's area of the dominant hemisphere (Fig. 3.25). The prime difficulty is a loss of understanding of the spoken word and often of the written word as well. Thus, two major forms of sensory aphasia may be separated, an auditory-receptive aphasia usually related to lesions in the superior temporal convolution, and a visual-receptive aphasia related to more posteriorly placed parieto-temporal lesions.

Patients with *auditory receptive aphasia* have trouble in understanding what is said to them. The problem is due to a failure in comprehension since auditory acuity as tested by audiometry remains adequate. The common presence of expressive difficulties as well in these patients again points to the undesirability of retaining rigid categories of classification.

Unlike the patient with expressive aphasia, the sensory aphasic's verbalizations may be fluent and, in fact, he may be unusually voluble. However, he uses language ungrammatically and often unintelligibly. Since he is not capable of monitoring his own verbal expression due to his difficulty in auditory comprehension, he may be unaware of the inappropriateness of his utterances. Verbal confusion and the substitution of wrong words or phrases (paraphasia) may result in a very disjointed form of speech disorder termed *jargon aphasia*.

In *visual-receptive aphasia* the understanding of written language is impaired. This difficulty is referred to as *alexia (or dyslexia)*, or sometimes word blindness. While the patient may be able to identify individual letters, he is unable to perceive words as meaningful wholes. Visual-receptive aphasia is often associated with visual field defects and also with expressive aphasia. Alexia may occur together with difficulty in recognizing objects under the syndrome of *visual object agnosia*. On the other hand, a syndrome of alexia without agraphia has long been recognized. Sometimes the alexia is also accompanied by a failure to name colours *(colour anomia)* and the ability to read numbers may be preserved while the ability to read letters and words is lost. Geschwind's (1965a) masterly analysis of the syndrome of alexia without agraphia forms a fine example of the use of the concept of the disconnection syndrome in analysing disorders of higher cortical processes (Ch. 7). It utilizes Wernicke's notion of the importance of the connections between different parts of the brain in the building up of complex activities. An example of the disconnection syndrome as the anatomical basis of the aphasias concludes this section.

Global or *mixed aphasia* refers to cases where there are both expressive and receptive elements present. These cases are usually severe in their symptoms and present extensive lesions on pathological examination.

Amnestic, amnesic, or *nominal aphasia* is characterized by the patient's inability to identify people or objects by their proper names. If shown a hairbrush the patient will be unable to evoke the name 'brush' though he will demonstrate both with words and actions that he is well aware of the nature of the object and will recognize the correct word when it is given to him. This ability to recognize the correct word when it is provided is not seen in patients with receptive aphasia. This form of aphasia is quite different from expressive aphasia. It does not have a precise localization though the lesion is usually behind the central sulcus.

It is the association between the object and its particular noun that is lost. If the deficit is marked, speech may be greatly reduced. When unable to find the correct word the patient may substitute colloquialisms and employ circumlocutions and periphrastic expressions to convey his meaning.

Some authors consider amnestic aphasia to be essentially a form of sensory or receptive aphasia and the responsible lesion is usually found in the posterior region of the superior temporal convolution on the dominant side.

The anatomical disconnection model. Geschwind (1969) has extended the anatomical model, first put forward by Wernicke, to provide understanding of the various forms of aphasia.

1. With a lesion in Wernicke's area, incoming auditory information will not be understood and since a lesion in this region interrupts the passage of visual information travelling forward from the visual association cortex, isolating this information from the anterior speech area, the patient will be unable to describe in words what he sees. Furthermore, since visual forms no longer arouse auditory ones because of the disconnection he no longer understands written language (Fig. 3.25).

2. A lesion in the principal connecting link between the comprehension area and the expressive area, the *arcuate fasciculus,* leads to abnormality in speech with the preservation of comprehension of both written and spoken speech. Such a disorder is termed *conduction aphasia* (Fig. 3.25). Since Wernicke's area is intact the patient can understand what is said to him. On the other hand with Broca's area also intact he will be able to speak spontaneously. The speech is often copious but is abnormal because of the isolation between the two major areas. However, since the connection has been broken between the receptive area and the motor speech area he will be unable to repeat what the examiner says to him. This disproportionate difficulty in repetition is said to be the principal characteristic of this disorder.

Furthermore, in order for the patient to carry out movements on command the information needs to go forward from Wernicke's area to the motor area and so the patient is unable to carry out such commands. As the pathway in the diagram shows, a lesion in the arcuate fasciculus will lead to bilateral difficulty in carrying out verbal commands since these are prevented from reaching the appropriate motor areas of either hemisphere.

3. When a lesion damages the left visual cortex and the posterior portion of the corpus callosum known as the splenium, the patient is still able to see stimuli in the left visual field corresponding to the intact right visual cortex though not in the right visual field. However, the information perceived by the right hemisphere can no longer reach the left hemisphere language areas so

that the patient cannot understand written language though, with the preservation of both Broca's and Wernicke's areas he can both comprehend and speak spontaneously. This disorder is termed pure alexia or agnosic alexia.

4. Sometimes even extensive lesions in the hemispheres may spare both Broca's and Wernicke's areas isolating them from the rest of the brain. Speech production and comprehension are both impaired but the ability to repeat spoken words is preserved. Such a disability is termed *transcortical aphasia*.

Further examples of the use of the anatomical model are given elsewhere and despite limitations this model 'most closely meets the criteria of efficiency in explaining the known data, efficiency in predicting new phenomena, or in design of important experiments and susceptibility to refinements that can be checked by observation or experiment'. (Geschwind, 1969).

Cerebral stimulation and speech. Stimulation of the human brain has confirmed the clinical findings relating lesions in various parts of the left hemisphere to disorders of language, e.g. mapping points where stimulation produced various effects has given essentially the same picture as lesion studies (Figs. 3.26 and 3.27).

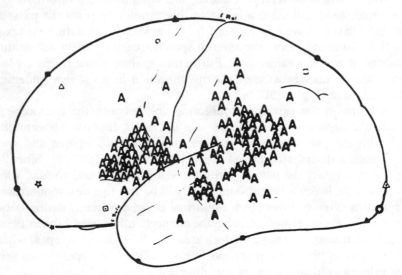

Fig. 3.26 Points at which stimulation produced aphasic responses (Fig. VIII-II, p. 130. W. Penfield and L. Roberts (1959). *Speech and Brain Mechanisms,* Courtesy of Princeton University Press).

Agnosia

It is a useful generalization to consider all the cortical territory behind the central sulcus as being concerned with getting to know the world around us. In line with the early name for the central sulcus—the fissure of Rolando— lesions in this region are still frequently referred to as retrorolandic lesions. In Luria's terms (Luria, 1973b) this is the second major unit of the higher nervous system, the one concerned with the reception, analysis and storage of information. It is divided into three major types of cortex. Firstly, primary projection areas which are modality-specific, i.e., serve only one sense modality such as vision, audition, or bodily sensation. Each of these areas is laid out in a somatotopic manner as described in Chapter 2. Secondly, projection—association cortex which is adjacent to a primary projection area and, while still concerned with only one sensory mode, organizes the incoming information into meaningful wholes. Finally, there is an area of cortex which is concerned

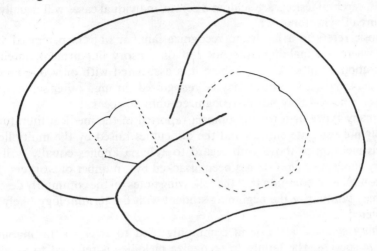

Fig. 3.27 Areas in which lesions have been shown to produce aphasic responses

with the integration of information from all sensory channels and, in this integrative sense, is supramodal. This cortex, which is specific to man, is found at the confluence of the parietal, temporal, and occipital areas in the region

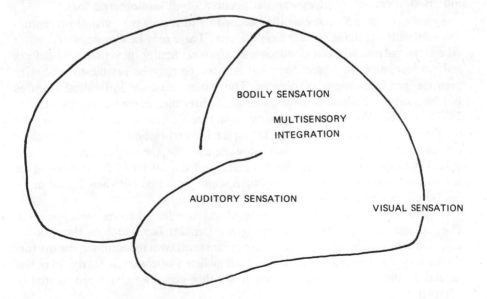

BODILY SENSATION

MULTISENSORY
INTEGRATION

AUDITORY SENSATION

VISUAL SENSATION

Fig. 3.28 The retrorolandic cortex and sensory systems

of the supramarginal gyrus. The major divisions of the postcentral or retro-rolandic cortex are shown in Figure 3.28.

Lesions of the postcentral area will give rise to simple or complex sensory or perceptual disturbances, and will affect one or more modalities, according to their location. Since, with the possible exception of some penetrating missile wounds, cerebral lesions are seldom discrete, individual cases will usually show a mixture of symptoms.

Agnosia refers to a failure to recognize familiar objects perceived via the senses where the inability does not rest on sensory impairment, intellectual deterioration or other cause. Where it is associated with only one modality, e.g. visual agnosia, an object may be recognized through other senses such as touch, or a person may not be recognized until he speaks.

The many types or forms of agnosia reported in the medical literature are probably not separate entities and the difficulties raised by the multiplication of labels mentioned above with regard to aphasia applies equally well here. The very concept of agnosia has been attacked by a number of workers. However, the term is so common that the following notes on the commonly described forms may familiarize the beginning student with the terminology likely to be encountered.

Auditory agnosia is the term commonly used to refer to the inability to recognize speech. The failure to recognize melodies is referred to as *amusia*. A careful analysis by Vignolo and others of patients' difficulties with different types of auditory material has led to a valuable distinction between semantic-associative difficulties on one hand, and auditory discriminative difficulties on the other (Ch. 5). As these difficulties show double dissociation with respect to the left and right temporal lobes they should prove of value as a diagnostic aid. Both forms of auditory agnosia occur without audiometric loss.

Visual agnosia has been classified according to the class of visual perceptual material with which the patient has difficulty. There may be *visual object agnosia* where the patient without disturbances of visual acuity or visual field defects fails to recognize the object for what it is, or he may be unable to recognize pictorial representations of objects. The patient can see individual features but he 'cannot combine these individual features into complete forms' (Luria, 1973b, p.116). Visual object agnosia is a rare clinical entity. However, the careful examination of a case by Taylor and Warrington (1971) showed clear cut dissociation between primary apprehension of the object via the visual modality (apperception) and the association of the object with meaning. This is close to the distinction made by Hebb some years ago between figural unity figural identity (Hebb, 1949).

A particular difficulty in recognizing faces is referred to as *prosopagnosia*. The patient may not only fail to recognize familiar faces such as those of his wife and children, he may be unable to recognize his own reflection in the mirror. There may be *agnosia for colours* which, when associated with dyslexia has special localizing significance. These and other visual agnosias are treated in Chapter 7.

Spatial agnosia. This form of disorder is sometimes referred to as visual or spatial disorientation. The patient is unable to find his way around in a familiar environment such as his own district or even his own home though he may recognize separate objects in the home quite well. There may also be defects in visual and topographical memory so that patients with this disorder are unable to find their way on a map or if asked to draw a map will produce one with topographical distortions and omissions.

Tactile agnosia or *astereognosis* refers to inability to recognize objects by feeling them. The relation of tactile agnosia to sensory defects is discussed in relation to lesions of the parietal lobes in Chapter 6.

Body agnosia, corporeal agnosia, or *autotopagnosia* is a lack of awareness of the body's topography, an inability to recognize or localize parts of the patient's own body. A special form of autotopagnosia is *finger agnosia* where the patient cannot point to, or show the examiner the various fingers of each hand. It forms one of the classical tetrad of Gerstmann's syndrome which, because of its important bearing on the notion of cerebral dominance or lateralization is discussed at length in Chapter 8. Body agnosia is also often associated with lack of awareness of disease or disability known as *anosognosia*, e.g., the patient fails to perceive or denies that his arm and leg are paralysed.

Sensory inattention, sensory extinction, sensory suppression, or *perceptual rivalry* denotes a failure to appreciate a stimulus when a similar stimulus is applied to a corresponding part of the body or to both halves of the visual field simultaneously. The patient is quite able to see and recognize things in any part of the visual field when they are presented alone or to report a tactile stimulus from either side of the body. It is only when the stimuli are presented simultaneously that the disorder comes to light. The inattention is for the stimulus opposite the side of the lesion. This phenomenon has been reviewed by Critchley (1949), Bender (1952) and Denny-Brown, Meyer and Horenstein (1952) and has been the object of numerous studies in the past two decades. These attest to the existence of the phenomena in a wide variety of sense modalities, e.g. vision, audition, pain, touch, temperature, pressure, taste, kinesthesis and vibration. The range of explanations is almost as wide ranging as the phenomena themselves. Birch, Belmont and Karp (1965a) felt that differences in threshold between the parts stimulated might be the most parsimonious explanation but a direct test of this hypothesis showed that this was not the case. Russell, Neuringer and Goldstein (1970) have suggested that such simple neurological tests as measuring for sensory suppression might form a useful part of the neuropsychologist's examination (Ch. 9).

Body image disorders may take various forms, e.g. unilateral motor, sensory or visual neglect; loss of awareness of one half of the body; anosognosia; undue heaviness of one half of the body, and sundry other signs and symptoms.

Apraxia

Apraxia is the inability to carry out purposive or skilled acts due to brain damage and which does not result from the numerous other reasons which may result in imperfectly executed movements, e.g., failure to comprehend what to do, weakness or paralysis, or sensory loss. Prior to the work of Liepmann, this disorder was thought to be secondary to agnosia. It is now recognized as a pure entity with a number of subsidiary forms, the principal ones of which are (1) *motor* or *kinetic apraxia*, (2) *ideomotor* or *ideokinetic apraxia*, (3) *ideational apraxia* and (4) *constructional apraxia*.

Motor apraxia is believed to be due to loss of the kinesthetic memory patterns or engrams necessary for the performance of the skilled act. This form of apraxia usually effects the finer movements of one upper extremity, movements such as doing up buttons, opening a safety pin, placing a letter in an envelope. Where there is associated weakness, the clumsiness of the movement is out of all proportion to the loss of power. This form of apraxia usually results from a lesion of the precentral gyrus on the side opposite to the side of the body affected.

Ideomotor apraxia is a condition in which the patient finds it difficult to carry out an action on verbal command but may do so automatically or almost fortuitously. He is unable to imitate actions that are demonstrated to him. The kinetic engram is preserved but is not available to the patient's voluntary recall. This form of apraxia is usually associated with a lesion in the supra-marginal gyrus of the dominant hemisphere.

Ideational apraxia is a disorder of the ideational part of the programme of movement, an inability to formulate a plan of action successfully. Portions only of an action sequence may be performed or the patient performs another action *like* the required one. Patients are able to imitate an action, i.e., where the plan of action is presented from the outside. The disorder is often said to resemble extreme absent mindedness. It is usually the result of bilateral and diffuse brain damage.

Constructional apraxia is a disorder of praxis which has received much more attention from neuropsychologists in recent years than the three major forms already outlined. Perhaps the major difference between constructional apraxia and other forms of praxic disorder is that special tests, albeit simple, are usually necessary to elicit it, while other forms are clinically apparent. With construct-ional apraxia the patient is unable to put together parts to make a whole. A detailed account of methods of testing for constructional apraxia is given by Critchley (1953) and recent reviews by Warrington (1969) and Benton (1969) examine all aspects of the disorder and its implications for localization. The deficit is discussed later in relation to parietal lobe dysfunction and testing methods are described in Chapter 9. A few examples of the patient's difficulties will suffice here.

On block design tests such as that of the Wechsler Adult Intelligence Scale (Wechsler, 1958) patients often have difficulty with the earliest and simplest designs and generally perform at a much lower level than other patients on this test. A poor performance on block design tests is not pathognomonic of the disorder since many patients with lesions in various parts of the brain will perform poorly on this test for a variety of reasons. However, an examina-tion of the quality of performance shows that patients with constructional apraxia have a greater number of constructional deviations in their attempts (Ben-Yishay, Diller and Mandleberg, 1971). Simple drawing tests such as copying geometric designs of varying complexity (Benton, 1962) or drawing common objects such as a house or clock face will elicit the difficulty though more complex tasks such as constructing a copy of a three dimensional model with blocks may have to be employed (Benton and Fogel, 1962).

Dressing apraxia denotes the condition where the patient is unable to clothe himself properly, more commonly leaving the left side partly or wholly unclad. It appears to be a reflection of the patient's neglect of part of his body mentioned above and is seen more frequently with parietal lesions of the non-dominant hemisphere.

The concept of the disconnection syndrome is also useful in understanding the anatomical basis of the apraxias. In the case of carrying out a skilled movement on verbal command there is a complex chain of events. Firstly, the auditory information is organized in Wernicke's area, i.e. the left superior temporal region if we are considering a right handed patient. From here the information travels to the motor association cortex in the frontal lobe and thence to the motor cortex which sends impulses to the appropriate muscle groups on the right side of the body to execute the command. If the patient is asked to carry out the action with his *left* hand, the sequence will have to be the same with the important addition that the information will have to travel from the left motor association area on the left to that on the right since the right motor region commands the left hand. Consequently a lesion of the anterior part of the corpus callosum, which carries these fibres between the left and right hemispheres, will render the patient incapable of carrying out verbal commands with his left hand while he is still able to carry them out with

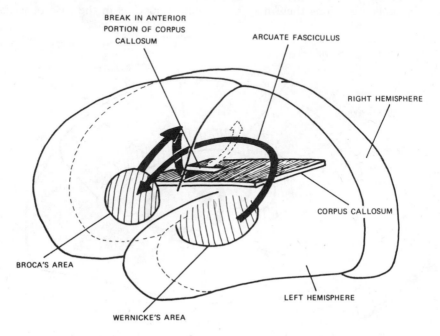

Fig. 3.29 Left sided apraxia produced by a partial disconnection in the anterior part of the corpus callosum

his right (Fig. 3.29). This disorder is often referred to as *left sided apraxia* and is one of the signs of commissural disconnection syndromes discussed in Chapter 8. Though apraxia may be seen in isolation it often accompanies other defects such as agnosia, dysphasia, and impairment of memory, and, despite the separation used here it may be difficult to decide in individual patients whether the defect of action is due to a lack of awareness, a lack of skilled movements, or some degree of weakness or ataxia of the affected limb.

Amnesia

Memory disorders are a frequent accompaniment of cerebral impairment. The range of symptoms covered under this heading, their evaluation and implication for diagnosis, and hence prognosis and treatment have been examined in numerous major publications in recent years (Delay, 1942; Russell and Nathan, 1946; Talland, 1965; Whitty and Zangwill, 1966; Talland and Waugh, 1969; Barbizet, 1970).

Clinical reports often refer to memory disorders under two principal subdivisions, *anterograde* and *retrograde amnesia*.

Anterograde amnesia is characterized by an inability to learn new information with an associated inability to learn new skills and to retain the knowledge of events after the onset of the amnesic period.

Retrograde amnesia is the difficulty in recalling events that occurred before the injury.

Memory disorders may be mild or severe, permanent or transitory, and may involve either anterograde or retrograde defects as their most obvious feature. On some occasions there may be a memory loss, as in the case of unilateral

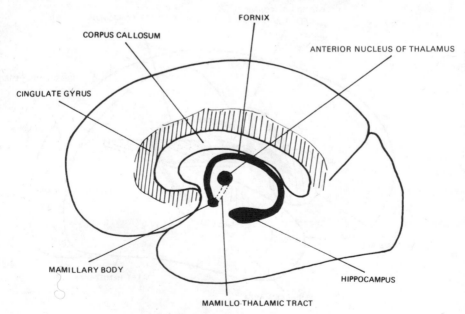

Fig. 3.30 Hippocampus-fornix-mamillary body complex

temporal lobe lesions, which is material specific (Milner, 1966) or referable to one cortical area, e.g., the so-called 'frontal amnesia' of Barbizet (1970). At other times, with severe, diffuse cerebral lesions there may be a severe impoverishment of all aspects of memory so that the patient becomes incapable of any effective thought processes. Such a severe state is called a *global amnesia*.

The syndrome originally known as Korsakoff's amnesic syndrome associated with the avitaminosis of chronic alcoholism is now known to occur with a variety of lesions which effect bilaterally the structures on the mesial surface of the hemispheres near the lower parts of the brain. Since many of these areas have intimate relationships with the temporal lobes this form of amnesia (now usually referred to as the amnesic syndrome) is discussed in Chapter 5. The structures concerned are part of the limbic system, the hippocampus, fornix, mamillary bodies, the anterior nucleus of the thalamus, and their related pathways (Fig. 3.30). The neuropathology of the condition is described by Brierley (1966). He points out that 'the retention and probably, to some extent, the recall of sensory impressions and experience are dependent upon the structural integrity of certain small and relatively well-defined regions of the brain' (p.150).

The principal clinical features of Korsakoff's syndrome are (1) an almost complete inability to learn new material with forgetting of newly presented material within a very short period even as short as ten seconds; (2) difficulty in recall of past events so that the patient is unable to give a satisfactory narration of his life history. This difficulty contributes to the patient's failure to adapt to the present; (3) preservation of early established skills and language so that the patient may be able to carry on his life only as long as the environment is a familiar one.

A translation of Korsakoff's classic paper of 1887 was published by Victor and Yakovlev (1955).

There has grown up over the years a clinical impression, often repeated in textbooks, that in amnesic patients memory for remote events is less impaired than memory for events closer in time. This proposition was tested by Sanders and Warrington (1971) using a questionnaire technique developed by Warrington and Silberstein (1970) and expanded by Warrington and Sanders (1971). They found that the duration of retrograde effects was very long indeed and that the effects were not, as frequently supposed, inversely proportional to the distance of the event from the present time or the onset of the amnesia. Such findings do not support an explanation of retrograde amnesia in terms of a theory of consolidation and they suggest that a unitary disorder could account for both anterograde and posterograde defects of memory.

Dementia

Dementia refers to a progressive and usually profound deterioration of all the intellectual processes. In the neurological literature it is often referred to as the *organic mental syndrome*. The principal features are impairment of memory, especially for recent events, loss of the ability to concentrate, lowering of abstract thought processes, and usually marked changes in the patient's personality. Among the latter are often striking changes in mood such as profound apathy or depression, or an elation of mood out of keeping with the patient's prevailing life conditions. Some of the changes such as the lack of inhibition, coarse behaviour, and sexual excess have much of the flavour of the behaviour seen after severe frontal lobe damage described in the next chapter under the frontal lobe syndrome. Errors of judgment are among the most frequently noted early signs of the dementing process. With the progress of the condition the person becomes neglectful of his appearance, dirty in his habits and finally incontinent. In the advanced stages, grandiose or persecutory delusions are common.

Many forms of organic brain disease and metabolic disorders affecting the nervous system give rise to dementia.

The multiplicity of disorders and diseases presenting as dementia is amply documented in recent works (Haase, 1971a, 1971b; Slaby and Wyatt, 1973; Wells, 1971). Table 3.1 provides a sample of the wide range of conditions which may be accompanied by widespread loss of intellectual function and this list is by no means exhaustive.

Table 3.1 Diseases causing dementia

1. Diffuse Degenerative Diseases of the Central Nervous System
       So-called presenile dementias
          Alzheimer's disease (including both senile and presenile dementia)
          Pick's
          Huntington's
          Parkinson's
       Senile dementia
       Other degenerative diseases
          Progressive myoclonus epilepsy
          Progressive supranuclear palsy
          Parkinson's disease
2. Vascular disorders
       Multiple infarct dementia
       Vascular stenosis
       Arteriovenous malformations
3. Trauma
       Open and closed head injuries
       Chronic subdural hematoma
4. Metabolic disorders
       Myxedema
       Wilson's disease
       Liver disease
       Hypoglycemia
       Cushing's syndrome
       Uremia
5. Brain tumours
6. Hydrocephalus
7. Infections
       Encephalitis
       Brain abscess
       Bacterial meningitis
8. Deficiency diseases
       Wernicke-Korsakoff syndrome
9. Toxins and drugs
       Metals

        Organic compounds
        Carbon monoxide
        Drugs
10. Diseases of unknown origin
        Multiple sclerosis

The nosological problems in dementia have been discussed by Hughes *et al.* (1973) who distinguish three principal groups, firstly, those cases with systemic causes, secondly, those cases with specific neuropathological changes, thirdly, a group of cases where 'a clinically apparent dementia is unrelated to an underlying basic disease and in whom no distinctive pathologic correlates are found at biopsy or autopsy'.

Accurate neuropsychological investigation may help to distinguish early cases of dementia from functional or psychiatric disorders. This is becoming of increasing importance since some of the causes are treatable and best results are to be expected in early cases, e.g. the surgical treatment of hydrocephalus by ventriculo-atrial shunt has been claimed to lead to a restitution of both mental and motor function by some workers but not by others (Salmon, Gonen and Brown, 1971). It is possible that early detection might be crucial in such cases.

De Jong (1973) has pointed out that the diagnosis of dementia may be misapplied to patients suffering from 'behavioural incompetence' due to other causes such as sensory (receptive) aphasia and retarded depression. One such case considered to be suffering senile arteriosclerotic dementia was remarkably improved by modified prefrontal leucotomy (Hohne and Walsh, 1970), demonstrating the not infrequent difficulty of distinguishing between severe retardation of behaviour by depressive illness and a true dementia.

Similarly, the recent recognition of 'subcortical dementia' where pathological processes in the subcortical structure appear to interfere with the activating and related mechanisms so that there is an excessive slowness in carrying out intellectual functions (Albert, Feldman and Willis, 1974) has important implications. These authors point out that. . . 'In ordinary human relationships, a 'normal' range of time is allowed for communication. If no response is forthcoming within this 'normal' range of time, one moves on to the next topic, assuming that someone 'doesn't know', or 'doesn't remember', or 'doesn't care'. In a clinical diagnosis if someone is shown to not know, or not remember or not care for a long enough time, he will surely be called demented'. (op. cit. p.129).

There are also other conditions, such as intracranial tumours, particularly those in the frontal region, which may give the appearance of generalized dementia when only a superficial examination is made. On closer examination the sparing of other aspects of behaviour should be noted.

Certain conditions giving rise to dementia such as drug addiction and alcoholism may have obvious causes while others such as lowered functioning of the thyroid gland may be easily overlooked at first. Because of the fact that their frequency may cloud the issue, senile changes are worth considering separately. The term 'senile dementia' is a particularly unfortunate one since it often carries the implication that the condition is due to the natural process of ageing with the result that, in many cases, no careful investigation is carried out.

It is also commonly assumed that senile dementia or senile psychosis is largely due to cerebral arteriosclerosis and the causative relationship between alteration in the efficiency of cerebral circulation and mental deterioration is still widely believed and taught. Numerous studies show that there is no simple clear cut relationship between cerebral changes in the elderly and demented behaviour. Postmortem examinations of large series of cases of people over 60 years of age, e.g. Raskin and Ehrenberg (1956); Gal (1959) show a lack of correspondence between brain damage and quality of behaviour. Gallinek (1948) not only observed in his study of senile psychosis that major cerebral changes could be noted at autopsy with no observable behaviour pathology antemortem but also that marked behaviour pathology was associated at times with minimal cerebral changes. He reported that many so called senile psychoses due to supposedly irreversible cerebral pathology were markedly improved by electro-convulsive therapy. This finding has been confirmed by Ehrenberg and Gullingsrud (1955) and others.

The studies of Kastenbaum (1965) and Volpe and Kastenbaum (1967) demonstrate that a change in the social treatment of elderly individuals will result in improvement in the behaviour of some deteriorated patients. This is in keeping with the reports of successful psychotherapy in elderly patients (Bowman and Engle, 1960). Finally the study of sociocultural influences shows that non-organic factors have a profound effect on the production of 'senile' or 'demented' behaviour.

A full discussion of the wide variety of deteriorated behaviour in the elderly will be found in textbooks of geriatric psychiatry. These remarks have been introduced to help dispel the assumption of a one to one relationship between brain damage in the elderly and deteriorated behaviour. It is not meant to imply that degenerative conditions play no part in the aetiology of some cases, even the major part.

4. The Frontal Lobes

Anatomy and functional organization

The frontal lobes are the most recently developed parts of the brain. In man they make up about one third of the mass of the cerebral hemispheres. It is only in the past three decades or so that we have begun to come to an understanding of the basic role which the frontal lobes play in many forms of human behaviour especially with regard to the regulation of complex activities. Much of this work has been greatly advanced by Aleksandr Luria and his Russian colleagues and the brief summary in this section owes much to this source (Luria, 1969; Luria, 1973a; 1973b). Other contributions are dealt with in later sections of this chapter.

The frontal lobes lie anterior to the central sulcus and may be subdivided into four major subdivisions: (1) the motor area which occupies the precentral gyrus; (2) the premotor area which lies anterior to the motor area and includes Brodmann's area 6 and part of area 8; (3) the prefrontal area (9, 10, 45, 46); (4) the basomedial portion of the lobes (9 to 13, 24, 32). These latter two divisions are often considered together as one 'prefrontal' region.

In Chapter 2 mention was made of the study of cytoarchitecture. This leads to a distinction in terminology which is often used in relation to the frontal regions. Some anatomists have grouped the finer subdivisions of cytoarchitecture as depicted by workers such as Brodmann into a small number of fundamental types which share common characteristics. Departure from the 'typical' six layered cortex allows a broad division first of all into cortex in which the granular layers (layers II and IV) are well represented or markedly absent. Cortex termed *agranular cortex* shows a lack of granular layers II and IV whereas layers III and V are very well developed. This agranular cortex is seen in the posterior parts of the frontal lobes anterior to the central sulcus and is characteristic of the motor cortex. Areas 4 and 6 together with portions of Brodmann's areas 8 and 44 belong to this type. Anterior to this the cortex may be divided into a number of fundamental types but as the granular layers are present in varying degree it might loosely be characterized as frontal granular cortex. This term gave its name to a symposium in 1964 and studies of frontal granular cortex might be said to be concerned with those frontal lobe functions which are not purely motor. The relative development of this

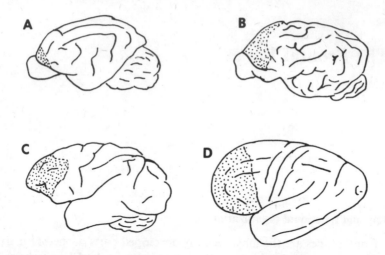

Fig. 4.1 The frontal granular cortex. A, Cat; B, Dog; C, Rhesus Monkey; D, Man. (Not drawn to scale)

type of cortex is shown in Figure 4.1.

The frontal regions have well-developed systems of efferent nerve cells leading from the cortex to lower brain centres and peripheral parts of the nervous system. The efferent projections from the frontal areas pass to the ventral and dorsomedial nuclei of the thalamus as well as to numerous other structures

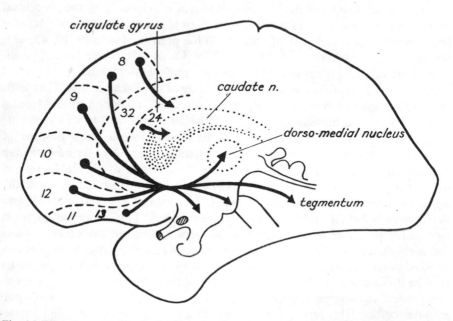

Fig. 4.2 Efferent connections in the frontal region (from E.G. Walsh *Physiology of the Nervous System*. (Courtesy of Churchill Livingstone) Figure has been modified from Le Gros Clark, the *Lancet*, 1948. ;Courtesy of eds).

(Fig. 4.2). Afferent fibres reach the frontal cortex over the thalamo-frontal radiation (Fig. 4.3).

Parallel to his division of the posterior zones into primary (sensory), secondary (association), and tertiary (supramodal or integrative) cortex, Luria perceives the organization of the frontal regions in a similar hierarchical arrangement *viz.*, motor cortex, premotor cortex (motor organization), and prefrontal cortex (higher integration). This leads to the concept of two types of syndrome (1) premotor and (2) prefrontal. This chapter is principally concerned with the latter.

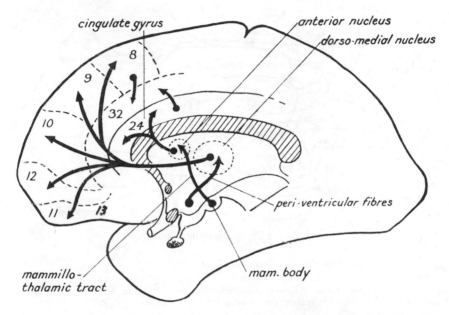

Fig. 4.3 Afferent connections in the frontal region (from E.G. Walsh *Physiology of the Nervous System.* (Courtesy of Churchill Livingstone.) Figure has been modified from Le Gros Clark, the *Lancet,* 1948. (Courtesy of eds.)

Luria also points out that the prefrontal regions serve as tertiary zones for the limbic system as well as the motor system. They have rich connections with, (1) the upper parts of the brain stem and thalamus, and (2) all other cortical zones. The richness of these connections is shown in Figure 4.4. Through the first set of connections the prefrontal areas particularly the basal and medial aspects of the lobes are intimately concerned with the state of alertness of the organism while the rich connections with the posterior receptor areas and motor cortex allow the lateral prefrontal regions to organize and execute the most complex of man's goal-directed or purposive activity.

From a clinical point of view the division of prefrontal cortex into lateral and basomedial (orbitomedial) regions may serve as a useful first approximation in the search for brain-behaviour relationships.

In the lateral (convexity) portions of the frontal lobes the character of the disturbances alters according to the placement of the lesions in the antero-posterior direction. With posterior frontal lesions adjacent to the motor cortex the disturbances are those of the organization of movements. As the lesions move forward they lead firstly to the disintegration of motor programmes and then to a disturbance of comparison of motor behaviour with its original plan. This latter disruption reminds us that not only must a programme of movement be organized and initiated, it must also be continuously monitored and neces-

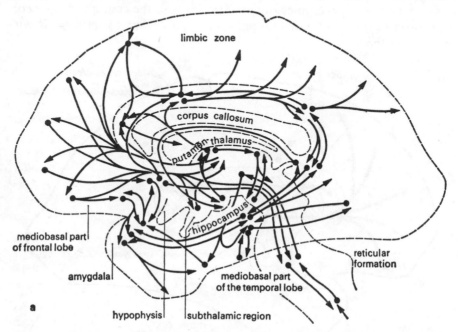

Fig. 4.4 Complete ramification of frontal lobe connections (in A.R. Luria. *The Working Brain*. Allen Lane Penguin (1973)After Polyakov; Courtesy of VAAP, Moscow, U.S.S.R.

sary adjustments made in the light of feedback from the activity for the sequence to be smooth and effective. 'All these disturbances are particularly marked in patients with lesions of the lateral zones of the left (dominant) frontal lobe which are closely connected with the cerebral organization of speech, and the disorganization of *speech activity* and of those *behavioural acts* which are especially dependent upon the participation of speech for their regulation (Luria, 1973b, p.222).

Speech disorders are particularly associated with lesions of the lower parts of the lateral cortex of the dominant hemisphere. Disturbance of speech from lesions of the posterior inferior area (Broca's area) is termed motor or expressive aphasia. There are other speech disturbances of a more subtle nature found with lesions anterior to Broca's area which are seen in patients who are not considered clinically to be suffering from aphasia. Reference is made to these in later parts of this chapter. Luria includes the following in such disorders of the left inferolateral frontal-cortex: (1) inability to make a spontaneous discursive statement, (2) difficulty in expressing a thought in discursive speech, and (3) 'verbal adynamia' or 'frontal dynamic aphasia'.

In the other major functional subdivision, the basomedial frontal cortex, the disorders are related to the state of activation of the subject and his affective responses. Luria (1973a, 1973b) has pointed to the recent research of the British and Russian workers on 'expectancy waves' in the electroencephalogram which, together with other evidence, shows 'that the frontal parts of the brain-cortex play an essential role in the regulation of the state of activation that arises as a result of some task given to the subject' (1973b, p.6). Extensive experience with psychosurgical lesions in the basomedial areas has confirmed earlier thought that these areas are concerned with the emotional life of the individual and with the control of inhibitions. These topics are also dealt with in what follows.

The frontal lobe controversy

Perhaps the most vexatious question regarding the frontal lobes has been the question as to whether they are more important for man's intellectual life than other portions of the brain. Since the introduction of psychological tests in the area of brain impairment around the 1930's much evidence has accummulated on both sides. This evidence is worth reviewing since it provides a number of lessons about making inferences based on incomplete information.

It seemed natural to some in view of the great development of the prefrontal regions in man that these regions should be concerned with his highest integrative functions. Many neurologists in the era before the introduction of psychological testing, had supported the notion of the paramount importance of the frontal lobe (Jackson, 1874; Phelps, 1897; Dana, 1915; Goldstein and Gelb, 1918; Dew, 1922; Papez, 1929; Worster-Drought, 1931) though there were those who were opposed to this notion (Feuchtwanger, 1923; Jefferson, 1937). Jefferson's six cases of frontal lobectomy not only appeared to demonstrate no apparent loss after operation but an improvement in some cases. . . 'those who showed no mental alteration before the operation were unaffected by partial removal of the anatomical frontal lobe. . .those who had mental symptoms were much better after the lobe had been excised.' Jefferson was opposed to the notion that the higher functions were 'localized' within the confines of the frontal lobes.

The care which must be exercised in making inferences from clinical material with 'presumptive' evidence of localization was given in a case reported several times by Brickner and one on which he based an interpretation of frontal lobe function. This patient who had undergone a partial bilateral frontal lobectomy for a meningioma, was found at autopsy very much later to have had multiple meningiomas including a very large parieto-occipital tumour. Brickner's case was also important as the author claimed that the patient did not appear to show any marked impairment of abstract thought, one of the higher intellectual functions which some writers, particularly Kurt Goldstein, felt was likely to be most affected by lesions in the frontal lobes. Commenting on Brickner's case Goldstein (1944) pointed to an important distinction which should be borne in mind.

'The underlying reason for this difference is seen in the fact that Brickner considered the use of abstract words as an expression of the ability to think in abstract terms or as a sign of abstract attitude. This is an assumption made very often, and I, myself, had the greatest difficulty in differentiating abstract thinking on the one hand and the concrete use of words with abstract meaning on the other'. (Goldstein (1936) had also been at pains to point out that the changes seen with frontal damage may be elusive to traditional examinations.

'. . .the personality changes characteristic of the frontal lobes are of a definite type and may easily be overlooked, because the methods of examination usually employed are unsuited to disclosing them. . .For these reasons the greater part of the literature is useless for answering the questions whether psychic disturbances occur in cases of lesion of the frontal lobe and if so, what these disturbances are.'

The first large study of intellectual changes with frontal lesions was that of Rylander (1939) who examined 32 cases of partial excision for either tumour or abscess. The tests of higher intellectual function, which included some which would be classified as tests of abstract thinking, were also given to 32 control subjects. There were highly significant differences between the operated subjects and the controls on most measures. The intellectual changes occurred in 21 of the 32 cases. This underlines the importance of not basing conclusions on a single case or small samples though it does provoke the question as to why some patients showed changes while others did not. In a second study of 16 cases with brain resections in the temporal, parietal, and occipital lobes Rylander (1943) found very few of the symptoms he had described in his earlier frontal series, e.g. there were no difficulties with 'abstract thinking, the power of combination, and acts involving judgement.' At a time when psychosurgical procedures were becoming popular he warned of the risk of mental invalidism after extensive frontal surgery particularly in those doing intellectual or other complicated work.

An early study of Halstead (1940) on the sorting behaviour of patients with frontal versus non-frontal locations disclosed a poorer performance on the part of frontal subjects.

Against this emerging support for the importance of the frontal lobes Hebb accumulated impressive evidence that frontal patients were not in fact inferior on intellectual tasks when compared with posterior lesions (Hebb, 1939a; Hebb and Penfield, 1940; Hebb, 1941; Hebb, 1945). The cases were made up of two right frontal cases, four left frontal cases, and one with extensive bilateral frontal lobectomy. Examination of the latter case (Hebb and Penfield, 1940) before and after operation failed to show post-operative deficits, in fact there was a striking improvement both clinically and psychometrically in this patient as well as lack of the traditional frontal lobe signs. They commented, 'It becomes evident that human behaviour and mental activity may be more greatly impaired by the positive action of an abnormal area of brain than by the negative effect of its complete absence' (p.431). Hebb (1945) considered there was evidence in some of the reported cases showing deficits after frontal lobe surgery that 'the deterioration they described may have been due to pathological complication and not to surgical lesion at all.' He did not deny that loss of frontal tissue might have important effects on behaviour merely that such changes had not been adequately demonstrated (Hebb, 1949). Goldstein felt that the frontal lobes were the structures which were most concerned with that complex set of behaviours which he termed taking up the abstract attitude. Because of the extensive nature of the controversy over abstract thinking and brain damage it is dealt with separately below. Speaking of Hebb's cases he remained sceptical . . .'However, I think these cases are not convincing because in none of them are such tests used by which the characteristic frontal lobe symptom can be disclosed.' (Goldstein, 1944). Although we have learned a good deal about the frontal lobe syndrome in the ensuing four decades it remains a truism of clinical practice that patients with frontal lobe lesions often appear essentially normal until they are examined with appropriate tests. Hebb's counterclaim (1945) was that Goldstein was placing emphasis on cases which supported his interpretations while disregrading those which were opposed.

In 1947 Halstead published his theory of 'biological intelligence'. This was based on factor analysis of a number of tests which appeared sensitive to the effects of cerebral impairment. One of the factors was a factor of abstraction. Among the tests in Halstead's battery, the Category Test had a particularly high loading on this factor. In keeping with earlier claims of lowered abstract ability after frontal lesions Halstead and his colleagues reported that abstraction loss in the form of high error scores on the Category Test was indeed greater with frontal involvement (Halstead, 1947; Shure and Halstead, 1958). Neither of these sources presents strong evidence upon which to make the general claims that were put forward. The first study presented only a small amount of data and both studies accepted levels of significance well short of those which have become conventional. An examination of Shure and Halstead's data shows that it is largely derived from Shure (1954) and that a direct test of the effect of size of lesion, laterality and locus of lesion (frontal versus non-frontal) in this original study revealed that all three main effects failed to reach significance in a $2 \times 2 \times 2$ Analysis of Variance. Using Shure and Halstead's data Chapman and Wolff (1959) employed their own method for re-estimating the mass of tissues removed in the 1958 study. To this they added other cases of their own where the extent and site of tissue removed could be clearly specified and where each case was restricted to one of the lobar divisions of the brain and where there was neither evidence of progressive disease nor other disorders. The findings showed that 'impairment was independent of site or side of the defect in the cerebral hemispheres but was directly related to the mass of hemisphere tissue loss. No one of the categories of highest functions was significantly or predictably impaired in relation to the site of defect, whereas all functions were progressively impaired with increasing mass of defect.'

During the 1950s Teuber and his associates accumulated a good deal of data, mainly but not exclusively on penetrating missile wounds, concerning the relative performance of frontal versus posterior lesions. Deficits were greater in frontal cases for a small number of visual tasks discussed below but the remainder of the tasks showed equal or greater impairment with posterior lesions. There tasks comprised: (1) complex visual tasks including sorting tasks (Teuber, Battersby, and Bender, 1951; Weinstein, Teuber, Ghent, and Semmes, 1955); (2) complex tactual tasks (Semmes, Weinstein, Ghent, and Teuber, 1954; Teuber and Weinstein, 1954); (3) visual and tactile discrimination learning (Battersby, Krieger, and Bender, 1955); (4) practical problem solving (Battersby, Teuber and Bender, 1953); and (5) the Army General Classification Test, a general intelligence test (Weinstein and Teuber, 1957; Teuber and Weinstein, 1958; Teuber, 1959). The poorer performance of the posterior group could not be explained on the basis of primary visual defects. Much of this and other evidence is comprehensively summarized in Teuber (1964). Supporting evidence against the pre-eminence of the frontal lobes in intellectual functions came from Birkmayer (1951) and Pollack (1960). Recently Black (1976) has confirmed Teuber's findings using subjects with penetrating missile wounds with the damage presumably restricted to one frontal lobe. The principal measures employed were the Wechsler intelligence and memory scales.

A good deal of insight into the reasons for the contradiction in the literature was provided by the two well designed studies reported by Reitan (1964). The studies used a wide variety of psychological measures and included the Halstead-Reitan group of tests, an Aphasia Screening Test, Reitan's Trail Making Test, an examination for sensory imperception, and the Wechsler-Bellevue Intelligence Scale. These tests were administered to 64 patients with focal lesions and 48 with diffuse cerebral involvement.

The first study required the psychologist to draw inferences from the psychological data in the absence of the neurological diagnosis. These inferences concerned three questions: (a) is the disorder focal or diffuse? (b) what is the location of the lesion? (left anterior, right anterior, left posterior, right posterior, diffuse, extrinsic tumour, vascular disease, trauma, multiple sclerosis). There was a fairly satisfactory degree of concurrence between the psychological and neurological ratings. For the purposes of the present section this means that the psychological test results must have been differentially influenced by the locus of the lesion, e.g. frontal versus non-frontal as well as the laterality and other factors.

The second study looked at the focal cases only and employed the formal comparison of test results between the *known* groups, i.e. intergroup mean comparisons using analysis of variance. Virtually no important differential features were revealed by this analysis. Reitan commented: 'Since the results of Study 1 could not have occurred unless the necessary information for the inferences was present in the data, the conclusion seems inescapable that the analysis was inadequate in Study 2'. It follows that the failure of other studies to show differential features between frontal and non-frontal patients cannot be taken to mean that such differential features do not exist. More sophisticated statistical techniques such as multiple discriminant function analysis or the taxonomic key approach to diagnosis (Russell, Neuringer, and Goldstein, 1970) may prove of greater value since they permit the most advantageous use of the pattern of results. On the other hand this method is probably less flexible than the use of qualitative features of the patient's behaviour on specially selected tests, some of these features being almost pathognomic of lesions in particular locations. The features which appear to be most characteristic of frontal behaviour are discussed in the remaining sections of this chapter and test procedures and analysis both general and specific are dealt with in Chapter 9.

The frontal lobe syndrome

Changes in personality after brain injury are most often noted after damage to the frontal lobes. These changes have been reported for well over a century and no description of what has come to be called the frontal lobe syndrome would be complete without reference to the case of Phineas Gage. The following summary which has appeared in many places is quoted by Kimble (1963).

Phineas P. Gage, an 'efficient and capable" foreman, was injured on September 13, 1848, when a tamping iron was blown through the frontal region of his brain. He suffered the following change in his personality according to the physician, J.M. Harlow, who attended him. "He is fitful, irreverent, indulging at times in the grossest profanity (which was not previously his custom), manifesting but little deference to his fellows, impatient of restraint or advice when it conflicts with his desires, at times pertinaciously obstinate yet capricious and vacillating, devising many plans for future operation which no sooner are arranged than they are abandoned in turn for others appearing more feasible. His mind was radically changed so that his friends and acquaintances said that he was no longer Gage.

Such gross changes are usually seen only with severe bilateral frontal damage but the lack of inhibition, impulsivity and lack of concern of such patients can be seen to a lesser degree in others whose injury is less severe. In its milder forms it could be taken to be within the extreme range of 'extraversion' if the examiner were not familiar with the patient's prior personality. Another of the characteristic features of the frontal syndrome is the mania for making puerile jokes referred to as *'Witzelsucht'*.

Many of these signs seen in the early months after head injuries fade with the passage of time though the more severe the injury the more likely it is that some personality change will remain. Both war injuries (Hillbom, 1960) and psychosurgery have provided potent evidence of the personality changes which accompany bilateral frontal damage.

The complex set of changes with bilateral frontal damage which comprise the frontal lobe syndrome are concisely expressed by Benton (1968). The first set of changes is related to what may be loosely termed personality: 'diminished anxiety and concern for the future; impulsiveness, facetiousness and mild euphoria; lack of initiative and spontaneity. (However, it may be noted that, while they are not mentioned prominently in group studies, anxiety states have been described occasionally in clinical case reports as a presenting symptom in patients with frontal lobe disease.)' The second set of changes may be termed intellectual: 'impaired integration of behaviour over a period of time, a deficit which for want of a better term has been called impairment in 'recent memory'; loss of the capacity to think in abstract terms; finally, inability to plan and follow through a course of action and to take into account the probable future consequence of one's actions, a deficit which is perhaps closely related to some of the observed personality changes as well as to the impairment in recent memory'. (Benton, op. cit. p.53). These various changes will be considered separately in the sections which follow though there is obviously a good deal of interaction between them. There is some evidence from lesion studies both in animals and man that there is at least a partial dissociation between the two major groups of symptoms (Warren and Akert, 1964). This is supported by the extensive literature on psychosurgery suggesting that the intellectual changes are more associated with damage to the dorsolateral connections while the personality changes are more associated with damage to the orbitomedial (or basomedial) regions (Girgis, 1971).

Lesion studies and intellectual changes

Abstract thinking

The question of the importance of the frontal lobes for abstract thinking is intimately connected with the controversy over whether these regions are more crucial than others for the highest integrative functions of man. The summary on theoretical formulations of abstraction in the monograph by Pikas (1966) would form an excellent background to research and reading in this area. This work also provided a summary of empirical studies to that time.

The central questions appear to be whether damage to the cerebrum leads to qualitative versus quantitative changes in what we might loosely term abstract thought processes and, if so, whether there are exclusive to frontal lobe involvement.

The foremost advocate of the qualitative position was Kurt Goldstein. In a large number of publications he put forward the notion that there are two qualitatively different modes of thought and behaviour, abstract and the concrete. The normal person is said to be capable of exercising both modes according to the demands of the situation while the brain damaged patient is restricted to use of the concrete (Goldstein 1936a, 1936b, 1939a, 1939b, 1940, 1942a, 1942b, 1943, 1944, 1959; Goldstein and Scheerer, 1941; Hanfmann, Rickers-Ovsiankina, and Goldstein, 1944). Several of these publications put forward the claim that impairment of abstraction was maximal with lesions of the frontal lobe.

Goldstein's central concept was that of taking up the 'abstract attitude'. There is no doubt that he conceived of the concrete and abstract attitudes as being a dichotomy although there are instances where he admits of degrees of abstraction and concreteness. Examples from his writings make this clear: 'In the concrete attitude we experience and recognize a given thing or situation immediately. Our thinking and acting are directly determined by the present claims upon us. In the abstract attitude we go beyond the current claims of objects or of sense impressions. Specific properties or situations are overlooked. We are oriented in our actions by a conceptual point of view which takes into consideration the demands of the entire situation'. (Goldstein, 1943). Or, again '. . .abstraction is separate in principle from concrete behaviour. There is no gradual transition from one to the other. The assumption of an attitude toward the abstract is not more complex merely through the addition of a new factor of determination; it is a totally different activity of the organism.' (Goldstein, 1940). 'There is a pronounced line of demarcation between these two attitudes which does not represent a gradual ascent from more simple to more complex mental sets. The greater difficulty connected with the abstract approach is not simply one of greater complexity, measured by the number of separate, subservient functions involved. It demands the behaviour of the new emergent quality, generically different from the concrete'. (Goldstein and Scheerer, 1941, p.22).

Operationally the 'abstract attitude' was defined by performance on a series of tests. These included the Weigl Colour-Form Sorting Test, and an object sorting test together with a block design test of the Kohs' type and the Goldstein-Scheerer Stick Test. In the monograph which gives the method of administration of the tests (Goldstein and Scheerer, 1941) Goldstein has presented a detailed treatment of his meaning of the term abstract attitude.

The abstract attitude is the basis for the following *conscious* and *volitional* modes of behaviour:

1. To detach our ego from the outerworld or from inner experiences.
2. To assume a mental set.
3. To account for acts to oneself; to verbalize the account.
4. To shift reflectively from one aspect of the situation to another.
5. To hold in mind simultaneously various aspects.
6. To grasp the essential of a given whole; to break up a given whole into parts, to isolate and to synthesize them.
7. To abstract common properties reflectively; to form hierarchic concepts.
8. To plan ahead ideationally; to assume an attitude towards the 'mere possible' and to think or perform symbolically.

Concrete behaviour has not the above mentioned characteristics. (Goldstein and Scheerer, 1941, p.4).

A reading of the examples provided in the monograph to explain these eight modes of behaviour reveals that Goldstein incorporated under one term many of the features of frontal behaviour which are considered under other headings in the remainder of the chapter. As some of these are considered characteristic of frontal behaviour by other workers it is regrettable as Battersby (1956) points out that 'Even in a comprehensive monograph describing details of the sorting test (and other allied procedures), no quantitative data were presented which would enable the reader to compare the relative effects of cerebral lesions in different locations.'

There is also a fundamental theoretical difficulty involved. 'The question of whether a more abstract level of functioning is only a quantitative extension of a more concrete level, and the two levels are hence continuous. . . . or is so qualitatively different from the more concrete functioning that it is discontinuous from it. . .is indeed an old—and yet unresolved one. It is, among other questions, the problem of reductionism versus holism, or relatedly of quantity versus quality, issues with which psychology—indeed all of science—has spent much effort. . .' (Harvey, Hunt, and Schroeder, 1961).

Quantitative versus qualitative change. A number of studies by Reitan and his colleagues have addressed themselves to the question of qualitative versus quantitative changes following brain damage. Reitan (1955a) has established the presence of striking group differences between brain damaged and control subjects on the ten tests of Halstead's Impairment Index and the Wechsler Bellevue Scale. He felt that 'if different kinds of abilities were used by the brain damaged subjects, the interrelationships or correlations between various tests would differ from the interrelationships between tests shown by the group without brain damage'. (Reitan, 1958a). Correlation coefficients were computed between each pair of variables for each group. A correlation of 0.85 was obtained between the matrices for brain damaged and control groups. Thus, while the brain damaged subjects showed definite impairment their abilities remained essentially of the same kind as nondamaged subjects. In a second study Reitan, 1959a), using the Halstead Category Test, found no significant differences in kind of response to subtests between the two groups though there was a clear difference in the mean error scores. This finding was extended by Doehring and Reitan (1962) again using the Category Test. Taking the ratio of errors on each subtest to total errors on the test they found no difference in the pattern of responding between left hemisphere, right hemisphere, and control groups. Earlier Simmel and Counts (1957) in examining the errors of temporal lobe cases and control subjects on the Category Test had reported that both groups reacted essentially alike to the stimulus material choosing the erroneous alternatives in much the same way.

Goldstein, Neuringer, and Olson (1968) pointed out that a difficulty with Kurt Goldstein's (qualitative) and Reitan's (quantitative) positions has been their failure to evaluate the possibility that *both* observations may be correct depending upon the kind of brain damaged patients and the abilities being evaluated. They employed concept identification problems both simple and complex of the type reported in Bourne (1966). They comment: 'The issue of quantitative vs. qualitative improvement of abstract reasoning in the brain-damaged is not independent of the subject's status, perhaps particularly his age, type of deficit, locus of lesion and problem to solved. Some brain damaged individuals behave as do the patients in Goldstein and Scheerer's case presentations. They seem to be completely incapable of adopting the abstract attitude. Others behave as did the typical subject in the 1959 Reitan study. They can apparently adopt the abstract attitude, but not as effectively as the non-brain damaged individual'. It is obviously important in the resolution of this problem to take the suggested factors into consideration. While the study just cited supported the importance of age and task complexity, the role of location of the lesion has been insufficiently explored.

Frontal locus and abstraction. There is a good deal of evidence that patients with frontal lesions perform poorly on so-called tests of abstraction. Many studies after psychosurgery in the forties and fifties showed such loss on a variety of tests (Fleming, 1942; Kisker, 1944; Rylander, 1947; Malmo, 1948; Yacorzynski, Boshes and Davis, 1948; Petrie, 1949; Grassi, 1950). That these changes might be more subtle with less radical operations has already been mentioned. One large study (Mettler, 1949; Landis, Zubin, and Mettler, 1950) reported only transient loss after psychosurgery.

Studies based on the examination of cases with other frontal lesions including excision of small and large portions of the frontal lobes have often described poor abstract ability defined by poor performance on one or more tests (Goldstein, 1936a, 1939, 1944; Rylander, 1939; Halstead, 1947; Shure, 1954; Shure and Halstead, 1958; Milner, 1963). These studies have often concentrated on the behaviour of individuals with frontal lesions without any comparable examination of patients with lesions in other locations or, where this has been done, e.g. in the Halstead studies, the evidence of a major difference is unconvincing. Teuber (1964) has cited several studies where patients with posterior lesions have performed at least as poorly as frontal patients even where sorting or categorizing tests have been used.

The unsatisfactory nature of this area of research lies in the unsatisfactory nature of many of the tests used and the unwarranted assumptions which have been made about the abilities which are felt to be central to their solution. A patient may fail on a test of abstract thinking for a number of reasons other than alteration in the ability to think abstractly. Milner's argument that the frontal patient may fail because of his inability to inhibit preferred modes of responding would appear to account for many of the failures described in the literature. When one looks at a complex test such as the Category Test one is not surprised at the failure of brain-damaged patients in general since so many factors appear to be crucial for good performance on this test. Some of these factors are introduced in the next section. While the present author feels that there is little doubt about the frontal patient's poor performance on abstraction tasks, it is inaccurate to ascribe the reason for failure to loss of abstract ability. There is now sufficient evidence on which to base a definitive study of group differences on these questions.

Planning and problem solving

One of the most helpful of Luria's contributions to neuropsychology lies in his conception of the frontal lobes at the summit of the brain's hierarchy. His point of view is nowhere more clearly expressed than in *The Working Brain*.

'Man not only reacts passively to incoming information, but creates *intentions*, forms *plans* and *programmes* of his actions, inspects their performance, and *regulates* his behaviour so that it conforms to these plans and programmes; finally, he *verifies* his conscious activity, comparing the effects of his actions with the original intentions and correcting any mistakes he has made.' (pp.78-80).

This higher form of man's activity has been referred to in other areas of psychology largely under the heading of thought processes, e.g. 'Thinking is a form of problem solving behaviour which involves the correlation and integration of critical events in time and space. It is characterized by (a) a period of preliminary exploration, (b) a pre-solution period of search, (c) a period of vicarious testing of tentative solution, (d) an act of closure and registry of a memory trace, and (e) appropriate action.' (Halstead, 1960). It has been the task of neuropsychology in the past decade or more to demonstrate the dependence of each of these major steps upon the integrity of the frontal lobes. This is not to say that there were no early contributions of worth, merely that converging lines of evidence in recent years have given us a better total picture of the complex functioning of the prefrontal regions. Some of the complexity can be gained from an examination of three areas (1) maze behaviour, (2) visuo-constructive activities, and (3) arithmetical problem solving. This is merely a convenient illustrative sample since planning and programming activities permeate virtually everything which man does.

Maze behaviour. As far back as 1914, in the days when mental testing was in its infancy, Porteus introduced a set of pencil and paper maze problems which have been in widespread use since that time and with which he worked in a variety of situations and with a variety of the world's peoples. (Fig. 4.5). One of the reasons for the continued use of the test must be that it measures some characteristic which is basic to man's intelligent behaviour. Porteus himself referred to this in a number of ways, e.g. as 'planfulness', 'planning capacity', or at another times as 'prerehearsal', i.e. a mental rehearsal of the act that the individual was about to perform. If we retain the simple term 'planning', it was this which Porteus considered was measured by the Maze Test and which he felt was a prerequisite to every intelligent act. (Porteus, 1950, 1958, 1959, 1965). Moreover he was to come to the conclusion based on his own studies and those of others that this factor was maximally represented in the frontal lobes. One of the earliest reports of extensive frontal lobectomy has remarked 'In so far as final conclusions from the first two cases . . . are justifiable it may be stated that maximal amputation of right or left frontal lobe has for its most detectable sequel impairment of those mental processes which are requisite to planned initiative'. (Penfield and Evans, 1935).

The advent of psychosurgery allowed Porteus to validate his long standing claim that the Mazes were a measure of planfulness. Patients undergoing classical lobotomy procedures showed a clear loss in this area when investigated clinically. Such patients also showed loss on the Mazes (Porteus and Kepner,

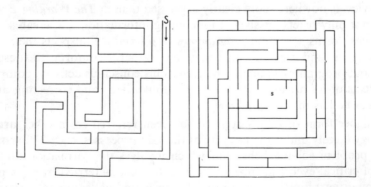

Fig. 4.5 Two examples from the Porteus Mazes (The Psychological Corporation, New York. Kind permission of D. Hebden Porteus.)

1944; Porteus and Peters, 1947). This finding was soon confirmed by others (Malmo, 1948; Mettler, 1949; Mettler, 1952; Petrie, 1949; Petrie, 1952a, 1952b; Robinson and Freeman, 1954). Failure of some workers to demonstrate such losses may have depended not only on the smaller magnitude of the lesion but also on the well known practice effect which such tests possess. This would account for findings such as those of Fabbri (1956), who demonstrated a slight increase in the quantitative score after transorbital lobotomy as well as a marked decrease in qualitative errors.

That losses on the Maze test are dependent on the location of the lesion within the frontal lobe has been shown by Crown (1952) and Lewis, Landis and King (1956). These authors demonstrated that posterior and superior lesions affected performance on the tests more consistently than did lesions in other sites. The work of Robinson on the other hand suggested that the extent of the loss might be related to the amount of the frontal lobe disconnected.

A different types of maze was introduced by Elithorn (1955) which appears sensitive to cerebral impairment. There samples of different degrees of difficulty are shown in Figure 4.6. The subject is instructed to find his way from the bottom to the top passing through the maximum number of dots, this number being printed on the form. The subject is instructed to keep to the dotted lines, told not to cross the white diamonds and that reversing direction is not permitted. Though a later study showed the sensitivity of the Elithorn Maze Test to brain damage there was no indication that frontal patients were differentially impaired (Benton, Elithorn, Fogel, and Kerr, 1963). However we have noted the same disregard for the rules in the face of their correct repetition by the subject and admonition by the examiner already noted for the electrical stylus maze. (See case summary patient 4, Ch. 9). A binary form of the maze for experimental work was developed by Elithorn, Kerr, and Jones (1963) while Gregson and Taylor (1975) have used a computer programme to generate a series of similar mazes where the dot density in the lattice has been controlled.

Visuo-constructive activities. These tasks are often performed poorly by patients with brain damage. Perhaps the most frequently used has been the Block Design task of the Koh's type which has found its way into popular aggregate measures of intelligence such as the Wechsler Scales. The Block Design test failed to live up to expectation as a universal indicator of brain damage but recent reappraisal would suggest that careful analysis of qualitative features of the patient's performance could reveal valuable indicators of brain impairment if the lesion is situated in the frontal or parietal regions.

Constructional difficulties are often all loosely referred to as 'constructional apraxia' (Ch. 6). In posterior lesions the difficulties arise because of a loss of spatial organization of the elements. Luria and Tsvetkova (1964) have demonstrated that frontal constructional difficulties arise through disruption of one or more of the steps mentioned at the beginning of this section, namely, *intention*, *programming*, *regulation* or *verification*. Lhermitte, Derousené, and Signoret (1972) provided confirmation of this by demonstrating how the performance of the frontal lobe patient may be facilitated by means of a programme provided by the examiner. As in the case cited in the section on psychosurgery a patient who was unable to execute a block design problem could do so immediately and without error when presented with a model or design where each constituent block was clearly delimited. In the words of Barbizet (1970) the examiner is here acting as the patient's frontal lobes by generating part of the programme for solution.

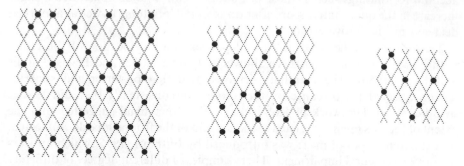

Fig. 4.6 Three examples from the Elithorn Maze Test (Courtesy of the author).

Other tasks are also improved when partial programmes are provided for frontal patients. This does not appear to be the case with lesions in other parts of the brain.

Lhermitte, *et al.* also employed the Complex Figure of Rey (Fig. 4.7, Rey, 1941, 1959; Osterrieth, 1944). The frontal patient's copying was much more adequate than his reproduction from memory. This was not, however, due to a primary disorder of memory. Following their poor reproduction from memory, the patients were given a structured sequence of the figure to copy.

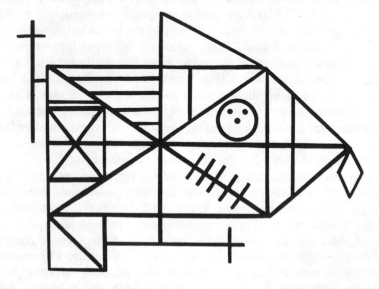

Fig. 4.7 The Complex Figure of Rey (Rey, 1959) (Courtesy of Les Editions du Centre de Psychologie Appliquée).

This began with copying the basic rectangle. They then had to copy a version consisting of the rectangle plus other features and more and more complete figures were given until the full figure was reached. The patient copied each of the more and more complete versions from the beginning so that by the time he had reached the full design he had experienced a sequential programme for its execution on a number of occasions. His later reproduction from memory was much improved. The improvement appears to be due more to the provision of a programme than to the sheer weight of practice. A control experiment of this sort is needed.

Arithmetical problem solving. With frontal lobe lesions there do not appear to be significant disturbances of well established operations such as addition and subtraction and none of the 'spatial' mathematical difficulties seen in parietal patients (Ch. 6). The essential difficulties are better described as those of problem solving or of 'discursive intellectual activity' (Christensen, 1975). Once again the patient may be able to repeat the problem but his actions suggest a form of amnesia. He seems to have forgotten how to generate and execute even a simple two or three step programme which would have presented no difficulty prior to his lesion. As in other areas of behaviour much of his difficulty arises through incomplete analysis and his inability to inhibit the first tendency aroused by the problem (Luria, 1966). A detailed analysis of the arithmetical problem solving ability of patients with frontal (and other) lesions is given in the French monograph of Luria and Tsvetkova (1967). Three sample problems likely to elicit difficulties are as follows: (from Luria, 1966)

'A. There were 18 books on two shelves, and there were twice as many books on one as on the other. How many books were on each shelf?

B. A son is 5 years old; in 15 years his father will be twice as old as he. How old is the father now?

C. A pedestrian takes 30 minutes to reach the station, while a cyclist goes 3 times as fast. How long does the cyclist take?'

Christensen gives a succinct summary of the behaviour of the frontal patient confronted with these problems. 'The patient only grasps one particular fragment of the problem; he does not make any plans but starts to carry out disconnected arithmetical operations with this fragment. The whole process of solution may be transformed into a series of impulsive, fragmentary arithmetical operations, frequently unconnected with the ultimate goal.' (p.188).

The patient often construes 'twice as many' and similar expressions as meaning 'multiply' without any regard for the context and so arrives at what appear ludicrous answers, e.g. in problem C (termed 'conflict' problems by Christensen) he arrives at the answer 90 minutes for the cyclist.

Error evaluation. One of the major changes in behaviour with frontal lobe cases is the patient's lack of full awareness of his deficits. Luria has referred to this as a 'lack of self-criticism' or 'lack of critical attitude towards one's own action' (Luria and Homskaya, 1963, 1964). He feels that this 'can be regarded as the result of a general loss of some feedback mechanism, a disturbance in signals of error, or an inadequate evaluation of the patient's own action. It can be reduced to a deficit in matching of action carried out with the original intention. . .' (Luria and Homskaya, 1964, p.355). In discussing their patient's inability to carry out compounded or symbolic instructions. Luria, Pribram, and Homskaya (1964) stress what has been pointed out several times already, namely that the failure is not one of understanding what is required. 'These incapacities seem not to depend on any difficulty in apprehending the instructions *per se:* they may however, be related to an inability, shown by our patient, to evaluate errors, especially self produced errors.' (p.278).

A most important increase in conceptualizing the nature of the frontal defect has been made by Konow and Pribram (1970). They describe a patient who made errors and, at the same time, gave clear indication that she was aware of making them. She was not, however, able to correct them. 'We therefore confronted her with a test in which one of us carried out the commands of the other, sometimes correctly and sometimes erroneously. The patient usually had no difficuty in spotting our errors. This was true even when they were embedded in rather complex serial performances.' (p.490). The important feature was the patient's inability to use such information to modify her ongoing programme of action. This analysis leads to an important distinction which should have marked implications for attempts to rehabilitate patients with frontal injury, i.e. the distinction between error recognition and error evaluation on one hand and *error utilization* on the other. The latter term is a clear expression of the dissociation between thought and action mentioned by many neuropsychologists in a variety of ways.

Luria has agreed that one basic factor contributing to the frontal patient's difficulties is his lack of the 'verbal regulation of behaviour'. In other words the patient's verbalizations (both internal and external) do not command his actions. Drewe (1975) specifically tested this proposition and found that while it might fit some of the findings it was unable to explain a good deal of the experimental findings in frontal subjects.

Rigidity and cerebral impairment

One of the most frequently mentioned features of the behaviour of brain damaged patients is a lack of flexibility in their approach to many situations. This has been noted in both clinical and psychological test situations. Particular studies express this in different ways, e.g. (1) lessening of the ability to shift from one concept to another when compared with normal subjects (Goldstein and Scheerer, 1941; Weigl, 1941; Aita, Armitage, Reitan, and Rabinowitz, 1947; Ackerly and Benton, 1948; Gleason, 1953; Halstead, 1959; Milner, 1963, 1964); (2) inflexibility, rigidity, perseveration or stereotyped behaviour (Nichols and Hunt, 1940; Rosvold and Mishkin, 1950; Appelbaum, 1960; Allison, 1966; Mackie and Beck, 1966; Allison and Hurwitz, 1967); (3) sensitivity to the effect of set or *Einstellung* (Kauffman, 1963). This list is by no means exhaustive but points to the common occurrence of a mode of behaviour we will term inflexible. There is no convincing evidence that all these descriptions refer to a unitary disability.

This type of behaviour has been described most frequently in association with tests of abstract thinking but has been found also in a variety of other test situations involving learning and problem solving as well as being reflected in the patient's everyday behaviour. Among the various test which have brought out the brain damaged subject's inflexibility have been the Goldstein-Scheerer tests, the Halstead battery, the Wisconsin Card Sorting Test, stylus maze problems, pegboard discrimination, paired associate learning, problem solving, and word association tests. The notion of inflexibility of behaviour in the brain damaged finds one of its clearest and most extensive expressions in the monograph of Goldstein and Scheerer (1941).

One fruitful experimental approach which has received little attention is to examine flexibility under the paradigm of negative transfer. The only direct examination appears to be that of Gleason (1953) who defined negative transfer as 'retardation in the acquiring of an activity as a result of being engaged in a prior activity'. Gleason found support for an increase in negative transfer in brain damaged subjects on several tasks – a pegboard discrimination task, a card sorting task, and a rotated stylus maze. He demonstrated that there was 'an application of old responses in new situations where such responses are inappropriate'.

There is considerable evidence that inflexibility is particularly marked after lesions of the prefrontal regions (Nichols and Hunt, 1940; Halstead, 1947; Ackerly and Benton, 1948; Rosvold and Mishkin, 1950; Luria, 1963, 1965, 1966, 1973b; Luria and Homskaya, 1963; Luria, Pribram, and Homskaya, 1964; Milner, 1963, 1964). Milner's findings suggest that such deficits may be more associated with lesion affecting the dorsolateral aspect of the frontal lobes rather than the orbitomedial regions. Such a finding may be in keeping with the reports of a number of psychosurgical studies which show little or no intellectual alteration when division of fibre pathways is restricted to the ventromedial quadrant of the frontal lobes (Malmo, 1948; Petrie, 1952; McIntyre, Mayfield and McIntyre, 1954; Bradley, Dax, and Walsh, 1958; Smith and Kinder, 1959; Walsh, 1960; Hohne and Walsh, 1970).

Despite this accentuation of the frontal lobe there is clear evidence that inflexibility is found with lesions in other parts of the brain (Critchley, 1953; Allison, 1966; Allison and Hurwitz, 1967). The latter authors point out that perseveration 'is not an occasional accompaniment of aphasia but. . .occurs in the majority of cases.' In fact sixteen out of their twenty four patients showed the symptom. The perseveration was linked to each patient's specific deficit, being elicited by tests related to the deficit but not by tests related to preserved language functions. Like many authors they comment that perseveration was facilitated by anxiety but was also seen in its absence. They also noted that in their series, absence of spontaneous talk was a frequent accompaniment of perseveration. In line with what has been said below on the verbal adynamia with frontal lesions one might suspect that the frontal lobes were affected in at least some of these cases. However, in a few cases where autopsy proof was available, perseveration existed in temporal lesions. With Critchley's observation of perseveration with parietal lesions one can be sure that inflexible behaviour is not seen solely with frontal lesions.

Perseveration or inflexibility appears to be most prominent when the task is difficult or the patient is fatigued. This is not surprising since these are the conditions under which such lapses are likely to appear in normal adults. It is when it becomes constant and pervasive that it provides one of the most valuable signs of early cerebral impairment.

In a number of communications Luria had provided evidence of motor perseveration with frontal lobe damage (Luria, 1963, 1965, 1966, 1973b; Luria and Homskaya, 1963; Luria, Pribram, and Homskaya, 1964). In 1965 he distinguished between two kinds of perseveration seen with frontal lobe damage which he considered to be associated with two different neuronal systems. The first type involves compulsive repetition of a movement that has been initiated but the patient is able to shift from one action to another. The second type represents what Luria terms an inertia of the programme of action itself. . . 'the patient, having once performed the required task, is incapable of switching to the fulfilment of any other task but continues even when instructed otherwise, to perform the first task on which he has 'stuck". (p.1). Type one is thought to be associated with deep seated lesions of the premotor zones involving the subcortical ganglia while the second type is associated with massive involvement of the anterior or basomedial portions of the frontal lobes. 'The only significant difference is that, whereas in lesions of the premotor zones the pathological inertia extends only to the effector components of the action, and performance of the programme as a whole is undisturbed, in massive lesions of the frontal lobes it extends to the scheme of the action itself, with the result that performance of the programme becomes impossible' (1973b, p.206). The validity of Luria's 'premotor syndrome' as a separate distinct entity has been strongly supported by the recent study by Derouesné (1973) of five cases of frontal tumour restricted largely to the rolandic/prerolandic area. Luria makes it clear that the patient who perseverates when given a verbal instruction does not fail through lack of understanding but because the verbal instruction does not regulate his behaviour as it does in normal subjects. . . 'it is not a matter of forgetting the instructions (the patient can reproduce its correct wording) but rather the loss of its regulatory role and replacement of the required programme by an inert motor stereotype' (1973b, p.206). This apparent disregard of instructions has already been mentioned. An extensive and detailed description of the tasks designed by Luria to elicit this behaviour together with examples of a typical patient's responses is provided by Luria, Pribram, and Homskaya, (1964). Luria's complete neuropsychological examination with explanatory texts has recently become available (Christensen, 1975).

As mentioned above, the question of inflexibility has been inextricably interwoven with the question of abstract thinking. A striking confirmation of the difficulty which frontal patients have with conceptual shifts was provided by Milner (1963). Using the Wisconsin Card Sorting Test she examined patients with static lesions in the frontal and temporal regions before and after cortical excision for the relief of epilepsy. Patients with dorsolateral frontal excisions were more impaired in their ability to shift than those with temporal excisions or those with orbitofrontal excisions even when combined with temporal lobectomy. There were no laterality effects shown in this study. Teuber, *et al.* (1951) using the same task had found that anterior missile wound patients were less impaired than posterior patients though in this study Teuber did not allow the prior mode of responding to be built up strongly before alternating the principle so that Milner's study is more conclusive for the effect of perseveration or inability to dissolve a prior mental set. As early as 1948 Grant and Berg showed that the 'amount of perseveration' shown on the Wisconsin Card Sorting Test is a function of the amount of reinforcement of original modes of response. Since then numerous studies have shown the effects of reinforcement on reversal learning, i.e. alteration of response set. It must also be remembered that behaviour on complex tasks of abstract thinking is determined by a number of factors some of which are affected more by frontal and others by posterior lesions. Milner (1964) has commented:

. . .'It would be a mistake to attribute the failure of the frontal lobe patients on the sorting task to a defect of abstract thought. Such patients frequently surprise the examiner by telling him that there are three possibilities: 'color, form and number', yet seem unable to recognize the possibility of change, once a particular mode of responding has become established. Thus they show a curious dissociation between their ability to verbalize the requirements of the test and the ability to use the verbalization as a guide to action' (p.86). She considers that the difficulty of the frontal patients on the WCST 'should perhaps be regarded as a special instance of a more general inability to change response set readily in accordance with varying environmental signals. . .' (1964, p.323).

Despite fairly wide acceptance of the notion that set-shifting difficulty is characteristic of brain damaged subjects, particularly of frontal lesions, the nature of the difficulty has remained unclear. Johnson, *et al.* (1973) suggest that this is largely due to the use of tasks varying in complexity both of stimulus and response as well as different types of abstraction task such as the Weigl Sorting Test (See above) or the reversal shift paradigm as examplified by the study of Phelan and Gustafson (1968). Their study suggests the need to study attentional and other general factors which may influence the performance of patients on tests used to elicit inflexible behaviour.

Intellectual loss and inflexibility. It has often been inferred that intelligence and behavioural inflexibility may be more closely related among brain-damaged subjects than among normals. Mackie and Beck (1966) examined this proposition in a study employing 20 brain-damaged subjects and an equal number of controls. Their results showed that a brain damaged subject may suffer intellectual loss without increased inflexibility and that inflexibility may exist in brain damaged subjects without general intellectual loss.

No examination of test inflexibility in brain-damaged subjects would be complete without taking into consideration factors which have been shown to influence the nature, extent, and frequency of such behaviour in normal subjects. Goldstein (1943), in offering a comprehensive treatment of the problem of rigidity, emphasized that it is a normal phenomenon. He distinguished two types of rigidity: (1) primary rigidity where the stimulus aroused a response system so strongly that the individual became incapable of altering his response set, and (2) secondary rigidity when the subject was faced with a situation with which he could not cope, and which enabled the subject to avoid difficult tasks which gave him an overwhelming feeling of helplessness – the so-called 'catastrophic reaction' (Goldstein, 1936). When Goldstein emphasized the fact that rigidity simply becomes exaggerated with brain damage he was referring to both these reactions. If these two areas are to be evaluated, then not only must we study traditional learning theory which examines factors influencing primary rigidity but also study the effects of the person's perceptions os his own successes and failures as exemplified in studies such as Feather (1966) and Nuttin and Greenwald (1968).

Inflexibility, general considerations. The psychological literature on rigidity or inflexibility should form a background for its study in brain damaged subjects. Reviews of aspects of rigidity are given by Cattell, Dubin, and Saunders (1954), Chown (1959), Fisher (1949), and Schaie (1955, 1958). Baer's (1964) factor analysis of a number of rigidity scales and other personality, perceptual, and aptitude tests suggested that rigidity cannot be represented by a unitary factor. This multidimensionality of the concept of rigidity is discussed in detail by Chown who cites the following definitions.

'The difficulty with which old established habits may be changed in the presence of new demands'. (Cattell and Tiner, 1949).
'The inability to change one's set when the objective conditions demand it' (Rokeach, 1948).
'Resistance to shifting from old to new discriminations' (Buss, 1952).
'Adherence to a present performance in an inadequate way' (Golstein, 1943).
'Lack of variability of response' (Werner, 1946).

Chown points out that while tests of rigidity can be classed under general headings, e.g. (i) tests of *Einstellung* or set, (ii) concept formation tests, (iii) tests of personality rigidity or dispositional rigidity, and (iv) tests of perceptual rigidity, there is a need for a study of the relationship between tests in these areas especially as there is a good deal of overlap apparent between some measures.

Since the presence of these several factors has been neglected or overlooked in many brain damage studies, it is not surprising that the relation between brain damage and inflexible behaviour is yet to be clarified.

Frontal amnesia

Clinical writers have stressed the frequency of memory impairment in patients with tumours of the frontal lobes. This is generally considered to be more marked for recent memory. Hécaen (1964) recorded an incidence of 20 per cent of isolated memory disorder in his own series of 131 frontal tumours while his survey of the literature revealed figures ranging from 29 to 73 per cent in other series. Unfortunately there is little if any psychometric detail provided in this material nor is there adequate information about the presence of memory disorder with regard to the relative location of the lesion within the frontal lobe. With the increase in knowledge of the neuropathology of memory disorders reported in the next chapter it seems possible that some of the memory defects seen with frontal lesions may be due to encroachment on connections between the frontal regions and the limbic or 'axial' structures. Certainly some patients with frontal lesions appear to have difficulty with learning new verbal paired associates though a true Korsakoff type of amnesia is rare (Hécaen, 1964).

Some writers consider that there is no true amnesia in frontal patients, i.e. no inability to register or to retrieve material given the proper conditions. In their views the memory disorder is only apparent, and the poor performance of frontal patients on some memory tasks is better seen as a disruption of complex forms of behaviour which reflects itself in numerous ways. One of the foremost advocates of such a theory is Luria. . . 'a lesion of the frontal lobes leads to gross disturbances of the formation of intentions and plans, disturbance of the formation of behaviour programmes, and disturbances of the regulation of mental activity and the verification of its course and results. In other words, while leaving the operative part intact, it leads to a profound disturbance of the whole structure of human conscious activity'. (Luria, 1973b, p.300). Thus the features of 'frontal amnesia' can be readily distinguished from amnesic disorders associated with temporal lobe lesions (Luria, Sokolov, and Klimkowski, 1967). In these latter cases the whole programme or general meaning is preserved so that 'patients who are unable to retain separate elements often can grasp the general meaning of a sentence or paragraph'. Frontal patients, on the other hand, suffer from a change in the total structure of behaviour which Luria (1971) believes is due to 'high distractibility on one hand and pathological inertia (of traces) on the other, resulting in a loss of programmed forms of activity. In such cases, there is no true amnesia, general or partial, and good retention of a series of items in any modality after 'free' intervals of two minutes or more is seen.

The defect of retrieval in these patients results from *an inability to create a stable intention to remember with failure to 'shift' their recall from one group of traces to another'* (1971, pp.372-373). There is an obvious overlap in this description with the discussions of inertia and rigidity elsewhere in this chapter.

Other writers have commented on the atypical nature of the memory difficulty of the frontal patient, Benton (1968) calling it 'impaired integration of behaviour over a period of time, a deficit which for want of a better term has been called impairment in "recent memory". . .' Barbizet (1970) agrees that simple registration and recall of both visual and verbal material is largely unaffected by 'frontal lesions'. 'In fact, only by means of memory tests in which the frontal patient must retain several facts simultaneously before he can accomplish a specific task are difficulties in recall and learning revealed, and these are often severe. .' (op. cit. p.83). The frontal patient, while possessing the information necessary to solve a problem, often acts as if he has forgotten the (correct) way to proceed. Barbizet recounts the following difficulty in a patient with resection of portion of the right frontal lobe for trauma.

Q: What is the length of one quarter of the Eiffel Tower?
A: After long hesitation, he said he did not know.

Q: What is the height of the Eiffel Tower?
A: 300 meters
Q: What is half of 300?
A: 150
Q: What is half of 150?
A: 75
Q: What is the length of one quarter of the Eiffel Tower, which measures 300 meters?
A: (after long cogitation) . . .200 meters (and despite many attempts he failed each time).' (Barbizet, 1970, pp.84-85).

Barbizet considers that the frontal memory defect is of a specific type, affecting particularly the use of previously acquired information. There is also a great similarity between his descriptions of the disorder and that of Luria 'The evidence seems to suggest that frontal lesions suppress the programs that govern the execution of the mental strategies that bring recall and memorization into play during the operation of any new task, whether it be the resolution of a problem or the learning of a piece of poetry.' (op. cit. p.87).

Frontal patients seem to have difficulty with voluntary learning or memorizing but when they are made to repeat material frequently by the examiner they show that they are quite able to acquire new information which they can also retain.

One specific study has been addressed to the question as to whether frontal patients, like retrorolandic patients, have specific short term memory deficits. Ghent, Mishkin, and Teuber (1962) found consistent negative results for frontal patients when they compared them with control and non frontal cases on a number of tasks with both immediate recall and delayed recall after 15 seconds. There were no significant differences between frontal and control subjects on conventional tasks in the form of recall of digits or recall of simple visual geometric forms or on specially devised memory for position tasks. These latter were created in an attempt to find, for use with human subjects, suitable tasks which might create an analogous situation to the delayed response paradigm which has presented such striking difficulty for frontal monkeys. With this in mind, stimulus material was chosen which 'could not be categorized readily with reference to a verbal or other framework,' Once again the frontal patients were not significantly different from controls. If this work is replicated it seems unlikely that frontal patients have a short-term memory defect in the usual sense.

Milner (1965) studied the effects of visually guided maze learning in patients with variously located lesions, both unilateral and bilateral. This stylus maze approximates the 'visible path, invisible stops' type of maze devised many years ago by Carr (Woodworth and Scholsberg, 1954). The patient had to find his way from start to finish by touching the boltheads with a stylus, moving one step at a time, errors being signalled by a click from the error counter. After working his way across the board once, he was required to repeat the procedure in blocks of 25 trials twice daily until the criterion of three successive errorless trials had been made. Parietal and left temporal groups were close to the performance of normal subjects but the right temporal, right parieto-temporal-occipital, and frontal groups were markedly impaired. It is highly likely that these various groups performed poorly on this task for quite different reasons.

Although the frontal patients were not more impaired on this task than some other groups, certain aspects of test behaviour were specific to the frontal lobe group. They acted on occasion as if they were unaware of the test instructions by frequently breaking the rules such as failing to return to the previous correct choice after making an error, moving diagonally against repeated instructions and back tracking towards the starting point. This latter type of behaviour led to frontal patients making the same error on the one trial. These qualitative differences may reflect the frontal patient's difficulty in inhibiting aroused response tendencies but it is interesting to note that Milner described a dissociation in some of her frontal patients on the WCST (above) and the stylus maze. One patient had many 'qualitative' errors on the maze but showed normal flexibility on the card sorting task. Two other frontal patients gave the reverse pattern.

In an earlier study Walsh (1960) had used a very similar maze in an examination of patients who had undergone modified frontal leucotomy in the orbitomedial quadrant. One of the most frequently reported changes reported after classical prefrontal lobotomy had been the inability of the patients to benefit from past experience. This was noticed not only in the clinical and social settings but had been remarked many times in studies using the Porteus Maze Test. 'Patients tended to make the same mistake repeatedly after the operation which did not happen before the operation, suggesting a loss in the ability to learn from errors' (Petrie, 1952). Fourteen clinically improved patients tested over a year after modified leucotomy were significantly inferior to an equal number of control subjects on both the stylus maze and the Porteus Mazes. The operated patients also had a greater number of the qualitative errors described by Milner though this comparison failed to reach significance.

Since the study mentioned above there have been many opportunities to observe this disregard of instruction on various forms of the stylus maze which have been used in our clinic. They are seen to a marked degree only in frontal cases and are particularly evident after frontal trauma particularly if this is bilateral. Though they may impede the progress of learning they do not always prevent the patient from reaching the criterion in a reasonable number of trials.

Verbal behaviour

Patients with lesions of the left frontal lobe often appear to have intact speech on superficial examination. However, careful examination will often bring out evidence of perseveration or, in severe cases, echolalia. Since some of the features may come out only on detailed examination it is advisable to follow a regular programme of examination in non-aphasic patients suspected of having localized cerebral pathology. Detailed descriptions of such examination have been given in Luria, Pribram, and Homskaya (1964) and Lhermitte, Derouesné and Signoret (1972). They are available in standardized form in the recently available and comprehensive manual for Luria's neuropsychological examination (Christensen, 1975). The following précis is taken from these sources:

The patient typically has no difficulty in repeating isolated words or simple sentences. He may also manage quite well with an unconnected series of words but often has much more difficulty if the word order is changed, e.g. he may repeat the set CAT—FOREST—HOUSE but have difficulty with the re-arranged sets CAT—HOUSE—FOREST and FOREST—TABLE—CAT, showing perseveration of the earlier order. When asked to name objects the patient names single objects readily but may have difficulty if the objects to be named are presented in various pairings, e.g. the series WATCH-PEN, SCISSORS-THERMOMETER, WATCH-THERMOMETER, SCISSORS-PEN may produce perseveration of earlier elements as the test proceeds. Such difficulties are exaggerated if the pairs are presented with only a small temporal separation.

Such difficulties are coupled with reduction of 'verbal fluency' described in the next section and with difficulties in what Luria has termed the verbal regulation of behaviour. These latter are brought out most clearly when a sequence of behaviour is called for. Two examples will suffice.

1. The patient is instructed to place in a line one black counter followed by two white counters and to continue doing this. Two attempts from a patient with a left frontal meningioma are shown (from Luria, *et al.*, 1964)

B.W.W.B.B.W.W.W.W.W.W......
B.W.W.B.W.B.W.W.B.W.

These incorrect attempts were made despite the fact that the patient was able to repeat the instructions perfectly. Though he appears to understand, neither his own internal language nor the verbal behaviour of others is capable of regulating his behaviour.

2. The patient has particular difficulty where there is apparent conflict in the instructions, e.g. 'Tap your hand once on the table when I tap twice and tap twice when I tap once.' He may be unable to do so or may begin correctly only to deteriorate rapidly into producing a random series or, more commonly, a rigid stereotype of tapping irrespective of the number of taps given by the examiner. The patient has no difficulty with echopraxis, i.e. simple repetition of movements in imitation of the examiner and, again, he is able to repeat the instructions signifying that he apprehended what was required of him.

Verbal fluency. Frontal patients' behaviour is often characterized by a general lack of spontaneity and voluntary action to which the term 'adynamia' has been applied. There is frequently an associated impoverishment of spon-taneous speech and a reduction in the patient's conversational replies which often shrink to passive responses to questions put to him. These responses often have an echolalic quality, e.g. 'Have you had your lunch?' Yes, I've had my lunch.' This verbal adynamia is often more marked after left prefrontal damage than elsewhere in the brain including the right frontal region. Luria (1973b) stresses that this form of reduction of speech cannot be regarded as an aphasic disorder. Though this may be only a matter of terminology the treatment of other language disorders accompanying frontal lesions is reserved for Chapter 9.

Milner (1964) employed Thurstone's Word Fluency Test in a comparison of left frontal, right frontal, and left temporal lobectomies. This test requires the patient to *write* as many words as possible in five minutes which begin with the letter S and then as many four-letter words which begin with C. Milner found that left frontal cases were much poorer than the other two groups. Since there was a marked difference between the left frontal and left temporal groups the effect would appear to be specific to the left frontal region and not due solely to involvement of the left (language dominant) hemisphere. Moreover, she found a double dissociation between the left frontal and left temporal groups on the task of verbal fluency versus two tasks of verbal recall. Left frontal patients performed poorly on verbal fluency but adequately on verbal recall of prose passages and paired associates while the reverse was true of the left temporal patients.

Benton (1968) confirmed and expanded these findings. His test of verbal associative fluency has been used in other studies and has become part of the Standardized Neurosensory Center Comprehensive Examination for Aphasia (Spreen and Benton, 1969). The patient is asked to say as many words as possible in one minute for each of the letters F, A and S with the proviso that names and other capitalized words are to be avoided and words with different endings but the same stem are not acceptable, e.g. eat, eaten, eating. Benton restricted his examination to the frontal regions, the lesions being mainly tumours classified in three groups, left frontal, right frontal and bilateral. On the verbal fluency test, left frontal and bilateral cases were both inferior to right frontal cases though there was no significant difference between the first two groups. Benton pointed out that the left hemisphere patients were 'ostensibly non aphasic' and felt that since the impairment was seen both in speaking as well as in writing (Milner, 1964) that it was a rather general higher-level language loss. Ramier and Hécaen (1970) confirmed the verbal fluency loss with left frontal lesions. They felt that the defect depended on 'the interaction of 2 factors: frontal lobe damage (defective initiation of an action) and left-sided lateralization of the lesion (verbal domain)'.

The following (Benton Word Fluency Test) case from our files shows the responses of a young woman of good education who had suffered severe left heimsphere damage with major accent on the frontal region. There were no obvious clinical signs of aphasia at the time of this examination.

The case typifies the frequent occurrence of difficulty in this form of word finding together with perseverations and failure to comply with the instructions. Lhermitte, *et al.* (1972) point out that the semantic and morphological perseverations which characterize the performance of frontal patients on this task are also seen in their attempt to define words.

Luria, Homskaya, Blinkov, and Critchley (1967) described a case with a deep left mesial frontal tumour which was also affecting the right side. In this case a disturbance of language became more evident as the tumour increased in size and the authors suggest that careful examination in the early stages of such

Benton Word Fluency Test

"F"	"A"	"S"
force	add	skin
fool	a	scoot
fiddle	alphabet	school
fink	adjective	skin (I said skin)
find	account	skittle
fool	advance	sun
Friday	answer	son
fink	animal	sound
fool		skin
find		skittle
fink		sun
fool		
Friday		

tumours might reveal certain 'pre-aphasic' signs. One of these is that psychological processes lose what the above authors termed their selective character. When asked to reproduce a sentence or word series the patient would interpolate additional associations which he was unable to inhibit. He also had difficulty in naming objects. Luria, *et al.* comment. . 'the naming of an object is a complex process, which includes singling out some leading features of the article, and also assignment to a certain category. This process necessarily includes the suppression of inappropriate alternatives, and a selective choice of proper designations. . .Often this sympton showed itself in a certain excess of detail in the replies indicating an impairment of inhibition of extraneous associations.' (p.111).

The present author has frequently observed this symptom in post-traumatic cases along with other obvious signs of frontal involvement. It is nicely demonstrated during psychological testing where a Vocabulary Test, such as that in the WAIS, is used. Here the patient has to give an appropriate definition of a series of words. If one can consider that in order to produce the correct definition the patient must at the same time inhibit competing response tendencies, the impairment of inhibition leads to many inappropriate responses. To the untrained observer these may appear to have the idiosyncratic quality of some psychotic verbalizations. However the patient may demonstrate during the examination that he is well aware of the correct definition, his difficulty being the inability to inhibit the competitors, some (but not all) of which may appear on association by sound with the word to be defined. i.e., what are referred to in the psychiatric literature as 'clang' associations. The inability in inhibiting aroused response tendencies is often evident in other aspects of the patient's behaviour. The following vocabulary responses are taken from one of the author's posttraumatic cases. The patient also showed impulsiveness, facetiousness and fluctuating euphoria.

DESIGNATE..........blow up something (detonate).

REMORSE.............woman singing a real sad song and she starts crying.

CALAMITY ....man is overcome with stone, rocks, everything.

FORTITUDE..........where all the soldiers are all going back to the fortitude because all the Indians attack.

TIRADE................(here the patient gave a long rambling description of disaster at sea, shipwreck etc. and finished by announcing. .'and this was all about a tirade wave.'

Many of this patients' other response were perfectly acceptable.

Perret (1974) has extended and clarified Hécaen and Ramier's hypothesis mentioned above, utilizing the concept of loss of control of inhibition. Perret found left frontal patients were significantly poorer than other patients both on a word-fluency test and on a modified version of the Stroop Test (Stroop, 1935) where the subject must make a response in which one category of response is pitted against another, e.g. name the colour in which a word is printed, the word itself being the name of a colour. The words BLUE, GREEN, RED and YELLOW were presented randomly in this way with the print colour never coinciding with the word, e.g. the word BLUE was printed in green. red, or yellow ink.

Right frontal patients performed more poorly than right posterior patients on the modified Stroop Test though the difference was small.

Perret considered that the basic difficulty which accounted for the exceedingly poor response by left frontal patients lay in the fact that for successful performance the patient must resist the habit of using words according to their meaning. In the word fluency test the subject is asked to search for words according to the beginning letter and not to the usual method of word finding related to meaning. 'Thus the tests may not have measured the ability to find words, but rather to *suppress the habit of using words according to their meaning.*' 'These results corroborate the hypothesis of the role of the frontal lobe in the adaptation of behaviour to unusual situations, the left frontal lobe being of fundamental importance when verbal factors are involved.' (pp.323-324).

Perceptual difficulties

The Aubert phenomenon. In 1861 Aubert described the following phenomenon which bears his name. When a subject is asked to align a luminescent rod to the vertical in a dark room he is usually able to do so with a fair degree of accuracy. However, if the subject's head is tilted (or both his head and body) the perceived vertical is displaced to the side opposite to the direction of body tilt and in proportion to the degree of head or body tilt. Several experiments (Forgus, 1966) have supported the notion that 'it is not tilt *per se* but the degree of muscular involvement, causing tonic imbalance, that is the important variable in these effects caused by the interaction of sensory and proprioceptive factors.' (p.192).

Teuber and Mishkin (1954) examined the Aubert effect in subjects with penetrating missile wounds in various locations. They found a 'double dissociation' on this task with regard to anterior (frontal) and posterior (parieto-occipital) lesions. Frontal patients had difficulty in setting the rod to the vertical with their head and body tilted (the visual-postural condition Fig. 4.8). Posterior lesion subjects had little difficulty on this task. On the other hand posterior subjects performed much more poorly on a visual-visual condition where the subject is required to set a black thread to the apparent vertical against an interfering background of visual stripes while their body was upright. On the simple visual condition for setting the rod and also on a simple postural task where the patient had to set his own chair to the vertical there were no major group differences (Fig. 4.8).

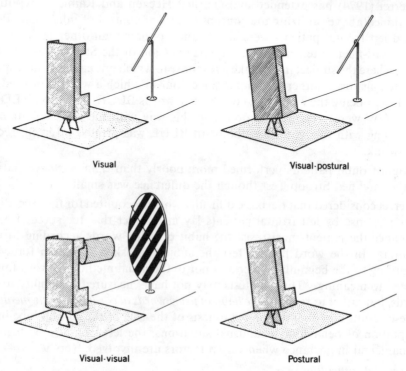

Fig. 4.8 Aubert experiments (Figure 20.6, p. 427 from Teuber (1964a) in J.M. Warren and K. Akert. *The Frontal Granular Cortex and Behavior.* Used with permission on McGraw-Hill Book Company.)

Visual search and analysis of complex material. Teuber's laboratory was also the first to demonstrate experimentally a 'subtle but lasting deficit in visual searching' (Teuber, Battersby, and Bender, 1949). Patients were required to point as quickly as possible to the matching stimulus when one of the forty-eight stimuli was displayed on a circular centre area (Fig. 4.9). Frontal patients were much poorer on this task than either control subjects or non-frontal lesion cases. Unilateral frontal cases, unlike the other subjects, also were disproportionately slower in finding objects in the side opposite the lesion.

An analysis of eye-movements in frontal subjects has appeared in a number of recent publications. Luria, Karpov, and Yarbuss (1966) examined eye movements in a patient with a large right frontal tumour and demonstrated a disturbance in the complex process of exploration of complex pictures. Chedru,

Fig. 4.9 Field of search test (Figure 20.4, p. 425 from Teuber (1964a) in J.M. Warren and K. Akert, *The Frontal Granular Cortex and Behavior*. Used with permission of McGraw-Hill Book Company.

Leblanc, and Lhermitte (1973) reported increased identification time for pictures in the contralateral visual half-field but found that the searching activity was similar in the two visual half-fields. They considered that the longer identification time might be accounted for by assuming that some alerting value was lost on the affected side by an alteration or disruption of occipitofrontal connections, an explanation similar to the disconnection hypothesis invoked elsewhere. Eye movements of the four patients studied were normal on verbal command and in following a moving target but differed from normals when complex pictorial material was used. Here preliminary visual exploration was reduced and almost compulsive fixation given to one or two details required for answering specific questions about the picture.

Luria (1973b) sees the failure of preliminary analysis as a basic reason why frontal patients fail to grasp the meaning of what he terms 'thematic' pictures. The type of behaviour deficit shown by frontal patients in this situation is very similar to that provoked by other problem solving situations. 'To understand the meaning of such a picture the subject must distinguish its details, compare them with each other, formulate a definite hypothesis of its meaning, and then test this hypothesis with the actual contents of the picture, either to confirm it or to reject it, and then resume the analysis.' (pp.213-214). The frontal patient will form an 'hypothesis' based on very little preliminary analysis, what Luria calls the 'impulsive hypothesis'. Since he fails to complete the other steps in the programme of action the patient will also be satisfied with his explanation, e.g. he does not carry out further exploration which would bring forth added information which would then confirm or disconfirm his hypothesis. Luria points out that the recording of eye movements in normal subjects reveals an alteration in the searching process when the subject is asked to answer different questions about a thematic picture such as the period of the picture, the age of the people depicted, their relationship to each other and so on. The frontal patient fixes on any point and impulsively gives the first hypothesis which comes into his mind: The non-analytical nature of the patient's behaviour is reflected graphically in his eye-movement record.

This type of behaviour with thematic pictures is often seen on the Picture Arrangement sub-test of the Wechsler intelligence scales. In this test the subject is given in random order a number of cards which when placed in the correct sequence will tell a logical story.

We have observed frontal patients to be uncritical in their arrangement, making few alterations in the positions of the cards and then telling a loosely connected story in which only one or two salient features are mentioned and the logical links between elements of the picture series are missing. On occasion the patient may state that he is quite satisfied with the random order as presented to him and then proceeds to tell a story which lacks the richness one would expect from his background or from an estimate of his intelligence based on tests of stored information which are relatively resistant to cerebral insult. At other times he describes some salient features of each card as though it were a separate unit and not part of a series. McFie and Thompson (1972) analysed the Picture Arrangement test in 143 adults with circumscribed cerebral lesions and found that, while patients with variously located lesions performed poorly on this test, the tendency to leave pictures in the presented order (in whole or in part) occurred more frequently with frontal than non-frontal lesions particularly on the right side. They felt that this tendency reflected 'a specific inability to correct a response in spite of evidence that it is wrong. .' (p.551).

There is little doubt that Luria's explanation of the frontal patient's difficulty with thematic pictures would apply equally well to performance on the Picture Arrangement test.

Reversible perspective. Cohen (1959) working in Teuber's laboratory with penetrating missile cases found that unilateral frontal cases experienced much fewer reversals of a double Necker cube (Fig. 4.10) than patients with lesions in other areas though all unilateral brain damaged individuals were inferior to

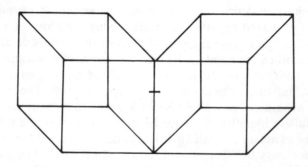

Fig. 4.10 Reversible double Necker cube

controls. The average number of reversals was smallest for the right frontal group. Rather unexpectedly, bilateral frontal cases showed the reverse phenomenon, reporting many more reversals than normal control subjects. The significance of these findings is uncertain.

Laterality and the frontal lobes

As far back as Jackson (1874) some writers have remarked on the greater disturbance of behaviour by left frontal lesions than by right though some studies, e.g. Rylander (1939) have found no difference associated with the laterality of lesion. Zangwill (1966b) pointed out that Feuchtwanger and Kleist had described certain higher level verbal difficulties in left frontal lesions which were not seen in right sided cases. These he summarized as: '(1) a certain loss of spontaneity of speech in the absence of articulatory disorder; (2) Difficulty in evoking appropriate words or phrases, amounting on occasions to frank agrammatism; (3) In some cases, definite impairment of verbal thought processes.' More recently attention has been addressed to the question as to whether the asymmetry of function of the two hemispheres is reflected in the frontal lobes as it is in the posterior parts of the brain (Ch. 8). A large study of unilateral frontal tumour cases by Smith (1966b) using the Bellevue-Wechsler Scale appeared at first to agree with Teuber's evidence that frontal lesions have less effect on test intelligence than lesions in other areas. Thirty one frontal cases had a mean I.Q. of 95.55 whereas 68 posterior cases had a mean I.Q. of 91.46. However a division into left frontal (14 cases) and right frontal (17 cases) revealed a significant mean I.Q. difference between the left (90.1) and right (99.5) cases. Smith re-examined Pollack's data on the Wechsler-Bellevue Scale for the latter's reported tumour cases and found a mean I.Q. of 86.25 for his 4 left frontal cases and a mean I.Q. of 103.5 for his 6 right frontal cases. Thus by grouping together all frontal cases an important difference has been concealed.

Smith also examined the ages of left and right frontal cases reported in several studies (Rylander, 1939; Halstead, 1947; McFie and Piercy, 1952a, 1952b) and found consistently younger ages for those with left frontal tumours. Together with clinical evidence that left frontal tumours appear to declare themselves earlier than right frontal tumours, Smith finds this a strong argument against the proposition that the disruptive effect of frontal tumours can be attributed to their larger size since the most disruption clearly comes from those of earlier onset, i.e. left frontal.

Finally, Benton (1968) has looked at the question of laterality effects in frontal lesions by utilizing tests meaningfully related to recent evidence of hemispheric asymmetry. He chose the following tests:
(i)   two 'left hemisphere' tests (a) verbal associate fluency (see below); (b) paired associate verbal learning.
(ii)   two 'right hemisphere' tests (a) three dimensional constructional praxis test (Benton and Fogel, 1962, Ch. 6); (b) copying designs, Benton Visual Retention Test.
(iii) two 'bilateral' tests (a) Gorham Proverbs; (b) temporal orientation. Al-

though only a small sample was available (8 right, 10 left and 7 bilateral cases) the findings strongly suggest that interhemispheric differences are reflected in the frontal lobes. Left frontal patients were inferior to right on the word fluency test while right frontal patients were inferior to left frontal on both the constructional praxis and copying tasks. Somewhat unexpectedly the right frontal group was inferior to the left on the proverbs task.

Neuropsychological examination of frontal lobe cases in recent years has strongly supported Goldstein's notion that the nature of frontal lobe deficits demands the use of appropriate tests for their elucidation. Tests which require the production of long-stored information or the routine use of long-established skills will seldom be helpful in eliciting frontal signs.

Personality changes and psychosurgery

Prefrontal lobotomy and its congeners

The birth of modern psychosurgery has been considered to date from November 1935, this being the date when Egas Moniz and Pedro Almeida Lima made the first attempt to alleviate mental suffering by operating on the human frontal lobes (Moniz, 1954). For various reasons, there was at first little interest shown in this new therapy by the medical profession as a whole, and the advent of World War II no doubt contributed to the slow progress made in this field during the ensuing years in Europe.

Following the publication by Freeman & Watts of their book *Psychosurgery* (1942) general interest in these techniques increased rapidly. The classical lobotomy of Freeman & Watts became the standard procedure in most centres,

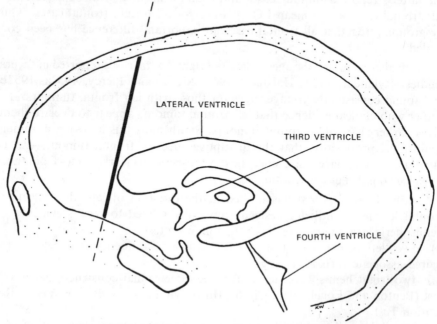

Fig. 4.11 Plane of Section in classical prefrontal lobotomy

and their finding that the dorsomedial nucleus of the thalamus degenerated when the frontal lobe was isolated provided an interesting and important connection between this work and the suspicions of earlier workers that connections between the frontal lobe and the thalamus provided 'for the addition within the prefrontal fields of affective impulses of thalamic origin' (Herrick, 1963).

The standard early lobotomy consisted of very radical division of the white matter of the frontal lobes in a more or less vertical plane just anterior to the tip of the frontal horn of the lateral ventricle (Fig. 4.11).

The extent of destruction of tissue can be seen in Figure 4.12 taken from Freeman & Watts (1948). The term lobotomy used by American and other writers means literally an incision into the lobe. English writers on the other hand preferred the term leucotomy, meaning a cutting of the white matter. The two terms can be taken to be synonymous though care should be taken in reading the literature to ascertain the placement and extent of the lesion in any given series.

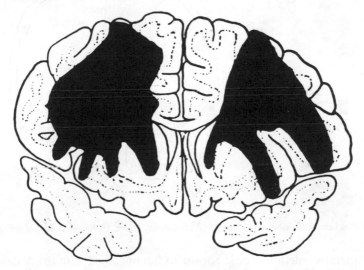

Fig. 4.12 Extensive lobotomy incisions (from Freeman and Watts. A.R.N.M.D. 27, 205, 1948)

Neurosurgeons and psychiatrists very soon became aware, following the early radical operations, that a percentage of patients showed a post-lobotomy syndrome which had many undesirable features. Indeed, in many cases where such a syndrome existed after operation, the second state of the patient appeared to be worse or less desirable than his pre-morbid one. Moreover the mortality rate was considerable in some series as was the incidence of post-operative epilepsy and intellectual deterioration. All this led either to an abandonment of the procedure by some or a search by others for a modified form of operation which would preserve any therapeutic value while minimising the risk of unwanted changes.

In England, Dax and Radley Smith described ventromedial leucotomy in 1943 and in 1945 using a special leucotome (the MacGregor-Crombie leucotome) performed the first selective leucotomies. In these, the upper, middle and lower portions of the frontal lobe were severally divided by sections in a plane parallel to the coronal suture. Other workers also reported that sectioning only the inferior quadrants produced equally good results as those occurring in the more extensive Freeman & Watts operation. From the early forties, the number and types of surgical intervention rapidly multiplied; but the accumulation of evidence seemed to suggest that the more important thalamo-frontal fibres to be severed were those in close proximity to the tip of the frontal horn of the lateral ventricle, and it was a minor variation of the lower section operation first performed by Dax and Radley Smith which formed the operative technique for a series reported by the present author over a very long period (Hohne and Walsh, 1970; Walsh, 1976).

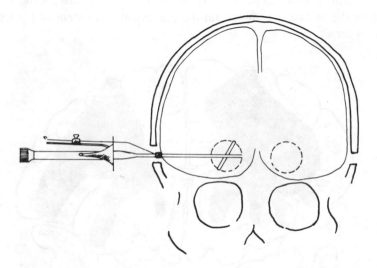

Fig. 4.13 Position of Section in orbitomedial leucotomy (from Hohne and Walsh, 1970)

This operative method would appear to be concerned with the destruction of much the same fibre pathways as the later method of coagulation by Grantham (1951) which also placed its circumscribed lesion just anterior to the frontal horn of the ventricle, in the lower medial quadrant of the frontal lobe. The procedure is described in detail by Bradley, Dax, and Walsh (1958). The placement of the lesions is shown in Figures 4.13 and 4.14.

These procedures had much to recommend them. Because of the absence of a large cortical scar, the danger of postoperative epilepsy was minimal. Secondly, if it was felt that further isolation of frontal cortex was necessary, a second operation could be performed to extend the lesion at another time. Thirdly, such operations seemed to be almost free of the type of postoperative change often referred to as the chronic frontal lobe syndrome, while producing equally effective symptomatic relief.

It would seem that if division of this bundle of thalamo-frontal fibres was the most important mechanism in producing symptomatic relief, then one would

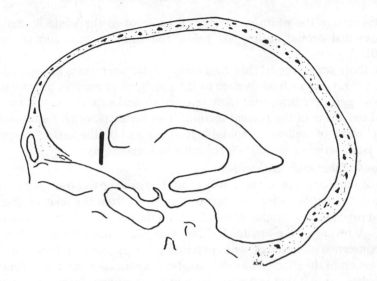

Fig. 4.14 Position of Section in orbitomedial leucotomy (from Hohne and Walsh, 1970)

expect most forms of leucotomy to have certain features in common, since the majority of operations interrupted part or all of this radiation.

Since this book is concerned with neuropsychological aspects of lesion studies the reader interested in the clinical effects of the countless psychosurgical operations may refer to *The Proceedings of the International Congresses on Psychosurgery* (the most recent of which was held in Madrid, 1975) or to the numerous books and reviews which have appeared on the subject over the past four decades of which the following is a sample (Mettler, 1949; Freeman and Watts, 1950; Greenblatt, Arnold and Solomon, 1950; Mettler, 1952; Petrie, 1952; Freeman, 1953a; Freeman, 1953b, Robinson and Freeman, 1954; Tow, 1955; Freeman, 1958; Robin, 1958; Tooth and Newton, 1961; McKenzie and Kaczanowski, 1964; Hohne and Walsh, 1970; Laitinen and Livingston, 1973).

Some operations aimed at largely sparing the thalamo-frontal radiation. Operations which isolated only parts of the frontal cortex have reported good results. The restricted orbital undercutting of Area 13 and part of Area 14 appears to have been as successful as many more radical procedures (Knight and Tredgold, 1955; Sykes and Tredgold, 1964).

During the 1960s numerous attempts were made to reduce the size of the lesion and to localize it more accurately by means of stereotactic surgery. These included electrodes, probes used for freezing, and the implantation of radio-active seeds. The latter method was introduced by Knight in 1960 and replaced his previous surgical method while placing the lesion in the same anatomical site. Results are reported by Knight (1965), Strom-Olsen and Carlisle, (1971), and Knight (1972).

In a brief but excellent review of psychosurgery Sweet (1973) commented on the more recent operations: 'On the assumption that some cerebral component of the limbic system was the appropriate target, lesions have been made in the gyrus-cinguli, in the white matter lateral to it, or in the white matter of the posteromedial orbital cortex just below the head of the caudate nucleus.' (p.1120).

Even more controversial than the fronto-limbic operations mentioned above are the operations such as damage to the amygdaloid nucleus in patients with violently aggressive behaviour. Any attempt to deal with this would move well beyond the scope of the present section. The material which follows is based upon a survey of studies on frontal leucotomy and on the author's experience with a large series of modified (orbitomedial) leucotomy.

The frontal lobes and personality*

One of the charges most frequently brought against psychosurgery is the lack of a proper scientific rationale. Part of this stems from the relative absence of detailed psychological studies of the effects on the person's internal organization or self. A review of the literature shows that the relatively few studies which have concerned themselves with psychological assessment limit this to an investigation of the effectiveness of operation in reducing anxiety or depression or in demonstrating that psychosurgery, in its 'modified' forms, does not have an adverse effect upon aggregate measures of intelligence such as the Wechsler scales. Remarkably few studies have been addressed to the question of the relation between personality change and a rationale for operation. In 1950 Freeman said: 'In order to establish a satisfactory result by psychosurgery, it is necessary to change the personality of the patient from his preoperative one or even his premorbid one.' A study of such changes might then not only increase our understanding of brain-behaviour relationships in the sphere of personality but also provide a better understanding of indication and contraindication for psychosurgery.

Early in our own series the rationale for selection was based on the belief that leucotomy becomes the treatment of choice in a patient with the symptom complex of what Arnot (1949) termed 'a fixed state of tortured self-concern', where this has been unrelieved over a long period by other measures. The concept of 'self-concern' as a favourable indication had also been referred to by others (Poppen, 1948; Freeman and Watts, 1950). With this background and knowledge derived from our early cases, a certain picture of the most suitable candidates for leucotomy gradually crystallized, and a constellation of personality features emerged, almost all of which were related to the patient's preoccupation with his self-concept. This was reflected in referrals in numerous ways. Thus, one patient might be referred as suffering from 'somatic delusions', or 'hypochondriasis' or even 'paraphrenia' while others were referred for 'persistent painful rumination' or 'anxious depression'. We agree with Robinson and Freeman (1954) that these are all aspects of concern over the self, the continuity of which can be modified by psychosurgery so that guilt-laden rumination about the past and fearful anticipation of the future are reduced in the direction of living more fully and contentedly in the immediate present.

In an attempt to assess the personality changes which followed operation the Minnesota Multiphasic Personality Inventory was administered to 100 consecutive cases before and after operation.

* This section is condensed from Walsh (1976).

The clinical scales of the inventory showed a marked decrease in group means after operation. This effect was differential, the most marked alterations being in the Depression, Hysteria, Psychasthenia, and Schizophrenia scales (beyond .001 significance level).

Against the generally favourable improvement on the MMPI one scale moved in an adverse direction. This was the Ego Strength (Es) scale which had been derived from the MMPI by Barron (1953). He felt that this scale reflected the ego strength or latent capacity for integration in the personality, the potential of the personality for coping with situations. The decrease in this scale after operation might support the frequently made claim that leucotomy may lead to a lessening of constructive forces within the personality. It is a reminder that even modified operations may not be carried out with complete immunity.

An item analysis showed that many items moved in the 'improved' direction following treatment. The most frequent improvement was in those items related to self-concern expressed either as general painful rumination, brooding or worrying or related to specific areas of dysfunction, most notably concern about mental health or concern over somatic complaints. Accompanying these changes was an improvement in items reflecting introversion. Items expressing depressive mood also showed marked improvement.

If these changes were the principal cause of improvement there should have been an overlap between the most frequently changed items and those taken from the most improved cases. This was the case, the items being those which expressed the central themes of self-concern, introversion, and depressed psychological mood in the most unambiguous manner.

Item analysis related to particular symptoms showed that anxieties, phobias and painful rumination were most affected, obsessions improved to a lesser degree, while hallucinations and delusions remained unchanged.

Since the main principle of selection was centred around the notion of tortured rumination about the self it follows that we would anticipate alteration in self-concern in successful cases. A comparison of 14 'most improved' with 14 'least improved' cases using Robinson's three tests of self-continuity (Robinson and Freeman, 1954) showed a highly significant difference on all measures when the patients were examined one to two years after operation. Those cases classed as improved showed significantly lower scores on the measures of self-concern than those classed as unimproved. One can conclude that a reduction in the capacity for the feeling of self-continuity may be regarded as a central mechanism of psychosurgery.

These findings have several implications: (1) it is only where the particular personality changes described are likely to lead to a better overall state for the patient that a rationale exists for operation; (2) not only are major frontal divisions which produce more drastic changes unjustified, even modified operations may be inimical where decreased self-concern might aggravate rather than help the patient's condition; (3) selection should be based on symptomatology rather than nosology.

This latter point seems particularly important. Reliance on traditional diagnostic categories in selection has often led to disappointing results since the symptom complex most likely to be favourably affected may be present in only few of the cases. The failure of frequently cited 'controlled' studies to show significant improvement after operation is misleading when an examination of the type of case operated shows a remarkable absence of rational principles of selection (Robin, 1958; Vosburg, 1962; McKenzie and Kaczanowski, 1964).

Follow up studies in series like the present suggest that operation is successful to the degree that the symptom complex of tense rumination is present. Where such symptoms form only part of the clinical picture, e.g. in what has been termed pseudoneurotic schizophrenia, only part of the condition will be helped. It would not be logical to expect otherwise.

Finally, the present author has had the opportunity of following a small number of patients for almost two decades. Clinical examination supplemented by psychological examination (including the MMPI in a few cases) demonstrates that the changes brought about by operation are still apparent.

The principal feature of modified leucotomy appears to be a modification of the personality in the direction of lessened self-concern. It is probable that this is the central factor by which various forms of prefrontal operation bring about symptomatic relief.

Cognitive changes with modified leucotomy

Less dramatic changes were observed in a small group of 14 patients on whom intellectual measures were taken. However, while these were not marked enough to trouble the patient they are of some theoretical significance in the light of recent studies.

It has been the general opinion that it was encroachment on the dorsolateral frontal regions which led to intellectual deficit following radical lobotomy. (Malmo, 1948; Petrie, 1952; Smith and Kinder, 1959). The only long term comparison of operation in these two areas strongly supports this notion. Hamlin (1970) showed that the long term losses of 'superior topectomy' patients (upper frontal lesions) on intelligence measures was appreciable whereas orbital topectomy examined after the same post-operative period of 14 years showed scores 'remarkably comparable to those of nonoperated controls' (p.307). Operation of all types confined to the orbitomedial area seem to have been relatively free of intellectual loss at least as measured by standardized tests. This is now understandable since such tests are greatly dependent upon long-stored information and skills. Most of them are not of the sort to elicit the subtle changes in the regulation of behaviour by the initiation and monitoring of appropriate plans of action which have been demonstrated with such clarity by Luria, Lhermitte, Milner and other neuropsychologists in recent years. The following characteristics now recognized by neuropsychologists as typically related to frontal lobe dysfunction were seen in the operated group: (1) lessened ability to formulate an adequate plan for the solution of a problem; (2) lessened ability to utilize information from their errors to modify subsequent action; (3) some inflexibility in conceptual behaviour.

The importance of the frontal lobes for the formulation, modification and execution of plans of action has been stressed by Luria and others over many years (Luria, 1973). Difficulties of this kind are well brought out by the Kohs block designs. Though this is a complex task which is also failed by patients with lesions in retrorolandic regions, an examination of the type of performance shows some pathognomonic features in frontal patients. Lhermitte, Derouesné, and Signoret (1972) point out that a number of steps are necessary in the solution of the block design problems, namely, preliminary analysis, generation of a programme, implementation and control of the programme and final comparison. Patients with frontal damage may fail at any stage often being blocked in their attempts at solution at the stage of preliminary analysis. . . 'il faut en effet, decomposer le modele en ses cubes constitutifs de facon a pouvoir choisir le nombre et les faces correctes des ces cubes. Sans cette analyse prealable, la reproduction des modeles est tout a fait impossible.' (op. cit. p.429).

The Goldstein and Scheerer (1941) version of the block design test was given to the operated subjects and a matched control group. If the subject could not complete the design with the small pictured example he was given a design equal in size to the four blocks he was to utilize in his construction. If he failed this he was given a design with the lines of the edges of the blocks superimposed on the design either in a reduced size or a larger version equal to the size of four blocks. No control subject needed any of this assistance whereas the operated subject often needed a partial programme for the solution, the divided diagram being of particular assistance to most subjects (Fig. 4.15). Design 10

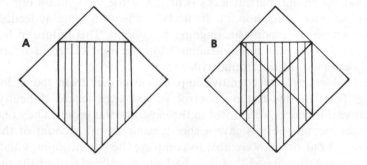

Fig. 4.15 Block design. A, undivided design; B, divided design.

shown in the diagram presented marked difficulty for nine of the fourteen subjects. Qualitative differences were seen in the experimental group. Several subjects expressed puzzlement that a particular design could be reproduced and even after completing the design exhibited uncertainty about it. Several other subjects successfully copied a design, expressed dissatisfaction, broke up the design and commenced again. Subject 14 had no difficulty up to design seven. After great trouble with this design she was given assistance in the form of a large undivided design, then a smaller divided design but still failed. After a long time she succeeded with the aid of the large divided design but volunteered the remark 'You're sure it is possible to get the *other* one right?'. She could see no apparent connection between the original design and the 'assisted' versions which followed. In view of the position and relatively small size of the lesions and the apparent preservation of the patients' intelligence, these signs take on added significance. They appear identical in nature though less pronounced than those described recently with massive frontal lesions. Design 10 also proved difficult for the patient described above by Luria and Tsvetkova (1964).

The second area of difficulty was seen on two maze problems. There was a slightly poorer performance by operated subjects than controls on the Porteus Maze Test. Such a loss has been reported frequently with frontal lesions and needs no further documentation. On a second type of maze, an electrical stylus maze (Walsh, 1960), the patient showed more of the qualitative types of error described by Milner (1965) in the section above though the difference between leucotomy and control subjects failed to reach significance. These errors reflected frequent failure to comply with the test instructions though patients showed very clearly on questioning that they understood the rules. Moreover the knowledge of their errors did not modify the patients' subsequent behaviour or, at least, did not do so as quickly as it did in control subjects. Similarly the patients often failed on problems of the Porteus Maze Tests by repeatedly entering the same incorrect alley while often remarking that their choice was going to be incorrect. In a minor way this seems to reflect the difficulty which frontal damaged patients have with inhibiting response tendencies once they have been aroused. The study of Konow and Pribram (1970) has made it clear that what the frontal patient lacks is neither error recognition nor error evaluation but error utilization, i.e. he finds it difficult to employ feedback from his own actions to modify his ongoing behaviour. This failure to learn from experience has become more meaningful in the light of recent neuropsychological dessection of the frontal syndrome.

The final example of cognitive impairment comes from the Colour-Form Sorting Test. In this test no control subject experienced difficulty. Again qualitative differences were noted in the experimental group. Only one of thirteen experimental subjects gave a spontaneous verbal account of the correct groupings. Four others were able to complete the two groupings and showed evidence when questioned that they had successfully classified the pieces and were able to shift from one group to the other. All the remaining subjects required further assistance.

Three of the experimental subjects were only able to shift to the second of the groupings after a considerable amount of verbal assistance and a demonstration of the second group by the tester. Two others were able to perform both groupings after explanation as well as demonstration on both colour and form groupings.

Three subjects were unable to complete either sorting irrespective of the amount of instruction and assistance given.

Only one of the subjects chose colour as the primary grouping.

The difficulties of scoring such material can be seen in Subject 1 who placed similar forms together and described them in terms of common objects. The request to sort them differently resulted in another grouping described as everyday objects. The subject was then presented with the proper colour groupings. Her response was: 'They don't fit just like that. They don't fit into a pattern according to size. You could have numbers, size, colours.' Despite this verbalization of an apparently high order of abstraction, she was unable to perform the colour groupings, and resorted to several form groupings the last of which was comprised of three groups of forms placed in a row. She explained that the pieces were ordered according to length. Her performance is a good example of what Teuber (1964) called the 'curious dissociation between knowing and doing'. The fact that the frontal patient may 'know' what to do does not necessarily mean that this knowledge will be translated into behaviour. Several other examples will demonstrate how difficult to quantify these changes in behaviour may be.

Subject nine first grouped forms together and gave a correct account. Asked to do it a second way, she persisted in separating the forms; but used them to represent concrete objects. Shown the colour groupings and asked to account for them, she replied: 'One of each shape in each group.'

E: 'What do they have in common?'

S: 'Shape in common. The number in the group.'

E: 'What would you call that group?' (pointing to green pieces)

S: 'The right-hand corner. There are two (groups) in the right-hand corner and two in the left.'

Such subjects cannot be said to have lost all ability to categorize or abstract yet they appear to have great difficulty with a distinction which normal individuals from eight years upwards perceive quite readily.

Subject five first sorted the pieces according to colour. When she could not perform the shift she was shown the form grouping; but because of her equivocal explanation she was shown the form groupings white sides up. She was then able to shift from one grouping to the other but in grouping forms turned up the white sides without hesitation. This could be taken as evidence of a tendency to perform in a concrete manner.

Subject six sorted four similar groups of three coloured pieces.

E: 'Why do they go together in this way?'

S: 'To form a pattern.'

E: 'What have the groups in common?'

S: 'All the same shaped piece. One of each.'

Finally she was coerced into describing the grouping according to colour. When asked to group them another way she immediately separated out three groups of forms.

E: 'What have you done?'

S: '(I) have formed a square in different patterns.'

E: 'What do the groups have in common?'

S: 'All consist of the same sort of pieces. Squares. Round. And what would you call that. .triangles.'

Subject four began by turning over the four squares to their white sides to represent a 'tile'. The four circles were placed together as 'rings' while the triangles were 'going to make an octagon; but I need another one.' The request to sort the pieces another way resulted in a more complex patterning. The demonstration of colour sorting seemingly made no sense to her, while the form sorting with the neutral (white) sides up evoked the following response:

E: 'Does that make sense?'

S: 'Only that you are sorting them out. .into one colour. .white.'

The relatively poor performance of patients on these tasks is in sharp contrast to the fact that these were clinically improved subjects coping with their occupations at their pre-operative level. However Goldstein (1944) pointed out that in everyday life much thinking runs in such familiar ways, i.e. learned patterns of responses, that frontal impairment may not be evident to the patient's physician or friends. Novel situations, on the other hand, particularly if they are complex, will make the loss apparent. The present findings confirm the axiom that patients with mild to moderate frontal lobe damage often appear essentially normal until one begins to test them. The results show that even orbitomedial operations are not completely free from intellectual changes. Fortunately the changes are not of sufficient degree to interfere with everyday life even in demanding occupations to which some of them have returned. If this operation does in fact spare the convexity connections (which is not certain) it argues for a conservative view of the partition of function within the frontal lobe which has been assumed in some publications.

All this, of course, is about an 'old' operation. It is to be hoped that similar or improved analyses of affective and cognitive change might be applied to the newer operations such as cingulate tractotomy especially as the personality effects may well be different and the behavioural changes brought about by the 'old' and 'new' modified operations might be differentially beneficial in different types of conditions.

5. The Temporal Lobes

Integrative functions of the temporal lobe

The organisation of the temporal lobe is very complex. It is related to the sense systems of olfaction and audition whose primary projection areas and areas of perceptual elaboration lie within its boundaries. It is also related to the visual system and serves to integrate visual perception with the information from the other sensory systems into the unified experience of the world around us. It plays an important role in memory in both its specific and general aspects. It contains systems which help to preserve the record of conscious experience. Finally, it has such an intimate connection with the structures of the limbic system which itself has far reaching connections, that its functional boundaries as well as its morphological boundaries are ill-defined. It is through this system that the temporal lobes help to provide part of the anatomical substrate for the integration of the emotional and motivational aspects of the organism with informational content coming from all those sensory systems situated behind the central fissure and, through its connections with the frontal lobes, with those systems for plans of action which are formulated in these regions. Because of this anatomical and functional complexity one must be cautious of over simplified conceptions based on an examination of lesions in specific parts of the temporal lobes. Williams says of temporal lobe syndromes. . . 'it is more true of this part of the nervous system than of any other that disturbances of the part must include consideration of the whole.' (1969, p.700). Therefore, the division of topics in what follows is an arbitrary one. It is particularly oriented to those disorders the examination of which will prove useful in the early diagnosis of lesions, as well as attempting to provide a basis for understanding the complex integrative functions which the temporal lobes serve. In the first section, the main areas deal with the effects of unilateral temporal lobe lesions on auditory perception, visual perception, intellectual changes and modality or material specific memory processes while the second séction deals with the complex disturbances of behaviour and experience caused by temporal lobe epilepsy and the non-specific disorders of memory which are such a prominent features of the mesial temporal lobe structures and their connections. For lack of space some areas such as the perception of time and the participation of the temporal lobes in the alerting mechanism will have to be omitted.

Anatomical features

The temporal lobe lies below the lateral cerebral fissure or fissure of Sylvius. The lateral surface is divided into three convolutions or gyri (superior, middle, and inferior gyri) by two sulci. The superior temporal sulcus runs approximately parallel to the lateral cerebral fissure beginning near the temporal pole in front and running back until, near its end, it turns upward for a short distance into the parietal lobe where it is surrounded by the angular gyrus. On the inner portion of the lateral sulcus the cortex of the superior temporal gyrus dips into the insula in several short horizontal convolutions known as the anterior transverse gyrus of Heschl. The middle temporal sulcus which is often in two disconnected parts, divides the middle from the inferior temporal gyrus, portion of which lies on the inferior or basal portion of the lobe. The artificial lines of demarcation of the boundaries of the lobe with the parietal and occipital lobes are shown in Figure 5.1. The posterior boundary is formed by an imaginary line joining the parieto-occipital sulcus to the preoccipital notch, and the superior boundary runs backwards from the upper end of the lateral sulcus to join the posterior boundary at right angles. Thus the temporal lobe merges into the visual cortex behind and the inferior parietal lobule above. The inferior parietal lobule is made up of the supramarginal and angular gyri. The supramarginal gyrus surrounds the ascending branch of the lateral sulcus.

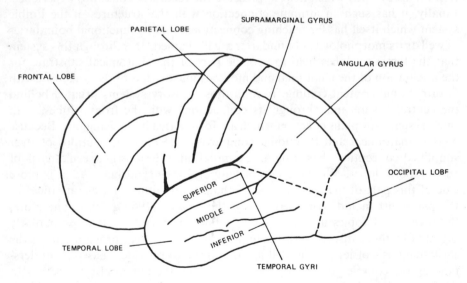

Fig. 5.1 Lateral aspect of the cerebral hemisphere

The inferior parietal lobule lies at the confluence of the parietal, temporal, and occipital lobes, i.e. with those posterior or retrorolandic portions of the cerebral cortex which are concerned with the various sensory systems of the body. As this area is rich in multisensory connections it is concerned with the integration of sensory information. Lesions in the lobule particularly in the dominant hemisphere, give rise to symptoms which are characteristically different from lesions in other areas. Whereas lesions in the primary projection areas and the association areas which surround them are modality specific, giving deficit in only one sensory system, lesions in the supramarginal and angular gyri disrupt 'the mnemonic constellations that form the basis for understanding the interpreting sensory signals. . . (which are based on) multisensory perceptions of a higher order' (Carpenter, 1972, p.17). Luria (1973b) has also given prominence to this area considering it as the crowning level of the hierarchically organized systems concerned with gnostic function.

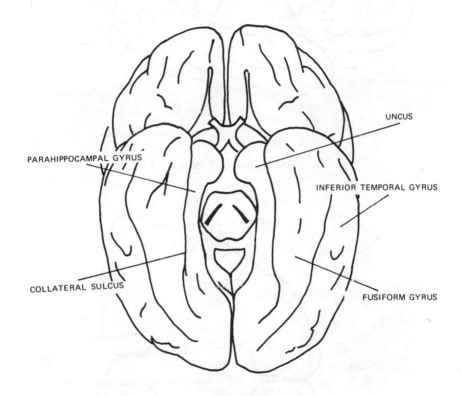

Fig. 5.2 Inferior or basal aspect of the brain

The inferior surface of the temporal lobe (Fig. 5.2) is also divided into three major gyri. Part of the inferior temporal gyrus occupies the lower lateral aspect of the lobe and is separated from the fusiform gyrus by the inferior temporal sulcus. The fusiform gyrus is separated from the hippocampal gyrus by the collateral fissure. The anterior portion of the hippocampal gyrus bends around the hippocampal fissure to form the uncus.

The mesial surface, largely the hippocampal gyrus, slopes downwards to the inferior surface (Fig. 5.3).

The cross sectional view (Fig. 5.4) relates the three surfaces to each other and should be of value in understanding descriptions of lesions in this area.

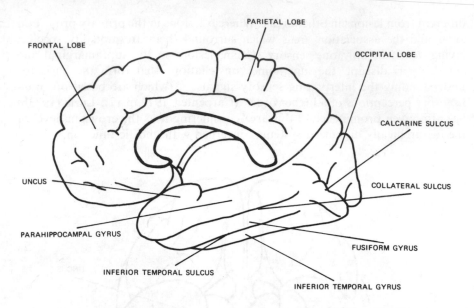

Fig. 5.3 Medial aspect of the hemisphere

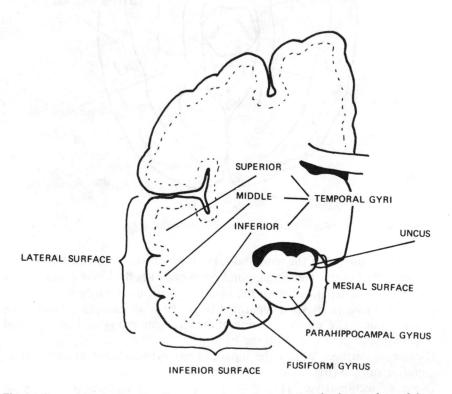

Fig. 5.4 Coronal (vertical) section through one hemisphere showing the three surfaces of the temporal lobe

Functional organization. The auditory system

The auditory cortex, like the cortex devoted to other sense modalities, may be divided into two zones : (1) the primary projection area for auditory sensation, and (2) the secondary or auditory association cortex.

Primary auditory projection

The primary projection area is largely buried in that infolded region of the cortex termed the insula which lies at the junction of the frontal and parietal lobes above and the temporal lobes below. This means that a portion of the superior surface of the temporal lobe is hidden from sight when the brain is viewed from its lateral aspect. This insular portion of the superior temporal cortex which serves auditory sensation is the transverse gyrus of Heschl (Fig. 5.5).

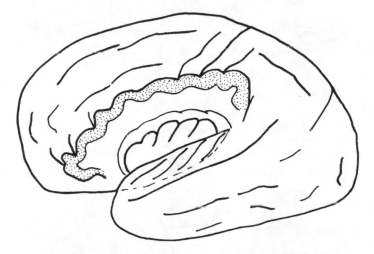

Fig. 5.5 Parts of overlying brain removed to show insular cortex

Auditory information is transmitted from the sense receptors in the cochlea of the inner ear via the auditory pathways. The pathways for auditory information in the brain stem are exceedingly complex and, even now, some of the details appear to be incomplete. The main features of the pathways (Fig. 5.6) are provided principally to demonstrate the fact that information from one ear may travel via a number of different routes to reach the auditory cortex of both hemispheres. After relaying at several points on the way auditory information reaches its final relay station in the medial geniculate body at the base of the thalamus from which it travels to the primary projection area in Heschl's gyrus.

Damage to the peripheral receptors or acoustic nerve results in deafness on the side of the damage; but damage in the principal auditory pathway in the brain stem – the lateral lemniscus (Fig. 5.6) causes a partial deafness since there are both crossed and uncrossed pathways in this tract.

There are certain similarities and also important differences in the transmis-

sion of photo- and phono- reception which are important in understanding
the effects of lesions in the two sense modalities of vision and audition. Both
systems relay their modality-specific information via specialized thalamic nuclei
and both auditory and visual cortex have a topological structure, i.e. the relationships of the stimuli as they impinge on the organism are preserved from
receptor to primary cortex. In the case of audition this is termed tonotopic
localization, Fig. 5.6. Fibres carrying impulses produced by high frequency
sounds are found in the medial portions of the cortex while the fibres carrying
information produced by low frequency sounds terminate in the lateral parts
of the auditory cortex.

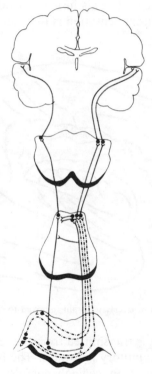

Fig. 5.6 The complex auditory pathways

In the visual system there is a partition of information from each eye, certain
fibres from each organ going to one hemisphere and other fibres to the other
hemisphere. (See Ch. 7 for further detail). In audition the fibres from the
receptor organ (the organ of Corti) in each ear are projected to *both* primary
zones of the auditory cortex. This representation is, however, not equal, each
ear being represented more strongly in the opposite hemisphere, i.e. the ears
are bilaterally but unequally represented in the cortex. Because of this bilateral
representation of each organ, complete cortical or cerebral deafness would
require lesions affecting both the transverse gyri of Heschl. Such a situation
is exceedingly rare. Unilateral lesions of the primary auditory zones of the

cortex do not have a marked effect on auditory acuity but careful testing reveals an elevation of auditory thresholds in the ear contralateral to the lesion.

Auditory association areas

The secondary or association areas of the auditory cortex give clear cut evidence of lateral specialization, the cortex of the hemisphere which is dominant for speech being particularly concerned with the analysis of speech sounds, while the auditory perception of non-verbal material including music appears to be mediated more by the non-dominant hemisphere. This partition or specialization of function is in accordance with what Luria (1973b) calls the law of progressive lateralization and forms an important aspect of the asymmetry of function dealt with in Chapter 8.

Auditory perceptual defects

Lesions in the auditory association cortex of the left side produce sensory or receptive aphasia. The difficulty arises only when the patient has to distinguish speech sounds and the older term auditory or acoustic agnosia is in some ways to be preferred since it points to the primary difficulty from which a number of other symptoms flow. However, usage is too well established to allow the change, and the term acoustic agnosia is best preserved for the inability to distinguish non-verbal sounds, which is associated with right hemisphere lesions. The disorder of phonemic hearing is produced largely by lesions affecting the superior temporal gyrus in the region adjacent to the primary auditory cortex of the left hemisphere. A phoneme is the smallest distinctive group of sounds in a language, and one of the principal tasks in learning a language is to distinguish readily between phonemes. The nature of phonemic distinction becomes apparent when we endeavour to learn a new language since the distinctive speech sounds are not the same in all languages and the difficulties which a person may have with learning a new language will depend on the phonemic distinctions which he brings to the task. The ease with which we are able to distinguish p and b in words such as peach and beach will be difficult for people whose primary language has but a single phoneme for these sounds.

It follows that a person who has an acquired difficulty in discriminating between similar phonemes will have difficulty in understanding spoken speech. Luria expresses this concisely – 'As words in his own language fail to be differentiated his attitude towards words in his native tongue will begin to resemble that to words in a foreign language' (Luria, 1973b). Since the patient's basic difficulty lies in auditory discrimination he is deprived of the regulation of his own speech via the monitoring of his own vocal productions. He is therefore unaware of his own defective speech and hence sees no necessity for correcting it. Moreover, if he has difficulty in producing the correct word to name an object, prompting him is of no avail since he is unable to fit the information into a phonemic system. Structured language disappears and is replaced by very fragmented utterances that have been called a 'word salad'.

The failure to distinguish the vital differences in acoustic content of words means that the patient will be unable to write material that is dictated to him whereas he may be readily able to copy verbal material when it is visually presented. An important exception to the inability to write words from dictation is in the ability to write words which have become so familiar that they no longer require precise analysis of their acoustic content. Prime examples of this conversion of words into motor stereotypes are the patient's signature and the most frequently used words in his trade or profession. Luria and his colleagues have pointed out that this is an example of how the cerebral organization of a process may change over time (Luria, Simernitskaya, and Tubylevich, 1970). In the process of learning to write words, careful acoustic analysis is needed at first but the motor aspects of writing become more and more automatic with use and less dependent upon auditory discrimination so that the writing of a familiar word comes to have a different neuronal or cerebral organization from a relatively new word. This means that lesions in different sites will have different effects and, once again, a careful qualitative analysis of the precise form of difficulty which the patient has (in this case with some words and not with others) will point more precisely to the location of the lesion.

As one moves away from the area surrounding the primary projection area for audition there is a decrease in phonological disturbances and, in the region of the middle temporal gyrus, the most prominent defect is one of audioverbal memory, an auditory amnestic aphasia. The characteristic feature of these memory disorders is the inability to repeat a series of words which has been presented acoustically despite the fact that the patient may be able to retain and repeat single words. With a series of words the patient may show a primacy effect (the reproduction of the first word given) or a recency effect (the reproduction of the last word given), other members of the series being lost. Luria, Sokolov, and Klimkovsky (1967) have analysed these distrubances of audioverbal memory and suggest that the fault lies in the increased mutual inhibition of the auditory traces. This hypothesis is supported by their finding that increasing the time interval between the presentation of members of the series greatly reduces or eliminates the difficulty. The extension of the time between words is thought to reduce the mutually inhibitory effects which adjacent members of the series have on each other. This type of finding is also relevant to an examination of the amnesic syndrome which follows bilateral mesial temporal lesions discussed below.

Left sided posterior temporal lesions sometimes lead to a difficulty in using words to name objects, the so-called nominal aphasia. The patient perceives the objects and their significance and can, usually in a round-about fashion known as circumlocution, describe their use or function. It is the association between the visual apprehension of a particular object and a particular word which is lost.

A second effect of lesions which disrupt the coordinated action of vision and audition in this borderland region between the temporal and occipital lobes is an inability to draw objects on verbal request ('Please draw a clock.') while retaining the ability to draw the same object when a copy is presented. It might be assumed that because of disconnection of portions of the auditory and visual regions from each other, that words no longer evoke images which would form the basis for executing a drawing of the object named.

So far we have dealt with difficulties which arise with the understanding of speech sounds. Man must also be able to discriminate and attach meaning to other environmental sounds. The finding of impairment in the recognition of these non-verbal sounds has been described in the literature for many decades under the term acoustic agnosia.

Unfortunately, this term has been used somewhat indiscriminately at times to refer to difficulty with the recognition of any kind of auditory material including speech. In his review of the earlier clinical literature Vignolo (1969) employs the term in its original sense of 'defective recognition of non-verbal sounds and noises'. He and his colleagues have addressed themselves to two major aspects of the problem of auditory agnosia, namely the relationship of auditory agnosia to aphasia, and the relationship of auditory agnosia to hemispheric location of the lesion. The two experiments described by Vignolo (1969) are summarized here in some detail. These experiments demonstrate the value of the clinico-experimental method in neuropsychology for testing hypotheses suggested by clinical findings. They have led to the concept of the double dissociation of auditory functions between the two temporal lobes. The practical diagnostic value of these findings is discussed at the end of this section.

In the first experiment a test of auditory recognition was given to normal subjects and to patients with unilateral temporal lesions both right- and left-sided. Left-sided patients were defined as aphasic if their scores fell below a certain point on one of a number of tests of aphasia. These aphasic patients were then further categorized into types and degrees of aphasia.

The auditory test required the subject to select from four pictures on a card the source of a common environmental sound played to him. The sounds were unambiguous, e.g., baby crying, ambulance siren, yapping dog. Four separate pictures were presented with each sound, each having the following categories of sound source: (1) the correct source (e.g. canary whistling), (2) acoustically similar source (man whistling), (3) similar class or semantic category (cock crowing), (4) unrelated sound source (train). Thus the subjects could have three types of misrecognition: acoustic errors, semantic errors and unrelated errors. The findings supported a distinction made by Vignolo between two different types of auditory agnosia. An inability to discriminate accurately the sound pattern produced a *perceptual-discriminative sound agnosia*, while an inability to associate the auditory stimulation with its meaning resulted in an *associative-sound agnosia*. As might have been anticipated, sound recognition defects were more frequently associated with marked receptive aphasia than they were with other types of aphasia. Thus auditory verbal comprehension and the recognition of non-verbal sound sources were closely related.

An examination of the type of error made by the aphasic and non-aphasic groups showed a highly significant difference with regard to the 'semantic' errors but not to the other types, i.e. 'auditory' or 'unrelated'. This strongly suggests that the difficulties in recognition by the aphasic patients were due, not to any inability to discriminate, but to an inability to associate the sound which had been perceived with its usual meaning. On the other hand, two patients with right hemisphere lesions who performed poorly on this test did so because of an increase in acoustic errors, i.e. their difficulty appeared to be discriminative rather than semantic-associative.

The second experiment strengthened and clarified this distinction. Two tests were employed. One, the Meaningful Sounds Identification Test was similar to the test employed in the first experiment, requiring the subject to select the correct pictorial representation of a well-known environmental sound. The second task, the Meaningless Sounds Discrimination Test, required the subject to discriminate between pairs of complex sounds which had been 'mixed' artificially in a sound studio. Again, groups of left- and right-brain-damaged patients, and normal subjects were used.

Each of the brain-damaged groups performed poorly on one of the tests the deficit varying according to the hemispheric locus of the lesion. Left sided damage was related to poor performance on the test of semantic association (Meaningful Sounds) while this group's performance on the discrimination test (Meaningless Sounds) was normal. The right hemisphere group reversed the pattern of deficit having a normal performance on the semantic-associative task and a very poor performance on the perceptual-discriminative test. In keeping with the findings from the first experiment, all patients with an exclusively semantic-associative defect were aphasic.

This double dissociation of function of the two temporal lobes with respect to auditory perception further supports the lateral specialization of function shown by the studies of material-specific memory defects, dichotic listening studies, and cortical stimulation of the temporal regions described elsewhere in this chapter, and the finding of asymmetry of auditory recognition is in keeping with the broader notion of cerebral hemisphere asymmetry of function reviewed in Chapter 8.

These findings also have a practical application in diagnosis since they appear to make an unequivocal distinction between unilateral lesions of the temporal lobes. In our own clinic a further meaningless sounds test has been developed by re-recording English words played backwards.

Dichotic listening studies

In 1954 Broadbent described the dichotic listening technique. This consisted of the simultaneous presentation of auditory material to the two ears by means of a stereophonic tape-recorder. The material consisted of pairs of digits and when three pairs of these were given in fairly quick succession, the subjects could normally repeat all six digits, usually reporting the three digits which had been presented to one ear followed by the three presented to the other. In right handed subjects (assumed to be left hemisphere language-dominant) the digits from the right ear were normally reported first. This may be assumed to be in keeping with the verbal nature of the material and the stronger contra-lateral representation of the auditory input mentioned at the beginning of the chapter. This finding is sometimes referred to as ear asymmetry or interaural rivalry. It might be better to avoid such terms since they focus attention on the periphery rather than on the asymmetry of processing by the two hemispheres.

Attention was directed to this area by the early work of Kimura. In her studies with Milner at Montreal (Milner, 1962) it had been found that certain aspects of the Seashore Measures of Musical Talents differentiated between patients who had undergone right or left anterior temporal lobectomy. In particular, right temporal lobectomy produced a marked deficit of tonal memory while left sided operations had no effect on this subtest. There was also a tendency for right sided cases to produce a general increase in error scores. These deficits appeared to be of a higher order or agnostic type since hearing as measured by audiometric testing was apparently unaltered. Following these findings, Kimura (1961a) employed Broadbent's dichotic technique in the assessment of temporal lobe damage. Patients with temporal lobe epilepsy were examined before and after lobectomy. Patients with temporal lobe seizures performed poorly before operation, but following operation the left-temporal group became much worse, while the level of performance of the right temporal group remained the same. These right sided patients, however, now reported more of the right ear digits than they had before operation. In more general terms, unilateral temporal lobectomy impaired the recognition of material by the contralateral ear. The fact that the left temporal lobectomy group performed very poorly is related to the verbal nature of the material used, i.e. the deficit is a function of the type of material presented. This point of view was strongly supported when Kimura (1964) developed her dichotic test using short melodic patterns instead of verbal material.

Kimura (1961a) assumed that the superiority of the right ear in dichotic listening (verbal) experiments was due to a direct relation between cerebral dominance and the verbal nature of the perception. However subsequent studies have shown that much of the effect can be accounted for by what has come to be termed the 'ear order effect' (Inglis and Sykes, 1967; Satz, et al., 1965; Schuloff and Goodglass, 1969). This effect represents a greater decay related to material reported from the ear which is reported second. The first ear report is closer in time to immediate apprehension of the stimuli while the second report is subject to decay in short-term memory (STM). In keeping with the Boston group's findings of more rapid STM decay in amnesic patients reported below Goodglass and Peck (1972) found that this ear order effect was greater in amnesic alcoholics than in either non-amnesic alcoholics or controls.

Clinical studies of amusia reported in the literature had often given equivocal findings with regard to the question of localization and, as Kimura pointed out, had often confounded any loss of musical recognition with verbal aspects of the test situation such as comprehension of verbal instructions, naming difficulties, and the like. The Kimura test consists of the simultaneous presentation to each ear of melodic patterns of four seconds duration. Each pair of melodies was followed by four single melodies and the subjects was asked to identify the position of the two dichotically presented patterns in the series, e.g. 'first and third', 'second and third', 'first and fourth'. Normal subjects were used and the usual dichotic digits test was given. Results showed a superiority for digits for the right ear.

The finding of better performance on the digits test in the form of more accurate reporting from the right than the left ear for patients with variously located lesions as well as normal subjects (Kimura, 1961a) highlights the importance of the left hemisphere for verbal material while the post operative findings are in keeping with earlier reports of difficulties which left temporal lobectomy subjects had with auditory verbal material (Meyer and Yates, 1955; Milner, 1958). Kimura's results strengthen the association between the right temporal lobe and a certain class of non-verbal sound pattern, namely music. Kimura (1967) pointed out that this auditory asymmetry for words and music has provided a new technique for the study of cerebral dominance. This dissociation is given added significance by Vignolo's analysis of auditory agnosia described above. These findings have been supplemented more recently by Goodglass and his colleagues (Schuloff and Goodglass, 1969; Sparks, Goodglass and Nickel, 1970). They found a bilateral decrement in auditory recognition with damage to either lobe which varied with the nature of the material presented – left hemisphere lesion cases showed a severe bilateral deficit with words as stimuli while right hemisphere cases showed a marked bilateral deficit with tonal sequences. In each case there was also a falling off in efficiency of the ear contralateral to the lesion for the other class of material, i.e. with left hemisphere lesions there was a right ear loss for tonal sequences while right hemisphere lesions there was a left ear loss of efficiency for digits. Sparks, Goodglass and Nickel (1970) consider the contralateral ear effects to be in the nature of extinction or suppression of simultaneously presented information corresponding to the damaged hemisphere, a finding that is reported elsewhere for both vision and touch. Similar findings have also been described with chronically brain damaged children (Goodglass, 1967).

Zurif and Ramier's findings (1972) come close to the same distinction made by Vignolo. Using dichotic digits and dichotic sequences of phonemes they found differences between left and right sided lesions suggesting that the left hemisphere is more concerned with the processing of phonological information while the right hemisphere is more concerned with the acoustic parameters of speech.

The question of whether primary sensory deficits contribute to the agnosic or so-called higher order defects is one which is frequently raised. In some instances there are those who doubt the existence of certain 'pure' syndromes such as visual object agnosia (Ch. 7) in the absence of a primary sensory deficit. As mentioned earlier, primary sensory deficits of cortical origin in audition are difficult to detect because of the bilateral representation of each ear in the cortex. Oxbury and Oxbury (1969) have compared the dichotic findings with digits in groups of cases in each hemisphere where the cortex of Heschl's gyrus was either completely removed or completely spared. Before operation the order of reporting the digits favoured the right ear, i.e. although digits arrived simultaneously the subjects most frequently reported those from the right ear before they reported those from the left. Left temporal lobectomy including Heschl's gyrus increased right ear errors but did not alter the order of report. Left temporal lobectomy sparing Heschel's gyrus reversed the order of report, i.e. left digits were reported before right; but there was no increase in errors.

Right temporal lobectomy including Heschl's gyrus did not increase errors and exaggerated the primacy of reporting right ear digits. Right temporal lobectomy sparing Heschl's gyrus led to no alteration on either measure. These data show clearly the importance of loss of the primary auditory cortex in producing the deficits.

Recently Berlin, *et al.* (1972) have studied the effects of staggering the time of arrival of stimuli at each ear. Using nonsense syllables they compared the performance of four patients with temporal lobectomies with one hundred normal subjects when the syllables arrived simultaneously and with various time delays from 15 to 500 milliseconds. Normal subjects tended to show better scores for the trailing stimulus when the time separation was 30 to 90 milliseconds. The small number of lobectomy subjects showed no such lag effect and demonstrated a further lowering of contralateral ear scores and enhanced ipsilateral ear function compared to their preoperative state irrespective of which lobe had been removed.

Finally, dichotic performance has been studied in a few instances where the interhemispheric fibres were interrupted either from agenesis of the corpus callosum or operative division of the fibres for the relief of epilepsy. Two studies (Milner, Taylor, and Sperry, 1968; Sparks and Geschwind, 1968) described failure to report digits presented to the left ear when dichotic stimulation was used in commissurotomy patients. Sparks and Geschwind's patient showed complete extinction of digits received by the left ear. The fact that the failure to report from the left ear in this patient was so much greater than any right hemisphere cases suggested the importance of the commissural pathways in dichotic stimulation. Two studies of agenesis of the corpus callosum (Saul and Sperry, 1968; Bryden and Zurif, 1970) report no auditory asymmetry nor is there any evidence of marked unilateral auditory effects with hemispherectomy (Curry, 1968; Bryden and Zurif, 1970).

The studies cited above are a sample only of the extensive studies which have been carried out on auditory asymmetry. A bibliography of dichotic listening studies has been provided by Richardson and Knights (1970).

Visual perception

The temporal lobes are neither concerned with the primary reception of visual information nor with its elaboration into meaningful wholes. They are concerned however, with the integration of visual experience with all forms of sensory information coming from the receptors of the other special senses and from the receptors of the bodily senses. Disturbances of all forms of perception of the individual's internal and external words are seen in all their complexity in temporal lobe epilepsy examples of which are described below.

The temporal lobes contain portion of the optic radiations which curve forward into the lobe after leaving the lateral geniculate bodies before looping back to their termination in the occipital lobes. Temporal lobe lesions thus produce visual field defects which characteristically affect the upper homonymous quadrants (see Ch. 7) but may sometimes produce a complete hemianopia

(Falconer and Wilson, 1958). Even in cases where no field loss was apparent to normal examination, changes were detected after temporal lobectomy in the form of raised flicker fusion thresholds for both left and right sided cases. Difference between the impact of the lesions according to the side have been demonstrated in a number of studies. Thus, Dorff, Mirsky, and Mishkin (1965) found that using the method of presenting two stimuli simultaneously one to each of the visual fields, the left temporal group was impaired in the right (contralateral) visual field, while the right temporal lobe group was impaired in both left and right fields.

Other studies have suggested that lesions of the right temporal lobe might produce disruptions of visual perception that are not shown by comparable lesions on the left side. Milner (1958) found that patients with right temporal lobe lesions had difficulty in recognizing objects from an incomplete pictorial representation of them, a difficulty which was not shown by patients with left sided lesions. Milner also described an impairment in right sided cases in the ability to recognize anomalies in pictures, e.g. a picture in which a painting is shown hanging on the wall inside a monkey house. However, using the same test—the McGill Picture Anomalies Test—Shalman (1961) failed to confirm this finding in a small highly selected sample. McFie (1960) described defects in the Picture Arrangement Subtest of the Wechsler Scale, again, restricted to right hemisphere cases. Kimura (1963), using tachistoscopic presentation, found that lesions on the right side impaired subjects' recognition when the material was unfamiliar while left temporal subjects were more impaired when familiar material was being presented.

Warrington and James (1967b) failed to confirm Kimura's general finding of impaired number estimation on tachistoscopically presented material with right temporal damage but did find significantly raised recognition thresholds in the contralateral left visual fields. Rubino (1970) found that right temporal lobe removal rendered the patient less able to identify meaningless visual patterns than did left sided removals.

Further support to the association of special defects with right temporal lesions was given by Lansdell (1962) who found right temporal lobectomy patients to be poorer on a design preference test than left lobectomy patients. In a later study, (Lansdell, 1968) he reported that right sided operations led to poorer performance also on a visuospatial abstract reasoning task that was relatively unaffected by left sided operations. The more extensive the removals were on the right side the greater were these deficits.

Though both temporal lobes are intimately concerned with perceptual processing it appears that the lateral specialization shown in auditory perception extends also to the visual modality in this area. From the sample of evidence cited the relationship between the side of the lesion and the nature of the perceptual deficit, however, is still far from clear.

Effects of anterior temporal lobectomy

The major contribution to our understanding of temporal lobe function has come from the numerous clinical and experimental studies which have been carried out in the past two decades in cases of temporal lobe epilepsy before and after removal of one temporal lobe. The effect of bilateral lesions is discussed in a later section of this chapter.

Intellectual changes

There have been frequent assertions that the differential effects of unilateral temporal lobectomy according to the side of the lesion are examples of what Blakemore (1969) calls 'the broad generalization that lesions occurring in the hemisphere of the brain which is dominant for speech produce deficits in performance on tasks which are essentially verbal in nature, while lesions in the non-dominant hemisphere produce performance impairments on essentially non-verbal (visual-spatial and perceptual-motor) tasks'. The question of the hypothesized hemispheric differences both with regard to the temporal lobes and other areas is the special theme of Chapter 8. It will be sufficient here to outline a sample of findings from the temporal lobectomy studies.

Left unilateral temporal lobectomy is often followed by dysphasia which is, however, transient in nature. Though language disturbance may cease to be clinically apparent, there are numerous studies which show that there are verbal deficits which are apparent for some time after operation when appropriate tests are employed. The early studies of Meyer and Yates (1955) and Meyer and Jones (1957) suggest that the decline in verbal intelligence test scores which has been found by studies such as Milner (1954, 1958) and Meyer (1959) after left temporal lobectomy are an aggravation of a deficit which patients with a left-sided lesion had before operation. The three latter studies reported no significant change in the verbal scales of the Wechsler Scale after operation on the right temporal lobe. Milner's data suggested that there was also no decline on the Wechsler Performance Subtests with right sided operations. However, Miller (1972) reinterpreted Milner's data in the light of the large practice effect from Form I to Form II of the Wechsler-Bellevue Scale which has been demonstrated by Gerboth (1950) and came to the conclusion that the data did in fact demonstrate a decline in Performance Scale score after right temporal operations. Blakemore and Falconer (1967) also described a lowering of the Performance Intelligence Quotient after right anterior temporal lobectomy. In one of the earliest studies of right temporal lobectomy Hebb (1939b) had noted a lowering of non-language abilities particularly those associated with visual form perception.

The general relation of verbal deficits with left, and performance deficits with right-sided lesions is supported by the studies of Lansdell (1962), Dennerll (1964) and Blakemore, Ettlinger, and Falconer (1966). On the other hand the verbal versus non-verbal character of deficits related to the laterality of the lesion was not confirmed by Parsons and Kemp (1960) though verbal-performance score differences have been suggested by more than one author as a method of predicting the laterality of the lesion (Balthazar and Morrison, 1961; Schmidt, 1961).

A rather different set of findings was reported by Halstead (1958) on 21 psychomotor epileptics subjected to small anterior temporal lobe resections. Firstly the results of operation of the left versus the right side did not support the contention that important differences exist between the dominant and non-dominant temporal lobes. Secondly, of major interest was the fact that a significant difference between epileptic patients and control subjects which existed on several intellectual measures before operation actually improved though impairment in relation to normal performance was still seen on some tasks. Such results may be due to the smaller nature of the operations compared with the larger temporal excisions in Milner's series and possible differences in the patient populations selected for operation. In discussion of Halstead's (1958) paper Cobb remarked concerning the post operative improvement on test measures—'it seems extraordinary, and, if it is true, it must be that the operation removes some noxious influence (if I may speak in very vague terms) that was actually impairing function.' A similar example of 'improvement of function' after removal of cerebral tissue is seen in the discussion of hemispherectomy in Chapter 8.

Several follow-up studies after anterior temporal lobectomy have shown recovery of both the verbal losses which follow left-sided operations (Meyer, 1959; Milner, 1958) and the non-verbal losses which follow right-sided ones within a year of surgery (Blakemore and Falconer, 1967). The latter study covers a period of ten years and it is difficult to reconcile this with the finding of Meier and French (1966) that, while performance scale scores one year after right-sided operations showed no decline over the pre-operative level, the scores at three years did show such a decline. Miller (1972) suggests that the different results again may be related to different operative techniques and subject populations. Certainly, there is a similar conflict of evidence over the recovery or lack of recovery of the material specific memory deficits with unilateral temporal lesions discussed in the next section.

Temporal lobe epilepsy

Complex partial seizures arising in the temporal region were outlined in Chapter 3. The term temporal lobe epilepsy was introduced by Lennox (1951). Part of the complexity of the syndrome no doubt lies in the spread of excitation from the numerous possible sites of origin of the electrical abnormalities though some regions such as the mesial temporal areas are more often involved than others. Williams points out that the way in which the term temporal lobe epilepsy is used 'reflects the difficulty we have in considering disturbance of complex functions in relation to equally complex structures which have a very extensive network of communications throughout the hemispheres. The phrase simply implies that the more evident origins of the disturbances are situated below the sylvian fissure. . .' (1969, p.700).

The complex symptomatology of temporal lobe epilepsy has been described in detail in its many guises by Lennox and Lennox (1960) and numerous other authors. The following two cases taken from the previously cited work of Williams are particularly illustrative of the multiform nature of the disorder.

A woman surgeon developed temporal lobe epilepsy as the result of head injuries caused by being knocked down by a car. The attacks were all heralded by appearance of a human face and shoulders clothed in a red jersey. The figure was intensely and distressingly identified with the patient. The hallucination would then topple sideways and disintegrate into discrete fragments like a jigsaw puzzle, the patient meanwhile experiencing extreme fear with an unnatural quality to it, followed by amnesia in which a general convulsion occurred. The patient had total amnesia for the accident, but it is incidentally interesting that long after the traumatic epilepsy became established she learnt that she had been wearing a red jumper when the car struck her. Here then is a visual hallucination identified with the self, compounded with an emotion, and having in it fragments of memory in time.

In another case a woman of thirty had had epilepsy for fifteen years. The attacks only happened when she was applying her eye shadow; then, her face close to the mirror attending fixedly to the eyes, the reflected image would change, becoming more intense and dominating her. She would then seem to see a scene with her grandparents and parents, which seemed to be vividly remembered from a former experience. The scene was visualized but was not seen as an hallucination—'it was in my mind's eye'. This visual memory was accompanied by unremembered words, the whole event being pleasurable and associated with a general sense of sexual excitement. This then is the experience of visual and auditory hallucination inter-mixed, related to past experience, and having visceral-sensory and emotional components, induced by a highly specific visual precipitant which must be closely identified with the self and also with sexuality.   (Williams, 1969,p.709)

Hallucinations and illusions of the temporal lobe

Disordered perception in the form of either illusions or hallucinations has been recognized as part of epileptic symptomatology for a very long time. If the perception refers to a person or object present in the environment we speak of an illusion or false perception. With temporal lobe attacks part or all of the object may be distorted, e.g., everything may appear visually larger or smaller (macropsia, micropsia) or the relative size of parts may appear distorted (metamorphopsia), or sounds louder or softer than usual. These distortions are often accompanied by a feeling that the person is somehow detached from his own body (depersonalization) or that things are unreal (derealization). Though these disorders are common in the visual modality they are by no means restricted to this sense. Hughlings Jackson's case with olfactory hallucinations was described in Chapter 3. These olfactory auras appear to be associated with the anterior and inferior portions of the lobe including the uncus. The odours are always described as being disagreeable or offensive, never pleasant, (Penfield and Jasper, 1954).

Hallucinations refer to perceptual experiences which do not correspond in any way to stimuli in the current environment. The patient is often aware of the 'unreal' nature of the hallucinated objects. The hallucination may be accompanied by emotional experiences which are usually unpleasant, though pleasurable feelings and even short periods of ecstasy have been described infrequently (Lennox and Lennox, 1960). Williams (1956) has examined these emotional experiences in epileptic subjects and related them to specific locations in the temporal lobe.

With temporal lobe disturbances there is a fresh interpretation of current experience. Simpson (1969) suggests that, for learning to take place, or to decide whether an object or situation is 'familiar', one must compare the present sensory input with the neural record of past experience. He interprets the data of temporal lobe epilepsy as demonstrating the presence in the temporal lobe of what he terms 'coincidence detection circuits'. If the comparison of the input with the record of the past produces a coincidence or familiarity response, the present stimulation will appear familiar even if nothing similar had occurred in the subject's prior experience. This is the well known phenomenon of *déjà vu* (seen before) which is experienced at times by normal subjects but more frequently and with greater vividness by some patients with temporal lobe epilepsy. On the other hand, a matching which produced a 'no coincidence' response leads to the experience of *jamais vu* or *jamais entendu* (never seen, never heard) even though the stimulus pattern or one very similar has been frequently encountered in the past. Penfield (1954) referred to these alterations in the perception of the present as 'interpretive illusions'.

On some occasions the hallucinations can be shown to be quite clearly related to prior experience and the evidence from cortical stimulation outlined below supports Penfield's contention that they are 'a reactivation of a strip of the record of the stream of consciousness'.

In 1938 Penfield produced for the first time an evocation of experience by stimulating the temporal cortex in a conscious human subject. These experiences were of two kinds. Firstly the evocation of an experience which the subject had undergone on a number of previous occasions during his epileptic seizures and, secondly, the production of previous happenings which had not been seen during the attacks but were also clearly related to specific prior experiences.

Penfield used the term *experiential hallucination* when the phenomenon occurred spontaneously, and *experiential response* when it was elicited by stimulation.

Several features stand out clearly in the very large number of cases where stimulation of the brain was employed (Penfield and Perot, 1963)—(1) despite the stimulation of practically every accessible spot on the cerebral cortex, experiential responses were evoked only from the temporal lobe (a total of 612 patients in Penfield's series were stimulated in non-temporal areas and produced not a single experiential response); (2) in almost all cases of evoked experiences, the patients were suffering from temporal lobe epilepsy; (3) only about eight per cent of temporal lobe cases stimulated gave rise to experiential responses; (4) responses were evoked from both sides of the brain but there was a marked asymmetry. Figure 5.7 shows the points in the two cerebral hemispheres where electrical stimulation produced an experiential response. The greatest concentration of the responses was in the superior temporal convolution of both hemispheres, with the frequency on the right side greater than that on the left. On the right side, too, the points giving rise to experiential responses extended more posteriorly along the superior temporal convolution and the posterior portion of the whole right lobe is productive while the corresponding regions on the left are almost silent to stimulation.

Auditory responses evoked by stimulation are shown in Figure 5.8. They are concentrated on the superior regions of the lobes with greater frequency on the right. Within this distribution no further finer topographical distribution was discovered, nor did there appear to be any separate effects related to laterality. The responses were most often a voice or voices though sometimes meaningful environmental sounds or music were elicited. The following case is condensed from Penfield and Perot (1963, p.639). The patient's verbatim responses are reported in full.

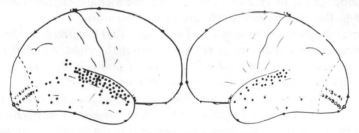

Fig. 5.7 Points on the lateral aspects of the hemispheres where stimulation evoked experiential responses (from Penfied and Perot, *Brain*, **85**, 595-697, 1963).

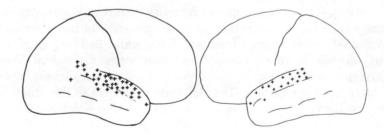

Fig. 5.8 Auditory experiential responses (redrawn from Penfield and Perot, 1963)

A 25 year old man with six year history of epileptic seizures which were at first characterised by vertigo and auditory experiential hallucinations and later changed their character to generalized seizures. Stimulation of a number of points on the cortex of the first or superior temporal convolution produced the following responses: STIMULATION 'Just like someone whispering, or something, in my left ear. It sounded something like a crowd.' REPEAT STIMULATION 'Again someone trying to speak to me, a single person. . . a man's voice. I could not understand what he said.' ANOTHER POINT STIMULATED 'Something brings back a memory, I could see Seven-Up

Bottling Company—Harrison Bakery.' ANOTHER POINT 'I am trying to find the name of a song. There was a piano and someone was playing. I could hear the song, you know. It is a song I have sung before but I cannot find out quite what the title of the song is. That is what I was trying to do when you finished stimulating!' REPEAT STIMULATION 'Someone was speaking to another and he mentioned a name but I could not understand it.' REPEAT STIMULATION "Yes, 'Oh Marie O Marie'—someone is singing it." REPEAT 'Someone telling me in *my left (contralateral ear)* (authors italics) Sylvere, Sylvere (the patient's name). It could have been the voice of my brother.' ANOTHER POINT 'It is a woman calling but I cannot make out the name.'

Combined auditory and visual responses were evoked on only very few occasions. Though also few in number experiences of music were more frequently reported from the right side and this is in keeping with clinical reports of amusia and the experimental findings on the greater importance of the right temporal lobe for the perception of music and the melodic elements of speech mentioned in this chapter and elsewhere in the literature.

Temporal lobe stimulation sometimes evoked visual experiences. There was an even greater preponderance of responses from the right side and the experiences were evoked over a much wider range of points in the right temporal lobe than was the case with auditory responses.

Though deep stimulation of the lobe has been employed on a small number of occasions no experiential responses have been evoked. The phenomenon seems to be restricted to cortical areas and then only in the vicinity of abnormally functioning tissue such as the neighbourhood of a temporal lobe focus.

Amnesia with cerebral stimulation

Two studies have reported transient memory disturbance with stimulation of the temporal lobe. Jasper (1958) produced amnesia during stimulation of the amygdaloid region in each temporal lobe, while Bickford *et al.* (1958) produced amnesia for recent events from stimulation of the deep posterior temporal region on either side. In this latter case the degree of amnesia depended on the duration of stimulation. The electrode placement in this study lay at the lateral border of the hippocampus, the importance of which is discussed in relation to the syndrome of axial amnesia which follows.

Memory and the temporal lobes

Probably no other area in neuropsychology has received such attention in the past two decades as the relation between memory and the temporal lobes. The impetus for such interest was provided principally by the accepted use of anterior temporal lobectomy in the treatment of temporal lobe epilepsy. The operation has been employed in cases where an abnormal focus is clearly localized to the temporal lobe and lateralized to one side. The resection typically includes the anterior six centimetres or so of the temporal lobe and the underlying structures, the uncus, amygdaloid nucleus, hippocampus, and parahippocampal gyrus.

The defects of memory associated with such surgical lesions may be considered according to the side of operation.

There is general agreement that removal of the left lobe interferes mainly with verbal memory and that the post operative changes are an exaggeration of verbal memory difficulties which may be demonstrated in temporal lobe epileptics before operation. Our own experience and that of others suggests that the temporal lobe abnormality needs to be present for a number of years before any deficit on memory tests is demonstrable. Milner has summarized her point of view (which is shared by many others) in the following way. 'It is now well established that a left temporal lobe lesion in the dominant hemisphere for speech impairs the learning and recognition of verbal material whether aurally or visually presented, and regardless of whether retention is measured by recognition, free recall, or rate of associative learning.' She cites her own work (Milner, 1958; Milner, 1962; Milner and Kimura, 1964) and Meyer and Yates (1955) in support of this view. Further support came from Weingartner (1968) who tested serial verbal learning after both right-sided and left-sided operations and found a learning deficit with left-sided lesions despite the visual presentation of the material. In short one major position with regard to the memory deficits after left temporal lobe lesions is that they are material-specific (verbal) but not modality-specific (auditory or visual).

Evidence for the opposite point of view was presented by Meyer (1959). Following an earlier study with Yates (1955) which demonstrated a severe impairment with aurally presented material for left-sided lesions and not right, Meyer specifically tested this proposition. He employed both visual and auditory (and tactile) modalities in an examination of learning with both verbal and non-verbal materials. Right-sided removals produced no post operative deficit, while left-sided removals produced a marked impairment of verbal paired-associate learning only with auditory presentation and not with visual. Several other studies (Luria, Sokolov, and Klimkovsky, 1967; Luria and Karasseva, 1968; and Warrington and Shallice, 1969) support the view that, while patients with left temporal or left temporo-parietal lesions may have difficulty with verbal memory for all forms of auditory material—words, letters, numbers—they have little or no difficulty with the same material presented via the visual modality. This apparent contradiction over material versus modality specifity remains to be resolved. There is no doubt of the greater sensitivity of verbal memory to left-sided lesions, the deficit being demonstrable with cerebral tumours (Meyer and Falconer, 1960) and after unilateral ECT on the left side but not on the right (Fleminger, de Horne and Nott, 1970; Pratt, Warrington, and Halliday, 1971).

Inglis (1970) suggests that the production of amnesic effects after ECT is probably related to the placement of the electrodes which are often sited over the temporal regions. He suggests that such effects will be diminished if the electrodes are kept as far away as possible from these sensitive regions. Where ECT is applied unilaterally it is suggested that amnesic effects will be verbal or non-verbal according to the side of placement but this hypothesis is virtually untestable since the tendency has been to apply unilateral ECT only to the non-dominant side. Squire (1975) has also demonstrated an impairment of recall from remote memory after ECT in the absence of changes in intellectual test scores. Since Inglis (1970) noted that ECT can produce signs of electrical disturbance in the temporal region Squire speculates 'that these same structures, which appear to be required for the storage and processing of newly acquired information, may also be required for the efficient recall of information from remote memory.' (op. cit. p.56)

Patients with temporal epilepsy in the dominant hemisphere have difficulties in recalling logical prose material under conditions of delayed recall and this difficulty is aggravated after left anterior lobectomy. Temporal lobe epileptics are regarded as being adversely affected by a divided attention situation but may not be significantly more so than a group of patients suffering from cen-trencephalic epilepsy (Glowinski, 1973). The selection of comparison groups in this area has received inadequate attention.

On the other hand, patients with non-dominant temporal lobe lesions and removals have no verbal memory defect but are impaired in memorizing pat-terned stimuli of a non-verbal nature both visual and auditory (Milner, 1962; Kimura, 1963). Maze learning has been shown to be impaired after right tem-poral lobe lesions whether tactually guided (Corkin, 1965) or visually guided (Milner, 1965) but this is not a specific loss since it appears with lesions in other parts of the right hemisphere. A qualitative examination may reveal different reasons for the failure of two groups such as frontal lobe and temporal lobe patients on the same maze test (Milner, 1964).

Blakemore (1969) questions the frequent assertion that the deficits after operation should be interpreted as learning deficits as such. He reports an earlier study of his in which he varied the rate of presentation of items by altering the time between words and between pairs in paired-associate learning. Patients after left temporal lobectomy showed the anticipated deficits at normal and rapid rates of presentation but, when the rate was slowed appreciably, the patient demonstrated that they could learn almost as well as before operation. Blakemore argues that the longer time intervals allow verbal mediation to be effective. The same findings would agree with the notion that the longer intervals may allow a dissipation of interference or inhibition in line with the argument advanced by Luria (1973b) above and considered with regard to the amnesic syndrome below.

The amnesic syndrome (Korsakoff or axial amnesia)

In 1889 Korsakoff described a collection of mental symptoms associated with a polyneuritis in patients suffering from chronic alcoholism. One of the prominent features of the mental disorder was a specific type of amnesia in which the patient was unable to retain for more than a few moments any of the information he was receiving, and consequently he was unable to learn anything new. His conscious state was clear and he retained a good deal of past events, though he tended to lose their chronological order, and there was a marked retrograde amnesia. Previously acquired habits were retained so that the patient managed to behave appropriately but only where no new be-haviour was required, even a slight variation of that which was familiar.

Not long after Korsakoff's description of the syndrome, autopsy reports described lesions in the mamillary bodies and other diencephalic structures. Numerous neuropathological studies since that time have emphasized the common occurrence of lesions in the anterior and other thalamic nuclei, the mamillary bodies and terminal portions of the fornix. Summaries are given by Talland (1965), Brierley (1966), and Talland and Waugh (1969). The lesions are produced only indirectly by alcoholism through a vitamin B deficiency, particularly of thiamine, and thus the syndrome has been described in other conditions causing thiamine deficiency such as a deficient diet, prolonged vomiting and other causes.

Soon after the discovery of the syndrome in alcoholics, several authors noted that the amnesia could be observed in other conditions without the polyneuritis. Bekhterev in 1899 provided the first link with the temporal lobes. 'At a meeting in St. Petersburg he demonstrated the brain of a patient who had shown a severe memory impairment as her earliest and most striking clinical abnormality; the main pathological finding was bilateral softening in the region of the uncus, hippocampus and adjoining mesial temporal cortex.' (Milner, 1966). It has been claimed since that time that this form of amnesia is produced whenever there is bilateral destruction of certain structures on the mesial or internal aspect of the cerebral hemispheres close to the central axis of the brain. For this reason the Korsakoff-type of amnesia has been called axial or mesial amnesia (Barbizet, 1970). The structures thought to be involved were the hippocampus, fornix, mamillary bodies, anterior nucleus of the thalamus, and the cingulate cortex, i.e. the causative lesions lie within what is known as the circuit of Papez (1937). 'The whole system constitutes a midline (or axial) functional structure intervening in memory processes.' (Barbizet, 1970, p.184).

Despite the frequent repetition of this generalization in the literature it is becoming clear that certain structures are much more intimately related to the production of the syndrome than others. Sweet, Talland and Ervin (1959) described the amnesic syndrome following transection of the anterior columns of the fornix in a patient suffering from a large colloid cyst of the third ventricle. Speaking of the possible theoretical basis of memory they commented

'Its availability to recall then depends on the complexity of its interrelationships with other significant memories or concepts, (i.e. on its 'embeddedness'). Within such a model, the hippocampal-fornix-mamillary system (which is increasingly implicated in 'motivational' or 'emotional' states), might operate in parallel to the primary perceptual system to add 'significance' to a perception and determine its 'embedding'... The hippocampal complex then would not be the 'site' of memory, but a necessary (though not sufficient) participant in that central process which makes an experience accessible to recall.' (op. cit. pp.77-78).

However such an attractive hypothesis gains no support from the results of similar operations where the fornix has been divided on a large number of occasions without any apparent effect upon memory. Added weight of evidence against the notion of the hippocampus-fornix-mamillary body complex as a unitary system related to memory is provided by studies of penetrating wounds of the brain, e.g. of nine fornical lesions reported in Lehtonen (1973) none had an amnesic syndrome.

On the other hand a very large number of studies has strongly implicated the hippocampus itself. Among the earlier studies were those of Grunthal, 1947; Glees and Griffith, 1952; Scoville and Milner, 1957; Terzian, 1958. Scoville and Milner (1957) examined cases who had undergone bilateral mesial temporal lobe resection and found memory loss in those operations which included the hippocampus and not in those with more anterior bilateral resections including the uncus and anygdaloid nucleus on each side. Serafetinides and Falconer (1962) demonstrated that unilateral removal of the hippocampus did not produce the syndrome. Piercey (1964) concluded, from his review of cases to that time, that severe memory defects of the Korsakoff type were produced only where hippocampal lesions were bilateral. Numerous studies over the past decade have only served to confirm this strong relationship. The occasional exceptions of apparently unilateral lesions producing an axial amnesia are discussed below.

A further landmark in the neurological basis of memory disorders was the report of Rose and Symonds (1960) of four cases of severe memory disorder occurring after recovery from what may be assumed to be viral encephalitis. Barbizet (1970) points to a similar post-encephalitic case reported by Hillemand in 1931 and whose memory disorder was essentially unchanged when he, Barbizet, examined the patient 36 years later. The features of these cases are essentially those of the amnesic syndrome namely, a gross defect of recent memory with difficulty in the registration of ongoing events, some retrograde amnesia, with relatively little impairment of other intellectual functions.

Further reports of post-encephalitic amnesia have become almost too numerous to mention, e.g. (Adams, Collins, and Victor, 1962; Leman, Loiseau, and Cohadon, 1963; Beck and Corsellis, 1963; Hall, 1963, 1965; Zangwill, 1966a; Barbizet, Devic, and Duizabo, 1967; Lhermitte and Signoret, 1972). By this time most neurologists will have encountered such cases. While many of the cases described in the literature have a profound, lasting amnesia a few cases of our own who have had a clear-out amnesic syndrome after a viral illness have gone on to complete or almost complete recovery.

The most common cause appears to be a necrotic encephalitis of herpetic origin causing bilateral hippocampal damage and sometimes other lesions. The neuropathological evidence is reviewed in some detail in Brierley (1966) and in Barbizet (1970).

With regard to the cingulate region Whitty and Lewin (1960) reported the amnesic syndrome in the confusional state which followed bilateral cingulectomy. However, no lasting amnesia was seen in the bilateral cingulate lesions following trauma in the series reported by Lehtonen (1973).

Perhaps the most interesting and productive clinico-anatomical examination of the amnesic syndrome stems from the work of Lhermitte and Signoret (1972). Taking the suggestion of Zangwill (1966a) that different forms of the amnesic syndrome may exist according to the location of the lesions in the axial structures they compared the performance of two classes of amnesic patients on several tasks. The alcoholic amnesic patient was considered to represent lesions in the region of the mamillary bodies and/or anterior thalamus while the post-encephalitic amnesia patient was taken to represent damage predominantly in the hippocampal areas. While each of these patients may be said to possess all the necessary clinical criteria of the amnesic syndrome the application of special tests showed special features in each group sufficient to tentatively consider them as belonging to two distinct sub-classes of the syndrome. The following table summarizes the principal findings.

Table 5.1 Differentiation of the amnesic syndrome according to locus of lesion

CLINICAL FEATURES	Mamillo-thalamic (Alcoholic)	Hippocampal (Post-encephalitic)
Delayed recall	May deny information was given	Says material has been forgotten
Confabulation	Present	Absent
Chronology (long term memory)	Disorganized	Satisfactory
Awareness of disorder	Lack of awareness or denial	No lack of awareness or denial

TEST FEATURES (after Lhermitte and Signoret, 1972)		
A. Learning of spatial disposition of objects		
Trials to criterion	Very many more than controls	Very many more than controls
Errors	Numerous	Numerous
Spontaneous recall	Nil	Nil
Cued recall	Good	Nil
B. Learning of a logically ordered spatial arrangement		
	Failure	Normal
C. Learning of sequentially presented material		
Sequence of words	Failure	Normal
Sequences of coloured counters	Failure	Normal

Note: In addition the two groups of patients showed qualitatively different types of errors during their learning trials on Test A.

In summary it seems that while both groups of patients have very great difficulty in learning new information and are unable to recall material spontaneously there is a double dissociation with regard to the two types of tasks used in this study as well as a qualitatively different type of error apparent in the learning attempts. The alcoholic (mamillo-thalamic) patients' difficulties are marked by an ability to store some information which, however, needs assistance for effective retrieval, and a difficulty with conceptual tasks which has been remarked by numerous writers such as Talland (1965). These conceptual difficulties are absent in the post-encephalitic group (hippocampal) who may be said to have a syndrome of 'pure forgetting'.

The impaired cognitive functioning of alcoholic Korsakoff amnesic patients also includes perseverative tendencies (Talland, 1965; Samuels, Butters, Goodglass, and Brody, 1971; Oscar-Berman, 1973). It is tempting to speculate that, because of the known association of lesions of the frontal lobes with conceptual difficulties and with perseveration, such deficits of the alcoholic group might be independent of their retention deficits, being based on functional or anatomical disruption of fronto-thalamic connections.

The material in this section demonstrates the wide variety of conditions which may produce the amnesic syndrome. A consideration of the remainder of the material in this section should reinforce the idea put forward by Williams (1969) that the temporal lobes are best thought of as bilateral structures morphologically and functionally related to the limbic lobe.

The amnesic syndrome with unilateral lesions. Despite the weight of evidence in favour of the amnesic syndrome being produced only by bilateral lesions, occasional reports suggest that unilateral lesions may produce the loss. Penfield and Milner (1958) reported two cases of the syndrome after unilateral anterior temporal lobectomy in the hemisphere dominant for language. They attributed this effect to the unsuspected presence of a lesion in the hippocampal region of the non-operated side so that what was a unilateral operation in one sense produced a bilateral lesion in another. Their contention was borne out in one case by the finding of a wasted hippocampal region in the non-operated hemisphere at post mortem and by the presumptive evidence of EEG abnormality in the other case in the side opposite the operation. Baldwin (1956) had previously described similar bilateral effects in unilateral left lobectomies only in cases with bilateral EEG abnormalities. Similarly, less severe amnesia was described by Serafetinides and Falconer (1962) after right lobectomy in cases with added left-sided EEG abnormalities. All these cases appear explicable in terms of the production of a *functionally bilateral* lesion by a unilateral operation.

In 1964 Dimsdale, Logue, and Piercy described the occurrence of a case of general amnesia after right lobectomy in which there had been no neurological evidence whatsoever of a lesion on the other side. The authors attributed the memory defect to the extensive nature of the operation. Milner however pointed to the authors' report of a verbal memory defect before operation as presumptive evidence of a left temporal lobe lesion which was then compounded with the right-sided lobectomy to produce the effect. In one of our own cases we have had confirmation that in fact clinical, radiological, and electrographic evidence may be negative while the hippocampus in the 'silent' temporal lobe may be completely wasted. This patient, who was a candidate in prospect for left-sided lobectomy, died of a cause unrelated to her epilepsy and the *right* hemisphere at autopsy showed wasting in the hippocampal region. Earlier psychological testing in this case had pointed to a lowering of function in certain non-verbal functions usually associated with the 'minor' hemisphere.

Finally the cases described by Stepien and Sierpinski (1964) are quite contrary to all the above findings. These three cases had a general memory defect before the operation and EEG evidence of abnormality on both sides. Removal of one temporal lobe, rather than aggravating the defect as Milner's hypothesis would suggest, resulted in a disappearance of the amnesia. These findings are difficult to reconcile with the numerous studies cited earlier.

Amytal ablation—the Wada technique. In 1949 Wada developed a method for determining directly the side of the hemisphere which played the major role in subserving speech functions. A temporary cessation or functional ablation was effected by injecting a solution of a rapidly acting anaesthetic agent into the internal carotid artery which supplies one side of the brain. This intracarotid sodium amytal injection technique produced the following evidence of functional loss

(1) hemiplegia, (2) hemianaesthesia, (3) half visual field loss (hemianopia), all on the side opposite the side of injection. If the hemisphere injected was dominant for language, dysphasia was also produced. These effects cleared within about five minutes though subtle changes in language function may be elicited on careful examination for as long as half an hour after the injection.

The amytal ablation technique has several advantages. Firstly, it allows the neurosurgeon to determine the lateralization of language function quite unequivocally, and to gauge the probable effects on language of operation in either hemisphere, since separate injections can be made on either side on two different occasions. The method has been used extensively to determine the anticipated effects on memory as well as language (Milner, Branch, and Rasmussen, 1962, 1964, 1966; Kløve, Grabow, and Trites, 1969; Kløve, Trites, and Grabow, 1970). The rationale for Milner's test of memory was based on an assumption derived from the findings stated above, namely that the loss of function in only one temporal lobe does not produce a generalized memory loss. However, if an unsuspected lesion is affecting the hippocampal zone of the opposite hemisphere, then amytal ablation of the temporal lobe should produce transiently the functional effect of a bilateral lesion. A generalized memory loss should be apparent for the time of the ablation and clear up as the effect of the anaesthetic agent wears off. Obviously the short time available, three to five minutes, limits the amount of testing possible. Milner (1966) presented strong evidence for the bilateral basis of the amnesic syndrome, e.g. each of three cases who had already been subjected to anterior temporal lobectomy showed a pronounced memory defect during the injection period when the other hemisphere was chemically ablated. Also, of the 216 injections some 27 cases of anterograde amnesia were produced and, in the 18 cases where the amnesic condition was most clearly produced, *all* occurred after ablation of the hemisphere contralateral to the side of the temporal lobe lesion. The value of preoperative testing under amytal ablation is one that should recommend itself because of the very drastic changes caused by bilateral lesions. 'The fact that there has been no incidence of post-operative memory loss in patients screened by this method, although the series included a number of cases of bilateral EEG abnormality furnishes some presumptive evidence of its validity.' (Milner, 1966). Despite these findings it is difficult to understand the anatomical basis involved. 'Branches of the anterior choroidal artery (which usually arise from the internal carotid) supply the pyriform cortex, uncus, posterior medial half of the amygdaloid nucleus, anterior hippocampus, and dentate gyrus. We do not yet understand the reasons for memory dysfunction (in cases with contralateral mesial temporal lobe abnormalities) after injection of amobarbital into the internal carotid artery, which perfuses only the anterior part of the hippocampal formation.' (Blume, Grabow, Darley, and Aranson, 1973).

The carotid amytal ablation technique has also been used in testing for lateralization of functions other than language. Bogen and Gordon (1971) looked at musical ability during depression of activity of the non-dominant (right) hemisphere in six patients. Injection of the right side caused a marked temporary disturbance of singing ability whereas in five of the six patients 'speech remained unaffected except for slight slowing and slurring of words and the presence of some monotonicity; the intelligibility and rhythmicity of speech were hardly affected.' Such a finding is in keeping with the evidence cited elsewhere of the greater importance of the non-dominant hemisphere in certain musical abilities.

On the negative side Serafetinides (1966) noted that visual recognition of geometrical designs was not affected by ablation of either side though he again confirmed the impairment of verbal recall with amytal ablation of the dominant hemisphere.

Opportunites for studying the effects of amytal ablation with specialized tests occur in only a few centres, the time during which testing may be carried out is restricted to only a few minutes, and the defects (such as hemianopia) produced by the injection make testing extremely difficult both on the reception and response sides, all of which restricts the amount of information produced to date.

The amnesic syndrome with vascular lesions. Alteration in memory is one of the very common accompaniments of vascular disorders. These memory problems may be of a transient or permanent nature. Occasionally, after several transient amnesic opisodes the patient may die of a massive vascular accident as in the case described by Whitty and Lishman (1966). The incidence of transient episodes of amnesia of vascular origin is difficult to estimate from the literature since so many of them go unreported. Material-specific memory disorders of probable cortical origin are seen frequently in association with disorders of gnosis and praxis.

More lasting disorders with many features of the amnesic syndrome have been described with axial vascular lesions, particularly due to thrombosis of both posterior cerebral arteries. A typical report is that of Victor, Angevine, Mancall, and Fisher (1961). Their patient who had been followed for a period of five years prior to death showed. . .

'a profound defect in recent memory and inability to learn new facts and skills. His general intellectual functions remained at a 'bright normal' level, although certain mild and relatively inconspicuous abnormalities were disclosed by the tests designed to measure concentration, shifting of mental set, and abstract thinking. He also showed an incomplete retrograde amnesia, covering the two-year period prior to the onset of his illness. His memory for remote events was virtually unaffected.' (op. cit. p.261).

Post mortem examination of the brain showed old bilateral infarctions in the inferomedial portions of the temporal lobes. Since that time further studies have described the association of serious memory defect in life with post-mortem evidence of bilateral infarction in the territory of the posterior cerebral arteries (Boudin, Barbizet, Derouesné, and Van Amerongen, 1967; Boudin, Brion, Pépin, and Barbizet, 1968; De Jong, Itabashi, and Olson, 1968, 1969). Two-thirds of a group of 31 patients with attacks of sudden loss of memory studied by Heathfield, Croft, and Swash (1973) were considered to have bilateral temporal lobe or thalamic lesions as the probable cause. In some of the patients there was 'clear evidence of ischaemia in the territory of the posterior cerebral circulation,' and these workers consider that this ischaemia is the cause of the majority of such sudden pervasive amnesias.

Most reports stress the presence of other neurological signs in these cases, particularly the presence of visual field defects. Benson, Marsden, and Meadows (1974) reported the acute onset of amnesia in ten patients, associated with unilateral or bilateral visual field defects. Once again clinical evaluation suggested the presence of an infarct affecting the posterior cerebral artery territory in each case.

Sometimes as in the cases reported by Geschwind and Fusillo (1966) and Mohr, Leicester, Stoddard, and Sidman (1971) there may be marked amnesia with damage to the left side only but there is, as yet, insufficient neuropsychological evidence about the nature of the amnesia in such cases to say whether a true amnesic syndrome can be produced by a unilateral lesion even of the dominant hemisphere. It is possible that, because of the common use of largely verbal or verbally mediated tests of memory, these unilateral (dominant) cases may only appear to be instances of the amnesic syndrome. One of our cases who suffered the sudden onset of amnesia after a brief period of unconsciousness has continued to have a profound learning and retention difficulty of material since the time of the episode some four years earlier. While having most of the features of the amnesic syndrome his difficulty with verbal material has always been much more severe than for non-verbal material many aspects of which are close to normal. In the absence of neuropathological evidence it is difficult to say whether such a case is due to unilateral or asymmetrical bilateral involvement of limbic structures. Certainly the memory disorder is more severe and incapacitating than the unilateral material specific deficits which have been described after unilateral temporal (anterior) lobectomy of the dominant hemisphere. This latter deficit is often thought to be due mainly to cortical involvement. Finally, Benson et al. (op.cit.) suggest that it is questionable whether circulatory abnormalities can produce a lasting amnesia without producing other clinical findings. They cite the absence of such autopsy-proven cases in the literature. The answer to this question hinges on the availability of pathological evidence which must be extremely rare in the few cases of 'vascular' amnesia without other significant defects.

Specific features of the amnesic syndrome. The amnesic syndrome has been the focus of a large number of studies in recent years. Material has been accumulating rapidly so that many points of uncertainty raised in reviews of neurological disorders of memory (Angelergues, 1969; Milner, 1970; Warrington, 1971; Warrington and Weiskrantz, 1972) are rapidly becoming clarified. Before considering these points in detail it would be of value to look at the general features of a typical case. Certainly no more intensive and prolonged series of investigations have been carried out than on one patient of Scoville's bilateral mesial temporal operation series. This patient, known as H.M., has provided a good deal of information because his amnesia has been almost completely free of other confounding effects such as intellectual deficit and has persisted almost unchanged over some two decades. These findings have been summarized by Milner (1970) and Scoville and Correll (1973) and many of the studies appeared in a special issue of *Neuropsychologia* (1968).

Immediately after the operation H.M. demonstrated both a retrograde and anterograde amnesia. The retrograde amnesia cleared but the patient was left with some confusion about the chronological order of events particularly with regard to a period of one to two years before the operation. On the other hand, the anterograde amnesia has remained severe with an almost total lack of registration for everyday events. He repeatedly re-reads the same papers and repeats tasks over and over without giving any evidence of having done them before. He fails to learn the location of his house or the location of objects within it. He is unable to learn the names of visitors even after they have been visiting the house frequently over some years and fails to recognize them.

On the other hand, H.M.'s immediate span of attention is normal. He can, provided there is no distraction, repeat a normal span of six or seven digits. This preservation of immediate memory in the clinical testing of amnesic patients had been reported many years earlier by Zangwill (1946) and has been confirmed frequently since. The preservation of intelligence can be seen in a reported Wechsler Intelligence Quotient of 118 some nine years after operation.

The marked degree of anterograde amnesia in this syndrome has led to a tendency on the part of some writers to overgeneralize and oversimplify the learning and retention deficit. There is now ample evidence that some learning and retention takes place even in such pronounced cases as H.M. Motor skills do not suffer to the degree shown by many other tasks. H.M. improved his performance with practice on a mirror drawing task even though he was unaware that he had done the task before (Milner, 1962). He also showed improvement on a number of manual tracking and coordination tasks (Corkin, 1968). Another amnesic patient of Starr and Phillips (1970) was able to learn and recall a new melody on the piano. Milner (1970) points out that this dissociation between different forms of learning is in keeping with the evidence for qualitative differences between kinaesthetic and other types of memory.

In 1962 Milner reported H.M.'s complete inability to learn a visually guided stylus maze of the type described in Chapter 4. However, when the number of choice points was reduced so that it fell within his immediate memory span, he demonstrated extensive saving in the number of trials to relearn the maze a week after the initial trials and a comparatively rapid relearning after two years (Milner, Corkin. and Teuber, 1968).

Finally, even with verbal material, it is possible for the amnesic patient to learn if the proper conditions are provided. Using their newly developed method of presenting partial information in the form of fragmented pictures and words to the amnesic subjects, Weiskrantz and Warrington found a relatively slow decline in retention compared with clinical impressions. In fact after three days there was no significant difference between amnesic patients and controls though the patients took longer to learn (Weiskrantz and Warrington, 1970a, 1970b). This learning by use of the fragmented or partial stimulus method was also demonstrated (again in H.M.) by Milner (1970) using Gollin's series of incomplete pictures (Gollin, 1960).

Short term memory and the amnesic syndrome. The common clinical finding of apparently normal short term memory in amnesic subjects with grossly defective long term memory has become for most workers an important part of the clinical definition of the syndrome. This is not to say that no abnormality in STM exists in these patients. Experimental studies of STM in amnesic subjects leave several matters unresolved.

In support of the dissociation of STM and LTM effects in amnesic patients two lines of evidence have been put forward by Warrington and her group (Warrington and Baddeley, 1974). Firstly, there are those studies which provide evidence that STM and LTM may be selectively impaired by brain lesions (Warrington and Shallice, 1969; Baddeley and Warrington, 1970; Shallice and Warrington, 1970; Warrington, Logue and Pratt, 1971; Warrington and Shallice, 1972). Secondly, Warrinton (1971) has reviewed the evidence from direct studies of STM in amnesic subjects. Her evidence appeared strong with regard to verbal short term memory, largely on the basis of her own studies. A summary of this evidence shows that, (1) immediate memory span is normal in amnesic subjects (Drachman and Arbit, 1966; Warrington and Weiskrantz, 1968; Wickelgren, 1968); (2) amnesic subjects show a normal decay function, i.e. their short-term forgetting is the same as normal subjects (Baddeley and Warrington, 1970); and they show a normal recency effect (Warrington, 1971).

However it is also becoming clear that short-term memory deficits may be present in amnesic patients (Cermak, Butters, and Goodglass, 1971; Samuels, Butters, Goodglass, and Brody, 1971; Goodglass and Pick, 1972). The conflicting evidence is difficult to understand since both groups employ the distractor technique of Peterson and Peterson (1959) to control for rehearsal. The suggestion by Warrington that the difference in the findings might be explicable in terms of more widespread lesions in the opposing studies is not supported by the published intelligence test levels by Butters and Cermak (1974) who further point out that the two groups are not strictly comparable because of the presence of post-encephalitic patients in Warrington's sample, and because her test procedures may have allowed some rehearsal during the delay periods. This matter remains to be resolved.

The position with regard to non-verbal short-term memory is not so clear. The lack of satisfactory evidence of the amnesic patient's performance on tasks requiring non-verbal short-term memory depends partly on the relative lack of suitable tasks. Several studies on H.M. appear to give conflicting results. The rapid forgetting of simple perceptual material reported by Prisko (Milner, 1970) and confirmed by Sidman, Stoddard and Mohr (1968) contrasts with the apparently normal short-term decay function for the recognition of tones described by Wickelgren (1968). The discrepancy may depend, in part on the nature of the test used. More recently Warrington and Baddeley (1974) have once again shown normal STM and poor LTM this time using visual stimuli which are 'not readily verbalisable' namely the location of dots.

If short-term memory deficits do occur in the amnesic syndrome the question arises as to whether they are modality or material specific or general. There seems little doubt that the long-term memory difficulties are general rather than specific though the difficulties often appear greater in the verbal sphere. The question with regard to specificity versus generality evokes the two major types of evidence cited concerning the presence or absence of short-term memory defects. Firstly, there are studies demonstrating that STM systems seem to be modality specific (Butters, Samuels, Goodglass, and Brody, 1970a, 1970b; Warrington and Rabin, 1971b; Warrington and Shallice, 1969, 1972). Secondly, specific tests of short-term memory in amnesic subjects have produced slightly conflicting results. Samuels, Butters, Goodglass, and Brody (1971) showed that Korsakoff alcoholic patients had severe memory deficits on both visual and auditory verbal STM tasks as well as a non-visual STM task employing non-sense figures when compared with normal subjects and non-amnesic alcoholic patients. In a second study using these three groups Cermak, Butters, and Goodglass (1971) again demonstrated that the span of retention for Korsakoff patients deteriorated much more rapidly than the other two groups for consonant trigrams, words, and triads of words. This study also showed that, despite the rapid rate of STM decay, some material could be transferred and maintained in long-term memory. In a more recent study Butters, Lewis, Cermak, and Goodglass (1973) have compared short-term retention, both verbal and non-verbal in three sense modalities, visual, auditory and tactile. This study, also with alcoholic amnesic patients, showed normal retention in each of the three modalities for non-verbal materials and a significant defect in all modalities for verbal materials. Confirmation of these findings would mean that the memory deficit is material-specific. This would be consistent with the hypothesis in the following section that verbal encoding difficulties may underlie the memory difficulties in amnesic patients.

Psychological theories of the amnesic syndrome. Following her studies of the amnesic syndrome after bilateral temporal lobe lesions, Milner put forward the theory that the difficulty experienced by the patient in remembering recently received information had as its basis a failure of the material to consolidate, in other words to pass from immediate or short-term memory to long-term storage. This simple and attractive hypothesis appears to fit the clinical facts so that the consolidation hypothesis continues to be repeated (Scoville and Correll, 1973; Feindel, 1974). Continuing experimental analysis of the amnesic syndrome has produced several lines of evidence to suggest that this explanation is not adequate—(1) there is evidence that material which the patient is 'unable to learn' on one occasion may appear spontaneously in a later examination. Warrington and Weiskrantz (1968) and Starr and Phillips (1970) both report the presence of these 'intrusion errors' in verbal learning. Though verbal associations may fail to be repeated on request it cannot be assumed that these items have not passed into storage. The 'forgotten' words may intrude themselves into later series when the patient is endeavouring to recall words from a new list. In our experience this can be commonly observed in testing on successive occasions with Forms I and II of the Wechsler Memory Scale, some responses from the Paired-Associate task on Form I being given to those of Form II administered on a second occasion. Warrington (1971) considers 'this is an example of proactive interference, and implies that some information is being stored for relatively long periods of time and that it has sufficient strength to interfere with new learning.' This alternative theory of interference has received further support from Warrington and Weiskrantz (1974) in an examination of the adverse effects of prior learning on subsequent retention in amnesic subjects. The interference theory is also favoured by Russian workers (Akbarova, 1972; Luria, 1973). Luria summarizes a number of studies by his group which he cites in support of a theory of retroactive inhibition or interference. 'The patient can successfully repeat and retain a small fragment (such as Tolstoy's story *The Hen and the Golden Egg*), but if he is then asked to spend a minute solving arithmetical problems, or if immediately after the first story he is asked to read another similar one (such as Tolstoy's *The Jackdaw and the Pigeons*), the traces of the first story become so inhibited that it cannot be recalled. The fact that this disturbance of recollection is based, not on total obliteration of the traces, but on their excessive inhibition by the interfering stimuli, is clear because after a certain time has elapsed, the traces of the "forgotten" story can suddenly and involuntarily reappear as a reminiscence.' (Luria, 1973b, p.65); (2) The difficulty which patients have in retrieving some material which was well-learned before the acquisition of their lesions suggests that if there is difficulty in consolidation it is by no means the only fault. Difficulty in retrieval must play a significant role. Sanders and Warrington (1971) employed a free recall questionnaire method and a multiple choice technique to examine patients' recall extending from recent times to a period over thirty years before and found that recall of events before the onset of the illness was more faulty than had previously been thought. This aspect of the disorder has received much less attention than the recall of more recent events such as the studies cited above; (3) even where amnesic subjects have learnt material to the same criteria as normal subjects, Warrington and Weiskrantz (1968) found that the amnesic patients' retention was impaired. Likewise, Cermak, Butters, and Goodglass (1971) using recognition procedures demonstrated that more of the original trace was present than could be recalled by the subject.

Warrington and Weiskrantz (1970, 1972) have strongly supported the retrieval hypothesis citing much of the above evidence and also their demonstration that retention conditions appear to have a differential effect on amnesic and control subjects. In 1968 they found that amnesic subjects showed evidence of some learning and retention, as measured by the savings method, when 'graduated reduced cues' were employed. Two sets of materials were used, (1) Gollin's incomplete figures (Gollin, 1960) and a comparable set of incomplete words. Such results do not lend themselves readily to the consolidation hypothesis.

The interference theory is not restricted only to memory within the same modality since Sherwood and McNamee (1967) have shown, again with Korsakoff patients, that a visual interference task affected the patients' ability to memorize orally presented digits while having no significant effect on control subjects.

The importance of the fragmented words test has been lessened by the findings of a recent study by Woods and Piercy (1974). Using two groups of normal subjects with two strengths of memory trace, one weak (after one week) and the other strong (after one minute) they found a comparable interaction between the method of testing and retention interval as Warrington and Weiskrantz found for the 'groups by test method' interaction with normal and amnesic subjects tested at one minute. With special regard to the fragmented words test they conclude: 'Whatever the distinctive features of this test of memory there seems no good reason for supposing that, compared with other tests, it produces effects in amnesics which it does not produce in normals.' (p.444).

The effectiveness of the cued-recall retrieval technique has been shown to be a valuable aid in differentiating between different forms of the amnesic syndrome (Lhermitte and Signoret, 1972) and the differential effects of cued recall for verbal material has again been replicated by Warrington and Weiskrantz (1974). Of particular interest in this latter study was the evidence that restricting the number of response alternatives proved more effective in amnesic than in normal subjects.

Warrington and Weiskrantz (1974) point out that, while most of the evidence makes it difficult to accept a simple consolidation hypothesis, an interference theory is only one of a number of alternative explanations. Among the possibilities they cite Gaffan's suggestion that the basis of the difficulty might lie in a loss of the normal ability to discriminate degrees of familiarity (Gaffan, 1972) i.e. that recognition memory is at fault. A similar point of view was expressed by Simpson (1969) cited in a previous section. Quite independently this approach had also been proposed by Mackay in discussion of an earlier paper describing a case of amnesia with anterior fornical division. .

'. . . recognition is affective, a feeling of familiarity . . . Recognition is the acceptance of an idea or an object as familiar. So perhaps, we have a reason why the fornix, so relatively insignificant a portion of the brain, is essential to memory, in that it is of crucial importance in affect and hence in the feeling of familiarity which is so necessary to recognition . . . the fornix is perhaps the supreme pathway for impulses subserving affect, [but] it need not be the only pathway. There may be other substitute routes by which some recognition, some feeling of familiarity, may be engendered upon the presentation of a more remotely familiar idea or object. In other words, old experiences, long since and often repeated, may be able to evoke, when newly experienced, a feeling of familiarity by means of other pathways than the fornix, while the re-presentation of more recent experiences requires the integrity for the affective function of recognition.' (In Sweet, Talland, and Ervin, 1959, pp.80-81).

More recently attention has been paid to other factors which may contribute to the retention difficulties of the amnesic patient. Chief among these are difficulties in encoding. Cermak, Butters, and Gerrein (1973) found that amnesic subjects are able to encode on acoustic, associative, and semantic levels but when left to their own preferences neglect semantic encoding in favour of the other two modes. The authors feel that this failure to employ semantic encoding may be at the basis of the amnesic patients' difficulty in retaining verbal material. Baddeley and Warrington (1973) cite evidence that semantic encoding is more efficient as measured by tests of retention than 'coding in terms of the sound or physical characteristics of the material.' They found in comparing different types of semantic coding that amnesic patients performed more poorly using visual imagery coding than on linguistically based coding strategies such as grouping according to taxonomic categories. This difficulty did not stem from an inability to form images since the amnesic patients were able to do so. Jones (1974) extended this finding by testing the use of imagery as a mnemonic aid in 18 cases of left temporal removals, 18 right temporal removals, two bilateral temporal cases (one of whom was H.M.) and 36 controls. Right temporal and control patients performed similarly, left temporal cases were able to compensate partially for their verbal memory deficits, while the two bilateral cases received no benefit from this aid.

The accumulation of evidence would support the position of Cermak and Butters (1972) that at least two factors are involved in the amnesic patients' memory problems—(1) an increased sensitivity to interference effects and, (2) a failure to verbally encode new information.

6. The Parietal Lobes

The middle third of the cerebral hemispheres strategically situated between
the frontal, occipital and temporal lobes, is closely related in function
to each of these regions of the brain. Partly as a result of this, a greater
variety of clinical manifestations is likely to result from disease of the
parietal lobe than from disturbance of any other part of the hemispheres.
It must be emphasized, however, that these phenomena require special
techniques for their elicitation; otherwise they may be easily overlooked
or discounted in a routine clinical examination (Jewesbury, 1969).

Anatomical features

The parietal lobe has two main surfaces one lateral and the other mesial.
The anterior border or lateral aspect is formed by the central sulcus while the
posterior border is formed by the parieto-occipital sulcus and a line drawn
from the end of this sulcus to the preoccipital notch on the inferolateral border
of the hemisphere (Figure 6.1). The lower border separates the inferior part
of the parietal lobe from the superior portion of the temporal lobe. It is made
up of the lateral sulcus and a line continued back from it to reach the posterior
line of demarcation.

Two well marked sulci lie within the parietal lobe. The post-central sulcus
delimits the post-central gyrus which is concerned with somatic sensation. The
intra-parietal sulcus runs roughly parallel to the lower margin of the lobe about
midway in the lobe separating it into a superior and an inferior parietal lobule.
The ends of two (sometimes three) sulci invade the inferior parietal lobule.
The anterior of these is the posterior branch of the lateral sulcus while just
posterior to it is the end of the superior temporal sulcus. The cortex of the
inferior parietal lobule around the end of the lateral sulcus is the supramarginal
gyrus, that around the superior temporal sulcus is the angular gyrus. Not
infrequently the sulci of the supramarginal and angular gyri are independent
of the lateral and superior temporal gyri.

The anterior border of the mesial aspect of the parietal lobe is formed by
a line which extends about midway through the paracentral lobule from the

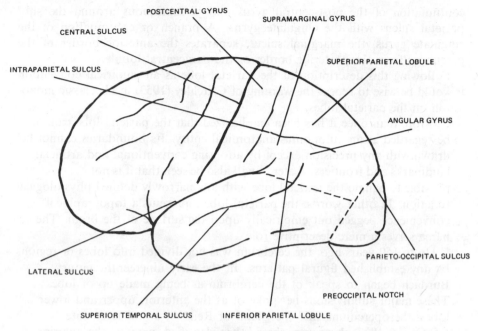

Fig. 6.1 Lateral aspect of the parietal lobe

point on the superomedial border of the hemisphere reached by the central sulcus, to the top of the corpus callosum (Figure 6.2). Thus only the posterior half of the paracentral lobule belongs to the parietal lobe. The posterior border is formed by the parieto-occipital sulcus which is usually very distinct. The region anterior to this sulcus is the precuneus which extends anteriorly to the

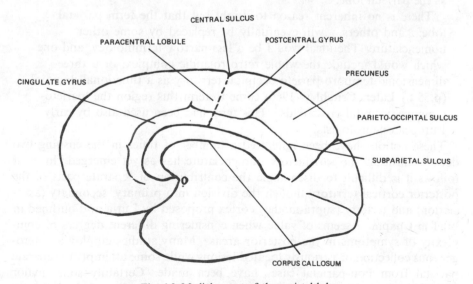

Fig. 6.2 Medial aspect of the parietal lobe

continuation of the post-central gyrus and is continuous around the sub-parietal sulcus with the cingulate gyrus. A branch or continuation of the cingulate gyrus, the marginal sulcus, separates the anterior border of the precuneus from the posterior border of the paracentral lobule.

Following this description of the parietal lobe as an empirical convention it would be wise to repeat the warning of Critchley (1953) in his classic monograph on the parietal lobes.

'More than once it has been emphasized that the parietal lobe cannot be regarded as an autonomus anatomical entity. Its boundaries cannot be drawn with any precision except by adopting conventional and artificial landmarks and frontiers. Later, it will also be seen that it is not possible to equate the parietal lobe with any narrowly defined physiological function. In other words, the parietal lobe represents a topographical convenience pegged out empirically upon the surface of the brain. The name serves a mere descriptive role. . .

Up to 150 years ago, the cerebrum was not divided into lobes or regions by any established figural patterns. In the early nineteenth century Burdach began to speak of the cerebrum as being made up of lobes. These major subdivisions he spoke of as the anterior, upper and lower lobes, the operculum, and the island of Reil. At a still later date (cf. Quain, 1837) there were three lobes identified, namely, the anterior, posterior and middle lobes, indicating the various positions of the brain as related to the fossae of the base of the skull. This system was adopted and recapitulated in text-books until 1850. Around that time, there developed a tendency to associate regions of the brain with the overlying cranial bones. Thus the anterior lobe became the frontal lobe, while the cortical territory underlying. . . (the)os parietalis became known as the parietal lobe. . .

There is no inherent reason to doubt but that the term parietal lobe. . .and others. . .will eventually be replaced by some other nomenclature. The ideal would be a less narrow terminology, and one which would include the whole retro-rolandic complex, or a three-dimensional temporo-parieto-occipital territory as a functional domain' (p.55 f.) Later, Critchley (1966) came to term this region the 'parieto-temporo-occipital crossroads.' This term had been used also by early European neurologists.

These notions have been reiterated a number of times in the ensuing two decades although no satisfactory nomenclature has as yet emerged. In what follows it is difficult to disentangle the contribution of separate parts of the posterior cortical territory though the division into primary, secondary (association) and tertiary (supra-modal) cortex proposed by Luria and outlined in brief in Chapter 2 seems of value when considering different degrees of complexity of symptoms in the posterior areas. Many studies employ a heterogeneous collection of variously located lesions while some attempts to separate parietal from non-parietal cases have been made. Certainly some major differences have emerged which are related to the laterality of the lesion in the territory behind the central sulcus.

Sensory and perceptual disturbances

The primary reception area for the numerous forms of somatic sensation has its principal locus in the post-central gyrus. The secondary or association cortex posterior to this is thought to deal with the elaboration of the discrete elements into meaningful wholes so that disorders with damage away from the 'somaesthetic' area tend to be more complex, i.e. tend to be cognitive in nature rather than simple disturbances of sensation. Further afield in the region of the 'temporo-parieto-occipital crossroads' the disturbances tend to be those which reflect a disruption of intersensory or cross-modal association and integration. Following this 'anatomical' division of deficits according to type of cortex three types of deficit have been selected for treatment: (1) somatosensory discrimination, (2) disorders of tactile perception, and (3) disorders of intersensory association.

Somatosensory discrimination

What is commonly called somatic sensation is made up of a number of separate modalities. Among these are touch, pain, temperature, body position sense or kinaesthesis, and vibration. The detailed organization of each of these is dealt with in tests of physiological psychology such as Geldard (1972) as well as in some texts of physiology and neurology. Some major texts do not treat the topic at all!

The somatosensory system is able to combine information from different modalities in different locations and with different temporal relationships. A treatment of these, however, is outside the scope of the present volume which is largely concerned with lesion studies.

The earliest neuropsychological studies of the cerebral basis of somatic sensation in man came from the examination of missile wounds to the head (Head, 1920; Holmes, 1927). The value of these studies suffered from the

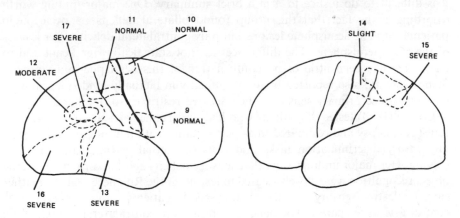

Fig. 6.3 Relation between severity of somatic sensory disturbance and site of lesion (Redrawn from J.P. Evans (1935) Research Publications. *Association for Research in Nervous and Mental Disease*, **15**, 331.) (Courtesy of the A.R.N.M.D.).

inability to accurately localize the site of the lesion for correlation with the results of their painstaking examination of sensory-perceptual capacities. The introduction and increasing use of cortical ablation for the removal of cerebral scars allowed Penfield's group to make the first serious examination of sensory defects following circumscribed ablation of cortical tissue (Evans, 1935). Employing the detailed examination procedure outlined by Head, Evans examined 17 cases, 9 posterior and 8 anterior (Fig. 6.3). Evans concluded from the examination of these cases that damage to the extra-parietal areas, the pre- and postcentral gyri and the central portion of the parietal lobe led to transient, if any, sensory dysfunction 'while limited excisions in the region of the supra-marginal gyrus caused extensive and permanent loss of somesthetic sensation.' Such limited case material supplemented by other smaller studies formed the basis for conjecture about the cortical basis of somatosensory function until the studies performed on penetrating missile cases after the Second World War. Numerous studies on such cases provided increasing evidence that performance on many complex sensory discrimination tasks depended on temporal, posterior parietal or parieto-temporo-occipital areas (Blum, Chow, and Pribram, 1950; Teuber, 1950; Battersby, 1951; Teuber, Battersby, and Bender, 1951; Teuber and Weinstein, 1954).

In 1956 Hécaen, et al. in a study of patients with surgical lesions of the minor hemisphere, reported that patients with parietal lesions showed no increase in sensory thresholds unless there was also involvement of the Rolandic region. They also noted difficulties with complex sensorimotor tasks such as using scissors, dressing, and making block constructions in patients with right posterior lesions as well as some of the visuospatial and body image disturbances described below.

One of the most extensive investigations of somatosensory changes after brain injury was that of Semmes, et al. (1960). This work summarizes a good deal of the work of this group on the effects of penetrating missile wounds and it is difficult to do justice to it in a brief summary. One major finding worth recording is the fact that this group found bilateral deficits on occasion in patients with left hemisphere lesions but only contralateral deficits after lesions of the right hemisphere. The difference was not statistically significant and to date there has been little or no confirmation of this hemispheric asymmetry. Semmes, et al., also reported bilateral difficulty in tactually guided learning in patients whose primary sensory deficit seemed restricted to one hand.

Corkin (1964) tested 95 patients who had undergone cortical excision for the relief of epilepsy and compared their performance with that of control subjects on sensory discrimination tasks and tests of tactual learning and problem solving. Her major findings were that sensory deficits and impairment in tactile object recognition were closely related to lesions in the Rolandic region of either side. No lasting sensory impairment was seen in patients whose pre- and post-central gyri were spared. The deficits were usually contralateral though some bilateral effects were produced by unilateral excisions. A wide range of measures such as pressure sensitivity, two-point discrimination threshold, and point localization were used. More complex functions such as tactually guided learning and problem solving showed deficits with removals in the right hemisphere regardless of location of the lesion within the hemisphere. Generalization from these findings is limited since left posterior parietal lesions were not specifically studied.

An extension of this work was reported by Corkin, Milner, and Rasmussen (1970). Tests of pressure sensitivity, two-point discrimination, point localization, position sense, and tactual object recognition were given to 127 cases of limited unilateral cortical removal. Pre-operative, post-operative and follow-up measurements were taken. This study confirmed the earlier report that lasting sensory loss was highly correlated with lesions of the postcentral gyrus and was particularly severe with involvement of the contralateral hand area. Normal scores were reported on patients with precentral lesions which did not encroach upon the postcentral hand area. Lesions of the parietal lobe outside the postcentral gyrus produced transient loss or no loss at all. Extra-parietal lesions produced little or no sign of somatosensory change. Ipsilateral sensory defects were found in 20 of the 50 parietal lobe patients and, unlike the finding of Semmes *et al.* (1960) showed no relation to laterality of the lesion but did appear to be related to the size of the lesion.

Disorders of tactile perception

The present summary is concerned largely with disorders of perception rather than sensation. For the latter, readers should consult neurological texts.

The term *astereognosis* has been employed to identify a form of tactile agnosia in which the patient is unable to recognize objects which he feels. If the disorder is to conform to the general concept of agnosia it should be a higher perceptual disorder in the presence of intact primary sense modalities. Denny-Brown, Myer and Hornstein (1952) considered the basic disturbance to be a failure to synthesize separate tactile sensations into the perception of form, a process they termed *amorphosynthesis*. Elsewhere they considered the difficulty to be one of inability to carry out a 'summation of spatial impressions' (Denny-Brown and Chambers, 1958).

There has been doubt as to the existence of this as with other forms of agnosia. Several neuropsychological studies have directed themselves in whole or in part to the problem. Corkin (1964) found that impaired tactual recognition was seen only in patients who also had somato-sensory deficits. This was confirmed in the 1970 study previously mentioned. . . 'Impaired tactual recognition of common objects reflected the sensory status of the hand, and, in this series of patients, there were no object-recognition deficits that were disproportionate to the sensory loss.' (p.57).

Semmes (1965) clarified the relation of sensory status to astereognosis in a study of left hemisphere, right hemisphere, and bilateral lesions. She found that impaired performance on tests of tactual shape discrimination was seen both in the absence as well as the presence of sensory defect. An examination of the cases without sensory defect revealed that the impairment was specific to shape, the discrimination of texture, size, and roughness being unaffected. The impairment was, however, related to spatial orientation even when this was measured by a visual task. 'It was suggested, therefore, that impaired shape discrimination after brain injury depends on a general spatial factor as well as on the status of somatic sensation.' (p.312) Either of these factors seemed capable of producing impairment of tactile form discrimination but when both were present the impairment was more severe suggesting that the factors are independent but additive. Semmes found that they tended to occur together in right hemisphere lesions and she assumed that this was because of the size of the lesion, a large lesion being needed to affect both sensation and orientation. 'Paradoxically although each of the factors is more localizable in the left hemisphere than the right and the parietal region is implicated for both, these factors show no tendency toward association. One must therefore assume separate foci for the two factors within the left parietal region' (p.312). Both specific testing of tactual recognition (De Renzi and Scotti, 1969) as well as the wealth of evidence cited later in the chapter would support the idea that the prime representation of the spatial factor which may contribute to astereo-gnosis has its major location in the posterior cerebral areas, particularly of the right hemisphere.

The only standard psychological measure of tactual form perception is the Seguin-Goddard formboard which has been adapted in the much used Halstead-Reitan battery of tests. Teuber and Weinstein (1954) showed that men with posterior lesions performed significantly poorer on this task than those with anterior lesions though all brain damaged subjects were significantly inferior to controls. This latter finding has been replicated many times by Reitan and his co-workers (Reitan and Davison, 1974).

Visual object recognition also appears to be related more closely to the right parietal regions than elsewhere. Warrington and Rabin (1970) found that a right parietal group was much inferior to others on a series of perceptual matching tasks of simple perceptual attributes but that this failure was not related to their poor performance on the Gollin incomplete figures test (Gollin, 1960) suggesting that failure of recognition of features (which was required in the matching tasks) could not account for impairment on the test of visual recognition. There was, however, a correlation between the performance on matching tasks and more complex tasks of spatial analysis such as Block Designs suggesting that there was a common spatial element involved in the two types of task but that this differed in complexity. A new test of object recognition was introduced by Warrington and Taylor (1973). This consisted of the recognition of objects photographed from a 'conventional' and an 'unconventional' view. The right posterior group was selectively impaired on this test compared to all other groups, having a very marked deficit whereas the deficit of other brain damaged groups compared with control subjects was much smaller. Right posterior subjects were again inferior on the recognition of Gollin's incomplete figures though not nearly as much as on the new recognition task. Other visuoperceptual tasks such as figure-ground discrimination showed no differ-ences between any of the brain damaged subgroups though all groups were inferior to controls.

Apart from tactile object recognition early studies (e.g. Battersby, Krieger, and Bender, 1955) suggested that tactile discrimination learning might not be more impaired with posterior lesions than with lesions in other locations though Semmes, *et al.* (1954) did find that patients with lesions of the parietal lobe, unlike other patients showed no transfer effect from one modality to another. This may reflect a loss of cross-modal association.

Both Corkin (1965) and Milner (1965) used visually guided and tactually guided maze learning in patients with variously located surgical lesions. Small parietal lesions had little effect upon performance while right hemisphere lesions either frontal or temporal produced a marked impairment.

A study of De Renzi, Faglioni, and Scotti (1970) showed that tactile searching like visual searching is poorer for the contralateral field for both left and right hemisphere lesions but that the poorest performances were made by the right posterior group.

Disorders of intersensory association

Studies on intersensory association or cross-modal integration are of interest because such integration or associations between different forms of sense information would appear to be basic to many higher functions. Damage to the region in which such integration is likely to take place, i.e. the area of conjunction of the temporal, parietal, and occipital lobes in the dominant hemisphere has often been said to produce the most marked losses of cognitive functions. Few studies relating cross-modal association problems with locus of lesion have appeared to date.

Butters and Brody (1968) found that patients with neurologically confirmed dominant parietal lobe damage were particularly impaired on cross-modal matching tasks (auditory-visual, tactual-visual, visual-tactual) whereas fronto-temporal patients were unimpaired either on intra-modal or cross-modal tasks. Deficits on the auditory-visual matching task were closely associated with reading difficulties confirming the notion that this cross-modal association is prerequisite for reading. Many of the parietal patients who were impaired on the visual-tactual and tactual-visual matching tasks were also impaired on copying tests which are often used to assess constructional praxis whereas those with mild or absent signs of parietal involvement showed little or no copying impairment. 'The possibility that certain kinds of intersensory associations or integrations may underlie some constructional apraxia disorders and other voluntary motor behaviour is intriguing and certainly deserving of further study.' (p.342)

Butters, Barton, and Brody (1970) found some impairment of cross-modal association (auditory-visual matching) in patients with severe parietal signs but none in those with only mild parietal signs. The care that must be exercized in interpretation of findings was highlighted by the subsequent finding that the impairment of right parietal patients on the auditory-visual task was associated with an auditory decoding problem rather than failure of cross-modal association. The inferred size of the lesions and the propinquity of the auditory association area make it possible that the difficulty arose from disruption of function in this area rather than from parietal damage.

Taking the data from these two studies it does appear that there is some evidence to support the contention that the left parietal area may be dominant for cross-modal associations.

Kotzmann (1972) compared the performance of 10 unilateral left lesion patients with 10 unilateral right and 10 control subjects on a tactile-visual recognition task. Subjects were asked to palpate two classes of objects and to choose the corresponding drawing from a multiple choice visual array. One set of objects was meaningful (pipe, eggcup, bolt, etc.) and the other meaningless (moulded nonsense shapes). The brain damaged groups performed more poorly than control subjects on both tactual recognition tasks. The meaningful/meaningless dichotomy was not related to the laterality of the lesion in any simple way. Left hemisphere subjects had about equal difficulty with the two tactual tasks while right hemisphere subjects performed more poorly on the meaningless task than on the meaningful. An extension of this work might shed further light on the asymmetry of function with regard to tactual perception in the same way that auditory perceptual studies have done for the different classes of auditory information described in the previous chapter.

Symbolic (quasi-spatial) syntheses

Luria in a number of publications has pointed to the importance of the 'tertiary zones' of the left hemisphere in relationships which are logical or symbolic in character. He argues that these relationships are 'quasi-spatial' in nature and this conception provides a basis for understanding what at first appear to be quite separately based disturbances. The first example is acalculia. Although the patient with a dominant parietal lesion can understand and remember a problem and may even think of certain rules which would be appropriate to the solution he is unable to carry out the necessary operations. As outlined below, if the description of the problem contains a number of symbolic relations the patient will have even further difficulty. The simplest examples may be found in the operations of addition and subtraction. The appropriateness of the term 'quasi-spatial' becomes apparent when it is realized that the significance of a number alters according to its spatial relation to other numbers, e.g. the figure 2 in the number 42 has a different significance from the 2 in 24. Luria provides the following example 'To subtract 7 from 31, as a rule we begin by rounding the first number and obtain the result $30 - 7 = 23$. We then add the remaining unit, placing it in the right-hand column, and obtain the result $23 + 1 = 24$. The operation is much more complex when we subtract a number of two digits (for example, $51 - 17$), when, besides observing the conditions just mentioned, we have to carry over from the tens column and to retain the double system of elements in the operative memory.' (1973b, pp. 154-155)

If one employs a series of mathematical operations of increasing difficulty (e.g. addition or subtraction of one figure numbers; addition or subtraction of two figure numbers; of three figure numbers; multiplication of two or three figure numbers) patients with lesions in this region will break down well below the level which might be expected of them from their educational or occupational level. For the 'spatial' reason mentioned above patients who have no difficulty with a problem such as 796—342 will fail repeatedly on seemingly similar problems, e.g. 534—286 as well as more complex mathematical operations since the 'spatial' or 'carry-over' element is essential for the solution of the second problem but not the first. The rather different characteristics which frontal patients experience with numerical problem solving have been described in Chapter 4.

The other major area of difficulty for patients with lesions of the dominant inferior parietal region is that involving the abstract logical relations of syntax. The communication of such relationships can be greatly affected by the sequence of words, by the introduction of relational terms such as prepositions of space or time, or by more complex syntactical structures. Note the completely different meaning of 'my wife's brother' from 'my brother's wife', or the difference between 'the bridge over the water' and 'the water over the bridge'. Identical words in different situations take on quite different meanings dictated by the structure of the whole. It is this significance of structure that may present difficulties for patients with lesions of the dominant parietal region though they show clear evidence of understanding the individual elements. The Token Test provides excellent opportunity for demonstrating these difficulties and is one of the reasons why this test is so sensitive to dominant hemisphere impairment.

The difficulty with logico-grammatical constructions forms part of 'semantic aphasia'. The numerous manifestations of aphasia are described in Chapter 9.

Disorders of spatial orientation

It will become obvious that the concept of spatial disorientation as employed in clinical neurology encompasses a variety of different disorders and even some of these, about which there is some consensus as to their validity as distinct entities, may well turn out on further investigation to be more complexly determined than is thought at present. The brief description of the commonly reported spatial disabilities which follows obviously overlaps in part with the preceding section on perceptual disorders and that on disorders of personal space or body schema which follows. The disorders in this section are mainly of the appreciation of spatial relationships between and within objects in extrapersonal space. The principal categories are: (1) disorders in the judgment of the location or orientation of stimuli both with respect to each other and to the person; (2) impairment of memory for location; (3) topographical disorientation and loss of topographical memory; (4) route finding difficulties; (5) constructional apraxia; (6) spatial dyslexia and dyscalculia.

Disorders of location and orientation

Benton (1969) suggests that a distinction might be made between impairment of localization of a single stimulus which could be termed a difficulty of 'absolute' localization, and difficulty with the perceived spatial relations between two or more stimuli which could be termed a difficulty of 'relative' localization. Paterson and Zangwill (1944) referred to 'defective appreciation of spatial relations in the visual field with or without impairment of visual localization in the strict sense' as *visuospatial agnosia*, in other words, a dissociation between 'absolute' and 'relative' localization. They also confirmed earlier reports of a tendency to overstimate the distance of very near objects and to underestimate the distance of far objects.

Absolute localization may be checked by asking the patient to point to a stimulus placed in different parts of the visual field. This test is usually failed only by grossly impaired patients. Localization difficulty has also been inferred from other tests such as the bisection of lines. The performance of 12 patients with parieto-occipital traumatic lesions on this bisection task and other spatial tests was described by Bender and Teuber (1947) with the addition of a further occipital trauma case a year later (Bender and Teuber, 1948).

Tests of more complex spatial relations often bring out difficulties when none are apparent on simpler tests. The multiple choice version of the Benton Visual Retention Test (Benton, 1950) (Fig. 6.4) would appear sensitive to the subtler changes in perception of spatial relations and has been relatively neglected in the study of parietal lesions since its introduction as a diagnostic aid (Benton, 1952) though Alajouanine (1960) employed it in his studies of occipital lobe patients. The visuospatial difficulties which many of Alajouanine's occipital patients had on this task remind us of the dangers of dealing rigidly with lobar divisions.

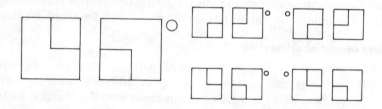

Fig. 6.4 Item 6 from multiple choice version of the Benton Visual Retention Test (from A.L. Benton (1956) *Archives of Neurology and Psychiatry*, **64**, 699, American Medical Association.

De Renzi, Faglioni, and Scotti (1971) have pointed out that spatial perception has been studied very often at a rather complex level, most tests having been derived from tests of intelligence or devised with various neurological symptoms in mind. For this reason they feel that 'it is difficult to disentangle the influence on performance of spatial as compared with praxic, intelligence, and memory factors' (p.490). They devised a very simple task where two rods jointed together could be placed at various orientations (angles) to each other. The subject's task was to align another pair of rods in the same orientation under the two conditions of visual, and tactile assistance. When tested in this way they found gross impairment was associated almost exclusively with posterior lesions of the nondominant hemisphere. They contrast this with the less striking asymmetry shown on more complex spatial tasks which are also poorly performed by a proportion of dominant posterior cases. Miller (1972a) comments:

It may well be that the important factor in determining whether an apparently spatial task is affected by left posterior lesions as well as right is the degree of verbal mediation used by the subject. Although a task may be spatial in nature, this does not prevent a subject from using verbal reasoning in its solution and to the extent that this occurs the task will be more liable to disruption by left-sided lesions even though the task may be particularly difficult to verbalize. (p.86)

Another simple test used by the Milan group was the reproduction of the location of a number of crosses drawn at random on paper, the measure of performance being taken from the sum of the distances by which the subjects' copies deviated from the originals (De Renzi and Faglioni, 1967). A right hemisphere group was inferior to a left hemisphere group on this task.

The significance of the right hemisphere for localization was again demonstrated by Faglioni, Scotti, and Spinnler (1971). Right posterior lesion patients were most impaired on a visual localization task. The fact that two separate versions of the task, one visual and the other tactile were both poorly performed supports the notion that many deficits produced by parietal lesions are not modality specific.

Perhaps a separate factor in dealing with spatial relations is the ability to carry out reversible operations in space. Two studies (Butters and Barton, 1970; Butters, Barton, and Brody, 1970) have employed a number of measures of this type. (a) the Stick Test—patient is shown a simple arrangement of sticks and asked to copy them under the two conditions of sitting alongside or opposite the examiner; (b) the Pools Reflections Test which is modelled after one of the subtests of Cattell's *A Culture Free Test* (Cattell, 1944). From a number of alternatives the subject must select the one which represents the reflection which the sample would present to the viewer (See Fig. 6.5); (c) The Village Scene test. Here the subject is shown the model of a village and is asked to choose the correct photograph representing the scene from six photographs one of which is correct and the others are similar views in which the spatial relationships of features of the scene have been altered before being photographed. Both these studies produced data which suggest that this type of task is performed poorly by patients with either left or right parietal lesions. Patients with lesions in other areas showed little or on difficulty with these spatial reversible operations.

There also appears to be a little evidence that a dissociation may exist between localization disorders and the topographical disorders of orientation and memory (Hecaen, Ajuriaguerra, and Massonet, 1951; Gilliatt and Pratt, 1952) each type of disorder being seen in isolation in some individuals. Marie, Bouttier, and van Bogaert (1924) described a right prefrontal tumour which produced marked spatial disorientation in the patient but 'l'absence de troubles dans les fonctions en quelque sort primaires de l'appréciation spatiale, chez ce malade.' (p.217).

Impaired memory for location

Very little systematic work has been done in this area. Impaired memory for location may form part of a general amnesic disorder or it may be seen in association with other spatial difficulties. However, an occasional patient is seen who performs adequately on the usual spatial tasks but who may encounter difficulty when asked to recall spatial relationships even after a short delay. Such difficulties have been described in occipital cases and right parietal cases by Alajouanine (1960) who used the multiple choice version of the Benton Visual Retention Test as a recognition memory task.

Loosely related to this area was the experiment of De Renzi, Faglioni, and Scotti (1969) who tested a large group of unilateral lesion patients on a simple memory for position task under visual guidance or tactual guidance. Though all brain-damaged subjects performed more poorly than controls there was no significant difference between the right and left hemisphere groups. The impairment was greater in those with visual field defects than those without. 'However, the finding that this impairment was significantly more marked on the tactile than on the visual memory test suggests that it is related to the concomitant injury of posterior areas of the brain rather than to the effect of the visual deficit.' (p.283).

Patients are seen frequently who have a disproportionate difficulty on the memory-for-location aspect of the Tactual Performance Test (TPT) of the Reitan Neuropsychological Test Battery. Though a large number of studies have been reported in which the TPT is demonstrated to be generally sensitive to cerebral impairment (Reitan and Davison, 1974) there is little or no available information on any differential effect of location of lesion on the memory aspect of the task. Since the patient is not advised in advance that he will be asked to recall the location as well as the shapes of the objects which he must place in the formboard (using only tactile information), inferences about individual patient's performances must be limited. It is a striking fact, nevertheless, that after the prolonged experience which this test gives, many patients with cerebral impairment will fail to recall correctly the location of even one of the shapes.

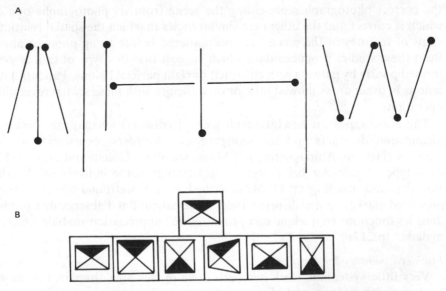

Fig. 6.5 A. Sample designs, Stick Test (from Benson and Barton, 1970)
B. Pool reflection item (from Butters et al., 1970).

A comparison of differences between the recall and copying versions of the Rey Figure (Rey, 1941; Osterreith, 1944; Rey, 1959) might also prove valuable in this regard.

Topographical disorientation and loss of topographical memory

Several different difficulties may be encompassed under this heading: (1) the inability to recall the spatial arrangement of familiar surroundings such as the disposition of rooms within the patient's house, or the disposition of furniture within a room; (2) The inability to recall and described well known geographical relationships with which the patient was formerly familiar. These and related areas are beginning to receive attention from neuropsychologists.

Benton (1969) considers the basic defect to be difficulty in calling up visual images—'We deal here with an impairment in "revisualization", a failure to retrieve long-established visual memories' (p.219) This is similar to the 'visual irreminescence' of Critchley (1953) which is mentioned in the next chapter in relation to lesions of the occipital lobes, particularly vascular lesions.

Compared with other aspects of spatial ability topographical orientation has received comparatively little attention. Ratcliff and Newcombe (1973) point out that most studies have been concerned with situations in which the patient can explore spatial relationships without gross changes in his own position, i.e. they have been more concerned with spatial agnosia.

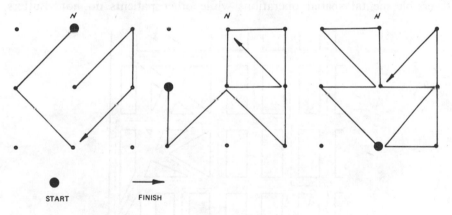

START   FINISH

Fig. 6.6 Items from a locomotor map following test (from Semmes *et al.*, 1955, courtesy of Dr Josephine Semmes).

In 1955 Semmes, *et al.* described an objective test of spatial orientation. This consisted of 15 diagrams of the type shown in Figure 6.6. The nine dots on each map represented nine circles on the floor of a room, the circles being some 137 cms apart. One wall of the room was designated as North and North was marked on the maps. With the map maintained in constant orientation to his body the subject was required to walk around each designated path. In this way the orientation of the person to the room was constantly changing. Both visual maps and 'tactile-only' versions were provided. Parietal lobe cases were significantly inferior to non-parietal patients and to control subjects. There was no difference between non-parietal cases and controls. Furthermore, as the disorder proved to be unrelated to perceptual modality (visual or tactile) Semmes *et al.*, felt that it was incorrect to label the difficulty as part of visuo-spatial agnosia. A second study (Weinstein, *et al.*, 1956) confirmed the poor performance of parietal subjects on the route finding task but, in this study, poor performance was also shown by frontal subjects though to a lesser degree. These frontal subjects also performed poorly on a test of personal orientation.

A later study (Semmes *et al.* 1963) extended these findings and compared the results on this test of extra-personal orientation with a test of personal space in which the subject was asked to touch parts of his own body in the order indicated by numbers on diagrams of the human body. Brain injury affected both tasks to an approximately equal degree. Statistical analysis showed that, though the two tasks were significantly related in the brain-injured group studied, there were also independent elements.

With regard to the locus of the lesion 'both personal and extra-personal orientation were impaired by lesions of the posterior part of the left hemisphere. Anterior lesions (particularly those of the left hemisphere) tended to impair personal but not extra-personal orientation, whereas the converse was the case for right posterior lesions' (p.769).

Two studies cited in the previous section (Butters and Barton, 1970; **Butters,** Barton, and Brody, 1970) have shown that parietal patients have difficulty with reversible mental spatial operations while other patients do not. Butters,

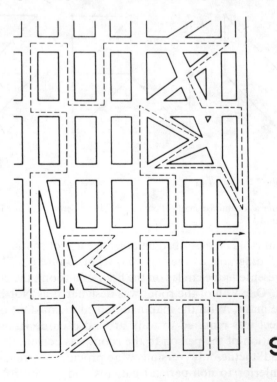

Fig. 6.7 Money's standardized Road Map Test of Direction Sense.

Soeldner, and Fedio (1972) extended these findings by including a test which cannot be performed by rotating an external object either at the concrete or the abstract level. In the test, Money's Standardized Road-Map Test of Direction Sense (Fig. 6.7) the patient needs the ability to rotate himself in imagery or on an abstract level. With the road map in a fixed stationary relationship he has to describe the right or left turns which would need to be made while following the route.

A comparison of left frontal and right parietal patients on this task allowed a test of Teuber's hypothesis that the frontal and parietal regions mediate qualitatively different spatial abilities (1) spatial orientation to external objects mediated by the parietal regions, particularly the right, and (2) spatial discrimination involving the subject's own body mediated particularly by the left frontal region. The study demonstrated a partial double dissociation between the two groups on the test of personal or egocentric space (Money's Test) and a test of extrapersonal space (the Stick Test described above). While the authors mentions a number of clinical, statistical and methodological restrictions there appears to be tentative support for Teuber's hypothesis.

Two early studies of Pierre Marie reported disorientation in space with major lesions of the frontal lobe comprising a traumatic left frontal case, a case of right frontal trauma, and a right frontal tumour (Marie and Béhague, 1919; Marie, Bouttier and van Bogaert, 1924).

In testing for difficulties in spatial orientation care should be taken in excluding topographical difficulties on the basis of verbal tests only. 'Long-standing associations of a purely verbal character may enter into the verbal descriptions and give an impression of the appreciation of topographic relationships which in fact the patient no longer possesses.' (Benton, 1969, p.221). Benton reports a case of De Renzi and Faglioni (1962) who was 'completely unable to make localizations on a map of Milan, nevertheless could name the streets and public buildings associated with a given locality as well as all the gates of the city. However, he could not specify the spatial relationships among the gates and his descriptions of routes were schematic and imperfect.' (p. 220-221)

Benton, Levin, and van Allen (1974) have recently made a more systematic study of this distinction. Geographic orientation was assessed in patients with unilateral cerebral disease using two types of task. The first required the localization of states and cities on a map of the United States while the second was a verbal test of the directional relations between places. Two subtests in this second (verbal) category failed to discriminate between left and right hemisphere cases or brain damaged subjects from controls on the map localization test. A 'vector' score was calculated showing a tendency of the subject to shift localization either toward the right or left part of the map. This score differentiated between the two hemisphere groups and suggested neglect of the visual field contralateral to the side of the lesion in some of the patients. These findings demonstrate the interaction of defects in producing impaired performance on complex tasks.

It has become evident that the relation between locus of lesion and topographical loss is less clear than with some other 'spatial' disorders. However the most frequent reports have been after posterior lesions, right, left or bilateral (Kleist, 1934; Brain, 1941; Paterson and Zangwill, 1945; Cogan, 1960; De Renzi and Faglioni, 1962; Hécaen, 1969).

Route finding difficulties

These patients, unlike some of those described above may be well able to give adequate verbal descriptions of familiar routes but are unable to execute them either by drawing or taking them in real life situations. The deficit is often described as one where the patient experiences difficulty in finding his way around the immediate environs of the ward or hospital or loses his way *en route* between the hospital and home. It is often difficult to decide how much of the difficulty is due to memory disturbance in a particular case without detailed examination. Some writers such as Brain (1941) and Gloning (1965) have explained at least one form of defective route finding on the basis of unawareness of, or inattention to the left half of space which results in a much higher proportion of right hand turns than would otherwise be the case. Others see it as part of an agnosia for one half of space, the socalled 'unilateral spatial agnosia' (Hécaen and Angelergues, 1963).

Little attention has been given to an analysis of the abilities necessary to adequate route following but they are obviously many and varied. For this and other reasons no standard neuropsychological tests have yet been developed. Some, such as the maze tests of Porteus (1965) and Elithorn (1955) which have been suggested for use in this area bear only a superficial resemblance to real-life route finding tasks. They are heavily dependent upon visual searching, visual planning and other factors discussed in Chapter 4 while they do not seem to have the necessary ingredient that the subject must operate continuously within a set of spatial coordinates which, for the most part, he must have internalized and to which he must make reference for the successful completion of his task. The type of maze problem used by Walsh (1960) and Milner (1965) eliminates the immediate visual cues of direction and a programmable maze of this type (the Austin Maze) which might be suitable for research in this area is in use in our clinic.

Constructional apraxia

The first modern description of constructional difficulties in patients with cerebral impairment is usually attributed to Kleist (Strauss, 1924; Kleist, 1934). After first considering certain drawing disabilities of neurological patients to be a form of 'optic apraxia' he later introduced the term 'constructional apraxia.' Moreover, Benton pointed out that Kleist insisted that this particular disorder was to be distinguished from others that were obviously rooted in visuoperceptual disorders and thought that the basis of the disorder lay in a disruption between visual and kinesthetic processes. This would accord well with what we would call today the general conception of a 'disconnection syndrome' alluded to in earlier chapters.

Many early investigators had felt that the failure of patients on certain tasks such as drawing and route-finding reflected a visuospatial disturbance. While many patients with constructional difficulties did have visuospatial problems there were also those who had for example, severe difficulties with drawing without showing a spatial deficit (Lhermitte and Trelles, 1933; Kroll and Stolbun, 1933; Mayer-Gross, 1935). Strauss (1924) defined a pure case of constructional apraxia as one with adequate form perception, perceptual discrimination and perceptual localization and absence of ideomotor apraxia or motor disability.

Later definitions include those of Critchley (1953), 'an executive defect within a visuospatial domain', and Benton (1967) 'an impairment in combinatory or organizing activity in which details must be clearly perceived and in which the relationships among the component parts of the entity must be apprehended if the desired synthesis of them is to be achieved.'

Constructional apraxia is often said to be the apraxia of the psychologist since it is more often revealed on neuropsychological examination than exhibited clinically. For this, and other reasons, numerous studies have been made of constructional disabilities in the past fifteen years. The present summary builds on reviews such as those of Benton (1969) and Warrington (1969).

The status of the concept of constructional apraxia

One of the most frequently asked questions is the following. Is constructional apraxia a single entity or are there separate, distinct types of disorder under this heading? In 1957 Ettlinger, Warrington, and Zangwill reported 10 cases in which right posterior cerebral lesions showed disturbances in spatial perception and manipulation. An investigation of the individual performances suggested the possibility of different varieties of constructional difficulty. Benton and Fogel (1962) pointed to the possible relation with the type of test employed or the activity under examination.

'Constructional praxis is a broad concept which has been applied to a number of rather different types of activities. These activities have in common the characteristic that they require the patient to assemble, join or articulate parts to form a single unitary structure. However, they may differ from each other in many respects, e.g. in complexity, in the type of movement and the degree of motor dexterity required in achieving the task, in the demands made on the higher intellectual functions, and in whether they involve construction in two or three spatial dimensions.'

Critchley (1953) had pointed out that three dimensional construction tasks appeared to be necessary since some patients with parietal lesions who had no difficulty on the commonly employed two dimensional tests displayed gross abnormalities of construction when the test moved into the third dimension. Such abnormalities could not be elicited by the usual clinical examination. Benton and Fogel confirmed this by demonstrating only a weak positive correlation between the performance of brain damaged subjects on a drawing test (Benton Visual Retention Test) and their newly constructed Three Dimensional Constructional Praxis task (Figure 6.8). Fourteen patients were adequate on the copying task but defective on the three dimensional task whereas another eight were adequate on the three dimensional task but showed defective copying.

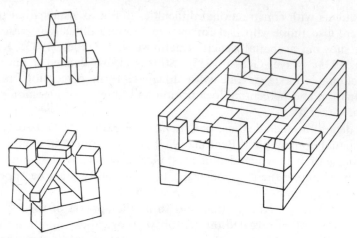

Fig. 6.8 Three dimension constructional praxis test (drawn from A.L. Benton and M.L. Fogel. (1962) *Archives of Neurology,* 7, 347-354. American Medical Association).

In a later study Benton (1967) addressed himself specifically to the question and, since it appears to be the only such study it is worth referring to in a little detail. Benton employed four apparently dissimilar tests—Benton Visual Retention Test, Stick-construction, Block Designs, Three Dimensional Constructional Praxis—and measured the concordance between various combinations of tests. The concurrence of failure varied from chance level upward for different pairs of tests but even the highest degree of concurrence fell well below perfect agreement. There was also considerable intraindividual variation in performance level on these tests. However, there did seem to be more relation between the last three tests than there was between any of these and the drawing test (VRT). Benton concluded that there may be at least two types of tests namely graphic tasks and assembly tasks and that empirical study may well reveal others.

The variety of tests which have been used to elicit constructional apraxia is great.

1.   spontaneous or free drawing. For a careful and detailed description with illustration of the common errors seen with drawing tasks the reader is referred to Warrington (1969).

2.   drawing from a model, e.g. Benton Visual Retention Test (Benton, 1962) as well as simpler clinical versions.

3.   stick pattern constructions, e.g. Stick Test, Goldstein and Scheerer (1941)

4.   block designs, usually modelled on the Kohs test (Goldstein and Scheerer, 1941; Wechsler, 1958)

5.   test of spatial analysis (mentioned above)

6.   three dimensional constructions (Critchley, 1953; Benton and Fogel, 1962)

7.   reconstruction of puzzles, e.g. (Benson and Barton, 1970) and the Object Assembly subtest of the Wechsler Adult Intelligence Scale (WAIS)

In view of the fact that many brain damaged patients fail on some of these and pass on others it is obviously unsatisfactory to use failure on any one as an operational definition of constructional apraxia as some writers have done. Since the WAIS is about the most widely used test in the assessment of higher functions it provides the most frequent opportunity to observe the dissociation which so often occurs between performance on the Block Designs and Object Assembly subtests. Obviously many tests, particularly Block Designs, are multi-factorial in nature and failure on such a test may arise from a number of causes which need to be explored if the significance of the failure is to be seen. The failure may rest on inability to visually analyse the model or be made difficult by disruption of the patient's spatial schemata or, as outlined above, be im-possible because the patient is unable to initiate and monitor a plan for the solution of the task.

Some of the factors which need to be taken into consideration in interpreting a patient's failure on constructional tasks have been mentioned in the study by Benson and Barton (1970) and are further discussed in relation to clinical assess-ment in Chapter 9. Benson and Barton suggest that the more general term 'constructional disability would be more appropriate for most findings, reserv-ing the term 'constructional apraxia' for the case having the features outlined by Kleist. Their study with a variety of tests showed that right hemisphere lesions produced more consistent disturbances than left, while posterior lesions of either hemisphere produced more consistent disturbances than anterior ones.

Laterality and constructional apraxia

Most early cases described as showing constructional apraxia had bilateral posterior lesions. Later, cases were described where constructional apraxia was seen together with one or more symptoms of the Gerstmann syndrome which suggested that the left or dominant parietal area was of importance as part of the substratum of constructional abilities. Still later, attention began to be paid to the role of the minor hemisphere when it was clearly demonstrated that unilateral right hemisphere lesions could produce the symptom (Paterson and Zangwill, 1944; Ajuriaguerra and Hécaen, 1960).

The first large systematic survey of laterality of lesion and constructional apraxia was that of Piercy, Hécaen and Ajuriaguerra (1960). In 403 consecutive cases with unilateral cerebral lesions 67 cases showed constructional apraxia. Of these, 42 had lesions on the right and 25 on the left. This represented 22.3 per cent of the right hemisphere cases and 11.6 per cent of the left. The dis-proportion between right and left cases was even greater for retrorolandic cases some 37.8 per cent of the right posterior cases showing apraxia against 16.1 per cent of the left. Since that time numerous studies have confirmed the much higher incidence of constructional apraxia with nondominant hemisphere lesions, e.g. (Benton, 1962; Benton and Fogel, 1962 Costa and Vaughan, 1962; Piercy and Smyth, 1962; Arrigoni and De Renzi, 1964).

Many studies have reported that constructional apraxia is not only more frequent with right hemisphere lesions but that it also tends to be more severe, i.e. patients show more grossly defective performances (Benton and Fogel, 1962; Benton, 1967; Gainotti, Messerli, and Tissot, 1972).

The assumption of a true relationship between lesions of the nondominant hemisphere and constructional apraxia has been seriously challenged by the study of Arrigoni and De Renzi (1964). While they also found a higher incidence of difficulties in right-sided lesions on each of three constructive tests in an unselected sample of hospitalized patients they felt that at least part of the difference might lie in the possibility that the lesions of the right hemisphere group were consistently larger. This possibility has also been alluded to by Costa and Vaughan (1962) and Benton (1965). Wolff (1962) had suggested that one reason for this might be the earlier presentation of dominant lesions because of language disturbances.

From their larger group Arrigoni and De Renzi matched left and right cases for severity of impairment using a reaction time measure which their earlier work had suggested was an index of cerebral impairment that was not affected by the location of lesion. The two groups of 44 patients produced the following findings (Table 6.1).

Table 6.1 Constructional apraxia and side of lesion

	Present	Absent
Right Hemisphere	27	17
Left Hemisphere	17	27

The difference was in the 'predicted' direction but was no longer significant (when tested by *chi square*). 'This result should make us extremely cautious in attributing a dominance (even if relative) to the right hemisphere with regard to constructive capacities.' (p.190) Benton (1969), in a summary of evidence to that time, pointed out that 'defective performance on the part of patients with left hemisphere disease is not at all rare. Thus, if right hemisphere "dominance" for visuoconstructive performance does exist, it does not appear comparable to the "dominance" for language performance exercised by the left hemisphere'. This does not mean that there are no qualitative differences between the two sides. In fact Arrigoni and De Renzi describe such differences.

Qualitative differences between the two hemispheres is the subject of Chapter 8 but numerous studies, including that of Arrigoni and De Renzi (1964) show characteristic differences in quality of performance on constructional tasks between left and right hemisphere cases (McFie and Zangwill, 1960; Piercy, Hécaen, and Ajuriaguerra, 1960; Warrington, James, and Kinsbourne, 1966; Gainotti, Messerli, and Tissot, 1972). The study of Warrington and her colleagues was directed to an examination of specially designed drawing tests which were rated by independent judges. Though there was no significant difference in degree of disability between the two groups they showed a dissociation of predominant types of error. 'The types of error made by patients with right hemisphere lesions suggest that these patients have difficulty in incorporating spatial information into their drawing performance, leading to disproportion and faulty articulation of parts of the drawing, while the patients with left hemisphere lesions seemed to experience difficulty in planning the drawing process, leading to simplified drawings of the model.' (p.82) Similar findings were described by Gainotti, Messerli, and Tissot (1972) who found left hemisphere cases produced simplified drawings which were helped by the presentation of a model for copying while the visuospatial disturbances of the right hemisphere cases were not helped to any degree by a model. The following table drawn largely from Warrington (1969) summarizes the main differences (Table 6.2).

Table 6.2 Laterality of lesion and characteristics of drawing

Right hemisphere	Left hemisphere
Scattered and fragmented	Coherent but simplified
Loss of spatial relations	Preservation of spatial relations
Faulty orientation	Correct orientation
Energetic drawing	Slow and laborious
Addition of lines to try to make drawing correct.	Gross lack of detail

Both Warrington (1969) and Benson and Barton (1970) have put forward hypotheses about the relative contributions of the left and right hemispheres to visuoconstructive tasks. '. . .right hemisphere lesions produce disorders of visuo-spatial perception while left-sided lesions disturb motor function (apraxia)' (Benson and Barton, p.21). . . '. . .the suggestion that the right hemisphere supplies a perceptual and the left hemisphere an executive component to the task.' (Warrington, p.80). Earlier studies had already suggested this hypothesis (Hécaen, Ajuriaguerra, and Massonet, 1951; Duensing, 1954; Ettlinger, Warrington and Zangwill, 1957; Ajuriaguerra and Hécaen, 1960; McFie and Zangwill, 1960; and Piercy, Hécaen, and Ajuriaguerra, 1960). Several of these studies are cited by both authors. The argument that the right hemisphere contributes a perceptual element is supported indirectly by studies showing that purely perceptual tasks (without a constructional component) are more poorly performed by patients with right hemisphere lesions (Chapter 8).

Results of constructional tests in a small number of patients who had undergone cerebral commissurotomy has been cited as additional evidence of the greater role of the nondominant hemisphere in constructional performance (Gazzaniga, Bogen, and Sperry, 1965; Gazzaniga, 1970). Though commissurotomy subjects may perform better when using the left hand (right hemisphere) than the right hand, the fact that performance was below par with either hand suggests bilateral but unequal representation of constructional abilities.

Constructional apraxia and locus of lesion
There seems little doubt that, if one can consider frontal constructional difficulties as forming a separate entity, the parietal lobe particularly on the nondominant side is most closely related with constructional disabilities which have the characteristics of the Kleist-Strauss formulation. Writers not wishing to be limited by the artificial lobar boundaries often relate constructional apraxia to the ill-defined area at the junction of the parietal, temporal, and occipital lobes, Luria's zone of overlapping. In a study of 105 cases with tumours to the temporal lobe Petrovici (1972) found a complete absence of constructional

apraxia in the 77 cases which were completely restricted to the temporal lobe, or in 4 frontotemporal cases. On the other hand the remaining 24 cases with added involvement of the parietal lobe or the parietal and occipital lobes, had 11 cases of constructional apraxia (4 left and 7 right).

A factorial study could be conducted to see whether the parietal, overlapping, and occipital areas contribute separate factors to the 'posterior type' of constructional disability. There are, however, anatomical and pathological reasons why this is difficult if not impossible.

Bilateral parietal or diffuse cerebral lesions lead to very marked disturbances both of constructional praxis and spatial orientation though they are often masked by accompanying organic dementia (Allison, 1962).

Associated disabilities. The most widely quoted study of disabilities associated with constructional difficulties is that of McFie and Zangwill (1960). They compared the visual-constructive impairment of 8 left hemisphere cases (all in the posterior parietal region) with that of right sided cases from earlier studies of the Cambridge group. Table 6.3 gives the quantitative features of the study.

Table 6.3 Comparison between left- and right-sided lesion (McFie and Zangwill 1960).

	Left		Right	
	No. examined	No. with disability	No. examined	No. with disability
Unilateral neglect	8	1	21	14
Dressing disability	8	1	15	10
Cube counting	6	(1)	7	6
Paper cutting	4	0	10	9
Topographical loss	8	1	18	9
Right-left discrimination	8	5	21	0
Weigl's sorting test	6	5	16	1

It is clear that there is a strong association between the first five symptoms and right sided lesions while the last two symptoms are seen almost exclusively with left sided lesions. McFie and Zangwill felt that their left sided cases corresponded more closely to the classical description of constructional apraxia whereas the difficulties encountered by the right hemisphere patients were more closely associated with visuospatial agnosia. As well as the difference in associated symptoms there also appeared to be qualitative differences in the constructional disabilities of left and right cases. Failure of a high proportion of left sided cases on Weigl's sorting test appeared to be part of a general intellectual impairment which was not seen with right sided cases. Gainotti, Messerli, and Tissot (1972) confirmed this relationship. In right sided cases there was no relation between constructional apraxia and mental impairment while with left sided cases there was a significant relationship between constructional apraxia, mental impairment, and ideomotor apraxia. A number of studies by Benton (Benton, 1962; Benton and Fogel, 1962; Benton, 1967) have shown a generally higher incidence of mental impairment in brain damaged patients with constructional apraxia than those without such apraxia. Despite this general relationship there were both patients with severe mental impairment who showed no defective praxis and patients with severe constructional impairment whose intelligence levels were around the level expected from their educational background. The impairment level was based on the work of Fogel (1962, 1964) using the difference between obtained and expected intelligence scores.

The problems which arise in the interpretation of the significance of associated disabilities are discussed by Warrington (1969).

Relation between visuoperceptive and visuoconstructive deficits

Two major hypotheses have been put forward in the literature over the past fifty years, firstly that visuoconstructive difficulties occur on the basis of perceptual deficit and, secondly, that at least the special form of constructional difficulty known as constructional apraxia is a separate entity. Some writers, from Kleist onwards, have put forward the notion that constructional apraxia depended on a lesion of the retrorolandic zone where the visual and somaesthetic modalities are integrated. Kleist himself postulated that the left hemisphere was the one mainly implicated in patients with constructional difficulties which were not on the basis of visuoperceptive defects.

Dee (1970) found that 42 out of 46 patients with constructional apraxia had significant visuoperceptive defects and was unable to demonstrate any hemispheric differences apart from the finding that three of the four patients with apraxia and no visuoperceptive defect had lesions in the left hemisphere. He concluded that most constructional apraxia is due to a disorder of visual perception irrespective of the side of lesion though he allowed that other explanations must be sought for the minority of cases without perceptual deficits. Further examination of the cases from the 1970 study by Dee and Benton (1970) showed that the patients with constructional apraxia also failed on a haptic-spatial task, supporting the contention of Semmes (1965, 1968) that many spatial disorders extend beyond a single modality and are not determined by primary sensory defect, i.e. they are multi-modal in character. Other studies, e.g. De Renzi and Scotti (1969) also suggest that posterior lesions may produce spatial difficulties embracing more than one sense modality. This seems reasonable in view of the anatomical model accepted here.

Frontal apraxia

Constructional difficulties with anterior lesions have been reported sporadically since the early finding of Pollack (1938) that frontal lesions may occasionally disturb constructional praxis. Luria and Tsvetkova (1964) summarized the difference between anterior and posterior lesions—

'In lesions of the parieto-occipital part of the brain the general factor underlying constructive disturbances is a loss of spatial organization of the elements. . . . . In lesions of the frontal lobes the general factor underlying constructive disturbances is a loss of programming and regulating of sequential behaviour . . . instability of the primary intention or program and to the inability to compare the results with the preliminary intention. . .' (p.95). This type of disruption has been considered in Chapter 4.

Spatial dyslexia and dyscalculia

This form of dyslexia may be clearly distinguishable at times from dyslexia of a symbolic nature. The patient can recognize letters and words but may be unable to read. At least part of this difficulty is attributable to difficulty with the continuous scanning movements necessary for reading. The disorganization in the directional control of eye movements varies a good deal from patient to patient but in severely disabled patients the fixations appear to be made at random so that fixation may jump from one part of a line to another and from part of one line to another line some distance away. Obviously a patient with this difficulty cannot make sense of printed material. In less severely affected cases the patient may skip only occasional words so that he is able to fill in the sense of what he is reading.

Some patients' reading difficulties appear to depend largely upon unilateral spatial neglect. For this reason spatial dyslexia is seen rather more frequently with right hemisphere lesions. Benton (1969) explains the effect in the following way: 'The patient initially fixates on a point which is at some distance to the right of the beginning of the line, reads to the end of the line and then returns to a point on the next line which is somewhat to the right of the beginning of the line. The result is, of course, that he cannot make any sense of what he reads and he soon becomes confused.' (p.219) This explanation is very similar to that usually employed in the explanation of reading difficulty of the hemianopic patient (especially those with a left half field loss) which is described in the next chapter.

The analysis of calculation difficulties and their significance is described in Chapter 8. Luria's interpretation of acalculia in terms of quasi-spatial synthesis has already been outlined above.

Hécaen (1969) divides the acalculias into three types which he believes have different mechanisms. These are (1) alcalculia based on an alexia of figures and numerals; (2) inability to do arithmetical sums (anarithmia); (3) dyscalculia of the spatial type. Hecaen and Angelergues (1961) found a predominance of left hemisphere lesions with the first two types and a predominance of right hemisphere lesions with the third. Approximately 24 per cent of 148 right hemisphere cases had this spatial acalculia compared with only 2 per cent of 195 left hemisphere cases.

Spatial disorders; some general comments

The hemispheric asymmetry of function with regard to spatial disorders is summarized in Chapter 8. Bender and Diamond (1970) remind us of the . . . 'extensive interrelationships among the various sensory-motor systems that characterize normal perceptual function. . . cerebellar, oculomotor and vestibular influences are prominent factors in visual function besides the visual projection system itself and the subject's state of alertness. It is not possible therefore to ascribe disturbances in perception of space to disease of the parietal lobe or, more specifically, to disease of the right parietal lobe' (p.184)

While one might agree with this statement if it means *only* to disease of the parietal lobe there is little doubt that the accumulated evidence indicts the right parietal lobe most strongly in certain disorders. There is some evidence, too, that the presence of residual perceptual and spatial deficits may be the principal reason why recovery after right hemisphere strokes is more difficult to achieve than after seemingly comparable lesions in the left hemisphere (Marquardsen, 1969; Hurwitz and Adams, 1972).

Finally, it is obvious that the concept of 'spatial disorientation' or even 'spatial difficulty' is a very gross one. Dee and Benton (1970) comment—'Assuming that spatial perception may be analyzed into "partial" functions, it would not be surprising to find hemispheric differences in the representation of such functions.' (p.270) It would also be surprising if these partial functions were not closely related to the specific outlying association areas of the different modalities.

Unilateral spatial neglect (USN)

Although unilateral spatial neglect was first described by Holmes (1918) in the visual modality and the phenomenon confirmed by Poppelreuter (1923) and Riddoch (1935), it was not until the detailed description by Brain (1941) of inattention for the left half of space in three patients with large right-sided parietal lesions that the condition attracted much attention. It has been variously defined but the essential features are expressed in the following definition of Gainotti, Messerli, and Tissot (1972, p.545). The 'syndrome consists of a tendency to neglect one half of extrapersonal space in such tasks as drawing and reading which require a good and symmetrical exploration of space.'

Laterality of lesion and USN

The first clear statement on a relation between laterality and neglect also came from Brain (1945) who considered that the deficit was very largely restricted to right hemisphere or non-dominant lesions. This point of view has

Table 6.4 Laterality and presence of neglect

	Dominant Lesion	Nondominant Lesion
Percentage	9	29
Clear presence of neglect	9	29
Testing precluded by aphasia	29	0
Neglect diagnosis uncertain	0	12
No evidence of neglect	62	59

received very wide support though Brain was aware that the apparently low incidence of report of USN in left hemisphere or dominant lesions might be due to the masking effects of other symptoms such as severe aphasia. A direct attempt to test this proposition was made by Battersby et al. (1956) during a study of 75 cases with unilateral space occupying lesions. The following table has been compiled from this study. *The authors suggest that the apparently high association between neglect phenomena and the nondominant hemisphere might be a spurious one. There are a number of factors which make comparison studies exceedingly difficult if not impossible. Chief among these are the characteristics of the groups under study, e.g. (1) the presence and degree of sensory deficits; (2) the presence and degree of dysphasia; (3) the presence of intellectual deterioration; (4) the relative size of the lesion. The sobering effect of the findings of Arrigoni and De Renzi (1964) with regard to laterality and another disorder (constructional praxis) has already been mentioned.

A brief review of studies since 1960 does lend weight to Brain's original hypothesis. In a study of other symptoms associated with constructional apraxia occuring in unilateral cases McFie and Zangwill (1960) found only one of their 8 cases showed neglect compared with 14 out of 21 cases which they found in a number of previous studies from Zangwill's laboratory (Paterson and Zangwill, 1944, 1945; McFie, Piercy and Zangwill, 1950; Ettlinger, Warrington and Zangwill, 1957). The right sided predominance was also reported by Piercy, Hécaen and Ajuriaguerra (1960). Hécaen (1962) reviewed a large number of retrorolandic cases which showed that only 4 out of 206 left hemisphere cases had the deficit as against 52 out of 154 right hemisphere cases. A much higher incidence of qualitative errors suggesting left hemi-inattention was found for right hemisphere cases than left hemisphere cases in Arrigoni and De Renzi's (1964) study of constructional apraxia. A specific test of the laterality hypothesis by Gainotti (1968) using a battery of simple tests showed that unilateral neglect is both significantly more frequent and more severe in patients with lesions of the right hemisphere than of the left. This finding was strongly confirmed in a later study (Gainotti and Tiacci, 1971) and other studies continue to add to the consensus. Oxbury, Campbell, and Oxbury (1974) for example, found no cases of neglect in their patients with either left hemisphere or brain stem strokes while 7 of their 17 right hemisphere stroke cases showed the symptom.

Not only has evidence of a quantitative difference between the two hemispheres gained support but the hypothesis has been advanced that qualitative differences also exist. Gainotti, Messerli and Tissot (1972) compared patients with unilateral lesions on various tasks of copying drawings. They described for the first time what appears to be a unique feature in the performance of some right hemisphere cases, namely, 'the tendency to neglect one half of a figure (on the side opposite to the hemispheric locus of lesion), while reproducing designs that are placed even more laterally on the neglected side' (p.546). Examples of this qualitatively different sign are shown in Figure 6.9.

The majority of references to neglect phenomena have been concerned with visuo-spatial neglect. Recent studies have shown that it can also occur in other

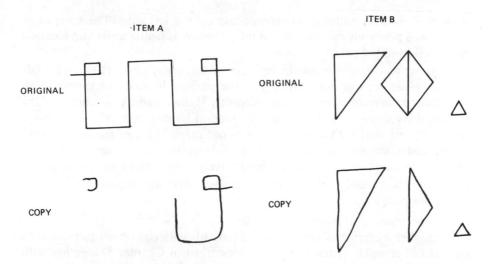

Fig. 6.9 Examples of copying defects in right hemisphere patients, (after Gainotti *et al.*, 1972 permission of the authors and the editiors, *Journal of Neurology, Neurosurgery and Psychiatry.*)

modalities. The finding of unilateral neglect in the tactile modality by De Renzi, Faglioni and Scotti (1970) suggested to those authors 'that hemi-inattention does not depend so much on perceptual and motor factors as on a mutilated representation of space' (p.202). Heilman and Valenstein (1972a) found 17 cases of auditory unilateral neglect in a ten month survey. Of 10 cases with positive brain scans, 9 were in the right inferior parietal lobule and one in the left frontal region. Though the defect became most apparent in test situations employing simultaneous stimulation it was not restricted to these, being apparent as an abnormal responsiveness when the patients were addressed from the neglected side. There was no loss of auditory acuity in these patients. There may also be an interaction between the nature of the task employed and the laterality of the lesion. Leicester *et al.* (1969) found that not only did neglect appear with lesions of either hemisphere but also that, with particular tasks, neglect occurred predominantly or exclusively with lesions of one hemisphere, e.g. a language related task of matching letters to an auditory sample showed neglect only on the right with dominant left hemisphere lesions. This study also revealed that neglect appeared not 'on every test, but only on those which, for some reason they could not do correctly.' (p.586)

Neglect and locus of lesion

Most studies of USN appear to implicate the posterior parts of the brain with particular emphasis on the nondominant parietal lobe. Recent studies have failed to give a definitive answer. Chedru, Leblanc, and Lhermitte (1973) found evidence of neglect in both left and right hemisphere cases with or without visual field defects, i.e. by implication anterior and posterior lesions. Using a visual searching task they found that all groups showed both prolongation of searching time especially for stimuli contralateral to the lesion and a tendency to begin visual exploration on the same side as the lesion. All right sided lesions showed a marked tendency to explore less on the left side. The severity of neglect was positively related both to the presence of hemianopia and location of the lesion in the parietal lobe.

Many writers have echoed the opinion of Battersby *et al.* (1956) who felt that while neglect was not restricted to the parietal lobe, it did appear to be restricted to the retrorolandic zones. Recently Heilman and Valenstein (1972b) described six cases of neglect in proven frontal lesions in a two year survey, demonstrating that such an occurrence is not rare. Three of the lesions were on the medial surface and three on the dorsolateral surface of the frontal lobe. The frontal cases appeared to be qualitatively very similar to the posterior cases with the exception that three of the cases were accompanied by a grasp reflex and paratonia.

Unilateral neglect and perceptual disorders

The higher incidence of impairment of patients with right hemisphere lesions on tasks of complex visual perception (described in Chapter 8) together with the higher incidence of neglect with right sided lesions has suggested the hypothesis that the two are causally related. Two experiments by Gainotti and Tiacci (1971) add weight to the hypothesis that some perceptual difficulties are due, at least in part, to unilateral spatial neglect. On an overlapping figures test right hemisphere patients made more total errors as well as more errors and omissions for figures lying to one side (left) of the midline than the left hemisphere group while there was no significant difference between the two groups for errors on figures lying to the right of the midline. Furthermore the right hemisphere group with neglect tended to overvalue drawings on the right half of the midline when asked to compare the size of two figures one to the left and one to the right. The authors suggest that the overvaluation may be due to a tendency to gaze to their right (now neglected) side invoking Piaget's theory of the 'fixation effect' (Piaget, 1969). . . 'the space of visual perception is not homogeneous, but the elements on which the gaze is mostly fixed are systematically overvalued' (Gainotti and Tiacci, 1971, p.456).

A much higher incidence of visual field defects has been found in right hemisphere groups with a higher incidence of visual spatial neglect (Battersby *et al.*, 1956; McFie and Zangwill, 1960; Hécaen, 1962). There is also a generally poorer performance on visual perceptual tasks by patients with right hemisphere lesions and neglect than by those with right hemisphere lesions without neglect (Oxbury, Campbell, and Oxbury, 1974). These authors employed a wide range of tests of visual perception and spatial analysis all of which showed a greater deficit in patients with neglect. However, the fact that some patients with clearly marked perceptual and spatial disorders showed no evidence of neglect suggested that while visuospatial neglect may be an important factor in producing impairments of perception and spatial analysis in patients with non-dominant retrorolandic lesions it certainly cannot be the whole answer.

The role of visual field defects in the disorders of visual perception which are so often associated with unilateral neglect has been the subject of frequent study. The Milan group has produced many studies showing that the perceptual deficits of nondominant lesions are almost always associated with visual field defects (De Renzi and Spinnler, 1967; De Renzi, Faglioni, and Scotti, 1969; De Renzi, Scotti, and Spinnler, 1969; Faglioni, Spinnler, and Vignolo, 1969; De Renzi, Faglioni, and Scotti, 1970). Ratcliff (1973) likewise found greatest impairment on a perceptual task for posterior right hemisphere lesions with visual field defects. Costa *et al.* (1969) inferred that the strong right position preference shown by their right hemisphere cases on Raven's Progressive Matrices was indicative of visual spatial neglect and this was strongly associated in their material with visual field defects.

Nature of the defect in unilateral neglect

At present no single conception appears adequate to explain all the findings. In view of the fact that neglect is not restricted to the visual modality De Renzi, Faglioni, and Scotti (1970) feel that neglect is based in a cognitive deficit which they view as a 'mutilated representation of space'. Gainotti, Messerli, and Tissot (1972) consider their findings indicate that their patients with neglect did not have a cognitive defect but that 'the core of unilateral spatial neglect consists in a peculiar disorganization of the type of synthesis of the sensory data which seems characteristic of the minor hemisphere.' (p.545). Such explanations are not mutually exclusive.

Leicester *et al.* (1969) feel that the same mechanism may underlie the predominance of disorders of the body image and spatial neglect which are seen with minor hemisphere disorders.

Finally, Heilman, Watson, and Schulman (1974) argue that the neglect syndrome may be a unilateral defect of arousal or alerting. In support of this they cite evidence from one human study (Heilman and Valenstein, 1972b) as well as studies in the macaque (Watson *et al.*, 1973; Watson *et al.*, 1973).

Measures of unilateral spatial neglect

Apart from the commonly used clinical tests of drawing and copying numerous measures have been employed, e.g. the omission of items on the neglected side of space with the Poppelreuter overlapping figures test (Critchley, 1953; Hécaen and Angelergues, 1963). Costa *et al.* (1969) derived an empirical position preference score from Raven's Coloured Progressive Matrices. Patients with right hemisphere lesions showed an overall poorer performance than other groups on the matrices for the side of their lesions than did patients with left hemisphere lesions.

It will be important to develop adequate standard measures of neglect particularly if the impression of Lawson (1962) is true that neglect may be amenable to rehabilitation.

Disorders of the body schema

Disorders of the body schema are usually attributed to impairment of parietal lobe function. Some observations would suggest that these disorders are more prominent with right parietal lesions than with left. Absence of the disorders of communication seen with left hemisphere lesions at least make the body schema disorders due to right hemisphere damage appear more apparent and striking. There are often associated motor and sensory deficits due to spread of the lesions to somaesthetic, visual, and motor pathways. The first systematic studies of disorders of 'the body image' were published by J. Lhermitte (1942, 1952). Only a sample of the most frequently seen syndromes will be outlined. These are (1) anosognosia (2) bodily agnosia (3) right-left discrimination, together with a consideration of the Gerstmann syndrome. The related area of unilateral neglect for external space has been treated separately above. Body schema disorders are dealt with more extensively by Frederiks (1969).

Anosognosia

This term means a failure to perceive illness. Its normal clinical usage implies a failure to perceive a defect or the denial of a defect and the term was introduced by Babinski (1914) in describing lack of awareness of hemiplegia. This association between denial or imperception of hemiplegia is a very common finding and in the majority of cases the paralysis is on the left side. In other words, the lesion is in the nondominant hemisphere. Nathanson, Bergman, and Gordon (1952) observed that some 70 per cent of patients with denial of unilateral paralysis had damage to the right hemisphere. Patients with this disorder may rationalize about their failure to use the paralysed limbs and sometimes even have the delusion that the limbs do not belong to them, i.e. they are seen as being outside the patient's own body image.

The term anosognosia has also been extended by some writers to the denial or imperception of other deficits so that qualifying terms need to be added. It is interesting to note that these phenomena may sometimes be dissociated, with unawareness or denial of one deficit but not another. Numerous reviews have appeared, e.g. Hécaen and Ajuriaguerra (1952), Critchley (1953), Alajouanine and Lhermitte (1957) and Frederiks (1969).

Anosognosia for hemiplegia (Babinski's syndrome) is almost always associated with acute, massive vascular lesions affecting the retrorolandic area with accompanying hemiplegia, hemianopia and hemianaesthesia. The middle cerebral artery is most often implicated as the seat of the trouble.

Related, but somewhat less striking, is the symptom of relative inattention to one side of the body. Once again this deficit is mostly for the left half of the body. It is also related in many patients to the neglect of one half of external space already described. It should be stressed that in these cases there is no weakness or paralysis though the patient may fail to move the limbs spontaneously such as not swinging the affected arm when walking. He may neglect the left half of the body when bathing, dressing, or combing his hair. Hécaen *et al.* (1956) found that patients with surgical lesions in the right posterior parieto-temporal area had marked difficulties with complex sensorimotor activities including dressing. One patient could dress store dummies at his work but had difficulty in dressing himself which may suggest that one of the fundamental deficits in dressing apraxia is unawareness of the position of the limbs. This may be part of the general unawareness of body parts. The so-called 'dressing apraxia' would appear to have a number of determinants only one of which is bodily inattention.

Lack of awareness of body parts

This disturbance of the body image declares itself in the patient's inability to name and localize parts of his own body. Methods of examination have been described in detail by Benton (1959). Common clinical tests include the following: (1) asking the patient to identify parts of the body named by the examiner or to move the named parts; (2) asking the patient to identify body parts on a diagram or on the examiner; (3) asking the patient to move parts shortly after the examiner has touched them; (4) asking the patient to touch one part of his body with another, e.g. 'place your (right) hand on your (left) ear.' This latter task is often known as Head's 'hand-eye-ear' test (Head, 1920) and forms part of many routine screening devices for higher function disorders, such as the Halstead-Wepman Aphasia Screening Test (Russell, Neuringer and Goldstein, 1970). Head's test is also commonly used for determining difficulties with right-left orientation.

One of the most commonly described disorders in this category is finger agnosia first described by Gerstmann in 1924 (see Gerstmann, 1930). It was defined by him in a later publication in the following way—'It consists in a *primary* disturbance or loss of ability to recognize, identify, differentiate, name, select, indicate and orient as to the individual fingers of either hand, the patient's own, as well as those of other persons.' (Gerstmann, 1957, p.866). Some writers would prefer a term like 'faulty finger localization'.

It was as a consequence of his early studies of finger agnosia that Gerstmann described the syndrome which bears his name and which led to considerable controversy (see below).

Finger agnosia has been studied experimentally by Kinsbourne and Warrington (1962). They examined 12 patients with this symptom using a number of specially constructed tests most of which require only minimal verbal response. Two of these tests are as follows:

1. *'The In-between test.* Two fingers are simultaneously touched. The patient is asked to state the number of fingers between the ones touched. Thus the answer may be 0, 1, 2, or 3 (Fig. 6.10, A)

2. *Two-point finger test.* The fingers are touched in two places. The patient judges whether the two touches are both on the same finger or on different fingers.' (Fig. 6.10, B). Warrington (1973) considers Test 1 the most clinically useful. Unlike the three studies cited below, Kinsbourne and Warrington maintained that the conjunction of the other Gerstmann symptoms with finger agnosia was more than coincidental.

Warrington cites Lunn's 1948 review of the published cases of finger agnosia. . . 'after excluding cases with widespread lesions and subjects with mixed handedness (they) found no case of finger agnosia with a right hemisphere lesion.' (p.273). There seems little doubt from the accrued evidence that finger agnosia is a sign *par excellence* of a dominant hemisphere posterior lesion.

Right-left disorientation

This disorientation reflects itself in confusion between left and right for all parts of the body. It is a complex disorder or set of disorders and its significance

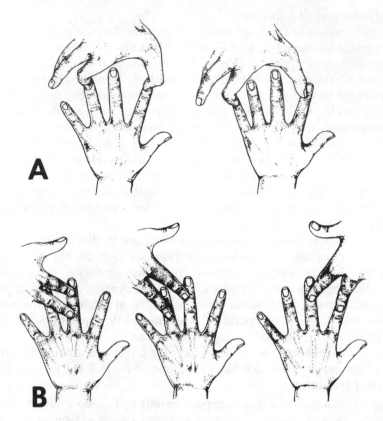

Fig. 6.10 A. The In-Between Test of Finger Agnosia
B. Two-Point Finger Test (from Kinsbourne and Warrington, *Brain*, 1962)

is still not yet fully understood. Many factors may be involved, apraxic, aphasic, and agnosic. Poeck and Orgass (1966) have stressed the role of aphasia though the deficit may be seen in the absence of clinically demonstrable aphasia. The complexity was brought out clearly in a factorial study of Poeck and Orgass (1967). Benton (1959) in a developmental study of lateral orientation in normal children has stressed the dependency of this type of ability on language. Like the other symptoms under discussion of right-left hemisphere malfunction, minor degrees of the disorder are difficult to establish since many normal individuals continue to have lateral confusion in adult life without any signs of cerebral impairment.

The Gerstmann syndrome

This syndrome was described by Gerstmann (1930) and consists of the four symptoms: finger agnosia, acalculia, right-left disorientation, and pure dysgraphia. This latter term refers to a difficulty in writing which is *not* associated with a reading disorder (dyslexia). Reading and writing disorders are outlined in Chapter 9.

The principal question is whether there is a relationship between the four symptoms such that they form a unique constellation which represents a syndrome in the usual sense or whether their association arises from biased sampling or other factors. The main arguments against a separate syndrome are outlined in the three studies which follow. Critchley in his William Gowers lecture, 1965, has commented elegantly upon the evidence for and against the syndrome. (Critchley, 1966).

The first major objective study to find against the validity of the Gerstmann syndrome was that of Benton (1961) whose designation of the syndrome as a 'fiction' attracted wide support. Benton studied the concordance between a number of deficits in a group of patients with cerebral disease arguing that the strength of concordance should be a measure of the viability of the concept of a syndrome. His summary is worth quoting 'Systematic, objective analysis of the performance of patients with cerebral disease on seven 'parietal' tasks (right-left orientation, finger localization, writing, calculation, constructional praxis, reading, visual memory) indicates that many combinations of deficits, including the known as the 'Gerstmann syndrome', may be observed. The syndrome appears to be no different from the other combinations in respect to either the strength of mutual interrelationships among its elements or the strength of the relationships between its elements and performances not belonging to it. These results hold both for patients with diverse cerebral conditions and for those with focal lesions of the dominant pariental lobe.

The findings are interpreted as indicating that the Gerstmann syndrome is an artifact of defective and biased observation. Further, a review of the pertinent clinical literature offers little support for its alleged focal diagnostic significance . . .' (p.181)

Benton's analysis was soon followed by another large study (Heimburger, Demeyer, and Reitan, 1964). Of 456 patients with cerebral disease some 111 showed one or more Gerstmann symptoms. Thirty three cases showed one symptom, 32 two symptoms, 23 three symptoms, and 23 showed all four. These four groups were then related to the nature and extent of pathology. Group 1 (one symptom only) tended to have small static lesions. An increase in the number of symptoms was paralleled by an increase in the extent and destructiveness of lesions up to Group IV (having all four Gerstmann symptoms). An analysis of Group IV also showed that the angular gyrus does not need to be involved as earlier writers, particularly Gerstmann himself believed. At least 3 of the 23 cases had autopsy confirmation of absence of a lesion affecting the angular gyrus. With regard to the localizing value of the Gerstmann symptoms Heimburger et al., found that the probability of a dominant hemisphere lesion increased with the number of symptoms but that they were of no value for localizing within the hemisphere. They concluded 'As to localizing significance, Gerstmann's syndrome has approximately the same degree of cogency as dysphasia.' (p.57)

The results of Poeck and Orgass (1966) supported the contention of the two previous studies that the syndrome does not occur in isolated form. They noted that the complete syndrome was rarely observed without dysphasia which they believed was the 'common denominator of the four symptoms.' 'The perform-ances which are disturbed in the so-called Gerstmann syndrome are closely related to language. However, aphasia also produces other behavioral deficits, appearing as 'concurrent' symptoms. It is therefore not justified to regard the four symptoms as a natural syndrome. They are an arbitrary partial grouping of the numerous neuropsychological disturbances resulting from lesion of the leading hemisphere.' (p.436)

The parietal lobes and short term memory

To date there is only a small amount of evidence about the localization of anatomical systems concerned with short-term memory dysfunction. Much of the work has been carried out by Warrington and her colleagues and reviewed by her in several articles (Warrington, 1971; Warrington and Weiskrantz, 1972; Warrington and Baddeley, 1974). The first report concerned one patient (K.F.) who had many years earlier received an injury to the left parietal region (War-rington and Shallice, 1969). This patient had a marked impairment of the ability to repeat auditory verbal stimuli which contrasted with much less difficulty with comparable visual verbal stimuli. This case suggested the possibility of modality specific short term memory defects. K.F.'s difficulty could not be accounted for by faulty auditory perception or speech defect. A further study of the same patient (Shallice and Warrington, 1970) confirmed the presence of modality specific STM defect. Later Warrington, Logue, and Pratt (1971) added two further patients with lesions in the left parietal region, this time employing 'psychological tests differentially loaded with short-term and long term memory components.' Results showed that (1) long term memory functions in audition were relatively intact while auditory STM was impaired and (2) the disability was specific to the auditory modality, visual STM (as measured by relatively normal decay function) being little affected. Peterson and Peterson techniques were used in all instances. Further testing of K.F. in 1972 confirmed his rapid forgetting in auditory STM compared with relatively normal visual STM (Warrington and Shallice, 1972).

Additional differentiation of the STM defect came with a study of K.F. and one other patient (Shallice and Warrington, 1974). Within the auditory mo-dality two tests were employed, one verbal (letters) and one nonverbal (mean-ingful sounds). The two patients exhibited a dissociation between these two tasks showing impairment on the verbal task but not on the nonverbal.

Against these studies supporting modal specificity is the study of Butters *et al.* (1970a). These authors compared the performance of frontal and parietal cases, both left and right, on a variety of short term visual and auditory tasks again employing the distractor technique. The right hemisphere group showed more severe impairment on visual STM tasks compared with auditory, while the two left sided groups (frontal and parietal) showed separate characteristics. Left frontal patients had predominantly registration but not memory deficits. Left parietal patients had memory deficits. However neither of the left groups showed modal specificity both visual and auditory material being affected.

Butters *et al.* consider their results can be interpreted 'as supporting the notion that the right hemisphere, especially the parietal region, is involved in the processing of visual information both verbal and patterned, while the left hemisphere is concerned with verbal material irrespective of sensory modality' (p.458). Further studies are needed to resolve this early apparent difference of findings.

Since a disproportionate impairment in the repetition of verbal stimuli is the most prominent symptom of 'conduction aphasia' Warrington considers that the results in her three patients with left parietal lesions adds weight to the anatomical basis of this syndrome which has been variously centred in the inferior parietal or temporo-parietal region. Many of the studies referring to the anatomical basis of repetition difficulty or conduction aphasia are given in Warrington, Logue, and Pratt (1971). Certainly, the obvious clinical feature on which these cases were selected was their marked impairment for repetition of digits on the Digit Span subtest of the WAIS.

Postural arm drift

A common clinical test used in neurological examination requires the patient to maintain a static position of the outstretched arms in a horizontal position with the eyes closed. In some brain damaged patients there may be considerable drift usually, but not always, towards the midline. Since this drift is so frequently seen with parietal lesions it has come to be called by some clinicians 'parietal drift'. Only one experimental study relating postural arm drift to localization and lateralization appears to have been made (Wyke, 1966). The findings of this study suggest that the more general term postural arm drift should be used since it is by no means uncommon with extraparietal lesions. All Wyke's patients with lesions of the parietal region showed significant drift compared with two-thirds of frontal and one-half of temporal patients. Left hemisphere cases showed some ipsilateral drift plus a more severe drift in the contralateral arm while right hemisphere cases showed only a contralateral drift effect.

7. The Occipital Lobes

Anatomical Features	Colour Agnosia
Cerebral Blindness	Pure Word Blindness (agnosic alexia)
Hysterical Blindness	Electrical Stimulation
Visual Agnosia	

Anatomical features

The occipital lobes form the most posterior portions of the cerebral hemispheres. On their inner or medial aspects there is a natural line of demarcation called the parieto-occipital fissure. On the lateral or convex surfaces there are no such gross landmarks and the occipital lobe merges into the parietal lobe above and the temporal lobe below (Figs. 7.1 and 7.2).

Following the discovery of the fact that the cerebral cortex varied in the cellular composition of its layers from place to place in the hemisphere, numerous attempts were made to map out regions of the cortex having similar distinctive structure. Such studies are termed *cytoarchitecture,* literally the architecture of the cells. One of the best known of such maps is that of Brodmann (1909). (Fig. 7.3). This difference in structure suggested difference in function and, while such a relationship has not been fully established for all areas, it appears to be largely true of the occipital region.

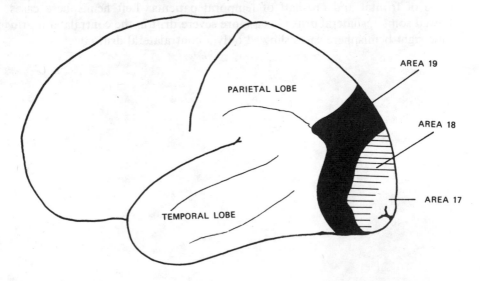

Fig. 7.1 The occipital lobe—lateral view

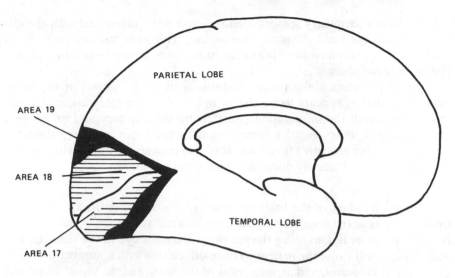

Fig. 7.2 The occipital lobe— medial view

Brodmann's method divided each occipital lobe into three areas having different cellular composition (areas 17, 18, and 19). Area 17 borders on the calcarine fissure which is largely on the medial aspect of the hemisphere and also covers the posterior pole of the hemisphere. This area is known as the striate area because of the striped appearance when it is sectioned. It is in this area that the neural fibres relaying information from the visual receptors in the retina reach their termination. Area 17 is the primary visual cortex. It is surrounded by area 18, the parastriate region, which, in turn is surrounded by area 19, the peristriate region which borders on the parietal and temporal lobes. (Figs. 7.1 and 7.2).

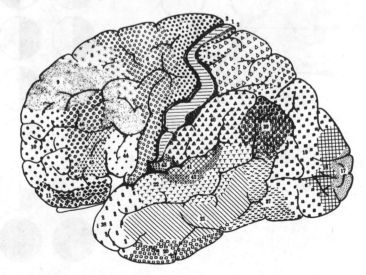

Fig. 7.3 Brodmann's cytoarchitectural maps. Lateral aspect of the left hemisphere.

Area 18 is a secondary sensory area believed to be concerned with the elaboration and synthesis of visual information. This area has numerous interhemispheric or commissural fibre connections with the corresponding area in the other hemisphere.

Area 19 possesses abundant connections with other regions of the hemispheres so that it appears to be chiefly involved in the integration of visual information with the information gathered by the auditory and other sense systems and it unites visual information with the brain systems subserving speech and other executive functions. It is also concerned, along with areas in the temporal lobes already discussed, with visual memory.

Visual pathways

An understanding of the basic anatomy of the visual pathways allows an understanding of the diagnostic significance of certain common defects of vision brought about by lesions along the pathways from the eye to the visual cortex. Such lesions will cause the patient to have difficulties with a number of psychological test measures, and an awareness of the nature of the visual defect will help in making correct inferences about the patient's performance on visuoperceptive tasks.

The lens of each eye focuses the stimulation from the outer part of each eye's visual field on to the inner half of each retina while stimulation arising

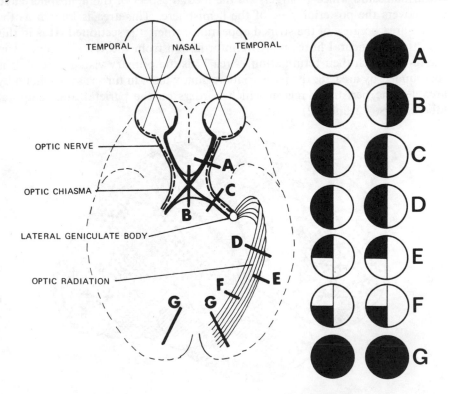

Fig. 7.4 The visual pathways with related field defects

in the inner halves of the visual fields goes to the outer halves of each retina. The terms 'temporal' and 'nasal' have often been used to refer to this division of the half fields of each eye and are included in Figure 7.4 so that the reader may understand texts where these terms occur, but, in what follows, the terms 'left (or right) halves of the visual field' will be used since they are less ambiguous in their reference than the terms 'temporal' and 'nasal'.

The fibres which relay information from the retina are gathered together in the optic nerve which travels back to join its partner in the optic chiasma. Here the fibres from the inner half of each retina cross over the midline and go on to enter the contralateral hemisphere while the fibres from the outer halves of each retina enter the hemisphere on the same side as the eye receiving the information. This means that each eye projects visual information to *each* hemisphere. Furthermore, there is a good deal of overlap between the visual fields of the two eyes so that most of the information (i.e., that seen by the two eyes in common) is analysed by both hemispheres. (Fig. 7.5).

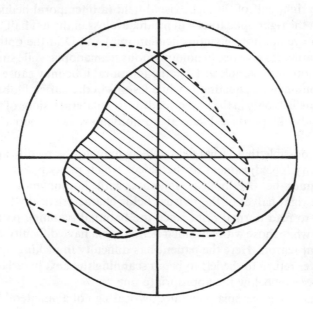

Fig. 7.5 Visual fields with area of overlap

From the optic chiasma the visual pathways extend backward to the lateral geniculate bodies. These bodies can be considered as special subdivisions of the thalamus. They relay the visual information to the visual cortex while the neighbouring structures, the medial geniculate bodies, relay auditory information to the primary projection area for audition situated in the temporal lobes.

The final part of the optic pathway is known as the optic radiation or geniculo-calcarine tract. From the geniculate bodies the pathway passes through an area called the temporal isthmus; then its fibres fan out to cover the upper and outer portions of the lateral ventricles before passing to the calcarine cortex.

A lesion in the temporal isthmus forms a good example of the widespread effects that a small lesion may have if it is strategically placed (Chapter 1). Not only does a small lesion in this location lead to an interruption of the visual pathways and hence to a visual field defect but also to somatosensory and motor changes since fibre pathways related to these functional systems are in close contiguity in this region (Nielsen and Friedman, 1942). Moreover, because of the asymmetry of function between the two hemispheres of the brain (see Ch. 8) two clinical syndromes are recognizable according to whether the left or right isthmus is damaged. With involvement of the left (dominant) side severe aphasia may accompany the above symptoms while damage to the right (non-dominant) side may produce anosognosia or delusions of the body schema as well as the visual, motor and sensory disturbances.

Visual field defects. Figure 7.4 represents the effect of lesions interrupting the visual pathways at various points. At A, a lesion produces blindness in the right eye. At B, a lesion will produce a loss in the left half of the left visual field and the right half of the right visual field (a bitemporal hemianopia). At C, a lesion in the right optic tract will produce a loss in the left half of the visual field or each eye (an homonymous hemianopia). At D in the optic radiation, complete lesions also give rise to homonymous hemianopia while smaller lesions in the radiation, for example at E, in the temporal lobe may cause loss only in the upper homonymous quadrants while lesions in the parietal lobe (at F) may cause visual defects only in the lower quadrants. Bilateral lesions of the occipital lobe (G1 and G2) produce bilateral homonymous hemianopia or cerebral blindness.

Since it is possible that visual field defects may not be readily apparent due to the capacity for adjustment to the defect which many patients show, they may sometimes be overlooked. Patients with homonymous hemianopia affecting the right halves of their visual fields characteristically have difficulty when asked to read normal print since the habitual scanning pattern is from left to right, while those with left sided hemianopia have difficulty with reading for a different reason. Here the patient has difficulty in picking up the correct line as his eyes return to the left to begin scanning the next line. He may begin on a line above or below the appropriate one.

Homonymous hemianopia is an unequivocal sign of a unilateral hemispheric lesion. Some would regard hemianopia as the *only* reliable sign of occipital lobe disease (Cogan, 1966; Gloning, Gloning and Hoff, 1968), since more subtle disturbances of visual perception tend to be associated with lesions spreading into neighbouring regions.

Less regular field defects are produced by partial lesions of the visual cortex or optic radiation such as those produced by penetrating missile wounds in wartime. The blind area in these cases is known as a *scotoma* and, particularly if small, may even pass unnoticed by the patient in much the same way as the normal or physiological blind spot in each eye becomes apparent only when the eye is fixated and visual targets are arranged so that they project into the retinal region of the head of the optic nerve where visual receptors are absent.

These traumatically produced lesions of the visual regions have been extensively studied by Teuber and his colleagues (Teuber, Battersby and Bender, 1960).

The borders of scotomata are usually ill-defined and vary with the attitude and attention of the patient and with the particular methods employed in testing.

Examination of the visual fields: The visual fields are routinely checked in the standard neurological examination. The commonly used method of clinical examination is termed *confrontation*. The patient faces the examiner and, with one eye shielded, fixates on the region of the examiner's nose while the latter checks various parts of the visual field by asking the subject to detect the presence or movement of the visual target, usually the examiner's fingers. This method readily picks out the more obvious field defects. More careful systematic examination is made with a tangent screen or retinal perimeter. These methods are described in standard textbooks in medicine and experimental psychology. Two further procedures may be of value.

1. Since it appears that in cases of tumour, field defects for coloured test objects invariably appear before that for black and white objects (Bender and Kanzer, 1941), Walsh and Hoyt (1969) have suggested that coloured targets be employed routinely. Such an examination is simple enough to be included in a small group of 'neurological' tests employed by the neuropsychologist (see Ch. 9), and may detect some lesions in their early development.

2. Flicker perimetry may also be sensitive to early lowering of visual efficiency though such testing is time consuming and needs special facilities not normally available in neuropsychological clinics. The method and its implications for localizing the site of brain damage were described by Parsons and Huse (1958).

Cerebral blindness

One of the most common causes of hemianopic defects is cerebral ischaemia produced by narrowing or occlusion of the posterior cerebral artery. The loss of vision for the contralateral half fields is a prominent symptom of a failure of the vertebro-basilar artery system to provide an adequate blood supply to the posterior regions of the cerebrum (Siekert and Millikan, 1955). Where the occipital lobes are affected on both sides a bilateral homonymous hemianopia or complete blindness results.

This blindness has often been termed cortical blindness but the term 'cerebral' is to be preferred since the underlying white matter is usually involved as well as the cortex. The blindness is often accompanied by other neurological signs and, even when the disorder appears to be clinically pure, careful examination will often reveal associated disorders. Since the prime cause is most often vascular in origin the blindness may follow a period of confusion or even unconsciousness due to the 'vascular accident' and testing of the patient may be rendered difficult because of residual confusion.

In patients with signs of vertebro-basilar insufficiency even the diagnostic procedure of arteriography may precipitate cerebral blindness. (Silverman, Bergman and Bender, 1961). In our experience this is accompanied on occasions by an amnestic syndrome of marked severity probably due to bilateral ischaemia of the medial temporal regions supplied by the *posterior* cerebral arteries.

In patients who survive the precipitating vascular episode, recovery of at least some visual function appears to be the rule (Silverman, Bergman and Bender, 1961; Gloning, Gloning and Hoff, 1968). This recovery is so frequent that it has led some workers to doubt the validity of earlier reports of lasting cerebral blindness. Of the 32 surviving cases of cerebral blindness in Gloning, Gloning and Hoff's, very large series of occipital lobe cases, all recovered some visual function though many stopped short of full recovery.

Restitution of visual function appears to take place in a typical order. Firstly the sensation of darkness becomes punctuated with elementary visual sensations or photisms. Next, the visual field becomes light but no form perception is possible. This is followed by the appreciation of primitive movement, i.e. the appreciation that the object is moving, or has moved, but not the direction or speed. Contours gradually emerge but are vague and unstable. Colour experience is the last to return. Even at this stage the visual processes may readily fatigue so that the percept appears to blur after some time. Some patients go on to recover their normal vision but others remain fixed at a stage of partial recovery.

Hysterical blindness

Hysteria or malingering may form a possible problem in differential diagnosis. True cerebral blindness shows a lack of both the menace and optokinetic reflexes where the other conditions do not.

The menace reflex is an eyeblink response produced by rapidly approaching the corner of the eye with a menacing object while the optokinetic reflex consists of jerky eye movements when the patient gazes at a rapidly moving series of objects such as a rotating striped drum.

The electroencephalogram has also proved of use in diagnosis in this situation (Bergman, 1967). Most normal subjects show the characteristic 9 to 13 cycles per second alpha rhythm in the posterior regions of the brain with the subject relaxed with his eyes closed, and this alpha activity disappears from the record when visual stimulation is received. This posterior alpha rhythm is absent in cases of cerebral blindness and is replaced by slow waves, and there is no response in the record to opening and closing the eyes. The presence of a normal, reactive alpha rhythm should contradict a diagnosis of cerebral blindness.

Anton's syndrome (denial of blindness)

It is characteristic of many though not all cases of cerebral blindness that the patient appears indifferent, fails to recognize, or even denies the existence of his defect. Post-mortem findings in Anton's case of 1898 showed bilateral softening of the brain in the parieto-occipital regions and he considered that the disconnection of the visual system from other parts of the brain to be the cause of the denial. Denial may also occur for incomplete blindness such as hemianopic defects and it is possible that one explanation may serve to explain both phenomena.

While denial may be verbally explicit, some of the patients examined by Gloning, Gloning and Hoff admitted their blindness while they were actually under examination but shortly after, again denied visual loss. This meant that the patient must need to invent fictions such as 'It is night now and there is no light in this room' or 'I am in a dark cellar'. (Gloning, Gloning and Hoff, 1968, p.13). Though there was a tendency for all patients to confabulate a true Korsakoff's syndrome was rare.

Denial occurs with other disorders such as hemiplegia (Babinski's syndrome) and we have also noted it on occasions after prefrontal lobotomy where the patient confabulates or rationalizes about the presence of the operative scars. Numerous psychological explanations have been put forward to explain this denial of illness or disability.

Nathanson, Bergman, and Gordon (1952) reported 28 cases of denial of hemiplegia in a series of 100 cases. The denial occurred with lesions in either hemisphere though more frequently with right hemisphere involvement. These authors considered that the denial of illness closely resembled the mechanism or rationalization or explaining away a defect, found in normal subjects. The difference appeared to be one of degree. In a similar vein Guthrie and Grossman (1952) pointed to the prior use of denial as a defense mechanism in their two neurological subjects while the denial of operation was considered by Paganini and Zlotlow (1960) to be a continuation of the use of this defense by their schizophrenic subjects. A low level of intellectual function also seems to be related to the production of denial (Fryer and Rich, 1960).

One difficulty in using these explanations for Anton's syndrome lies in the fact that in some cases where blindness and hemiplegia co-exist, there may be denial of one disability with acceptance of the other. Such a dissociation of the denial of one defect and not another needs to be taken into consideration in a theory which endeavours to explain all forms of denial of illness or disability.

Adaptation to visual field defects: At first sight it is a remarkable thing that persons with quite extensive field defects behave in everyday situations as though their vision was close to normal. The fact that patients are little incommoded by homonymous hemianopia has been commented on by numerous authors and is the subject of a study by Gassel and Williams (1963) who found that 'the visual function was little impaired, impaired transiently or defective on few occasions in most patients; and the ability to compensate for the visual field defect was remarkable' (Gassel, 1969, p.672).

Since the time of World War 1 when many patients with traumatic damage to the posterior regions of the brain were examined, cases have been described where the patient demonstrates the phenomenon which has been termed *completion*. If a patient with a hemianopic defect is asked to fixate a point and a card is introduced with, say, half an object depicted on it until the border between the 'half drawing' and the blank portion of the card coincides with the division between the patient's visual field and visual defect he may 'see' the whole object (Fig. 7.6). Similarly he may 'see' the whole of the examiner's face despite the fact that while the patient was looking at the examiner the latter had placed a card in front of a portion of his face. Examination of this completion phenomenon has produced both different findings and different types of explanation to explain the findings. (Fuchs, 1938; Lashley, 1941; Pollack, Battersby and Bender, 1957; Warrington, 1962). Gassel and Williams (1963) suggest that the hemianopic field loss functions as an extensive blind spot. 'The hemianopic field is an area of absence which is discovered rather than sensed, its presence is judged from some specific failure in function rather than directly perceived.' (1963, p.258). For this reason the deficit may not be discovered by the patient who is often vague about the nature of his impairment.

Gassel further believes that the completion phenomenon is an illusion which is a function of a number of factors which include expectation on the patient's part, his attitude, and the testing conditions.

In his discussion of the nature of visual field defects King (1967) points out that incomplete figures (Fig. 7.6) have been as effective as complete figures in eliciting completion (Pollack, Battersby, and Bender, 1957), thus disproving the hypothesis that the phenomenon may be accounted for by remaining visual function in the affected area.

With regard to the locus of the lesion Warrington (1962) has pointed out that completion occurs more commonly though not exclusively in patients with parietal lobe lesions.

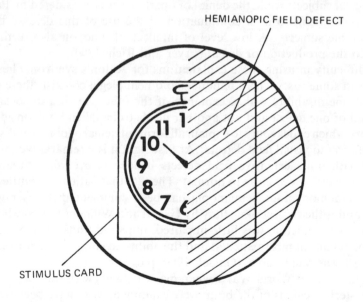

Fig. 7.6 Completion phenomenon

The opposite of completion is the phenomenon of *extinction* or *suppression*. Here a stimulus may be seen when shown singly in any part of the visual field, i.e. no visual field defect exists in the normal sense of the term. However, if the stimulus is paired with a similar stimulus and the pair are *presented simultaneously* each to a half-field corresponding to the two cerebral hemispheres, the stimulus in the half-field corresponding to (contralateral to) the affected hemisphere may fail to be reported. Such a finding will be of value in early diagnosis. The recent Neuropsychological Key approach to diagnosis employs tests of extinction or suppression of simultaneous stimulation among its measures (Russell, Neuringer and Goldstein, 1970). These authors believe that more subtle deficits may be detected by this means, the suppression or sensory imperception tests being part of their general rationale of comparing the perceptual functioning of the two hemispheres with each other to determine the lateralization of the lesion.

Apart from being found on routine neurological examination, visual field defects may be discovered on occasions for the first time when a patient has to deal with visual analysis and synthesis of configurations required for successful performance on some psychological tests, e.g. the patient may find difficulty with the Block Design or Object Assembly subtests of the Wechsler Adult Intelligence Scale, one of the most frequently employed tests in neuropsychological assessment. The difficulty with the seemingly easy material of these tests may surprise the patient who has adjusted well to everyday situations in which eye movements and other strategies may have minimized the defect or even rendered him completely unaware of it.

Gassel (1969) argues that the way in which the hemianopic patient adapts to his defect is similar to the operations of visual perception in the normal subject where the imperfections of the eye as an optical instrument do not interfere with the perception of the external world because of rapid eye movements and shifts in attention, both of which are usually carried out without the conscious awareness of the perceiver. 'Thus, in both normal vision and that of patients with homonymous hemianopia what is "seen" is really a conflation of a series of events in space and time, which also involves memory and expectation.' (Gassel, 1969, p.674). In other words the eye-brain analyzer is able under normal circumstances to convert a less than perfect set of data into a picture of what is 'out there' in the world and has the ability to continue doing so when the information is further reduced or degraded by visual field defects.

Visual agnosia

Visual-agnosia refers to a failure to recognize objects through the visual sense where there is neither a primary sensory loss nor mental deterioration. The essence of the disorder, as outlined by Freud (1891) when he introduced the term 'agnosia', was a disruption of the relationship between things themselves and the person's concepts of these things ('object concepts'). This notion distinguished the disorder from the group of aphasias where there was a disruption in the relationship between the concept of the object and the word used to signify it. The essence of these agnosic defects as Williams points out is 'not so much in non-awareness of the stimuli as in misrecognition of their meaning.' (Williams, 1970, p.58).

A number of separate forms of visual agnosia have been described as occurring in a pure form, i.e. in isolation from other defects. The validity of these claims is examined at the end of this section. The forms which have attracted most attention, particularly in recent years are (1) visual object agnosia; (2)

simultaneous agnosia, or simultanagnosia; (2) visuospatial agnosia; (4) agnosia for faces, or prosopagnosia; (5) colour agnosia; (6) pure word blindness, or agnosic alexia.

Whatever the status of these separate forms of visual agnosia or even of the validity of the concept of visual agnosia itself, the deficits described are important indicators of lesions in the occipital lobes, and hence the necessity for understanding the manner in which these forms of recognition disorder may present themselves and the tests which might elicit them.

The impaired recognition of spatial relationships sometimes called spatial or visuospatial agnosia has been described in Chapter 6.

Visual object agnosia

This is a failure to recognize objects when presented via the visual perceptual modality with preservation of recognition by other modalities such as touch. Gassel (1969) notes that there is often some difficulty in drawing objects from memory or in describing them so that defective visualization may play a part in these patient's symptoms.

Sometimes patients with visual object agnosia are able to use objects which they have failed to recognize but are unable to state the function of the object when shown it. This clearly distinguishes the condition from a similar deficit seen in amnesic aphasia where the patient, while unable to find the correct name for a thing, is well able to describe its use. Again, this demonstrates that an examination of the qualitative details of a patient's deficit may prove useful in localizing the causative lesion.

Most authors indict the lateral aspect of the dominant occipital lobe as the source of the difficulty. Kleist (1934) pointed to the importance of area 19 on the left side while Nielsen (1937) felt that, while left side lesions were more often the cause, visual agnosia for objects (or mind blindness as it was called earlier) could also occur with lesions of the right occipital region if the lesion lay in the 'cortex of the second and third convolutions'. (Fig. 7.7). He later considered that visual agnosia resulted from interruption of fibre connections between both striate areas and the area of the left occipital region depicted. This hypothesis is supported by the fact that cases with lesions of the left occipital lobe and the posterior portions of the corpus callosum—the splenium —do show agnosia. Some patients with a lesion confined mainly to the splenium of the corpus callosum have been found to have a marked visual agnosia for objects which fall in the half-fields contralateral to the so-called minor or non-dominant hemisphere, e.g. right-handed patients with left hemisphere dominance for language have difficulty only in their left visual fields (Tresher and Ford, 1937; Akelaitis, 1942; Gazzaniga, Bogen and Sperry, 1965). Improved experimental techniques of testing since the advent of cerebral commissurotomy in man have clarified and extended the earlier findings (see Chapter 8).

One of the requirements for a diagnosis of visual agnosia would be the absence of primary sensory defects such as loss of acuity since, in the sense of Freud's definition, the diagnosis depends on a dissociation between levels of visual function, higher order functions being compromised while

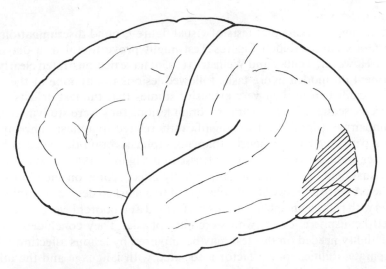

Fig. 7.7 The area in either hemisphere thought by Nielsen to be important in producing visual object agnosia.

primary sensory functions remain intact. A review of the literature shows that, while obvious defects of visual acuity may be absent, various perceptual disorders are very frequently present in the case of visual object agnosia. In the extensive report of Gloning, Gloning and Hoff (1968) which studied 241 cases of occipital lobe disorder, two findings are pertinent here. Firstly, only three cases of visual agnosia for objects were encountered in the total series and, secondly, each of these cases suffered also from a number of other perceptual disorders.

Cases described as visual object agnosia have been poorly documented on most occasions. Recent observations have suggested that this form of agnosia, although rare, may be explained in terms of a visual-verbal disconnection syndrome (Benson, Segarra and Albert, 1974; Albert, Reches and Silverberg, 1975).

Simultanagnosia

This form of visual agnosia consists of an inability to appreciate more than one aspect of a stimulus configuration at a time. Single aspects can be identified and pointed out from a stimulus array when it is presented again, suggesting clearly that the subject can identify and remember single features or objects even quite complex ones. In what appears to be a related disorder, some subjects are able to recognize still pictures but cannot understand a succession of pictures in a moving film. The difficulty in both cases appears to be one of synthesis.

Luria described such a case of difficulty with visual synthesis when the patient was shown a picture of a pair of spectacles. 'He is confused and does not know what the picture represents. He starts to guess. "There is a circle. . .and another circle. . .and a stick. . .and a cross-bar. . .why, it must be a bicycle"' (Luria, 1973b, p.116). Luria points out that these patients have particular difficulty if drawings are overruled with lines or presented against 'optically complex backgrounds'.

Such findings suggest that tests of visual figure-ground discrimination such as the Gottschaldt Hidden Figures Test might prove useful in a diagnostic battery. However, Teuber and Weinstein (1956) have demonstrated clearly that impairment on hidden figure tasks followed lesions in any lobe of the brain. They concluded from their very extensive studies that the test deficits were a non-specific sequel of the penetrating brain lesions they were studying. Moreover, impairment on the test was significantly related to aphasia since aphasic patients performed more poorly than non-aphasic brain-damaged subjects. This latter finding was confirmed by Russo and Vignolo (1967) who found that while visual field defects did not appreciably affect scores on the Gottschaldt Test, the presence and severity of aphasia did to a marked degree. Furthermore, patients with right hemisphere lesions performed at a poorer level than patients with left hemisphere lesions who were not aphasic. They concluded that the type of ability needed on this test may be impaired by lesions affecting at least two separate abilities, one a factor associated with language and the other a visuospatial factor related to the non-dominant hemisphere. This second aspect is in keeping with the accumulation of recent evidence supporting a major role for the non-dominant hemisphere in subserving visuospatial and visuoconstructive abilities.

An experimental study of three cases of simultanagnosia was made by Kinsbourne and Warrington (1963). Thresholds of recognition were determined for single stimuli and for two stimuli simultaneously exposed. While the thresholds for single stimuli were not altered significantly, there was invariably a long delay before the second stimulus was perceived. This delay in processing the second stimulus was seen as the basis of the deficit and is in accord with the hypothesis put forward by Birch, Belmont and Karp (1967) to account for visual extinction. These authors considered that extinction of response to a stimulus on one side occurred because the unaffected hemisphere processed its sensory input in advance of the damaged one and that the more highly organized processes of the intact hemisphere actively interfered with the more slowly integrating processes of the damaged side.

Bay (1953) attributed the disorder to a lowering of visual function which produced constriction in the visual field so that, in effect, the patient was functioning with tubular vision. Bay's position on visual agnosia is outlined below.

Agnosia for faces (prosopagnosia)

While patients with this disorder are able to recognize that a face *is* a face and may be able to identify the individual features, they are unable to identify the face as belonging, say, to a relative or friend. In some cases there is even difficulty with recognition of the patient's own face in the mirror. Charcot had described a case in which a patient held out his hand in excuse to another person for having bumped into him when it was, in fact, his own reflection (De Romanis and Benfatto, 1973). Hoff and Poetzl appear to have first described the condition in 1937 under the title 'amnesia for faces'. The term 'prosopagnosia' was introduced by Bodamer ten years later (Bodamer, 1947).

The condition rarely occurs as an isolated defect, being associated often with such other disorders as simultanagnosia and colour agnosia. The rarity of the defect in sufficiently pronounced form to be remarked clinically is shown by the occurrence of only one case in the series of Gloning, Gloning and Hoff (1968). However, some degree of deficit in the recognition of human faces is much more common when tests of this ability are introduced in the examination of patients with posterior lesions. Where facial recognition is poor, visual field defects are almost always present, usually in the form of hemianopia.

Location of the lesions. A good deal of attention has been directed to this question. In some studies there has been direct (post-mortem) or presumptive evidence of bilateral lesions in the occipital lobes. Gloning, Gloning, Jellinger and Quatember (1970) reviewing six cases concluded that either a bilateral lesion was present or a unilateral lesion was accompanied by involvement of the corpus callosum. They reported post-mortem evidence of bilateral softenings of the brain in the region of the lingual and fusiform gyri in a case which had shown prosopagnosia and other marked signs of visual agnosia but normal visual acuity. Gloning, *et al.* agree with Bornstein that clinical findings alone are insufficient for the purposes of localization (Bornstein, 1963, 1965; Bornstein and Kidron, 1959). A review of the literature by De Romanis and Benfatto (1973) reveals a relative scarcity of autopsy information only eight cases with such evidence being reported in the period 1958 to 1970. In five of these the lesions were bilateral and in three cases unilateral (two right and one left) with the corpus callosum also being implicated in four of them.

In study of unilateral lesions, prosopagnosia has been reported more frequently with right sided lesions though it does appear to occur with left sided ones (Beyn and Knyazeva, 1962; Hécaen and Angelergues, 1962; Bornstein, 1965; Tzavaras, Hécaen and Le Bras, 1970). De Romanis and Benfatto (1973) reviewed 112 cases described in the literature to that time. Of these, 42 appeared to have lesions in the non-dominant hemisphere, 41 were bilateral, while 29 had dominant hemisphere lesions.

The disability not only appears with greater frequency but in more severe forms in patients with right sided lesions (Warrington and James, 1967a; Benton and Van Allen, 1968). Thus, faulty recognition of faces can be added to the growing list of deficits whose frequency and severity is strongly associated with right hemisphere lesions (Benton, 1965). The increasing acceptance of the posterior regions of the right hemisphere as the most important site for the production of impairment of facial recognition is questioned by the findings of the study by Benton and Van Allen since performance level on their test of identification of unfamiliar faces was not related to the *intrahemispheric* locus of lesions.

In view of what has been said earlier on the nature of functional systems (Ch. 1) it may be illogical to search for a single, narrowly localized site for the production of the deficit in all cases, rather, the processes underlying the complex perceptual task of facial identification may well be affected by lesions in different locations, though the right posterior regions are obviously of paramount importance.

Nature of the defect. There is still no agreement as to the nature of the defect in these cases. The most fruitful line of research is in the relationship of prosopagnosia to other forms of visuoperceptual disturbance. Many regard it as merely one form of disturbance of the visual recognition process, an inability to discriminate complex visual configurations especially those that cannot easily be verbalized (Gloning, Gloning, Jellinger and Quatember, 1970). If this is so, testing of patients with prosopagnosia should reveal difficulties with other complex perceptual material. De Renzi and Spinnler (1966b) found defects in recognizing both abstract figures as well as photographs of human faces in patients with right hemisphere lesions while De Renzi, Faglioni and Spinnler (1968) describe a marked case of prosopagnosia who was also impaired on tasks requiring the discrimination of complex visual patterns. On the other hand, Tzavaras, Hécaen and Le Bras (1970) found no correlation between poor performance on tests of facial recognition and a range of other tests of a complex perceptual nature from which they concluded that the hypothesis of the existence of a separate entity of prosopagnosia was supported.

A rather different hypothesis has been advanced by Warrington and James (1967a) who suggest that there may be two types of problem in patients with difficulty in recognising faces, one a perceptual difficulty associated with parietal (or occipital lesions) and the other a memory difficulty associated with temporal lesions. The notion of impairment of visual memory contributing to the disorder has been given verbal support by Gloning, Gloning, Jellinger and Quatember (1970) and some factual support by Tzavaras, Merienne and Masure (1973). The latter authors described a case of prosopagnosia, dysphasia and memory problems in a left handed patient with a left temporal lesion. Repeated testing suggested that his difficulty with the recognition of faces was not one of perceptual discrimination but a failure in the storage of information. Several studies have shown that prosopagnosia may exist in the presence of a normal performance on tests which assess the capacity to discriminate faces (Assal, 1969; Tzavaras, Hécaen and Le Bras, 1970; Benton and Van Allen, 1972).

Many writers agree that the fault in prosopagnosia lies in the disturbances of visual synthesis or the integration of received sensory data (Benton and Van Allen, 1968; Pallis, 1955; Gloning, Gloning and Hoff, 1968). Since visual fixation is necessary for such synthesis, it is possible that difficulties in fixation might lead to impairment of facial recognition. This suggestion has been put forward by Gloning and his colleagues (Gloning, Haub and Quatember, 1967, and Gloning, Gloning, Hoff and Tschabitcher, 1966) who felt that the prime difficulty lay in identifying the 'eye-region' of the face but they later describe a case with very marked prosopagnosia who had no such difficulty, (Gloning, Gloning, Jellinger and Quatember, 1970). The argument which Luria (1973b) presents on the role of fixation difficulties in simultaneous agnosia might well be applied also to agnosia for faces.

Colour agnosia

Acquired disturbances of colour vision are an important sign of occipital lobe involvement. The basis of the various disturbances of colour sense is still poorly understood but several distinctions will prove clinically useful. Colour agnosia seems to comprise at least two separate entities, namely, visual agnosia for colours and a defect of colour naming.

The patient with agnosia for colours has difficulty in identifying colours in practice. He is unable to match colours or order them in series as in Holmgren's colour sorting test with skeins of wool (Goldstein and Scheerer, 1941) or, if he can manage the task, finds it a good deal more difficult than normal subjects. In keeping with the general philosophy of the term agnosia no primary sense disability is apparent, e.g. on testing with a pseudoisochromatic chart such as that of Ishihara (Lhermitte, Chain and Aron, 1965). As with other visuognostic disorders colour agnosia is often associated with visual field defects particularly right homonymous hemianopia in this case. Disorders of colour recognition have been reported more frequently with lesions of the dominant hemisphere (Kinsbourne and Warrington, 1964).

The colour naming defect is believed by some to be a specific defect (Nielsen, 1962). The patient who performs normally on the Ishihara and Holmgren tests is unable to name the colour of an object or to recognize it when it is given to him. Though this defect may occur as part of a more general dysphasia it does occur with no observable language difficulty. The failure to recognize the name when given distinguishes it from the amnestic aphasia described earlier. Critchley (1965) has described in detail the features of colour agnosia which distinguish it from other forms of colour blindness.

The relation of colour agnosia to aphasia is one which has to be examined in each case but there is so far little direct support for Geschwind's hypothesis (Geschwind, 1965a, 1965b) that colour naming is secondary to language defect. If they understand the instructions aphasic patients usually do not show abnormalities on tests of colour vision (Alajouanine, Castaigne and De Ribaucourt-Ducarne, 1960).

The nature of the deficit seems to depend to some degree on the type of test administered. Recently the Milan group has developed a test in which the patient is required to colour outline drawings of objects having a definite colour, such as cherries, the national flag, and so on (De Renzi and Spinnler, 1967). They found that difficulty with this task was particularly associated with lesions of the left hemisphere. This finding was confirmed by Faglioni, Scotti and Spinnler (1970) and Spinnler (1971), both studies showing that the main defect related to this test was receptive aphasia, and in both studies there was a positive relationship with the Weigl test of conceptual thinking. They concluded that this ability to associate a drawing with its colour can be viewed as an aspect of the aphasic's impairment in mastering concepts (Spinnler, 1971). As Gassel (1969) remarks *colours*, separate from *coloured objects*, involve a degree of intellectual abstraction' so that the relationship with Weigl's test is not surprising.

The greater difficulty with this task for patients with left hemisphere lesions was not found by Tzavaras and Hécaen (1970) though these workers did find a correlation between the degree of deficit in left hemisphere patients and the presence of receptive aphasia.

Colour imperception as distinct from colour recognition defects may be more associated with the right rather than left hemisphere defects especially in the presence of visual field defects (Scotti and Spinnler, 1970).

Pure word blindness (agnosic alexia)

This form of reading difficulty consists of failure to recognize words without evidence of dysphasia such as speech and writing disorders. These latter conditions are treated under disorders of language (Ch. 9). Reading difficulties with language disturbance could be designated aphasic alexia.

Agnosic alexia has also been termed alexia *without* agraphia since, unlike the dysphasic patient, the patient can write either spontaneously or to dictation. The visual basis of the difficulty becomes apparent when the patient is unable to copy printed material and is unable to read a sentence from a card in front of him which the examiner has just read and the patient has clearly understood. Where the disorder is not very gross the patient may have difficulty only with longer words and a careful search in these cases may reveal elements of simultaneous agnosia. Sometimes the patient can recognize single letters and may even be able to spell whole words without understanding them, the so-called spelling alexia.

Pure word blindness provides a further example of the explanation of neuropsychological symptoms in terms of a disconnection syndrome. Such an explanation has been used to account for the first case of agnosia without alexia described by Dejerine in 1892 as well as more recent cases (Geshwind, 1965; Walsh and Hoyt, 1969). Several findings make such an explanation more easily understood. (1) there is a highly significant correlation between pure word blindness and colour agnosia (Gloning, Gloning and Hoff, 1968). These authors point out that this relationship has been reported frequently since it was first noted by Poetzl in 1928 and suggest the term 'Poetzl's syndrome' for the association. (2) in some cases (37 per cent of those of Gloning *et al.*) the reading of numbers is not disturbed, (3) a right homonymous hemianopia is almost always present.

The concurrence of symptoms is explained by a lesion which damages the left occipital region and the splenium or posterior portion of the corpus callosum which connects both occipital lobes (Fig. 7.8). Both these regions are supplied by the posterior cerebral artery, and infarction in the distribution of this vessel is almost the sole cause of the syndrome since other lesions are most unlikely to affect both areas so completely and exclusively (Walsh and Hoyt, 1969). Since the regions concerned with the nonvisual aspects of language are supplied by the other main arteries these latter functions remain unaffected.

Visual information received by the right occipital lobe cannot reach the language hemisphere (left) because of the interruption to the interhemispheric fibres in the splenium (Fig. 7.8). Thus, while they can see, these patients are unable to interpret or speak about what they see. The preservation of the patient's ability to write spontaneously is accounted for by the fact that nonvisual stimuli from both hemispheres can reach appropriate language centres over intra and interhemispheric connections. The patient is, however, unable to transcribe printed material.

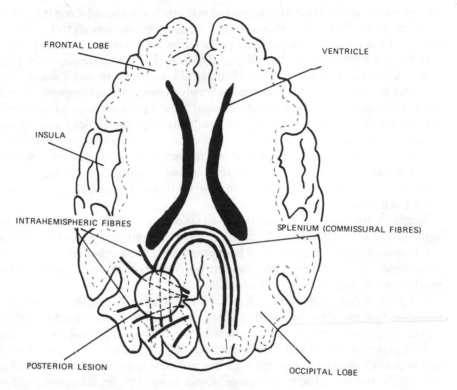

Fig. 7.8 Horizontal section with lesion in the left occipital lobe producing alexia without agraphia

The importance of the splenium of the corpus callosum in the production of this syndrome has been emphasized by numerous authors (Kleist, 1934; Alajouanine, Lhermitte and De Ribaucourt-Ducarne, 1960) and is shown by cases where the callosum has been divided in the removal of cysts of the third ventricle (Tresher and Ford, 1937; Maspes, 1948) or in the more recent operation of cerebral commissurotomy for the relief of epilepsy (Gazzaniga, Bogen and Sperry, 1962, 1965; Geschwind, 1962, 1965b, 1965c). These patients showed alexia only in the left visual field since this information is transmitted to the right occipital lobe and cannot reach the language centres in the dominant hemisphere over the severed commissural fibres. For a similar reason removal of the occipital lobe of the language dominant hemisphere has been shown to produce lasting word blindness (Ajuriaguerra and Hécaen, 1951).

Anatomical evidence supporting the suggestion by Geschwind that the lesion in agnosic alexia affects the visual cortex of the dominant hemisphere and the splenium of the corpus callosum without affecting other regions such as the supramarginal gyrus is given by Cumming, Hurwitz and Perl (1969).

The sparing of the reading of numbers may be accounted for by the preservation of associations such as those developed by counting on the fingers. These associations of somaesthetic with visual information could still reach the language hemisphere over the intact interhemispheric pathways anterior to the splenium. By contrast, the naming of colours is not spared since it involves no associations beside the visuo-auditory ones. 'A colour has no feel, smell, or taste and has no fixed associations but its name'. (Geschwind, 1965a, p.99).

A further refinement in the study of disconnection mechanisms underlying alexia comes from a case of Greenblatt (1973). In this case and a similar one reported by Ajax (1967) the focal lesion involved only the ventro-medial aspect of the left occipital lobe and the splenium of the corpus callosum. Greenblatt's patient had alexia without agraphia but no hemianopia and colour naming was preserved. He puts forward the hypothesis that. . .'within each occipital lobe, the inferior association tracts and the ventro-medial (lingual and fusiform) gyri are necessary for reading. Visual-verbal colour naming, on the other hand, apparently may be served either by the dorsal or by the ventral outflow paths from the calcarine cortex.'

Similarly, the careful symptomatic analysis of a case of agnosic alexia, colour agnosia and severe naming difficulties in a patient with left posterior cerebral artery ischaemia by Lhermitte and Beauvois (1973) has further emphasized the importance of intrahemispheric as well as commissural connections in the production of symptoms in such cases.

Likewise, Albert, Yamadori, Gardner and Howes (1973) propose a functional disconnection between the visual, auditory and motor systems used in the understanding of written language as a possible basis for their patient's symptoms.

This patient who had had a tumour removed from the left temporo-occipital region showed alexia without agraphia but was able to spell words presented to him orally and was able to recognize words from their letters spelled out to him though he was unable to spell words presented in written form and was unable to carry out written commands. It seems important, as in this case, to establish whether the patient has preservation of capacities which are intramodal (within the auditory-oral system) or intermodal (visual-auditory), or both.

The fact that left hemisphere lesions are paramount in the production of acquired reading disabilities does not imply that the right hemisphere plays no important part in reading. Faglioni, Scotti and Spinnler (1968) have shown that there is a clear dissociation between the effects of left and right hemisphere damage on the subject's performance on visual recognition of verbal material.

Again, as shown for the temporal lobes with regard to auditory material, the dissociation is between the semantic-associative capacities of the left hemisphere and the perceptual-discriminative capacities of the right. An integration of both sets of functions is necessary for effective reading.

Status of the concept of visual agnosia: There has been a movement in recent years away from the acceptance of visual agnosia in its early accepted sense as a clinical entity to the position that there are patients with varying degrees of difficulty with visual recognition not all of which can be accounted for by a single deficiency. The definition of agnosia as a higher order loss without evidence of disturbance of primary visual functions will depend upon what is accepted as a 'primary visual function'. Bay, in a series of papers (e.g. Bay, 1953) has put forward the notion that visual agnosia is due to a combination of faulty visual clues due to lowering of visual function plus an ineffective interpretation by the patient of the visual information he has. Bay claims that the lowering of visual function can be demonstrated by refined means of testing where normal tests such as retinal perimetry may show the fields to be normal. His theory has received some support (Critchley, 1964; Bender and Feldman, 1965) though there are also a number of objections. Gassel (1969) points out that the findings such as those of Bergman (1957) and Williams and Gassel (1962) demonstrate that many patients with marked visual field constriction do not have disturbances of visual recognition.

Gloning, Gloning and Hoff (1968) do not believe that dissociation of primary and secondary visual functions exists at all in the sense that Freud first suggested. Their own series of cases gives strong support to this view only three cases with visual recognition difficulties occurring in 241 cases when those with severe visual disturbances or mental deterioration were excluded. As Critchley remarks 'cases of visual agnosia though a commonplace in medical textbooks, represent—let us admit—an extreme rarity in clinical practice.' (Critchley, 1964, p.281).

The rarity of the pure 'syndrome' of visual agnosia should not prevent neuropsychologists from examining the fundamental difficulties which give rise to all forms of visual recognition disorder.

Visual hallucinations

Visual hallucinations are described frequently in conditions affecting the occipital lobes (Allen, 1930; Paillas, Cossa, Darcourt and Naquet, 1965; Gloning, Gloning and Hoff, 1968). The essential characteristic of these hallucinations is their elementary nature. More organized visual hallucinations of people, objects and scenes usually indicate that the excitation is arising in or has spread to neighbouring regions particularly the temporal lobes. Elementary hallucinations or photisms have been described by a number of authors (Lhermitte, 1951; Ajuriaguerra and Hécaen, 1960; Gloning, Gloning and Hoff, 1968). The latter authors found 55 cases of elementary visual hallucinations in their series. These were almost exclusively projected to the half-field contralateral to the lesion and consisted of points, stars, flames, flashes, wheels, circles and triangles. A few cases of photisms with lesions outside the occipital lobes were reported and each of these seemed to be due to irritation of the visual pathways.

Elementary hallucinations have been well documented with focal epileptic seizures originating in the occipital lobes (Penfield and Jasper, 1954; Russell and Whitty, 1955; Lhermitte, 1951). Again, the sensations are referred to the contralateral half-field.

Electrical stimulation

The findings of studies of spontaneously occurring hallucinations in posterior cerebral lesions have been very strongly confirmed by the results of stimulation, in that complex visual experiences, most frequently that of a person or group of persons, are produced from the temporal, temporo-occipital or parieto-occipital regions but not from the visual cortex itself. Gloning, Gloning and Hoff (1968) reported no hemispheric difference in the incidence of complex visual hallucinations for their lesion cases. This is in marked contrast to the stimulation findings reported by Penfield and Perot (1963) where visual hallucinations of prior experience were elicited overwhelmingly from the right hemisphere (Fig. 7.9).

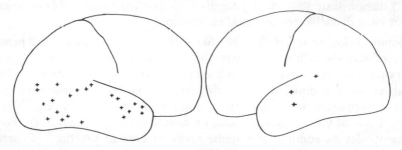

Fig. 7.9 Visual experiential responses evoked by stimulation (from Penfield and Perot, 1963)

The content of the hallucinations when complex may be determined by prior experience. A male patient of Gloning, Gloning and Hoff who had been a philatelist saw postage stamps in the hemianopic parts of his visual field while one of our patients who had been a forestry officer saw predominantly scenes with trees. As is often the case, the hallucinations were vividly coloured, the patient describing them as colours he had not seen before 'colours such as they bring out for new cars each year'. They were so vivid that they prevented the patient getting off to sleep.

Sometimes the experimental hallucination elicited by stimulation is very similar to that experienced by the patient during an epileptic seizure. The following case is condensed from Penfield and Perot (1963).

Case 3—a 12 year old boy with a three year history of seizures. The pattern of his attacks was
1. visual sensation (coloured triangles);
2. experiential hallucination—visual;
3. automatism. . .after the visual sensation usually he would see a robber, or a man with a gun, moving toward him. The man was someone he had seen in the movies or the comic strips. . .(stimulation of several points on the right temporo-occipital cortex produced the following references). 'Oh gee, gosh, robbers are coming at me with guns! . .Pain in my forehead, and there was a robber. He wasn't in front, he was off to the left side' . . .'Yes, the robbers, they are coming after me' . . .'Oh gosh! Here they are, my brother is there. He is aiming an air rifle at me.'

The very wide experience of Penfield and his colleagues with brain stimulation (Penfield and Rasmussen, 1950; Penfield and Jasper, 1954; Penfield and Perot, 1963) show that lights, shadows, colours, movements and other elementary visual sensations occur on stimulation of the occipital lobe (areas 17, 18, 19) and never complex figures or scenes. The fact that Foerster (1936) described the evocation of figures or scenes on stimulation of area 19 might be accounted for by the spread of excitation to regions in front of the occipital lobes.

8. Hemispheric asymmetry of function

The concept of cerebral dominance

The most significant discovery leading to the notion of cerebral dominance was the finding by Dax, Broca and others of a strong relationship between lesions of the left hemisphere and disorders of language namely disorders of expression, comprehension, reading, and writing. For many people the concept of cerebral dominance remained confined to the lateral specialization for language at least until recent times. However, there were notable exceptions. One of these was the great English neurologist Hughlings Jackson. In 1864, that is not long after Broca's first report Jackson commented 'If, then it should be proved by wider evidence that the faculty of expression resides in one hemisphere, there is no absurdity in raising the question as to whether perception—its corresponding opposite—may not be seated in the other.'

Benton (1965) pointed out that extension of the concept of dominance beyond the sphere of language seemed to be required by the findings of Liepmann and Gerstmann in the early part of the present century. Liepmann had first described *apraxia* 'the inability to perform a skilled act or series of movements, this disability occurring within the setting of preserved comprehension and adequate sensory and neuromuscular capacity.' (Benton op. cit. p.334). A particular form of this disorder termed ideomotor apraxia Liepmann found to be associated with lesions of the left hemisphere. In this disorder the patient was unable to carry out a skilled act on verbal command. Subsequent reviews have supported Liepmann's notion that ideomotor apraxia is associated exclusively with lesions of the left hemisphere. Gerstmann's 'syndrome' has been discussed in Chapter 6 but, despite the doubtful status of the syndrome itself, there is no doubt about the strong association of each of the component symptoms or signs with disorders of the left hemisphere—and their almost complete absence in right hemisphere disease.

While these findings enriched the range of disorders associated with lesions of the left hemisphere it has been argued that both ideomotor apraxia and the Gerstmann symptoms may be conceptualized as due to a language deficit (Poeck and Orgass, 1966; Brewer, 1969). Brewer reminds us of the recent evidence showing that many 'ostensibly non-verbal tasks' are verbally encoded by the subject so that failure on such a task is only enlightening when we are sure how the subject normally goes about the task. 'Thus, given the current state of knowledge, it is possible to hold the extreme hypothesis, that all tasks showing left-hemisphere dominance are due to an underlying linguistic deficit'. (Brewer, 1969).

For a long time many neurologists, while accepting the evidence for lateralization of language, were unwilling to admit that the other hemisphere, often termed 'minor' or non-dominant, might also have areas of specialization in which it excelled. Several converging lines of evidence have made it clear that the right hemisphere does, indeed, have such distinctive functions. Zangwill (1961) was one of the first to assemble evidence as to the functions of the minor hemisphere and he defined the principle of cerebral dominance as follows:

'As ordinarily understood, this principle states that certain higher functions, in particular speech, are differentially represented in the two hemispheres—and are liable to be disturbed, predominantly if not exclusively, by damage to one alone. Further, it has long been accepted that the dominant hemisphere is typically that contralateral to the preferred hand—though many exceptions to this rule are known, particularly among the left handed' (p.51).

This question of the relationship between lateral hand preference and hemispheric dominance for language has only recently become clarified and will be considered first. This will be followed by the principal lines of evidence which have led to a clearer understanding of the functioning of the two hemispheres. These include (1) the evidence from naturally occurring cerebral lesions including agenesis or absence of the corpus callosum, (2) commissurotomy studies, and (3) hemispherectomy. The emerging knowledge of asymmetry derived from the pathological material is then reinforced by a number of recent studies which demonstrate asymmetry of cerebral function in normal subjects notably for auditory and visual perception. The chapter concludes with a brief consideration of the concept of cerebral dominance in the light of this knowledge.

Dominance for speech and hand preference

Very soon after the introduction of the concept of dominance with the classic formulation that the left hemisphere was dominant in right handed individuals and *vice versa*, numerous exceptions were found to the second half of the formula. Study of right handed aphasics revealed well over 90 per cent to have lesions in the left hemisphere. On the other hand numerous studies of left handed aphasics while varying somewhat in their findings have tended to show a much lower proportion of left hemisphere lesions and a higher proportion of right hemisphere lesions than in the right handed groups. Even in groups of left handed individuals the left hemisphere appears to be the site of the lesion in 60 per cent or more of the cases. There is also evidence to show that often (but certainly not always) aphasia tends to be less severe and prolonged in left handed cases (Chesher, 1936; Conrad, 1949).

Such facts have been thought by some to reflect a bilateral representation of speech in left handers (Subirana, 1958; Zangwill, 1960). Support for such a contention comes from the examination of left handers using the Wada technique.

Benton (1965) points out that the category of left-handedness poses a number of problems if one is to utilize such a category for correlation with pathology. Some 'left-handers' are indeed more skilful with their left hand than with the right and employ it for preference. Other 'left handers' in fact both employ the right hand more and are more skilled with it. A third and much larger category is much closer to ambidexterity.

The Wada technique. The introduction of the intracarotid sodium amytal test by Wada (1949) has allowed a more definitive statement to be made on the lateral representation of speech. This technique has been extensively employed at the Montreal Neurological Institute where several hundred cases have been studied, the injections on the right and left sides being carried out on separate days. Most of the subjects have been under consideration for surgery and the greater number were left handed or ambidextrous patients together with a smaller number of right handed patients for whom the lateralization of language was in doubt (Branch, Milner, and Rasmussen, 1964; Milner, Branch, and Rasmussen, 1966; Milner, 1974).

In the first report there was a marked difference between the findings for right handed and non-right handed patients (Table 8.1).

Table 8.1 Relationship of handedness to speech lateralization (From Branch *et al.*, 1964)

| Handedness | No. of Cases | Speech Representation | | |
		Left	Bilateral	Right
Left	51	22 (43%)	4 (8%)	25 (49%)
Ambidextrous	20	12 (60%)	6 (30%)	2 (10%)
Right	48	43 (90%)	0 —	5 (10%)

Several points emerge clearly from these findings. Firstly, there is an absence of bilateral representation in right handed subject. Secondly, there is a difference in lateralization between the two non-right handed groups. The left handed group has a high percentage of right hemisphere representation and a small percentage of bilateral representation while the ambidextrous group has by far the highest percentage of bilateral representation and a much smaller percentage of right hemisphere speech representation. Grouped together the total non-right handers showed 48 per cent of left, 38 per cent of right, and 14 per cent of bilateral representation.

A closer examination showed a further difference when the non-right handed group was divided into those having clinical evidence of early left hemisphere damage (within the first five years of life).

The difference between the two non-right handed groups seems to imply that in some cases at least the left handedness is a reflection of early left hemisphere damage. Milner also draws attention to the 'impressive tendency for speech to become organized in the left hemisphere', some two-thirds of normal left handers having speech representation in the left hemisphere and even 30 per cent of those left handers with gross early damage to the left hemisphere still have the major representation of language on the left side.

Table 8.2 Handedness and carotid-amytal speech lateralization (From Milner, 1974)

Handedness	No. of cases	Speech Representation		
		Left	Bilateral	Right
Right	95	87 (92%)	1 (1%)	7 (7%)
Left or ambidextrous WITHOUT early left hemisphere damage	74	51 (69%)	10 (13%)	13 (18%)
WITH early left hemisphere damage	43	13 (30%)	7 (16%)	23 (54%)

Warrington and Pratt (1973) in examining transient dysphasia following electroconvulsive therapy applied unilaterally found strong confirmation for predominant language representation in the left hemisphere in about 70 per cent of left handers, (Lansdell, 1962). Hécaen and Sauguet (1971) have examined the differential characteristics of aphasia in left handers according to the side of the lesion. Left handers with left hemisphere lesions tend to have aphasic disturbances as happens with right handers. However, they have a lower frequency for comprehension and writing defects and a higher frequency for reading difficulties. Disturbances of other functions from left hemisphere lesions, e.g. disorders of calculation, perception and praxis are similar in the two groups. With right hemisphere lesions left handed patients, unlike right handed, have a high frequency of disturbance of language both oral and written, while the disorders of calculation, perception and praxis are again similar in the two groups.

These authors also found a difference between left handers according to the presence or absence of left handedness in the family history. In those with a positive familial history of sinistrality, language disturbances occurred with similar frequency with either left or right hemisphere lesions whereas language disturbances were almost absent with right hemisphere lesions where there was no familial history of left handedness.

The importance of a family history of sinistrality in relation to laterality differences in both right and left handers has been reported in recent years for both auditory and visual perception (Zurif and Bryden, 1969; Hines and Satz, 1971).

Lansdell (1962) found that not only did the right hemisphere become dominant for speech in some cases of early left hemisphere damage but that this right hemisphere also became involved with the verbal factor in intelligence.

These few facts merely serve to introduce the general question of hand preference and cerebral asymmetry. More extensive treatments are provided by Subirana (1969) and Levy (1974a).

The remainder of the chapter is devoted to a summary of some of the main areas that have extended our knowledge of functional asymmetry between the hemispheres.

Unilateral lesion studies

No attempt has been made to present an exhaustive coverage of lesion studies related to asymmetry of hemispheric function. However, most of the principal areas are outlined and these may be supplemented by reviews such as: Mountcastle, 1962; Hécaen, 1969; Subirana, 1969; Milner, 1971; Benton, 1972; Dimond and Beaumont, 1974; Kinsbourne and Smith, 1974; Schmitt and Worden, 1974; Joynt and Goldstein, 1975.

In reviewing lesion studies there is a tendency to concentrate on lateral differences rather than similarities in function. This often leads to a devaluation of the role of one of the hemispheres in the particular function under scrutiny. Before beginning our review of the evidence for separate functions attributed to the minor hemisphere it would be wise to remember that there is no convincing evidence for absolute control of any complex psychological process by either hemisphere. 'The idea of cerebral dominance for a function must be revised, since it appears that there may only be a hemispheric proponderance rather than dominance for a certain behaviour. Thus there are relative rather than absolute contributions from the two hemispheres. This makes it more imminent that we categorise behaviour in its component operations if we wish to make sense out of localisation studies on brain behaviour correlations'. (Joynt and Goldstein, 1975, p.172).

Visual perception and asymmetry

The following is a sample of the very large amount of information which has accumulated since the sixties about the asymmetry of function of the hemispheres with relation to visual perception. A good deal of it tends to support the hypothesis of a special role for the minor hemisphere which is the complement of the left hemisphere's specialization in verbal symbolic processes.

Stereopsis. The development of random dot stereograms by Julesz (1964) has presented us with a technique for the study of depth perception where monocular cues to depth and form can be eliminated as well as eliminating figure-ground contours. Carmon and Bechtoldt (1969) compared the stereoscopic vision of subjects with unilateral lesions using the Julesz technique. Left hemisphere subjects showed no deficits compared with normal controls. Those with right hemisphere lesions showed significantly more errors and longer response times than either of the other two groups. Using essentially the same procedure but different clinical groups Benton and Hécaen (1970) have strongly replicated these results.

Figure-ground discrimination. In his studies of perceptual defects after penetrating missile wounds Poppelreuter (1917) developed the overlapping figures test. The subject is required to demonstrate his ability to name or outline a number of figures in overlapping drawings (Fig. 8.1) or to select from a number of alternatives the complex figure in which a simpler figure has been 'embedded' (Fig. 8.2).

A number of studies of soldiers with penetrating missile wounds (Poppelreuter, 1917; Golstein, 1927; Teuber, Battersby, and Bender, 1951) as well as patients with cerebral tumours (Battersby, Krieger, Pollack, and Bender, 1953) have shown that difficulty with tasks like the Gottschaldt Hidden Figure Test is a common accompaniment of cerebral lesions. Subsequently, Teuber and Weinstein (1956) and Russo and Vignolo (1967) have demonstrated an asso-

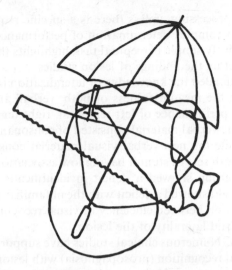

Fig. 8.1 Overlapping drawings test (after Poppelreuter, 1917)

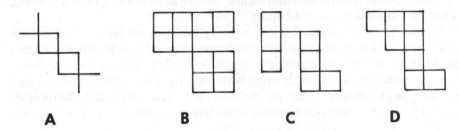

A   **B**   **C**   **D**

Fig. 8.2 Typical item in embedded figures test. Figure A is embedded in B and D but not C.

ciation of this defect with the presence of aphasia. The latter study compared patients with unilateral right and left lesions with each other and with controls. The presence of aphasia and of visual field defects was checked in each case. While there was a significant association with both the presence and severity of language disorders, visual field defects did not affect scores significantly. Furthermore, considered as single groups, the left and right hemisphere cases did not appear to differ. However, right brain damaged patients did significantly worse than non-aphasic left brain damaged patients, these latter performing very much like the control subjects. Russo and Vignolo suggest that poor performance may be related to the impairment of at least two specific abilities namely a language ability and a perceptual factor, the latter being 'preferentially subserved' by the right hemisphere. Poeck *et al.* (1973) confirmed the finding of a disturbance on the Gottschaldt test with lesions of either hemisphere. They suggest that there is a 'common underlying functional disturbance of the visuospatial type associated with the retrorolandic part of both hemispheres'. They point to the recent evidence from both normal and commissurotomy subjects (see below) which shows that different forms of information processing are utilised by the two hemispheres, i.e. 'non-verbal strategy predominates in visual information processing, unless there is a specific requirement for inner verbalization'. Such complex determination of performance on what appears at first to be a relatively simple perceptual task highlights the care which must be taken in interpreting the findings of lesion studies.

Rubino (1970) extended the knowledge of lateralization in visual perception by greatly reducing the meaningfulness of both 'verbal' and figural material and comparing the performance of left temporal, right temporal and normal control subjects. The verbal material consisted of consonant vowel-consonant trigrams (CVC) while the non verbal visual material consisted of randomly generated figures, both sets of stimuli having low association value (meaning). The left temporal group showed a deficit in identification of the nonsense syllables while the right showed a deficit with the unfamiliar figures. Thus there appears to be a relation between efficiency of visual recognition, the nature of the visual material and laterality of the lesion.

Facial recognition. Numerous clinical studies have supported the association of disorders of facial recognition (prosopagnosia) with lesions on the posterior part of the right hemisphere (Hécaen and Angelergues, 1962; De Renzi and Spinnler, 1966b; Warrington and James, 1967a; Benton and van Allen, 1968). This topic was discussed in Chapter 7.

Milner (1968b) considered that a memory factor might be involved in such disorders but De Renzi, Faglioni and Spinnler could find no evidence for a memory factor being a determinant of prosopagnosia. Warrington and James (1967a) found that locus of the lesion within the right hemisphere had an effect on the type of difficulty. Right parietal cases were more affected in the recognition of new faces while right temporal cases had more difficulty with well known faces.

Visuospatial perception and related functions. Over the past three decades a very large number of studies has produced evidence for the relatively greater importance of the right than the left hemisphere for the perception of spatial relationships. The following is a representative sample of such significant papers: Paterson and Zangwill, 1944; McFie, Piercy and Zangwill, 1950; Ettlinger, Warrington, and Zangwill, 1957; Piercy, Hécaen, and Ajuriaguerra, 1960; Whitty and Newcombe, 1965; Milner, 1965; Warrington and James, 1967b; Newcombe, 1969; Warrington and Rabin, 1970. Much of the relevant material has been reviewed in Chapter 6. A few further points might be made.

In order to establish the exact nature of the visuospatial defect which appears to be associated with right posterior lesions it is necessary to show dissociation of the defect from others, e.g., the recent study of Taylor and Warrington (1973) demonstrates that while patients with right posterior lesions are inferior to other groups on a spatial task of position discrimination they are not inferior on other discrimination tasks such as size and shape. Such studies will help to specify the nature of the defect more precisely.

A second factor which clouds the issue as to what is lateralized is the degree of complexity of the task, hence the degree to which sundry factors dependent on different areas (and hemispheres) may enter into the performance. Many of the tasks mentioned in Chapter 6 involve space perception at a rather complex level. De Renzi, Faglioni, and Scotti (1971) point out that this makes it difficult 'to disentangle the influence on performance of spatial as compared with praxic, intelligence and memory factors'. These authors found that with a very simple test such as visual (or tactile) judgment of the orientation of a single rod in space, only the right posterior group performed poorly, other brain-damaged groups performing very much like controls. Also the fact that there was no significant difference in effect for the different sense modalities stresses the truly 'spatial' nature of the defect. 'It appears, therefore, that when spatial perception is tested at a very basic and simple level. . . there is almost a complete dominance of the posterior region of the so-called minor hemisphere. This result must be contrasted with the less striking asymmetry of function shown in more complex spatial tasks—for example, route finding, copying drawings, block designs— that are failed also by patients with damage to the left posterior area' (p.489). Miller (1972a) reminds us that 'it may well be that the important factor in determining whether an apparently spatial task is affected by left posterior lesions as well as right is the degree of verbal mediation used by the subject. Although a task may be spatial in nature, this does not prevent a subject from using verbal reasoning in its solution and to the extent that this occurs the task will be more liable to disruption by left-sided lesions even though the task may be particularly difficult to verbalize' (pp.86-87).

The issue of task complexity has been handled by Orgass et al. (1972) in a different manner. They began by looking at factor analytic studies of visual cognitive processes in normal subjects and then selected tests related to the three most consistently found factors. The three factors were (1) speed of visual closure (Street's Figure Completion Test), (2) flexibility of visual closure (Gottschaldt Embedded Figures Test) and (3) perceptual speed (form recognition test). Performance on these tests was then related to the lobar and hemispheric locations of lesions, and the presence of aphasia and visual field defects. The presence of field defects can be taken to indicate the presence of a posterior hemispheric lesion. In keeping with other studies cited above, aphasia was related to factor (2) (Gottschaldt's Test) while there was no significant relation to laterality, location or presence of field defects. However, the combination of a right-sided lesion with the presence of visual field defect gave significant impairment of the other two factors, namely, speed of closure and speed of recognition. Since neither laterality nor presence of VFD were alone significant the authors conclude that 'the presence of VFD in the patient with right-sided lesions does not act on test performance as a defect in visual function but stands for a critical localization of lesion'.

Finally, Ratcliff and Newcombe (1973) pointed out that a distinction should be made between visuospatial tasks such as those cited above where the subject can explore spatial relations without any major changes in his position, and tests such as Semmes' locomotor map-reading task (Ch. 6) which measure the subject's topographical orientation ability in a dynamic situation. Using a 'static' task of the first kind they confirmed the expected inferior performance of those with right posterior lesions. However, on the 'dynamic' map-reading task those with unilateral posterior lesions and bilateral frontal lesions were unimpaired, only bilateral posterior lesions showing a lowered performance. They suggest that while the right hemisphere obviously plays an important role in spatial perception 'it does not bear exclusive responsibility for the maintenance of spatial orientation'. The locus of the lesion related to topographical orientation is unclear and may be clarified by the specification of task variables as well as clarification of concepts of personal or egocentric versus extrapersonal space along the lines of the study by Butters, Soeldner, and Fedio (1972). Certainly disorder of topographical orientation has been described after both left and right frontal lesions (Marie and Béhague, 1919; Marie, Bouttier, and van Bogaert, 1924) as well as with right, left and bilateral posterior lesions (Kleist, 1934; Brain, 1941; Paterson and Zangwill, 1945; Cogan, 1960; De Renzi and Faglioni, 1962; Hécaen, 1969).

Visual search. De Renzi, Faglioni, and Scotti (1970) found that in a visual search task where the subject had to seek out a number from a random array on a board, normal subjects were slightly better when the item was on the left than on the right of the midline. This difference was much exaggerated in the presence of left hemisphere damage. With damage in the right hemisphere subjects were much better when the number was on the right than on the left. This suggests that injury to one hemisphere may impair visual exploration of the contralateral field.

Tactile perception

Somatosensory changes. The most extensive study of somatosensory changes after lesions in various parts of the cerebrum is that of Semmes *et al.* (1960). These authors examined a large number of patients with brain injuries caused by penetrating missiles in wartime. The group employed a wide range of measures such as two-point threshold, point localization, and pressure sensitivity. One of their findings has relevance to the question of asymmetry of function namely, that they described some bilateral somatosensory deficits after lesions of the left hemisphere but only contralateral deficits after lesions of the right hemisphere. Since this finding has been reported in a number of places it should be pointed out that the differences found were small and did not reach statistical significance and that subsequent workers have not confirmed it though there has been only a small amount of work done in this field.

Sensory dominance. In the study of Semmes *et al.* (1960) right handed subjects tended to show a differential sensitivity to pressure stimulation, being more sensitive to pressure on the contralateral (left) hand than on the right. In a subsequent study Weinstein and Sersen (1961) showed that this 'sensory dominance' varied in a complex manner with the patient's familial history of handedness. Thus lateral hand preference and 'sensory dominance' are not inextricably related. The situation is analogous to crossed aphasia occurring with right hemisphere lesions in some right handed subjects. It is important to state the nature of the function being affected when employing the term dominance since the present evidence shows that cerebral dominance cannot be a unitary function.

Size discrimination. Tactual size discrimination was found by Teuber and Rudel (1962) to be affected by lesions in either hemisphere but was more frequent with right-sided lesions. The deficit appeared to be independent of sensory loss though more severe if this was present.

The information from penetrating missile wounds needs to be interpreted with caution because of the somewhat uncertain nature and extent of the lesions. Another major source has been the study of patients undergoing restricted resection of cortical tissue for epilepsy (Corkin, 1964, Corkin, Milner, and Rasmussen, 1964). Sensory defects appeared to be strictly related to damage to the pre- and postcentral gyri and were mostly for the contralateral side of the body. However localization by the patient of a point on the patient's body touched by the examiner (point localization) often showed bilateral effects with unilateral lesions.

Astereognosis. This defect refers to the inability to appreciate the identity of three dimensional objects by touch. As with other forms of agnosia this disorder should by definition occur in the absence of sensory loss. The existence of pure astereognosis must be seriously in question in view of Corkin's finding that impairment of tactile object recognition occurred only in those cases with sensory deficits due to lesions in the vicinity of the central sulcus. Semmes' findings on patients with missile wounds was less clear (Semmes, 1965) though she agreed that astereognosis was probably not a clinical entity. She employed tests of roughness, texture and size, together with tests of tactile shape discrimination, in examining patients with right hemisphere, left hemisphere, and bilateral lesions. Deficits of shape discrimination were noted with and without the presence of sensory defect. These deficits were related to spatial orientation 'even when this was assessed by a purely visual task'. This finding suggested that shape discrimination may depend on a general spatial factor as well as on the integrity of somatic sensation. Where both factors are affected the disorder is likely to be severe. Semmes' evidence suggested that the factors were organized in a different way in the two hemispheres though this has not been clarified in the ensuing decade.

In contrast to the apparently greater impact of left hemisphere lesions on the sensory system than right hemisphere lesions, Weinstein (1965) found the reverse to be true of the motor system. Using a test of finger movement ('finger oscillation') Weinstein found that lesions of the right hemisphere near the central sulcus tended to produce bilateral slowing with a more marked contralateral effect whereas left central lesions resulted in contralateral slowing only.

Other recent studies have lent weight to the greater importance of the right hemisphere in tactile perception. Carmon and Benton (1969) and Fontenot and Benton (1971) tested the perception of the direction of tactile stimulation applied to the palms of the hand. A significant proportion of patients with right hemisphere lesions showed bilateral impairment on this task whereas patients with left hemisphere lesions showed significant impairment only in the contralateral hand. Similarly Boll (1974) found that the right hemisphere lesions gave rise to both ipsilateral as well as contralateral defects in tactile form perception, tactile finger localization, and the perception of finger tip number writing. Left-sided lesions produced much smaller defects.

In the previously mentioned study of De Renzi, Faglioni, and Scotti (1970) performance on a tactile, as well as a visual, search task was performed most poorly by those with right posterior lesions.

The weight of evidence suggests that the right hemisphere plays a particularly important role in mediating tactile perception.

Auditory perception

Asymmetry effects in auditory perception have been treated in Chapter 5. These related particularly to the work of Milner, Kimura, and others which has demonstrated the superior processing of speech sounds by the left hemisphere and of nonlinguistic stimuli by the right hemisphere. Such a dichotomy is supported by such studies as that of Faglioni, Spinnler, and Vignolo (1969) described in detail in the same section.

Research with the dichotic listening task has proliferated so greatly since Kimura's work in the early sixties that two issues (1, No.4 and 2, No.5) of the journal *Brain and Language* have been devoted to this topic and the reader is referred to these as well as earlier references for a coverage of the main developments.

Temporal perception

The perception of temporal order has been the subject of only few studies in brain-damaged individuals (Efron, 1963; Carmon, 1971) and even in these studies, perceptual and amnestic processes were possibly confounded. One study (Carmon and Nachson, 1971) seems to have shown a clear cut difference between lateralized lesion groups. Those with left hemisphere lesions were significantly impaired in the identification of the order of both visual and auditory stimuli as compared with normal controls and those with right hemisphere lesions. The left hemisphere may specialize in temporal perception just as the right specializes in spatial perception.

Memory and learning

Reference has already been made to the effects of unilateral temporal lobectomy on memory and learning in Chapter 5. Dominant temporal lobectomy leads to difficulty in the learning and retention of verbal material whether apprehended via visual or auditory perception and whether tested by recall or recognition (Meyers and Yates, 1955; Milner, 1958; Blakemore and Falconer, 1967; Milner, 1967; Milner and Teuber, 1968). Resection of the non-dominant temporal lobe leads to difficulties with non-verbal material both visual and auditory. 'Non-verbal' in this sense can be taken to mean those stimuli which are difficult to encode verbally (Kimura, 1963; Milner, 1968b). Milner has also shown that patients with right temporal removals have difficulty with visually or proprioceptively guided maze learning (Corkin, 1965; Milner, 1965).

Apart from the temporal lobectomy material only a few studies have concerned themselves directly with laterality and memory. De Renzi and Spinnler (1966a) tested patients with lateralized lesions on two tasks of the recognition of familiar figures, one immediate and the other delayed. The registration of familiar visual patterns in this study did appear to be related to the left hemisphere. In the delayed memory test, poor performance was related to the presence of visual field defects and the severity of the lesion but was not related to the presence of aphasia.

Boller and De Renzi (1967) compared 60 patients with left hemisphere damage with 40 patients with right hemisphere damage on two visual tasks, one easily verbalized (meaningful) and one not easily verbalized (meaningless). The left hemisphere patients were inferior on both tasks though, when the scores were adjusted for the scores obtained on two language tasks the difference between the left and right groups decreased. The importance of aphasia in lowering the scores appeared to be about as great for the meaningless task as for the meaningful. The authors interpret this as showing 'that, whenever possible, patients try to transform meaningless figures into meaningful ones'.

Warrington and Rabin (1971) using a recognition task of recurring figures similar to that devised by Kimura (1963) found no significant difference between left and right hemisphere groups though there was a trend in the predicted direction, right hemisphere patients tending to perform more poorly than left. A consideration of other factors tended to suggest that while temporal and right parietal patients were equally impaired on the recognition memory task the deficit had an amnesic basis in the temporal group and a perceptual basis in the parietal group.

Emotional reactions in unilateral lesions

Two forms of emotional reaction have been described with lateralized lesions. These are particularly evident during certain examinations when the patient is confronted with failure. The first type of emotional response was termed 'the catastrophic reaction' by Goldstein (1939b) who noted that it was particularly associated with dominant hemisphere lesions. Goldstein noted that these reactions were 'not only "inadequate" but also disordered, inconstant, inconsistent and embedded in physical and mental shock'. The patient appears not only emotionally distressed but develops signs of incipient physical collapse such as pallor and sweating. It is important to recognize the onset of this catastrophic reaction since, apart from the patient's comfort, his performances may be further reduced for some times afterwards and a true picture of his present capacities may not be elicited. '. . .after a catastrophic reaction his reactivity is likely to be impeded for a longer or shorter interval. He becomes more or less unresponsive and fails even in those tasks which he could easily meet under other circumstances. The disturbing after-effect of catastrophic reactions is long enduring'. (Goldstein, op. cit. p.37). The second type of reaction is one of indifference to such major disorders as hemiplegia, seen more frequently with right hemisphere lesions (Hécaen, Ajuriaguerra and Massonet, 1951; Denny-Brown, Meyer, and Horenstein, 1952). These related reactions to stressful situations such as those produced by difficulties encountered during psychological testing have been systematically studied in a large series of cases by Gainotti (1972). He lists the following symptoms with their association to laterality: symptoms more frequently seen with left-sided lesions were 'anxiety reactions, bursts of tears, vocative utterances, depressed renouncements, or sharp refusals to go on with the examination'. With right-sided lesions the following were more common: 'anosognosia, minimization indifference reactions and tendency to joke, and expressions of hate towards the paralysed limb'. Gainotti strongly reinforced what had been said by Goldstein and others, namely that catastrophic reactions were found most often in aphasic subjects after repeated failure of their attempts to communicate. 'They seemed due, as Goldstein argues, to the desperate reaction of the organism, confronted with a task it cannot face'.

Motor impersistence

In 1956, Fisher described a syndrome which he considered 'akin to apraxia' the central features of which were the inability to *maintain* the eyes closed and the tongue protruded though these actions could be carried out adequately for a short period. The disorder was strongly associated with left hemiplegia, i.e. with lesions of the minor hemisphere and, though often transient, persisted in some cases for years. Some degree of mental impairment was always present. Fisher was aware that the grouping of several manifestations as a 'syndrome' needed substantiation. He suggested hypotheses which might explain the several signs, e.g. failure to maintain a motor set, interference with the persistent control of a motor act or distractability.

Though of theoretical interest the value of impersistence as a clinical observation is minimal since it appears to be seen only in the presence of unequivocal lateralizing signs. The disorder is reviewed in Joynt and Goldstein (1975).

Bilateral effects from unilateral lesions

Apart form the effects caused by permanent damage to functional systems, cerebral lesions may often bring about effects due to alteration in neighbouring or remote areas. These effects may alter with time particularly in areas adjacent to the damaged tissue because of resolution of oedema and other reversible changes. The term *diaschisis* was used by von Monakow (1911) to denote functional disturbances in situations anatomically remote from the lesion (Smith, 1974). Smith points out that consideration of diaschisis may help to resolve some of the apparently conflicting results described in the literature. His extensive studies of patients with vascular lesions reveal a high percentage of patients with bilateral hemisphere dysfunction and this itself is also affected by the size of the lesion and the age at which it occurs.

Such observations are not rare, e.g. sixteen out of eighteen patients with left hemiplegia in a study by Belmont, Karp and Birch (1971) showed disruption of movement of the intact side when bilateral function was called for but not when the movement was required only from the intact side.

Bilateral effects from unilateral lesions may involve at least three classes of effect. Firstly, the effect of disconnecting an association area of one hemisphere from the association cortex of the opposite side. Many examples of interhemisphere disconnection effects are provided in the later sections of this chapter. Secondly, the possibility of interference or inhibitory influences is suggested by the improvement in function following removal of pathological tissue as mentioned in the section on hemispherectomy. Thirdly, recent studies have demonstrated that reduction in cerebral function may follow alteration in hemispheric blood flow. A reduction in blood flow and metabolism in *both* hemispheres has been shown to occur following unilateral cerebral lesions both vascular and neoplastic in origin. A summary of evidence on diaschisis has been given by Smith (1975 pp.70-73).

Hemispherectomy

The operation of hemispherectomy might more correctly be termed hemidecortication since not all the hemisphere is removed in most instances. Usually parts of the deep nuclear masses such as the thalamus and striate complex remain untouched. The nature of the operation varies according to the indication for operation. Two major conditions have appeared to date. These are: (1) infantile hemiplegia, and (2) extensive invasion of the hemisphere by neoplastic disease. Because of the very great difference between these two types of cases they are treated separately here. A more extensive general review of the evidence from hemispherectomy has been provided by Dimond (1972).

Infantile hemiplegia

The earliest report of removal of a very considerable proportion of one hemisphere for the treatment of uncontrollable epilepsy associated with hemiparesis of early onset appears to be that of McKenzie (1938). This was followed by the series reported by Krynauw from Johannesburg (1950a, 1950b). The complex problems posed by using such material to provide evidence about brain function is indicated by the following description of indications for operation given by Carmichael (1966) and cited in Dimond (op. cit.). 'The patient must first of all have a hemiplegia. This should affect the arm more profoundly than the leg, and the patient usually suffers from fits which do not prove amenable to medical treatment. The patient frequently has behaviour disturbances in the nature of being difficult to handle, personality problems, temper tantrums and rages.'

The most striking feature of early reports apart from clinical improvement was the absence of mental deterioration that might be expected on *a priori* grounds from such massive removal of cortical tissue. Krynauw's first report (1950a) described 12 cases with 'improvement of mentality' as adjudged by clinical evidence though no psychometric evidence was presented in support. Cairns and Davidson (1951) reported three cases with no evidence of intellectual loss but rather an improvement in scores on tests such as the Wechsler-Bellevue, and Stanford-Binet scales. Such improvement strongly supported the frequent claim by Hebb and others mentioned earlier (see Ch. 4) that the deficits seen after operations on the brain might often be due to the effect of residual pathological tissue rather than simply due to loss of brain substance. Presumably where the pathological tissue was radically removed as in the present cases of hemispherectomy there was no longer any interference effect so that residual healthy brain tissue was permitted to function at an optimal level thus providing an explanation for the seemingly 'paradoxical' effect that the brain could perform better after hemidecortication than before. In the decade which followed, this point of view received further support in the finding that these cases of infantile hemiplegia seemed to benefit much more from complete hemispherectomy than from partial removal (McFie, 1961). Studies such as the latter also indicated that the capacity of the remaining hemisphere to mediate the normal functions of both hemispheres was restricted in scope.

Perhaps the most outstanding feature of the cases operated upon for infantile hemiplegia is the remarkable degree of 'functional plasticity'. Reports such as that of Obrador (1964) show that sensori-motor functions, praxis, and language are largely preserved whichever hemisphere is removed. It seems that either hemisphere is capable of mediating most of these functions though mental activity usually remains at a fairly low level together with lack of drive and initiative.

The evidence from the cases of hemispherectomy in early life supports the general evidence from other studies of early brain damage in favour of some potential for transfer of function from one hemisphere to another being possible in early life with transfer becoming more difficult as the higher cortical functions become more established.

Gardner et al. (1955) made a comparison of residual function following hemispherectomy for tumour in adults and for infantile epilepsy in children. The deficits were much more devastating in the adult cases. Similar reports of the lessened impact on younger cases has been given by Hillier (1954) and other writers. The greatest effects in the later cases are seen in language and other higher cortical functions. Once these are well established they are not easily transferred. The question as to how young the patient must be for any major transfer or compensation of function to occur is still an open question. The optimal age appears to vary with different functions but some writers (e.g. McFie, 1961) would place the crucial point before the end of the second year of life. In a study of hemispherectomized patients which employed dichotic listening techniques, Netley (1972) suggested that compensation may be restricted to a period as early as 17 months. Against this may be placed two recent long-term follow up studies.

The first is a case of hemispherectomy performed for epilepsy at the age of $5\frac{1}{2}$ years and reported 21 years later by Smith and Sugar (1975). This case provides impressive evidence of the brain's ability to utilize residual tissue in the remaining hemisphere as the basis for high level ability in both the verbal and non-verbal spheres. Before operation at $5\frac{1}{2}$ the patient's mental age was 4.0 years with marked speech defect but normal verbal comprehension. Four months after operation his mental age was close to his chronological age and his speech 'which earlier had been practically unintelligible, had rapidly become normal'. When tested at 8 years 8 months, his mental age was 7 years 10 months. Since that time further progress has continued and his scores on a wide variety of tests both verbal and non-verbal are now at, and in some cases well above, the normal range. Some extracts from Smith and Sugar's table of his test performance 15 and 21 years after hemispherectomy are shown in Table 8.3.

In addition to these and other good performances on psychometric measures the patient's performance on all language modalities at these two examinations was normal (speech, comprehension, reading and writing).

This article also provides an up-to-date discussion of the evidence for and against the concept of 'functional plasticity' after early brain damage. Le Vere (1975) points out that restoration of function after apparent loss is insufficient evidence on which to claim that functional reorganization of neural tissue has taken place and points to evidence supporting the notion that 'the nervous system, like other biological systems is quite stable and incapable of the plasticity required to mediate functional reorganization.' No doubt further evidence will be sought by proponents of this viewpoint.

The second is a case studied over many years by Damasio, Lima, and Damasio (1972). This patient was not a case of infantile hemiplegia but had a normal development until the age of five at which time she sustained a severe head injury resulting in left hemiplegia. She developed left focal seizures seven years after

Table 8.3 Test performances after left hemispherectomy (Condensed from Smith and Sugar (1975).

Age	21	$26\frac{1}{2}$
Post-operative Interval (years)	$15\frac{1}{2}$	21
WAIS Weighted Scores		
Information	13	16
Comprehension	19	19
Arithmetic	9	15
Similarities	12	15
Digit Span	7	9
Digit Symbol	8	10
Block Design	11	9
Picture Arrangement	10	9
Object Assembly	8	12
Verbal I.Q.	113	126
Performance I.Q.	98	102
Full Scale I.Q.	107	116
Peabody Picture Vocabulary	125	137+
Benton Visual Retention	7	8

injury and these increased in frequency and some thirteen years after injury she was showing aggressive and disturbed behaviour. Two years later right hemispherectomy was performed for the frequent, uncontrollable *grand mal* seizures. The result of surgical intervention was 'dramatic relief of intractable epilepsy, the recovery of personal independence, and. . remarkable improvement of motor and sensory capabilities'. Such a case demonstrates that alternative systems may be brought into play even when the lesion had occurred as late as five years. The authors suggest an interference or inhibition hypothesis similar to that suggested by Smith below for recovery of motor and language function following hemispherectomy for tumour in an adult patient. Damasio *et al.* comment: 'Removal of the right diseased hemisphere rid our patient of a "squalid nuisance", stopping its deleterious effect on the rest of the brain and disclosing a normal, partially duplicated left hemisphere.' The partial duplication of function is evidenced by the patient's normal performance on a number of tasks of a visuoperceptive, visuospatial and visuoconstructive nature normally thought to be dependent upon the integrity of the right hemisphere.

It should be pointed out that the essential difference between this case and those of infantile hemiplegia is the presence of perfectly healthy tissue in both hemispheres for some years prior to a major lesion of one side. The case presents a number of other features in the adaptation after operation which need further study but it is obvious that age of occurrence should not in itself be a contra-indication to operation.

Hemispherectomy for infantile hemiplegia has decreased over the last decade though some recent reports seem to suggest that the main clinical features are all improved (French, Johnson, and Adkins, 1966; Breschi, D'Angelo, and Pluchino, 1970; Wilson, 1970). Discussion of the reasons for and against such operations is beyond the scope of the present text.

Adult hemispherectomy

The first case reports of removal of almost a complete hemisphere for ex-tensive invasion of the brain by malignant tumour were given by Dandy (1928, 1933). The effects can be discussed in relation to the concept of cerebral domin-ance for language.

Firstly, an early report of removal of the left (dominant) hemisphere (Zollinger, 1935) showed that not all language was lost. Zollinger's patient retained an elementary vocabulary which was partially increased by speech training. No other formal neuropsychological examination was carried out partly because of the patient's adynamia or unwillingness. Death of the patient 17 days post-operatively prevented follow-up. A second case of dominant hemispherectomy reported by Crockett and Estridge (1951) survived four months, and although severely impaired, also showed improving capacity for speech as well as verbal comprehension.

These findings were supported by the more detailed examination of a case followed for more than seven months by Smith (Smith, 1966c; Smith and Burklund, 1966). Immediately after the operation the patient showed the anticipated signs of right hemiplegia, right hemianopia and severe aphasia. On later examinations the patient showed continuing recovery of language func-tions, not total abolition which might be expected on the belief that the left hemisphere played the 'dominant' role in such functions. 'Since these functions are not abolished, and since speaking, reading, writing and understanding language show continuing improvement in E.C. after left hemispherectomy, the right hemisphere apparently contributes to all these functions, although in varying proportions (i.e. receptive language functions were initially less im-paired and have shown greater recovery than expressive language)'. (Smith, 1966c, p.470). The patient preserved the ability to sing old songs suggesting that the right hemisphere plays an important role in this area. This finding would be in keeping with evidence from studies of restricted lesions and from brain stimulation mentioned earlier.

Smith's patient also showed preserved learning ability as shown by an in-creased score of $2\frac{1}{2}$ years on two testings with Porteus Maze Test at a ten-day interval some six months after operation. The patient was also able to solve abstract as well as concrete mathematical problems and was close to normal on non-language tests of higher mental functions. Smith and Burklund (1966) take these good performances to indicate 'either that these functions are not exclusively or predominantly 'localized' in the adult dominant hemisphere, or that, following removal of this hemisphere, the right hemisphere has the capacity to amplify previously smaller contributions to these functions. . .'.

A case of hemispherectomy for epilepsy of late onset described by French, Johnson and Adkins (1961) similarly supports the cases operated for tumour in demonstrating capacity for both language comprehension and some expression.

Hemispherectomy on the right (non-dominant) side has been carried out much more frequently. Early reports such as those of Dandy (1928, 1933) and Rowe (1937) commented on the sparing of intellectual ability at least with clinical tests and the standard intelligence tests of the day. Rowe's case showed a post-operative intelligence quotient on the Stanford-Binet scale in the 'superior adult' range, not greatly different from that which she showed before operation. As with other reports there was also return of considerable motor function and some sensory function on the opposite side of the body. The mental changes noted in this case included impairment of recent memory, emotional instability and loss of inhibition. Mensh et al. (1952) were impressed with the extreme variation in performance of their patient with non-dominant hemispherectomy as well as the numerous disturbances reflected in psychological tests. Though verbal facility and vocabulary remained good their patient showed 'concreteness and perseveration of ideas, confused and psychotic-like thinking, clang associations, mingling of old and new information,. . .self-reference. . .and extremely compulsive behaviour.' Smith (1967) also noted extreme variability in one case of right and one of left hemispherectomy and pointed to this as a common finding in the clinical reports of some 40 non-dominant hemispherectomies to that time. Improvement in contra-lateral motor function was also frequently reported. In 1969 Smith reported on three non-dominant cases examined from one year to 30 years after operation. All three cases showed specific non-language defects in keeping with similar reports by Austin and Grant (1955) and Bruell and Albee (1962). Smith notes that while, impairment of language functions after dominant hemispherectomy is more severe than the deficits of non-language functions after non-dominant resection, the impairment is still 'subtotal'. 'In all reported cases, no single specialized hemispheric function was totally abolished'. The finding of relatively greater impairment (of speech) with left hemispherectomy than the impairment (non-verbal) after right hemispherectomy suggests a greater degree of specialization for speech functions.

There is a major difference between the effects of partial hemisphere lesions and hemispherectomy which has implications for theories of brain dysfunction. This difference is seen with regard to both motor function and speech. If one assumes that a gain in function is never produced by removal of cerebral tissue, the most plausible explanation seems to be that the improvement is produced by removal of interference or inhibition. One of Smith's three cases (1969) had been totally unable to lift his left leg from the bed and was barely able to move the left arm on command for one month before operation. Immediately after recovering from anaesthesia he promptly lifted his left leg on command. His voluntary arm movements were also improved though still impaired. Smith commented—'This suggests that the more severe or total defects in other specialized hemispheric functions or the presence of unique defects reported in certain cases with lateralized lesions may reflect interference with or inhibition of the role of the opposite hemisphere or of caudally inferior ipsilateral structures in such functions'. The presence of speech after left hemispherectomy demonstrates (though the evidence is scanty) that the nondominant hemisphere may have limited command over the executive apparatus of speech if the inhibiting influence of the dominant hemisphere is removed. A few hints from the commissurotomy evidence in support of this notion have already been mentioned in the literature.

A bilateral effect rising from a unilateral lesion has also been evoked to explain unusual combinations of symptoms such as the case of Gazzaniga *et al.* (1973). This patient who had a presumed unilateral lesion in the left hemisphere suffered from pure word blindness but was also unable to make an auditory-tactile match. The authors suggest that 'the damaged left hemisphere may have an interfering effect on the potential linguistic capacity of the nondominant hemisphere', a very similar explanation to that suggested above for hemispherectomy. No doubt as more lesion cases are subjected to careful neuropsychological examination further examples of bilateral effects will be reported.

Finally, the report of Gott (1973) of three hemispherectomy cases all with memory quotients below normal suggests that two communicating hemispheres are probably necessary for normal memory functioning. The similar claim of Sperry with regard to the poor memory of some commissurotomy patients is mentioned below.

Agenesis of the corpus callosum

On rare occasions the major neocortical commissure, the corpus callosum, fails to develop, a condition termed agenesis. A summary of the literature with representative cover of much of the literature in neuropsychological studies has been provided by Dimond (1972). Apart from the rarity of the condition the usefulness of this material in the study of hemispheric asymmetry is restricted by a number of factors such as the completeness or otherwise of the agenesis and the presence of associated abnormalities of the cerebrum. The fact that no dramatic manifestations may be present during life is demonstrated by the cases where the agenesis is revealed for the first time at post-mortem. Furthermore, most of the cases described in the literature until recently have failed to use sophisticated examination procedures (such as those developed in the study of commissurotomy) which would allow disconnection effects to be demonstrated if present. Some authors (e.g. Russell and Reitan, 1955) have felt that this was probably the case for most of the earlier studies which claimed an absence of symptoms unless the callosal agenesis was associated with other brain anomalies. The question of clinico-pathological correlation in these cases has been re-examined recently by Loeser and Alvord (1968a, b).

Since the sixties, detailed examination of a small number of cases of agenesis has been carried out. Jeeves (1965a) examined three acallosal cases with particular reference to tasks requiring bimanual manipulation and co-ordination.

He found all three subjects inferior to suitably matched controls on a variety of such tasks and the ante-mortem evidence including radiological studies seemed to suggest that absence of the callosum was the only major anomaly present. Other cases of partial or complete agenesis studied by Jeeves (1965b) varied in their ability on motor co-ordination tasks. Even where the everyday level of motor ability of some of these subjects was close to the norm for their age sensitive tests involving integration of the two hands showed a poorer performance for acallosal subjects.

A single case studied by Solursh et al. (1965) confirmed the difficulty of integrating tactile or proprioceptive information across the midline. Like commissurotomy subjects this boy could identify by touch with the corresponding (contralateral) hand, objects presented to either hemisphere (i.e. to either half visual field) but was unable to do so with the ipsilateral hand. Despite this, fairly clear indication of transfer of information presented solely to one hemisphere was obtained in other situations. Incomplete compensation for the lack of the major organ of transfer of learning seems to have taken place. Extra-callosal pathways appear to be limited in the ability to which they can enter into the transmission of information from one side to the other.

In another patient with complete absence of the corpus callosum Saul and Sperry (1968) could find no evidence of callosal symptoms despite the use of tests developed in the study of split-brain subjects. However they also found indications that absence of the callosum hampered the patient 'in those activities in which the specialized nonverbal and spatial faculties of the minor hemisphere would normally reinforce, complement and enhance the verbal and volitional performances of the major hemisphere.' (Sperry, Gazzaniga, and Bogen, 1969, p.288).

Ettlinger et al. (1972, 1974) in a comparison of patients having partial or total developmental absence of the corpus callosum with control subjects found a conspicuous lack of impairment in the acallosal subjects. Their tests included the following: intermanual tactile matching; depth perception; tachistoscopic visual identification and matching; spatial localization and dichotic listening. The absence of a pronounced laterality effect which had been found in commissurotomy subjects had also been reported by Bryden and Zurif (1970). The fact that their subject performed in a manner very similar to a group of normal subjects suggested that alternative pathways for adequate listening could be developed in cases of agenesis.

Because of the heterogeneous nature of the clinical material it would be unwise to speculate about the mechanisms and alternate pathways used for compensation. However the observed enlargement of the anterior commissure in a small number of callosal subjects has led some authors (Saul and Sperry, 1968; Ettlinger et al., 1974) to speculate that at least some of the tasks such as cross-matching might utilize this tract.

The intelligence of callosal subjects covers a wide range. The majority are below the norm on intellectual measures with a few cases at or above normal. Once again it is difficult to disentangle the contribution of any associated cerebral abnormalities and there does not appear to be any common pattern in the small amount of psychometric data available. The common depression of intellectual measures would lead many to agree with Dimond's suggestion '. . .in the early stages of development the absence of the corpus callosum places the individual at a disadvantage for which it is difficult subsequently to compensate. This condition does depress intellectual function and the employment of subsidiary pathways cannot totally compensate for this disadvantage'. (p.66).

Cerebral commissurotomy

Around the turn of the present century neurologists had described clinical syndromes which they felt were due to lesions of the corpus callosum. The best known of these were the syndromes of alexia without agraphia (Dejerine, 1892) and that of left hand apraxia (Liepmann, 1906). The first disorder has been described in Chapter 7 and the disconnection theory argues that the syndrome is explained by an isolation of the speech areas of the left hemisphere from the right visual cortex. The second disorder was described in Chapter 3 and finds a similar explanation in terms of isolation of the dominant hemisphere language centres from the right motor cortex. Only a few reports of this kind were available until the introduction of surgical division of the corpus callosum for the prevention of the lateral spread of an epileptic discharge (van Wagenen and Herren, 1940). The first commissurotomy operation involved section of the corpus callosum together with bilateral section of the fornix. The operation proved beneficial in some cases and a considerable number of psychological studies of the effect of partial (15 cases) or complete division (9 cases) of the corpus callosum were soon reported by Akelaitis (1940; 1941a, b, c; 1942a, b; 1943; Akelaitis, Risteen, and van Wagenen 1941, 1942, 1943). These were completely negative, i.e. they provided no support for the concept of a hemisphere disconnection syndrome. This state of affairs remained until Myers began his classic studies on callosal section in animals in the early 1950's

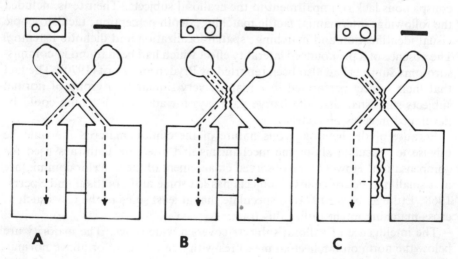

Fig. 8.3 Split brain experiments in animals. A, normal animal; B, optic chiasma divided; C, optic chiasma and commissures divided.

(Myers, 1955, 1956, 1959, 1961, 1965). Beginning with cats, callosal experiments continued with monkeys and chimpanzees and finally, specially designed tests were applied by Sperry and his colleagues to human patients who had undergone division of the main commissures of the brain for the relief of epilepsy. The principal findings of the Sperry group are set out below.

In keeping with the findings of Akelaitis, split-brain animals behaved quite normally in most of their activities. However, the story was quite different if steps were taken to restrict information to one hemisphere at a time. With tactile information this can be achieved readily because the tactile information is normally conveyed almost exclusively to the contralateral hemisphere. With vision the fact that each eye presents information to both cerebral hemispheres (Fig. 8.3 A) presented a problem if the principal aim is to restrict information to one hemisphere only, for the purpose of studying the single hemisphere's capabilities. In animals, this was simply achieved by dividing the optic chiasma in the midline so that direct transmission of information from each eye to the contralateral hemisphere was no longer possible (Fig. 8.3 B).

The first experiments of this kind were carried out by Myers (1955, 1956) and may be described briefly as follows. (1) the chiasma sectioned animals had one eye occluded while it learns a visual discrimination via the other (Fig. 8.3 B); (2) after discrimination training the occluded eye was uncovered and the 'training eye' was occluded; (3) the animal showed very rapid discrimination learning via the 'untrained' eye.

In a second stage the same procedure was repeated, this time with commissurotomy (callosal division) added to splitting of the optic chiasma (Fig. 8.3 C). In this second stage the animal reacted as if it had not seen the problem before, i.e. transfer of memory and learning from one hemisphere to the other was prevented by division of the corpus callosum. It took the animal just as long to learn the discrimination with the second eye as it had with the first.

Of course, splitting the optic chiasma does not form part of the commissurotomy operation in man. The operation is generally restricted to division of the two major forebrain commissures, the corpus callosum and the anterior commissure together with the interthalamic connection (or massa intermedia) where this exists. This latter structure is not a commissure but consists of grey matter. It is a variable structure seen only in a proportion of human brains and its exact role is uncertain.

In man, study of response to visual information by each hemisphere is achieved by taking advantage of the orderly projection of fibres from the two halves of each retina (Fig. 8.4).

It can be seen that with eyes fixated on a central point information to the left of this point is projected by each eye *only* to the right hemisphere (A) while stimuli to the right of the midline project *only* to the left hemisphere (B). This is, of course, true only for the moment of fixation. In normal viewing the presence of both voluntary and involuntary eye movements would mean that stimuli to either side of the midline would be transmitted to *both* hemispheres. In order to prevent this, the technique of half field (or hemi-retinal) projection has been used. With the subject fixating a central point the stimuli to be studied are projected to either half field at an exposure so brief (tachistoscopic) that eye movement is not possible. This achieves a functional split of the optic projection in much the same way as achieved by surgical division of the chiasma in animals. It should be stressed that the projection in the studies which follow is to the half-field, left or right (hence to the corresponding contralateral hemisphere) and *not* to the left eye or right eye.

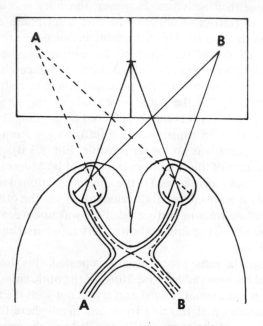

Fig. 8.4 Projection of visual information

The use of such specialized techniques in the study of commissurotomized man was reported by Sperry (1961), Gazzaniga, Bogen and Sperry (1962) and Sperry (1964). The discrepancy between the early studies of Akelaitis and those of Sperry, Bogen, Gazzaniga and their colleagues which are still continuing may be accounted for by a number of factors among which the more important would appear to be differences in completeness of section of the corpus callosum and sophistication of experimental techniques used in post-operative testing. Goldstein and Joynt (1969) carried out a follow-up of one of Akelaitis' patients who had been operated upon some 27 years earlier. They found lasting defects in interhemispheric transfer of information with no evidence of any reorganization of function.

Despite the small number of patients who have been studied with 'split-brain' techniques the extensive testing, often ingenious, which has been carried out has led to a fairly consistent picture of the hemisphere disconnection syndrome. The peculiar anatomical condition of the brain has allowed a variety of hypotheses concerning brain function to be tested in a way that would not otherwise be possible. The literature is already very extensive and the following main features are condensed from Sperry, Gazzaniga, and Bogen (1969) and Gazzaniga (1970). This is followed by more detailed consideration of some topics together with recent findings.

Vision

Using the tachistoscopic half-field technique a marked difference is noted between the two sides. Material which is presented to the right half-field (left hemisphere) can be read or described at about the preoperative level. Material in the left half field can *not* be described in speech or in writing. This has held true over hundreds of replications for tachistoscopic presentations of 100 milliseconds or less. 'This is not true if objects are merely held in the left field or shown with longer exposure times, presumably because very rapid eye movements bring stimuli on the left into the right half field. Failure to find the foregoing left field defect in the Akelaitis studies seems best ascribed to the fact that tachistoscopic projection was not used in visual testing.' (Sperry *et al.*, 1969)

Though commissurotomy patients could not speak about what was in the left half-field they could use non-verbal responses such as pointing to a matching stimulus or selecting the name of the object from a list. There is no hemianopia. The right hemisphere is unable to utilize the apparatus of speech for responding.

Earlier experiments revealed the independence of the two visual fields in memory as well as perception. The dissociation between things falling in the two half-fields has been utilized to great effect in the elegant 'chimera' experiments described below.

In the early experiments where two objects were presented simultaneously on the screen one in each field, the response was shown to be dependent on the request made. If the subject was asked to reach behind the screen and retrieve the object from a number of others with his left hand he would select the object presented to the left half-field (right hemisphere/left hand). If asked to name the object he would invariably name that in the right half-field. This occurred even when the subject was still in the process of retrieving the object with his left hand. 'When asked to confirm verbally what item was selected by left hand, subject names incorrectly the *right* field stimulus.' (Sperry, *et al.*, op. cit) Such gross discrepancy attests powerfully to the independence of the two hemisphere-eye combinations.

Touch

Here the task of object recognition (stereognosis) gave similar results to that in vision. Objects felt with the right hand (but not seen) could be named and described. Using the left hand the patient could recognize the presence of an object but was never able to name or describe it. Experimenters found that it was important to control for auditory cues such as those arising from moving the object on the table surface thus producing information which could alert the left hemisphere to the nature of the object which could then be named.

As with vision, a variety of tests demonstrated that the object felt with the left hand had been perceived and remembered by the right hemisphere. The subject could retrieve an object previously felt by the left hand from a mixed group of objects even after several minutes. The problem then is not one of stereognosis or tactile object agnosia but a unilateral anomia.

The independence of the two hemispheres for tactile information is shown clearly where integration is required for solution of a problem such as the simple jig-saw puzzles of Gazzaniga (1970) (Fig. 8.5).

INTERMANUAL TACTILE COMPARISON

JIGSAW PATTERN	ONE PATTERN IN EACH HAND		BOTH IN L H	BOTH IN R H
	L H	R H		
1	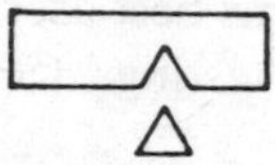 Not Completed		Correct	Correct
2 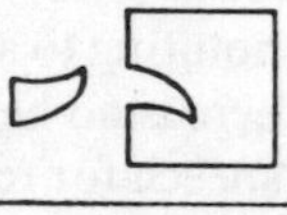	"		"	"
3 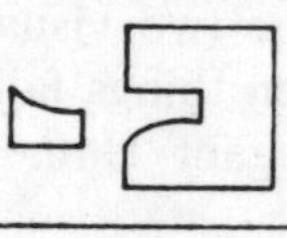	"		"	"

Fig. 8.5 Intermanual tactile comparison Figure 28, p. 87, M.S. Gazzaniga, *The Bisected Brain*, 1970. (Courtesy of Plenum Publications Corporation.)

The subjects could fit together simple two piece jigsaw puzzles with either hand separately but not when intermanual transfer was required by placing one piece in each hand. It is noteworthy that when stylus maze learning problems were used there was complete intermanual transfer.

When information has to be integrated between two modalities such as vision and touch the commissurotomy patient only succeeds where the information is processed in the same hemisphere. The subject cannot retrieve an object with his right hand if it is flashed to his left visual field. This tactile-visual match is not possible since the information from the two sense modalities is divided between the two hemispheres. For the same reason other forms of intermodal association are impossible.

Language

Language comprehension. Much interest has centred on the minor hemisphere's capacity for language comprehension. The use of auditory material is complicated by the fact that both ears present information almost equally to both hemispheres and it is not possible to devise an auditory procedure analogous to the half-field visual technique. It is possible that since the dominant hemisphere hears the same material as the non-dominant hemisphere it may facilitate the latter by some means other than the major commissures. With this reservation in mind it does seem that the nondominant hemisphere possesses a fair degree of language comprehension. Patients are able to retrieve with their left hand objects named or even described by function. They may also be able to indicate which name read aloud corresponds to an object flashed in the left half-field.

Comprehension of written material has also been tested by the split-field technique. The right hemisphere appears to comprehend limited word classes particularly concrete nouns. Patients did not comprehend verbs in the left-half field nor were they able to act upon simple one-word verbal commands such as 'nod'.

The major hemisphere always shows normal comprehension of all orally and visually presented material in the commissurotomy subjects.

At first sight the commissurotomy evidence appears to be at variance with large numbers of lesion studies, e.g., left hemisphere lesion cases with aphasia often seem to have less verbal comprehension than one might expect from the commissurotomy studies.

Relatively small lesions confined to the left hemisphere have been described as producing word-blindness or word-deafness (Geschwind, 1965a, 1970; Luria, 1970; Gazzaniga, 1972). It might have been expected that if the right hemisphere was intact the patient should show at least the amount of comprehension shown by the right hemisphere in commissurotomy subjects. Two explanations have been offered. The first and more plausible explanation suggests interference with right hemisphere function from the left sided lesion by way of the commissural pathways. The second explanation suggests that, because of their long-standing epilepsy, commissurotomy subjects may have developed a stronger bilateral representation of language.

Language expression

All visual and tactile material presented to the left hemisphere could be named or described normally by the commissurotomy patient. On the other hand, with the few exceptions mentioned below, subjects were completely unable to use verbal responses when material was presented to the right hemisphere. The fact that this was an 'aphasia' rather than an 'agnosia' was readily demonstrated by the subject's adequate non-verbal responses.

Perception of chimeric figures

One of the most subtle techniques for testing the perceptual abilities and control of motor response by each hemisphere is the method of chimeric stimuli described by Levy, Trevarthen, and Sperry (1972). The technique is based on the observation by Trevarthen and Kinsbourne that commissurotomy patients tend to complete material across the midline in a similar way to some hemianopic patients (Ch. 7). For example, when only half a stimulus was presented in such a way that the edge of the half-stimulus coincided with the vertical meridian, the commissurotomy patient often responded as though perceiving a whole stimulus. This completion process was particularly strong in completion to the left when verbal report was used and in completion to the right where the subject was asked to draw the stimulus (Trevarthen, 1974a, b).

Chimeric stimuli consist of a composite joined at the vertical midline comprising the right half of one stimulus and the left half of another, e.g. the left half of one face and the right half of another. Other stimuli constructed by Levy *et al.* were 'antler' patterns, line drawings of common objects, and chain patterns. (Fig. 8.6).

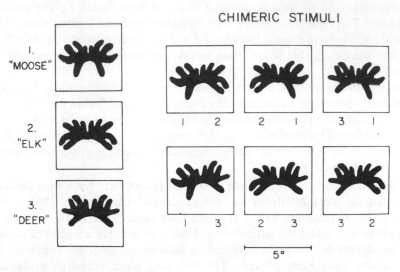

Fig. 8.6 Chimeric stimuli (from Levy, Trevarthen and Sperry, 1972)

The composite stimuli were exposed briefly in a tachistoscope and the subject was asked to indicate what he had seen. Three modes of response were used (1) pointing with the left hand, (2) pointing with the right hand, and (3) naming the stimulus.

When using pointing responses the subject had in front of him an array of the original stimuli from which the chimeras had been constructed. In the case of naming, the choice stimuli were removed, the subject having been taught assigned names for each of the faces and the different types of 'antlers'. (Fig. 8.6).

Levy *et al.* pointed out that 'recognition of faces appears to be strongly gestalt-like in nature and a face is relatively resistant to analytical verbal description.' They also noted the clinical finding that most patients with difficulty in facial recognition seem to have lesions in the right hemisphere. (This difficulty, or prosopagnosia, has been reviewed in Chapter 7). This suggested that the disconnected right hemisphere might be superior at this type of task. This hypothesis of asymmetry of function favouring the right hemisphere was strongly supported for all four sets of stimuli (faces, antlers, drawings, and patterns) *irrespective of which hand was used for pointing.* However, when the response was changed to verbal naming there was a reversal in favour of the visual information going to the left hemisphere. When pointing was employed the 'completed' stimulus from the left half of the visual field was favoured, while naming was significantly biased in favour of the right visual field. The asymmetry of function when naming faces, while significant, was not as striking as with pointing and there was a higher proportion of errors. The authors commented 'It was evident in the hesitancy and incidental comments of the subjects as well, that the left hemisphere found this kind of task extremely difficult and *was inclined to describe the distinctive features of the right field face instead of naming it as a unit.*' (op. cit. p.66 italics added by present author).

The implication of this set of experiments is of such significance that the authors' summary is worth presenting in full:

Visual testing with composite right-left chimeric stimuli shows that the two disconnected hemispheres of commissurotomy patients can process conflicting information simultaneously and independently. Which hemisphere dominates control of the read-out response was found to be determined primarily by the central processing requirement rather than by the nature of the stimuli or whether the response is ipsilaterally or contralaterally mediated. Where the task needs no more than visual recognition, a visual encoding ensues, mediated by the right hemisphere and based on the form properties of the stimulus as such rather than on separate feature analysis. On the other hand, where some form of verbal encoding is specifically required, the left hemisphere takes over and attempts a visual recognition based on nameable analytical features of the stimulus. Stimuli having no verbal labels stored in longterm memory and which are resistant to feature analysis were found to be extremely difficult for the left hemisphere to identify. We conclude that each of the disconnected hemispheres has its own specialized strategy of information processing, and that whether a hemisphere is dominant for a given task under the test conditions depend upon which strategy is the more proficient.' (Levy, Trevarthen, and Sperry, 1972 pp.75-76).

Visuospatial functions

One of the striking pieces of information supporting the notion of lateral differences in visuospatial functions came from early reports of studies on two commissurotomy patients (Gazzaniga, Bogen, and Sperry, 1962; Bogen, and Gazzaniga, 1965; Bogen, 1969a). Both these patients were able to write with either hand before surgery the left being the non-preferred hand. After commissurotomy both patients lost the ability to write with the left hand but preserved the ability to write with the right hand. There was, however, a dissociation between their writing and drawing abilities. Though both patients could copy drawings better with the right hand before operation, after surgery they were each better at this task when using the left hand. This visuospatial superiority of the so-called minor hemisphere was also seen in better performance of Block Design problems with the left hand. Where verbal instructions were used superiority reverted to the right hand.

The difficulty with writing has been termed by Bogen (1969a) dysgraphia and the copying difficulty dyscopia. Bogen is careful to point out that dyscopia signifies a difficulty in following a 'visual instruction (that is copying from a model) rather than drawing from verbal instructions.'

Further insight into the nature of the right hemisphere's superiority has been provided by three experiments by Nebes which demonstrate that the effect extends to the tactile modality as well as the visual and also to the synthesis of information between these modalities. Nebes (1974a) put forward the hypothesis that the right hemisphere 'attends to the overall configuration of the stimulus situation, synthesizing the fragmentary chunks of perceptual data received from sampling of the sensory surround into a meaningful percept of the enviroment. The right hemisphere is thus viewed as giving spatial context to the detailed analysis carried out by the major hemisphere' (p.156).

In his first experimental test of this hypothesis (Nebes, 1971) the subject was required to judge from visual or tactile appreciation the size of circle from which arcs of various size (80°, 120°, 180°, 280°) had come. Tactile-visual, visual-tactile, and tactile-tactile conditions were employed. Four of the five commissurotomized patients tested performed significantly better with their left hand on all three versions, i.e. both on intramodal and crossmodal tasks. In a second experiment (Nebes, 1972) the subject was required to select from a number of tactually presented shapes the one which would be formed from a visually presented fragmented figure. These visual figures each depicted 'a geometric shape that had been cut up and the pieces drawn apart, maintaining, however, their original orientations and relative positions.' Once again commissurotomized subjects proved far more accurate with their left hand than with their right. Control experiments showed that neither difficulty with tactile discrimination nor the intermodal nature of the tasks were significant factors determining the poor performance but rather the 'Gestalt' requirement of the task. The third experiment (Nebes, 1973) utilized the well known Gestalt principle of proximity. Here an alteration in the spacing of the uniform stimulus units gives rise to two differing percepts, e.g. in Figure. 8.7 the figure on the left

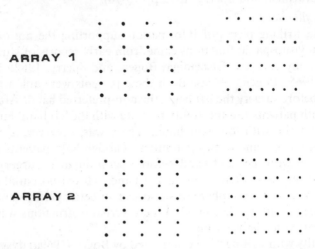

Fig. 8.7 Gestalt figure (Figure 1, p. 286, R.D. Nebes (1973) *Neuropsychologia*, **11**, 285-289. (Courtesy of Pergamon Press Ltd.)

is perceived as columns of dots whereas the figure on the right is seen as rows. Commissurotomy subjects (three in number) were presented tachistoscopically with one of these figures to either the left or right half-field of vision and were required to signal either vertical or horizontal organization by finger movements. All three subjects were more accurate with displays in the left half of the visual field 'suggesting that in man the right hemisphere is more competent than the left in perceiving the overall stimulus configuration inherent in the spatial organization of its parts' (p.285).

Such experiments provide strong support for the position that the right hemisphere functions much more efficiently in situations where synthesis of configurations is required from fragmentary information. Nebes (1974b) considers that this ability of the right hemisphere 'can be viewed as a spatial function in which, from limited data, we infer the structure and organization of our environment without having to submit the whole sensory array to a detailed analysis' (p.12). He points out that the results of his experiments taken together with the data from the chimera experiments suggest that it is the type of information processing required in a given situation which determines whether one hemisphere or the other will be 'dominant' or function in a superior manner. 'If only visual recognition is called for, even if the material is verbal, it is the right hemisphere which acts. If, however, a verbal transformation is demanded, even if the material is non-verbal it is handled by the left hemisphere.' If this suggestion is true (and there is already experimental support for it) then it will enable us to understand why certain contradictions in the literature have arisen on the basis of patients' performance on verbal versus non-verbal tasks. It will also enable tests to be designed which should have greater value in the prediction of laterality of localized lesions in either hemisphere.

Auditory perception

Differences have been noted in the testing of commissurotomy subjects under dichotic conditions. Firstly, there is a marked lowering in the number of digits correctly reported from the left ear (Milner, Taylor, and Sperry, 1968; Sparks and Geschwind, 1968). This difference is also seen after right temporal lobectomy though to a less marked degree. On monaural stimulation subjects showed equal efficiency for the two ears. Milner *et al.* extended this finding by presenting pairs of competing instructions simultaneously to each ear. The subject was told, for example, to pick up an object from a group of objects hidden from view but on each occasion separate objects were named to the left and right ears. Under these conditions the subjects showed a strong preference to pick up objects named through the left ear with a relative neglect of item named in the right ear. This suppression or neglect of information coming to the right ear varied from subject to subject and with the conditions of testing. Subjects also had some difficulty with naming the objects picked up with the left hand. They tended to misname them and often gave the name which had simultaneously presented to the right ear. The authors conclude that the 'dissociation between verbal and left-hand stereognostic response indicates a right-left dichotomy for auditory experience in the disconnected hemispheres'.

Language expression and the minor hemisphere

Extensive examinations of commissurotomy patients seemed to give very strong support to the contention that the right hemisphere is mute. 'Information perceived exclusively or generated exclusively in the minor (right) hemisphere could be communicated neither in speech nor in writing; it has to be expressed entirely through nonverbal responses' (Gazzaniga, 1970, p.125). This led Levy and her colleagues to ask the question, 'Does the minor hemisphere suffer from expressive aphasia because it cannot wrest control of the linguistic expressive mechanisms from the left hemisphere, or is the right hemisphere simply incapable of thinking of words?' (Levy, 1974, p.165).

In an attempt to answer such a question Levy, Nebes, and Sperry (1971) had tested the ability of the surgically separated right hemisphere to spell out words. Two commissurotomy patients were asked to use their hidden left hand to rearrange plastic letters to form a meaningful word. Both patients were able to arrange the letters into words but were unable to name the word they had 'spelled out'. They performed very poorly when asked to write the name of an object felt with the left hand whereas they were able to draw the object readily. These patients were also inferior in left-handed writing of verbs as compared with nouns. Levy *et al.* considered that there were two major factors accounting for poor performance in expression (here written expression) by the right hemisphere, (1) dominance by the major hemisphere over the motor mechanisms for expression and, (2) an intrinsic limitation in the processing of language. They comment, 'Our results suggest that though there are two aspects of language expression—central conceptual dominance and peripheral motor dominance—there is a fairly direct relationship between the two. When a hemisphere is intrinsically better equipped to handle some task, it is also easier for that hemisphere to dominate motor pathways' (Levy *et al.*, p.58). When the effect of the dominant hemisphere is removed as in dominant hemispherectomy the positive but limited power of the minor hemisphere over expression becomes apparent.

Evidence for vocalization originated by the minor hemisphere is commissurotomy patients is almost non-existent. Butler and Norrsell (1968) reported that one patient tested three years after section of the anterior commissure and corpus callosum appeared to be able at times to name simple words presented in the left visual field. They employed a technique by which eye movements actuated a shutter to shut off the projector if the patient changed fixation. In this way the stimulus was kept in the left visual field for a much longer time than with the usual tachistoscopic method. Possible explanations of this finding have been put forward by Gazzaniga (1970).

In an examination of right hemisphere language and speech capacity in commissurotomy patients Gazzaniga and Hillyard (1971) could find no confirmation for expressive capacity in the right hemisphere. There was, moreover, virtually no syntactic ability shown by their tests, even the limited amount of comprehension by the right hemisphere on pictorial-verbal matching tasks being limited to the affirmative-negative dimension. Other workers (Trevarthen, 1969; Milner and Taylor, 1970; Teng and Sperry, 1973) have mentioned situations in which the right hemisphere has appeared to initiate fragmentary utterances in split-brain testing.

Gazzaniga (1970) noted that while object nouns appeared to be comprehended best of any words flashed in the left visual field nouns derived from verbs were not comprehended at all. Words containing more than one morpheme also presented difficulty for the right hemisphere. Caplan, Holmes, and Marshall (1974) failed to confirm this hypothesis, namely, that while simple nouns are represented in the right hemisphere agentive (verb-derived) nouns or bi-morphemic nouns are not.

Memory

Numerous studies by Sperry and his associates have demonstrated that each hemisphere has the capacity to store information for subsequent retrieval and this capacity is directly related to the specialization of each hemisphere. However, this does not mean that the memory abilities of split-brain subjects remain normal. Milner and Taylor (1972) tested commussurotomy patients' tactile recognition memory by asking them to feel an object then select it tactually from a group of four after delays of up to two minutes. Two classes of objects were used (1) everyday objects to which verbal labels could be readily attached, rubber band, key, coin, scissors, and (2) 'non-verbal' tactile nonsense shapes. In six out of the seven subjects there was a marked superiority for the left hand. This was taken to mean that complex perceptual information can be remembered without the necessity for verbal encoding and it is the right hemisphere which specializes in this regard. The combination of these two findings seems to imply that 'both cerebral hemispheres normally participate in such tasks, but with the right playing the preponderant role.' Milner (1974) points out that concentration on the evidence of hemispheric specialization derived from commissurotomy studies and the parallel studies of asymmetry in normal subjects using similar experimental techniques may lead to an overemphasis of the functional differences between the two hemispheres. She reminds us that unilateral lesion studies have demonstrated that there is a parallel organization of function on the two sides of the brain which is in danger of being overlooked. Recently Zaidel and Sperry (1974) examined a total of ten commissurotomy patients on six standardized tests of memory. An examination of the data suggested that the processes which mediate the initial encoding as well as the retrieval of contralateral engrams involve co-operation between the hemispheres and so depend upon the commissural connections.

The present selection of commissurotomy evidence has focused on those areas which have been most closely examined. Other areas which have been less systematically explored include emotion, volition, and consciousness. Incidental reports related to these have occurred throughout many of the studies mentioned. Much of the material to that time was reviewed by Lishman (1971).

The 'Strange Hand' sign

Brion and Jedynak (1972) have reported a new sign of callosal disconnection which they term *la main étrangère*. 'The patient who holds his hands one in the other behind his back does not recognize that his left hand belongs to him.' They stress that this is not a matter of failed tactile recognition but a failure on the patient's part to recognize that the hand he is holding actually belongs to himself. Two patients when asked to write with their left hand were able to do so but expressed amazement and were unwilling to believe that they themselves had done the writing.

Functional asymmetry in normal subjects

The hemispheric asymmetry of function demonstrated in lesions studies and after commissurotomy has been supported by studies, particularly of auditory and visual perception, in normal subjects.

Visual perception

The typical experiment in this field has employed tachistoscopic presentation to the separate half fields of vision corresponding to each cerebral hemisphere. Thus a superiority of perception (as measured by speed or accuracy) in one half-field compared with the other argues for a special 'dominance' of the particular hemisphere for a particular class of percept. A sample of findings is presented in Table 8.4. Recent summaries reporting visual perception asymmetries include White (1969), Milner (1971), White (1972), Kimura (1973) and **Kimura and Durnford (1974)**.

Table 8.4 Perceptual asymmetry in vision

Left half-field superiority	Right half-field superiority

Number and location of dots
    Kimura (1966, 1969).
Depth perception/ slope of line
    Durnford and Kimura (1971).
Facial recognition
    Rizzolatti, Umilta, and
    Berlucchi (1971) Hilliard (1973).
Shape recognition
    Dee and Fontenot (1973).
	Verbal material
	    Mishkin and Forgays (1952);
	    Heron (1957; Terrace (1959)
	    Wyke and Ettlinger (1961);
	    Bryden and Rainey (1963);
	    Bryden (1965); Kimura (1966);
	    McKeever and Huling (1971);
	    Bryden (1973); Hilliard (1973).

Auditory perception

Asymmetries in auditory perception have followed the early work of Kimura using the dichotic listening technique of Broadbent. Table 8.5 presents a small sample of such findings.

Table 8.5 Perceptual asymmetry in audition

Left ear Superiority	Right ear superiority

Melodies
    Kimura (1967)
Environmental Sounds
    Curry (1967); Knox and
    Kimura (1970).
Two-click threshold
    Murphy and Venables (1970)
Pitch patterns
 Darwin (1971)
	Verbal material
	    Kimura (1967); Shankweiler
	    and Studdert-Kennedy (1967);
	    Darwin (1971).
	Human voice recognition
	    Doehring and Bartholomeus
	    (1971).

While some attempt has been made to be representative, it should be pointed out that difficulties have been encountered in attempts to replicate some of the above findings. Bryden (1973) found that stable laterality effects for non-verbal visual material are difficult to obtain, and also reminds us that unequivocal evidence of cerebral dominance for language is lacking in these normal subjects. Finally, the relation between the visual and auditory asymmetries has received little attention to date. However, the general tenor of the results in these studies of perceptual asymmetry accords well with the other evidence for asymmetry presented in this chapter.

Information processing

Space does not permit an adequate review of the growing research which utilizes the information processing approach to the study of the relative efficiency of each hemisphere or related topics such as the interaction between attention and hemispheric asymmetry. Many of these have employed reaction time methods on samples of the normal population to test hypotheses derived from neurological findings. It should be remembered that models of cerebral organization based on results of lesion studies, naturally or surgically induced, may be misleading. Reviewing relevant literature on reaction time studies in normal subjects Moscovitch (1973) concludes that 'a model of cerebral organization based on the split-brain evidence cannot properly describe the functional organization of the cerebral hemispheres of normal people' (p.113).

Of more direct interest to the clinical emphasis of the present chapter are studies which show focal impairment of reaction time with unilateral lesions. The first major study appears to be that of De Renzi and Faglioni (1965) who demonstrated greater impairment of simple reaction time with lesions of the right hemisphere. These patients were appreciably slower when using their preferred hand to respond than a left hemisphere group even where the latter used the non-preferred hand. These findings were supported by Benson and Barton (1970). On the other hand at least two studies fail to support a hemispheric difference (Benton and Joynt, 1959; Tzavaras and Tzavaras, 1974). The reasons for the discrepancy are discussed by Howes and Boller (1975). These authors suggest that lesions of the left hemisphere produce an increase in reaction time in a 'non-specific' way while there seem to be focal regions in the right hemisphere (in the region of the basal ganglia or posterior parietal region) which appear to have a specific effect which is present even in patients with no evidence of contralateral motor involvement.

Dominance revisited

As evidence has accumulated regarding the specialized functions of the two hemispheres, attempts have been made to characterize the different contributions of each hemisphere. Bogen (1969b) traced the emergence of the various dichotomies from the time of Hughlings Jackson up to his own classification. His table is produced below.

Table 8.6 Some dichotomies distinguishing between the two hemispheres (From Bogen, 1969b)

	DOMINANT (left) HEMISPHERE	MINOR (right) HEMISPHERE
Jackson (1864)	Expression	Perception
Jackson (1874)	Audito-articular	Retino-ocular
Jackson (1876)	Propositioning	Visual imagery
Milner (1958)	Verbal	Perceptual or non-verbal
Zangwill (1961)	Symbolic	Visuospatial
Bogen and Gazzaniga (1965)	Verbal	Visuospatial
Levy-Agresti and Sperry (1968)	Logical or analytic	Synthetic perceptual
Bogen (1969b)	Propositional	Appositional

Bogen points out the difficulty which we have in the present state of our knowledge in characterizing the ability of the right hemisphere. His earlier dichotomy (a combintation of those of Milner and Zangwill) was abandoned because of the evidence of some verbal capacity in the right hemisphere. He proposed the use of the provisional term 'appositional' for right hemisphere function. 'This term implies a capacity for opposing or comparing of perceptions, schemas, engrams, etc. but has, in addition, the virtue that it implies very little else. If it is correct that the right hemisphere excels in capacities as yet unknown to us, the full meaning of 'appositional' will emerge as these capacities are further studied and understood' (Bogen, 1969b, p.149). Though much more information has accumulated since then it is still difficult to select a pair of terms to epitomize the lateral differences in function. Perhaps this is just as well since, as Milner (1974) points out it would be wrong in studying hemispheric differences in function to overlook the large amount of evidence from both neurological and neuropsychological studies which demonstrate that 'similarities as well as differences exist between corresponding areas, in the two hemispheres', i.e. there is what she aptly terms a complementary specialization of the two hemispheres with regard to psychological functions. The question then is one of relative rather than absolute dominance. Benton expressed this in the following way: 'Dominance denotes *asymmetry* in hemispheric function, i.e. the two hemispheres subserve particular functions to an unequal degree. Theoretically the degree of inequality with respect to a particular function might be either *absolute* (one hemisphere exclusively mediating the function) or *relative* (one hemisphere being the more important in the mediation of the function). All available evidence suggests that absolute inequality is rare, the more common relationship being one of relative inequality' (Benton, 1975, p.9). Some authors would prefer to specify the particular function being considered rather than speak of one hemisphere as 'the dominant one' (e.g. Poeck, 1975).

Finally, the evidence from some commissurotomy studies coupled with studies of normal subjects has supported the notion that one of the major differences between the functioning of the two hemispheres lies not so much in the specialization for different types of information or for different psychological functions but rather in the different strategies and modes of central processing which each hemisphere employs.

In summarizing the evidence on asymmetry of function in the brain Levy concludes (1974a, p.167).

. . .the human cerebral hemispheres exist in a symbiotic relationship in which both the capacities and motivations to act are complementary. Each side of the brain is able to perform and chooses to perform a certain set of cognitive tasks which the other side finds difficult or distasteful or both. In considering the nature of the two sets of functions, it appears they may be logically incompatible. The right hemisphere synthesises over space. The left hemisphere analyzes over time. The right hemisphere notes visual similarities to the exclusion of conceptual similarities. The left hemisphere does the opposite. The right hemisphere perceives form, the left hemisphere, detail. The right hemisphere codes sensory input in terms of images, the left hemisphere in terms of linguistic descriptions. The right hemisphere lacks a phonological analyser; the left hemisphere lacks a Gestalt synthesizer. . . . This description of hemispheric behaviour suggests that the Gestalt Laws of Perceptual Organisation pertain only to the mute hemisphere. If so, the adaptive functions served by these organisational principles are likewise restricted to the mute hemisphere, just as the adaptive functions served by language are restricted to the verbal hemisphere.

9. Neuropsychological Assessment

General considerations.

Attacks on the validity of drawing inferences about normal psychological mechanisms by analysing behaviour disrupted by neurological lesions have become less frequent as modern neuropsychology has developed. 'The criticism that inferences about normal brain mechanisms cannot be based on the study of mechanisms in an abnormal organism is so general as to be self defeating. The bounds of normality resist definition. The same argument can be applied to individual differences within a normal population, so that one is driven to admit findings derived from the behaviour of any one individual as relevant to none other' (Kinsbourne, 1971, p.287). The value of the study of pathology might be assailed with the same objection but the study of physiology and pathology have proved mutually enriching in advancing our biological concepts and it is reasonable to expect that the study of lesion cases and general psychology will interact in the same way. There is already evidence that they are beginning to do so. In the last chapter, for example, it was noted lesion studies were the first to bring to light the differences in function which characterized the individual cerebral hemispheres. The nature of these differences has been clarified by experimental studies in neuropsychology and parallel studies in normal subjects. Converging lines of evidence from these separate sources have clarified our ideas on the notion of information processing in the brain.

Assumptions implicit in early studies of 'brain damage' or 'organicity' and the conceptual and practical shortcomings have been reviewed on a number of occasions. The reader is referred to Yates (1954), Meyer (1957), Smith (1962a), Yates (1966), Kinsbourne (1971) and Reitan and Davison (1974). Because the issues are far from resolved they will be reviewed briefly in the first sections of the present chapter.

With increasing evidence of the specific effects of localized lesions there may be a tendency to overlook general or non-specific effects. Earlier Yates (1966) pointed out that brain damage may produce different types of effect in any individual; (a) a general deterioration in all aspects of functioning; (b) differential (group) effects, depending on the location, extent etc. of the damage; and (c) highly specific effects in certain locations. Yates pointed out that for this reason single tests of brain damage were likely to prove unsatisfactory. An exception to this would be the discovery of both specific and general effects from a single perceptual task described by Teuber and Liebert (1958).

A widely used notion that has been accepted uncritically is the assumption that a test validated on clearly defined brain-damaged groups may be useful for the day to day purposes of clinical diagnosis. Yates (1966) points out that even if care is taken to control the numerous methodological factors outlined below, the fact that the test was validated on groups with clear cut cases may mean that its predictive validity may be quite low. If it can identify 'only those subjects whose brain damage is obvious, then the test serves no useful purpose, since it confirms what needs no confirmation.' (Yates, 1966). Study of the literature had led Heilbrun (1962) to observe that a significant proportion of predictive hits seemed to come from those instances in which the neurological symptoms were fairly clear. 'A crucial study would be one in which the neuro-logical group is made up entirely of subjects for whom neurologists disagree as to diagnosis or are unable to make a diagnostic statement at all at the time the psychological measure is obtained and for whom retrospective diagnosis is possible.' (Heilbrun, 1962, p.513). Such predictive validity studies are few in number. One such study is that of Matthews, Shaw and Kløve (1966). These workers tested the predictive validity of a number of measures from the Hal-stead-Reitan Battery and the Wechsler scales on a group of subjects all of whom were initially suspected of neurological disease but in whom only half were subsequently confirmed as neurological, the other half being allotted to a non-neurological diagnosis. The authors rather nicely refer to the latter group as 'pseudoneurologic'. Even in this more difficult diagnostic situation some of the measures discriminated at a high level. Further studies of predictive validity are obviously necessary. Yates (1954) also reminds us that many forget that even where a test shows a highly significant group difference it may still be of little clinical use because of an unacceptable level of misclassification.

Another shortcoming of psychological studies in this area might be termed the principle of multiple determination. 'Behavioural deficits are defined in terms of impaired test performance. But impaired test performance may be a final common pathway for expression of quite diverse types of impairment.' (Kinsbourne, 1972). Smith (1975) takes as an example what is probably the test most frequently reported as showing decrement with brain damage in sundry forms and locations, namely the Digit-Symbol Substitution Test, 'the responses are the end product of the integration of visual perceptual, oculomo-tor, fine manual motor, and mental functions.' It is therefore important to be aware that low scores on this test may be due to disturbance in any of the functions involved or any combination of them. This concept forms a very important factor in application of the experimental investigation of the single case outlined below. It is unfortunate that not only are so many psychological tests in use in neuropsychology multifactorial in nature but that, in many cases, the exact nature of the functions which determine a successful outcome is unknown.

Closely allied to the notion of multiple determination is that of multiple pathways to the goal. Many psychological tests are concerned solely with whether or not the subject can reach the goal. 'The flexibility of cerebral mechanisms is such that the solution of most test items can be reached by many devious routes. The method the subject uses in tackling a problem will in general provide more information as to the character of a skill or of a psychological deficit than will the knowledge as to the subject's success or failure' (Elithorn, 1965).

Smith (1962) has challenged the next assumption, namely that any sizeable cerebral lesion will lead to demonstrable psychological defects. He points to the frequently reported presence of major neurological lesions at autopsy which were unsuspected during life. Other patients with classical signs of neurological disorder have shown no evidence of any lesion at autopsy. The first type of evidence should remind us of Teuber's dictum that 'absence of evidence is not evidence of absence.' In the present imperfect state of our knowledge we should not interpret negative signs on our tests to mean that symptoms do not have a neurological foundation. Looking back over the hundreds of studies with negative results we cannot fail to note that most of them failed to show evidence of neuropsychological disorder because the tests were either too crude or inappropriate. The fact that neurological lesions can be found at autopsy does not mean that they *would have* remained undiagnosed if the patient had presented himself and had been subjected to an *appropriate or relevant examination*. The growth of neuropsychological knowledge means that less and less of the brain is silent to examination or, as McFie (1972) put it 'much of the brain (is) demonstrably occupied with psychological functions.' There are also disorders which do not intrude very much upon the patient's everyday living or occupation and thus are not likely to be presented in the form of complaints to physicians. A prime example is constructional apraxia, often called the apraxia of the psychologist since the deficit is only elicited under the special conditions of psychological examination. It might be anticipated that as an adequate neuropsychological assessment becomes an integral part of neurological investigation these 'negative' cases will occur less frequently. Perhaps the exceptions will be cases where, as in the case of slowly-growing meningiomas, the lesion allows gradual adaptation to take place. Finally, the less dramatic symptoms might be construed both by patient and physician as 'nervous' or 'functional' in origin and their true nature not revealed because of inadequate examination.

The assumption which seems to be the most difficult to eradicate from psychology is that of the unitary concept of brain damage. Despite the enormous growth of evidence in the neurosciences over the past few decades about the specificity of function in the several parts of the brain, clinical journals of psychology have continued to publish studies on the validity or otherwise of tests for 'organicity' or 'brain damage' as though lesions of different nature and size, in different locations in the brain will reflect themselves in poor performance on simple tests. The naiveté of this approach is in part the failure of some psychologists to look at the evidence from behavioural neurology and neuropsychology.

Roles for neuropsychological assessment

The best known role has been in assistance in neurological diagnosis. The two most commonly asked questions concern (1) the presence or absence of neurologically based cerebral impairment, and (2) the lateralization and localization of the lesion. Those who are familiar only with the findings from the psychometric approaches described in the following section may well agree with Solomon and Patch (1971): 'Despite claims of some psychologists to the contrary, it has not been established that psychologic tests can localize brain lesions or other organic disease except in a gross way. Although these tests often can determine whether an organic lesion is present or absent, they cannot localize the specific lesion.'

It should be remembered that the clinical neuropsychologist is seldom in the position of being asked to provide a definitive diagnosis. However, it will be argued that if he accepts the role of applied scientist rather than technician he will be in the position of offering what at times is crucial information with regard to diagnosis. The neuropsychological examination is an integral part of the neurological examination and must be seen in this context. It would be valuable if sensitive behavioural measures could be refined so as to promote the earlier diagnosis of some cerebral lesions. There is encouraging evidence that behavioural measures may be able to detect impairment which is too subtle to be detected by many current neurological procedures.

The second role lies in the assessment of cases where the diagnosis has already been verified. A systematic and comprehensive documentation of the patient's mental functions is of value in following the progress of patients suffering from cranio-cerebral trauma, cerebrovascular disorders and the numerous other neurological conditions in which mental symptoms may form a prominent part. This role should not be thought of simply as a mechanical documentation but rather the examinations should be seen as providing *understanding* of the ways in which the neurological condition has affected the individual patient. Such an understanding should aid in designing the total management of the patient.

Neuropsychological assessment also provides an important method of evaluating various forms of treatment such as neurosurgical procedures and drug therapy. The neurosurgical procedures include resections for tumour and epilepsy, the insertion of shunts in cases of so-called normal pressure hydrocephalus, and the special procedures loosely referred to as psychosurgery. Assessment is also valuable in checking progress after vascular surgery such as endarterectomy for stenosis of the vessels supplying the cerebrum. The principal drug therapies at present are those for the treatment of epilepsy and Parkinsonism.

The last major role and one which has only recently begun to develop is rehabilitation. A more detailed understanding of the manner in which the neurological disorder has affected the patient should come from a careful examination of the deficits. It will be apparent in some cases that the nature of the patient's deficits will preclude certain forms of rehabilitation altogether or will make some methods more desirable than others. Even in the rudimentary state of our knowledge about the restitution of cerebral function a systematic appraisal should be preferable to the blind application of rules of thumb.

Where rehabilitation procedures make specific claims objective assessment procedures will allow such claims to be tested. In most rehabilitation centres rather strenuous efforts are directed to the obvious sensory and motor deficits and one suspects that a good deal of progress is due to spontaneous recovery rather than to the application of special regimes often put forward on doubtful theoretical bases. This is not meant to suggest that all means should not be attempted but that they should be subjected to scientific evaluation if progress is to be made. Some individuals make substantial improvement after marked structural damage to the brain while others with apparently minor injuries fail to make the progress expected of them. Systematic study of individual cases with the recently acquired knowledge of brain-behaviour relationships might begin to open up what has been a very barren area. Certainly this knowledge has so far received little attention. The clinical impression mentioned below that in traumatic cases those with persistent signs of frontal lobe involvement tend to do poorly in rehabilitation even after apparent recovery of sensory and motor defects needs systematic evaluation. At the same time there is a need to apply the very great wealth of material which psychology has gathered on cognitive development to ascertain whether methods similar to those used in the acquisition of concepts in children could be applied to the retraining of cerebrally impaired adults.

Symptoms and syndromes

The significance of a patient's symptoms and signs can be understood in the context of the notion of a functional system (Ch. 1). A functional system in the brain consists of a number of parts of the brain, particularly but not exclusively cortical together with their fibre connections. The system operates in a concerted manner to form the substratum of a complex psychological function. This systemic concept allows a new approach to the use of psychological tests in the diagnosis or assessment of neurological conditions, an approach which parallels the study of other bodily systems.

It will be apparent that if a psychological process is served by an anatomical system which is spread out in the brain then the psychological process will be vulnerable at a number of different points some of which may be widely separated. Such a finding was, in fact, one of the seemingly powerful arguments used against the early localizationists. If, for example, speaking or writing or perceiving could be altered by lesions in sundry locations, then these functions could not be localized. The argument turns, of course, on what is meant by 'localized'.

The modern notion of a functional system also incorporates the notion of regional specialization within the system and it is this which increases its value both in theoretical explanation as well as application to the individual case. While damage anywhere in the system will lead to some change in the function which the system subserves, the *nature* of the change will be dependent upon the particular part of the system which is damaged or the set of connections which has been disrupted since each part contributes something characteristic to the whole. It is thus necessary to look carefully at the *nature* of the changes in a psychological function to determine how they are related to the location and character of the lesions.

This multiple significance of what appears at first to be the same symptom or symptom complex begins to render meaningful the apparently conflicting findings of many early studies and, at the same time, allows symptoms or signs to have localizing value. To take a common example, psychologists have long observed that the Kohs block design test is often performed poorly by many, but certainly not by all, brain-damaged subjects. Poor performance on this test could result from a disruption of what might rather loosely be termed constructional praxis. It could also be performed poorly because of visual and other difficulties but if these are excluded and poor performance of the block design task is taken as an operational definition of constructional apraxia, the regional significance still remains to be determined. Here observations during testing will be of help. Constructional deviations are particularly prominent in right hemisphere lesions and markedly so where there is a right posterior locus. Ben Yishay *et al.* (1971) have described these errors in terms of deviation from the square format of the design to be copied—'broken squares; rectangles; linearly placed horizontally, vertically, diagonally; irregular shapes—patterns wherein the individual blocks are improperly aligned with respect to one another and with the horizontal and vertical planes.' An example is shown in Figure 9.1.

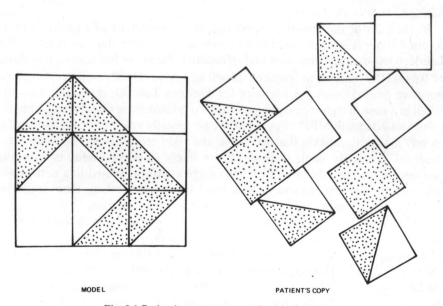

MODEL   PATIENT'S COPY

Fig. 9.1 Patient's attempt at copying block design

An equally poor score on the block design test may be obtained by a second patient with a right frontal lesion. However, such a patient will usually show fewer constructional deviations and his difficulty may be shown to be dependent upon incomplete preliminary investigation of the problem as in the case examined by Luria and Tsvetkova (1964) cited in Chapter 4. In this case the frontal patient is helped by the provision of a design card upon which the outlines of the four (or more) constituent blocks have been drawn. On the other hand the right parietal patient tends to benefit little from this procedure. The 'partially solved' block design problem apparently has no more meaning in his shattered visuo-spatial world than the original. As mentioned elsewhere the nature of the observations which will be of value and the tests which will be applied must rest on a knowledge of the findings emerging from research studies.

Approaches to the assessment of brain damage

It will be assumed in what follows that the reader has at least a general familiarity with the development and nature of psychological assessment particularly with regard to the construction, norming and standardization of commonly used tests such as the Wechsler scales together with some appreciation of the reliability and limitations of psychological measurement. Further detail can be gained from sources such as Holt (1968), Matarazzo (1972), Zimmerman, Woo-Sam, and Glasser (1973), and Anastasi (1976). The present topic of neuropsychological testing can be found in Williams (1965), Mittler (1973), and Smith (1975). Conceptual and methodological difficulties related to the assessment of the neurological patient are clearly discussed by Kinsbourne (1971).

Single tests of brain damage

In the light of the growing knowledge about specificity of function and its cerebral bases it is surprising to find single tests of brain damage (such as the Bender-Gestalt) still being used and advocated. Negative findings such as those of Rosen (1971) are all to frequent. Bruell and Albee (1962) even demonstrated negative findings with the Memory for Designs Test (Graham and Kendall, 1960) in a case of right hemispherectomy. To paraphrase Garron and Chiefetz (1965) an adequate MFD copy does not necessarily rule out brain damage; it merely makes it unlikely that lesions in the right temporo-parietal region are involved. The only single tests which are likely to prove useful as screening procedures for the detection of brain damage are those related to a nonspecific lowering of cerebral efficiency. The most likely areas where these could be developed might be vigilance, reaction time and new learning.

While single tests used against an assumption of a unitary concept of brain damage are to be decried there may be very practical reasons why some might like to employ them as steps in what Wechsler (1958) termed 'the method of successive sieves'. The extensive work of McFie (1969) and others shows that the Digit-Symbol subtest of the Wechsler Scales shows impairment with lesions in any location. The Symbol-Digit Modalities Test (Smith 1973, 1975) has added to the substitution test an opportunity to compare the patient's performance utilizing two independent response modalities, written and spoken. Though false positives rule out its use alone, the almost complete lack of false negatives in studies of large numbers of brain damaged patients make it an excellent screening device.

A second example might be Reitan's Trail Making Test. Though not intended for use on its own, its brevity and the fact that it yields a high percentage of correct identification for brain damage (Korman & Blumberg, 1963, Rosen, 1972) make it a possibility for screening purposes. A good performance would greatly lower the likelihood of impairment while a poor score should lead to further testing.

Similar reasoning might be applied to the 'Mini-Mental-State' test of Folstein, Folstein and McHugh (1975).

'Psychometric' versus 'Clinical' approaches.

It is now over two decades since Meehl published his monograph on clinical versus statistical prediction (Meehl, 1954). In this he outlined the theoretical assumptions and implications inherent in the two approaches which still appear to divide psychologists. This division is as apparent in the assessment of cerebral impairment as it is in other areas of clinical endeavour. In a number of papers, some with provocative titles but all with serious intent, Meehl clarified the issues and greatly advanced our understanding about drawing inferences from psychological test data (Meehl, 1956a, b; 1960, 1961). He felt that it would be possible to produce 'cookbooks' which would allow an automatic clerical or mechanical evaluation of the test data carried out by the use of explicit rules set out in the 'recipes'. This would mean that the newcomer could be about as efficient in this phase of clinical practice as the more experienced clinician. The clinical method Meehl saw as involving 'the clinician's personal experience, skill and creative artistry.'

In propounding the use of the actuarial approach Meehl (1956a) felt that an initial layout of research time could result in a cookbook whose recipes would encompass the great majority of psychometric configurations seen in daily work.

For our present purposes the most commonly adopted approaches to assessment have been divided into a rough dichotomy of 'psychometric' versus 'clinical' in Table 9.1. A brief discussion of each follows.

Table 9.1 Methods for inferring psychological deficit

Psychometric	Clinical
Level of performance	Qualitative Changes in Performance
Differential score methods	Abstract thinking
Quotients and Indices	Rigidity
Wechsler's Deterioration	Spatial Rotation
Index. Hewson's ratios	Detection of Syndromes
Halstead/Reitan Impairment	Experimental Investigation of the Single Case
Index	
Scatter patterns	
Verbal-Performance differences	
Taxonomic Keys	
Statistical Weighting	
Multiple Discriminant Function	
Analysis	

Differential score comparisons

In 1930, Babcock introduced the notion of comparing the performance of the patient on tests such as vocabulary which seemed to be relatively impervious to cerebral impairment with tests such as those involving new learning or motor speed which seemed to be almost universally lowered. Tests which 'held up' in the face of cerebral disorders were thought to provide a useful index of the patient's premorbid intellectual level and thus could serve as a basis for comparison of his present performance on other tests. Babcock's notion reached its most popular expression in Wechsler's Deterioration Index (Wechsler, 1944) originated to quantify lowering of performance with age. Wechsler subtests which held up with age were: Vocabulary, Information, Picture Completion, and Object Assembly. Don't Hold tests were: Similarities, Digit Span, Digit Symbol and Block Design. The Deterioration Quotient was expressed as:

$$\frac{\text{Hold-Don't Hold}}{\text{Hold}}$$

From this position it was but a short step for some to equate deterioration in this sense with cerebral impairment from any neurological lesion. The transition was especially easy for that large number of psychologists who accepted uncritically the unitary concept of brain damage. Terms such as 'organicity', 'brain damage' and 'the organic brain syndrome' tended to suggest what Smith (1975) described recently as 'a relatively uniform pattern of disturbances. . . regardless of the nature, locus, age, or dynamics of the underlying cerebral lesion, age of the patient, and other factors'. Even disregarding these objections, application of the Deterioration Quotient was largely unsuccessful. Studies in favour of its efficacy in diagnosis are difficult to find while those reporting the index as unsatisfactory are numerous.

The ratio method was extended by Hewson (1949) who developed a number of different ratios only some of which might reach an 'organic' level in particular cases or groups. Bryan and Brown (1957) pointed out that Hewson's method departed not only from Wechsler's Deterioration Index but also from the various differential score techniques such as those of Babcock (1930) and Rapaport (1945) which have all assumed that certain subtests or group of subtests would remain relatively fixed while others would show substantial changes. Smith (1962b) using unequivocal cases with neoplastic lesions found that over seventy per cent gave non-organic ratios.

The Halstead-Reitan impairment index. In 1947, Ward Halstead published his theory of 'biological intelligence'. This theory had arisen from his study of cases of brain damage using a variety of measures which came to be termed the Halstead battery of tests. Some tests have been dropped from the battery and others modified but there is a remarkable constancy some thirty years later. A great amount of information on the battery has been generated for both children and adults particularly by Reitan and his colleagues and the recent book by the users of this method is very well documented (Reitan and Davison, 1974). The tests themselves have been described by Reitan (1966b).

The method consisted essentially of deriving a cutting score from each test which discriminated satisfactorily between brain damaged subjects and controls. Criterion groups were heterogenous collections of brain damaged subjects. Each of the ten tests reaching the cutting point contributed 0.1 to an index of impairment, i.e. the value of the index ranged from zero (no impairment) to 1.0 (very gross impairment). Interpretation of intermediate values of the index (e.g. 0.4) is difficult. Validity of the index and the constituent subtests in the battery can be examined in Reitan and Davison *op. cit.* One of the favourable features of the battery approach is the fact that it has been shown to be capable of distinguishing between 'neurologic' and 'pseudoneurologic' patients (Matthews, Shaw and Klove, 1966).

The Halstead-Reitan battery does not necessarily limit the psychologist to a strict actuarial approach, i.e. the Impairment Index only. It can also form the basis for clinical prediction. Relatively inexperienced recent graduates with some teaching and clinical training in interpretation based on the battery were shown to be superior both to the Impairment Index alone and considerably better than even experienced clinicians using the WAIS, the MMPI, and the Bender-Gestalt test (Goldstein, Kleinknecht and Deysach, 1973). A fair degree of competence can be obtained with only a short course at the graduate level at least with regard to the diagnosis of laterality (Lewinsohn, 1971).

Scatter patterns

Many users of the Wechsler-Bellevue Scales, particularly in the fifties, attempted to develop methods which would relate differential performance on the subtests to diagnostic categories such as 'schizophrenia', 'psychoneurosis', and 'brain damage'. Closely allied to these were factor analytic studies of the scales in relation to brain damage. Varying success met these attempts (Allen, 1949; Wittenborn and Holzberg, 1951; Cohen, 1952; Jastak, 1953; Cohen, 1955; Jackson, 1955). Wechsler (1958) himself pointed out the difficulties in these approaches and the frequently false assumptions upon which they were built. Though he did not use the term he likened the diagnostic process to the syndrome approach in medicine employing medical analogies (1958, p.170). Deviation of the separate subtests was considered against the individual's mean subtest score hence the common translation of his method as a scatter pattern. Most psychologists found the method of little use in clinical practice.

Differential impairment on verbal and non-verbal tests. A common assumption regarding psychological assessment is that a differential performance on 'verbal' versus 'nonverbal' tests necessarily reflects the lateralization of the lesion. Such a relationship has often been claimed for the Wechsler intelligence scales. This may be expressed in the following terms. Patients with left hemisphere lesions will show relative impairment on the Verbal portions of the scales while conversely patients with lesions in the right hemisphere will show relative impairment on the Performance subtests. Furthermore, patients with diffuse damage will show no such differential effect.

The evidence for this proposition is conflicting. Some studies appear to lend support to the general contention (Reitan, 1955b; Kløve and Reitan, 1958; and Reitan, 1963; Satz, Richard, and Daniels, 1967; Parsons, Vega and Burn, 1969; Simpson and Vega, 1971; Black, 1974), while others have seemed to confirm one side of the formula but not the other. Most of these are reviewed in Guertin, Ladd, Frank, Rabin and Heister (1966). More serious reservations about general acceptance of the hypothesized relationship come from studies such as Smith (1965; 1966), and McFie and Thompson (1971). Smith's results are most impressive containing as they do a large number of brain tumours whose nature and location were verified at operation or autopsy. His results quite clearly show that despite the inclusion of 28 patients with 'readily discernible language disorders in the total of 92 left hemisphere cases somewhat less than one quarter had lower verbal than performance scores (weighted scale scores).' Smith points out that there are various factors which must be controlled before a clear interpretation can be made of the relation between Wechsler subtest scores and laterality of lesion. He pointed to Wechsler's own evidence (1944) that as full scale I.Q. decreases from 120 to 75 the proportion of patients with higher performance than verbal quotients increased from 21 to 74 per cent. Smith also criticized most workers for a too ready equation of performance on the two component scales with verbal and nonverbal intelligence a distinction which Wechsler himself was careful to avoid.

Smith also pointed to the importance of other factors such as composition of groups with regard to nature and development of lesion, age at onset, and location within the hemisphere, factors he has discussed elsewhere (Smith and Kinder, 1959; Smith, 1962 a, b).

Perhaps psychologists should substitute some term such as 'non-verbalizable' for non-verbal. Though somewhat clumsy this term would remind us that many so-called non-verbal tests require verbal-symbolic functions for their solution so that it is quite misleading to make inferences about laterality of lesions on the basis of tests crudely categorized at their face value.

As pointed out elsewhere, brain lesions may have both general and specific effects. Some tests are affected by laterality and some are not (Satz, 1966). In the WAIS four of the five Performance Scale items are timed and so any lesion, irrespective of location, which would tend to depress the brain's efficiency is likely to result in a lowered score on these items. If we then assume that the Performance Scale also possesses material which is sensitive to impairment of right hemisphere function such as visuospatial and visuoconstructive tasks while the Verbal Scale is sensitive to language disturbance, certain common findings become clearer. In some left sided lesions the non-specific effect on the Performance Scale may outweigh the specific effect on the Verbal Scale while in some right sided lesions the specific and general effects are additive leading to a marked differential effect. This might mean that where the Verbal Scale is much less than the Performance Scale a left sided lesion is highly probable whereas a Performance Scale lower than the Verbal may be produced by a lesion of either side though the probability of a right sided lesion appears to increase with the magnitude of the difference. Certainly the finding of no difference should not be construed as lack of evidence of a lateralized lesion.

Finally the question of base rates has received almost no attention in the studies cited though tables for these Verbal-Performance differences are available (Field, 1960; Fisher, 1960).

For practical purposes one can only conclude that the presence or absence of a verbal-performance differential can only be interpreted in the light of the numerous factors which may have contributed.

The taxonomic key approach

This method is described by Russell, Neuringer, and Goldstein (1970). It is an outgrowth of the extensive use of the Halstead-Reitan neuropsychological test battery and is the best developed attempt to apply the actuarial approach to the diagnosis of brain damage.

The approach takes its theoretical basis from modern biological taxonomy being greatly influenced by Sokal and Sneath (1963). One of the principal advantages is the departure from the unitary concept of brain damage, a movement from a 'monothetic' to a 'polythetic' system of classification. Russell *et al.* cite Beckner (1959) on the nature of the polythetic grouping. '(a) each member "possesses a large but unspecified number of properties" in the group; (b) each property "is possessed by large number of these individuals"; (c) no property is necessarily possessed by every member of the group' Russell *et al.* (p.19).

In applying this philosophy to the assessment of brain damage Russell *et al.* have constructed a number of keys which attempt to allot the particular case to one of a number of groups, brain-damaged or non brain-damaged; left hemisphere, right hemisphere, or diffuse damage; acute or congenital brain damage. In order to do this two procedures are necessary (1) the application of a fixed and extensive battery of tests which includes essentially the Halstead-Reitan Battery, the Wechsler Adult Intelligence Scale and a number of neurological measures of sensory and perceptual functions; (2) the processing of the scores through the various keys.

The sources which were used to generate the keys were quite varied and included: (1) lectures and workshops in neuropsychology; (2) individual clinician's 'rules of thumb'; (3) psychologists' reports; (4) statistical information from reports in the literature. Thus there was some attempt to make the decision-making process quite explicit. The principal advantage claimed is that it enables someone with little training and experience in neuropsychology to make accurate decisions in the difficult area of the psychometric diagnosis of brain damage. Some might feel that the limited amount of information might be obtained much more economically by other means. One attempt to deal with the relatively long administration time of this lengthy battery has been to employ testers and, in such a mechanical operation, there seems little reason to employ highly trained psychologists. There is to date little information about the usefulness of the method though the Halstead-Reitan battery itself is widely used and the key method could be used with little extra expenditure of time.

An inspection of the keys reveals that while the approach is termed neuropsychological, much of the contribution to diagnosis appears to come from neurological findings incorporated in the weightings, e.g. sensory suppression, finger tapping, presence of hemianopia, rather than from the more psychological measures. One wonders about the reaction of a neurologist informed that the patient suffers from brain damage lateralized to the right hemisphere when he is already aware that a 'one-point indicator'—'(f) A left homonymous hemianopia is found' (Russell *et al.*, p.44).

The formulation of the keys has been derived from clearly defined groups. It remains to be seen whether it will be useful in cases where the symptoms and signs are less well defined. This may depend (as would the extension of the method to other questions) on the expenditure of a good deal more research effort.

Multiple discriminant function analysis

This is the most sophisticated weighting technique so far attempted in the application of the psychometric approach to diagnosis. It has been applied with varying success to the scores derived from the Halstead-Reitan battery (Wheeler, 1963; Wheeler, Burke and Reitan, 1963; Wheeler and Reitan, 1963; Goldstein and Shelly, 1972). The method consists essentially of an attempt to answer the question: What weightings should be applied to each of the scores to effect the maximum separation between the groups? The procedure has a number of advantages and disadvantages and it is likely that MDFA will be restricted to clinical research settings for the time being.

Two comparative studies have been noted. Goldstein and Shelly (1972) found that stepwise discriminant function analysis was not very much better at distinguishing between brain-damaged and non brain-damaged groups than the more simple measure the Average Impairment Rating of the Halstead-Reitan battery. It was about as effective as the taxonomic key approach. Birch (1975), has recently extended these findings.

Qualitative changes in performance

Some people who expressed dissatisfaction with the early psychometric approaches pointed to the frequent occurrence of certain qualitative alterations in behaviour with cerebral impairment. They felt that these 'organic signs' were important indicators of brain impairment. The two most frequently mentioned were alteration in abstract thinking and inflexibility or rigidity of behaviour. A third type of behavioural response the 'catastrophic reaction' has already been mentioned. An added sign, that of spatial rotation is also briefly mentioned.

Abstract thinking. The numerous changes subsumed under the term 'abstract attitude' (Goldstein and Scheerer, 1941) have been discussed in Chapter 4. With the increasing realization that many tests of abstract thinking involve numerous other factors in their solution the controversy as to whether abstract thinking is more dependent upon the integrity of the frontal lobes has lost much of its fire. Certainly the presence of concreteness of behaviour in its numerous forms should raise the question of organic impairment whenever it occurs. Simple tests like the Weigl Colour-Form sorting test will often bring these forms of behaviour to the fore in a short time.

No reference to changes in abstract behaviour would be complete without mention of the Halstead Category Test which has been shown on innumerable occasions to give highly significant differences between organic and control groups (Halstead, 1947; Shure, 1954; Reitan, 1955a; Simmel and Counts,

1957; Shure and Halstead, 1958; Reitan, 1959a; Fitzhugh and Fitzhugh, 1961; Kløve, 1963a, b; Matthews, Shaw, and Kløve, 1965, 1966; Vega and Parsons, 1967; Tureen, Schwartz, and Dennerll, 1968). Representative studies of the reliability and validity of this test are given by Shaw (1966) and Reitan and Davison (1974). The Category test appears not only to discriminate between groups of subjects with and without brain damage but also provides a fair indication of the severity of impairment in individual cases. The test is somewhat lengthy and this, together with the need for special apparatus, means the test is used infrequently apart from the users of the Reitan battery. Experiments by Kilpatrick (1970) and Boyle (1975) suggest the test could be reduced by more than half while still retaining most of its effectiveness.

Rigidity. 'Lack of flexibility in behaviour refers to a somewhat heterogeneous collection of signs referred to by various authors as 'inflexibility', 'rigidity', 'perseveration', and 'stereotyped behaviour' (Nichols and Hunt, 1940; Aita, Armitage, Reitan and Rabinowitz, 1947; Rosvold and Mishkin, 1950; Appelbaum, 1960; Kauffman, 1963; Allison, 1966; Mackie and Beck, 1966; Allison and Hurwitz, 1967). A whole group of studies has referred to the particular difficulty which some impaired subjects have had in shifting readily from one concept to another (Goldstein and Scheerer, 1941; Weigl, 1941; Armitage, 1946; Ackerly and Benton, 1948; Halstead, 1959; Milner, 1963, 1964). These examples are by no means exhaustive and this difficulty has been found in a wide variety of test situations and in everyday life.

One promising approach to an experimental analysis of inflexibility was under the paradigm of negative transfer i.e. 'the retardation in the acquiring of an activity as a result of being engaged in a prior activity' (Gleason, 1953). This would allow the experimental manipulation of a number of variables so that the 'application of old responses in new situations where such responses are inappropriate' can be studied (Gleason, op. cit.). Employing a number of different tasks in this way would also allow an examination of the generality of a rigidity factor in brain damage to be tested, together with the question as to whether inflexible behaviour is more a feature of damage in certain locations rather than others. Though there is a deal of evidence that at least certain forms of inflexible behaviour are particularly prominent after frontal damage (Nichols and Hunt, 1940; Halstead, 1947; Ackerly and Benton, 1948; Luria, 1960, 1971b; Milner, 1963, 1964; Luria and Homskaya, 1963) there is also evidence that it is also seen after non-frontal and diffuse damage (Critchley, 1953; Allison, 1966). Finally, experimental studies in normal subjects have shown that a number of factors contribute to the production of rigidities (Allison and Hurwitz, 1967). These factors include fatigue, age, and task difficulty and no examination of rigidity in brain damaged subjects would be complete without appraisal of these factors.

Spatial rotation. It has been noted that brain damaged subjects will often rotate their version of a block design copying task even where their copy is correct. This anomaly in visuoconstructive performance has been studied extensively by Shapiro and his colleagues in a series of publications from the early fifties and a number of suggestions offered in explanation (Shapiro,1951b,

1952, 1953; Shapiro *et al.*, 1962). This anomaly has been used in the form of a rotation score in the Minnesota Percepto-Diagnostic Test (Fuller and Laird, 1963; Fuller, 1967).

Detection of syndromes

Medical science has long been accustomed to noting configurations of signs and symptoms termed syndromes which are then taken to be indicative of a particular disease or lesion. Not all signs or symptoms are of equal importance and the weighting of the different elements is often an idiosyncratic process 'being unformulated outcome of the interaction of medical instruction and clinical experience.' (Kinsbourne, 1971). However psychology in particular has developed multifactorial statistical procedures which should be capable of demonstrating whether a particular set of signs and symptoms possesses the cohesion necessary for designation as a syndrome with its implications of aetiology and prognosis. Though tests such as cluster analysis and other measures of concordance have not yet been applied in neuropsychology they might well prove useful in the future.

For some time English workers have suggested that the syndrome concept should be used in the area of cerebral impairment.

. . .the assessment of intellectual deterioration calls, not for a single
valid standardization test, but rather for a flexible test procedure and
awareness of the relevant syndromes. This view is justified by a
consideration of the multiform effects on intellectual performance of
focal and diffuse cerebral lesions and also by a consideration of the focal
disturbance of intellectual function already recognized by neurologists
and utilized in diagnosis (Piercy, 1959).

As far as cases of suspected cerebral lesion are concerned, the psychologist
can tell the neurologist whether or not the patient's performance resembles
that of a typical case of lesion in one of the major cerebral lobes; and the
neurologist can combine the information with evidence from other procedures in arriving at his assessment. (McFie, 1960).

Thus the psychologist should be concerned with patterns of impairment and as his knowledge of syndromes increases he will, when confronted with certain symptoms or signs, often look for the association of other features to confirm or disconfirm the presence of a particular syndrome. This medical model seems particularly applicable to neuropsychology.

It is obvious that this method of thinking can be extended beyond the syn-dromes of the major cerebral lobes, useful as these undoubtedly are. Other areas suggest themselves. Disconnection syndromes are already the subject of a good deal of study and much benefit could be derived from more careful neuropsychological analysis of the various cerebral arterial syndromes whose gross clinical features are well known. In Chapter 7 mention was made of the frequent association of a recent memory disorder in association with visual deficits (particularly cerebral blindness) produced by insufficiency in the pos-terior cerebral circulation. The unity of this syndrome is seen in relation to the territory irrigated by the arteries rather than the symptoms reflecting a functional impairment common to them all as is often the case. A similar example with qualitatively different types of functional disturbance would be the middle cerebral artery syndrome since the territory of this artery embraces several different functional areas of the cortex.

It is apparent that this approach will only be appreciated by those who have the basic anatomical and neurological knowledge which is one of the prerequisites to the study and practice of neuropsychology. The neuropsychologist has two main roles: (1) sharpening the definition of known syndromes and developing procedures for their more certain detection, and (2) the discovery of fresh syndromes.

Experimental investigation of the single case

One of the most important drawbacks to almost every form of psychometric approach is the loss of valuable information particularly loss of the qualitative features of responses. Shapiro (1951) quoted Schafer 'A test response is not a score; scores, where applicable, are abstractions designed to facilitate intra-individual and inter-individual comparisons, and as such they are extremely useful in clinical testing. However, to reason—or do research—only in terms of scores or score patterns is to do violence to the nature of the raw material. *The scores do not communicate the responses in full*' (italics added). Reitan's (1964) study mentioned in Chapter 4 shows clearly that, utilizing the same test data, clinical prediction can be superior to formal or psychometric methods. This may have been due to loss of qualitative features in individual responses or complex *intra-individual* patterns of response lost when only levels of performance were used. Shapiro has pointed out also some of the major difficulties and limitations inherent in the application of standardized validated tests in the clinical diagnostic setting. His comments are as pertinent today as they were twenty-five years ago though, as he pointed out recently (Shapiro, 1973) very few serious attempts have been made in the intervening period to overcome these difficulties by application of his recommended solution, namely, the experimental investigation of the single case. It may be that the few published studies cited by Shapiro do not represent fully the clinical use of the method. The fact that is lends itself particularly well to the neurosychological elucidation of syndromes is shown in the work of Luria and other European workers.

The whole process is summarized succinctly by Shapiro (1973). After reminding us of the scientific concept of error in psychological measurement he argues that this should prevent us from making unwarranted generalizations from the data but should not prevent us from using observations in a systematic way to advance our understanding of the individual case.

The awareness of error makes us look upon any psychological observation not as something conclusive but as the basis of one or more hypotheses about the patient. One's degree of confidence in any hypothesis suggested by an observation would depend upon the established degree of validity of that observation and upon other information about the patient concerned.

If one or more hypotheses are suggested by an observation, then steps must be taken to test them. In this way further observations are accumulated in a systematic manner. It should then become possible to arrive at a psychological description in which we can have greater confidence. The additional observations may in turn suggest new hypotheses which have in turn to be tested. We are thus led to the method of the systematic investigation as a means of improving the validity of our conclusions about an individual patient (Shapiro, 1973, p.651).

Working hypotheses may arise from generalizations which have emerged from the research literature. Clinical neuropsychology is becoming very rich in this regard as evidenced by the sample provided in Chapters 4 to 8 which, while representative, is far from exhaustive. As this work grows, converging lines of evidence make the generalizations more secure and thus facilitate the implementation of crucial tests of the various hypotheses, e.g. the evidence on asymmetry of hemispheric function makes the testing of laterality of lesions more open to systematic investigation. This experimental method should help to reduce much of the error arising from the use of ordinary standardized psychological tests. As mentioned elsewhere, these tests often have a complex determination and the experimental method will aid in deciding between equally attractive hypotheses concerning the cause of poor performance.

Shapiro considers that this process will not have wide appeal as it tends to be time consuming. In fact, in our experience, it is often more economical than the application of a routine battery of tests many of which may be irrelevent to the questions being asked. Since in clinical practice certain questions tend to recur frequently, trainees quite soon recognize the most likely hypotheses and the most productive tests to be used in particular situations. Subsequent case evaluation in the light of neurological or neurosurgical knowledge continually improves the process.

In busy clinical practice, time is an expensive commodity and on some occasions the clinician has to tender an opinion after less than ideal examination of the patient. In this situation his report should make it clear to the referring source that the opinion consists 'of the hypotheses which the applied scientist thinks best account for the data at his disposal, and which he would choose to test next if he had sufficient time and suitable means' (Shapiro, 1973, p.652). The term *suitable means* often takes the form of appropriate tests. In some cases these do not exist but this situation is becoming rare as neuropsychology develops and clinicians working in a particular field are likely to acquire the tests which prove useful in answering the most common hypotheses. Some suggestions as to what should prove useful in the armamentarium are given at the end of the chapter, the emphasis being strongly upon tests which have shown themselves of value and are economic of time and readily available. Very popular standardized tests such as the Wechsler Adult Intelligence Scale (or a short form thereof) and the Wechsler Memory Scale may well provide the central hypothesis which can then be tested by other procedures. Sometimes the whole or part of the answer lies in testing that has already been carried out on the standardized tests. Psychologists trained in one of the psychometric traditions often ask what are the newest or latest tests for brain damage. It can often be pointed out that they already have significant information in the tests they commonly employ but being largely unaware of the developments in neuropsychology they are unable to recognize its significance.

As Ley (1970) comments, the criticism that the method is time-consuming is valid 'only in so far as one thinks that: (i) the method will produce findings of sufficient value, and (ii) that there are more valuable things for clinical psychologists to do.' Economy of time must be seen in relation to the importance of the question being asked.

A partial answer to the question of time was originally tried by Ward Halstead who employed trained testers who were not psychologists. This use of psychological technicians has become popular in some American clinics. For obvious reasons this met with little enthusiasm. Even in the single case method less experienced testers could carry out much of the routine testing provided that the experienced neuropsychologist controlled the decision-making or successive steps in the investigation and the examiners (e.g. psychology graduates in training) are trained to record all the qualitative features of the patient's responses so that the same interpretation is possible as if the experienced clinician had carried out the investigation himself. If no significant information is lost in the process there can be little objection to a method which has worked so well in clinical medicine for so long. There is an added advantage in that it may force the neuropsychologist to make explicit to himself and others the nature of his decision making processes.

Methodological considerations

The following brief outline is intended to serve two purposes: (1) to set out a number of factors which have been poorly controlled or completely ignored in many studies and which have led to numerous apparent differences in results; (ii) to remind us that most of these factors may greatly limit the validity of many approaches to the individual case if they are not taken into account. Apart from the effects exerted by the many variables mentioned below the effects of interaction between them is largely an unknown quantity. However, Kinsbourne (1971) argues that many of the difficulties encountered by earlier workers arose 'largely because investigators fail(ed) to use the everyday concepts and methods of human experimental psychology.'

Characteristics of the lesion

The *nature* of the pathological process may have a marked effect on the kind and degree of impairment it produces, e.g. a benign tumour such as a meningioma causes effects largely by pressure on the cerebral tissues whereas a malignant tumour such as a glioma causes much greater impairment because it invades the cerebral substance itself. Lesions of different nature such as trauma, neoplasm, atrophy, and vascular lesions will all vary in the effects they produce by interruption of fibre tracts, increase in intracranial pressure and alteration of cerebral blood supply.

The effects of a lesion do not alter in direct proportion to its size. This interacts with other factors such as the location, a small strategically placed lesion often producing much more disruption of function than a large lesion in another location. In the past, correlation of behavioural changes with location of lesion often had to depend on 'inferential' diagnostic procedures in neurology, such as electroencephalography, arteriography, and pneumoencephalography, procedures which were themselves somewhat uncertain. With the advent of computerized axial tomography a more direct visualization of the site (and sometimes the nature of the lesion) should lead to a sounder basis for neuropsychological correlation.

Acuteness of dysfunction has been clearly demonstrated to be of importance in a wide range of studies by Reitan and his colleagues (Fitzhugh and Fitzhugh, 1961; Fitzhugh, Fitzhugh, and Reitan, 1961, 1962, 1963). Whereas acute lesions generally show marked and easily observed changes, more chronic lesions may not. Slowly developing lesions such as benign tumours or vascular insufficiency may be so insidious in their onset that they are easily overlooked.

Patient characteristics

The principal factors usually considered are age, intelligence and education.

Since the present text has concerned itself exclusively with findings on adult subjects the documented differences due to onset of lesions in childhood will not be reviewed. At the other end of the life cycle care must be taken to evaluate the effects of ageing on the various tests employed. In patients over middle age at least some of the tests employed should have age norms. Psychology has accumulated data on the decline of function with age and this should be consulted. Heron and Chown (1967) have shown systematic variation in a wide variety of tests. This subject has been reviewed ably by Williams (1973). The importance of interaction between neurological factors and the normal processes of ageing should not be overlooked, nor should the social and environmental influences be neglected since these may have a profound influence in the ageing patient.

The comparative effect of ageing in patients with and without brain damage has been studied by Reitan and his colleagues. Though the conclusions may be specific to the type of tests used it is worth noting that 'the rate of advancing impairment with age was approximately comparable in both the groups with and without brain damage' (Reitan, 1962b). The nature of the test made a significant difference in the degree of impairment both for normal ageing (Reed and Reitan, 1963) and ageing brain-damaged subjects. 'Younger groups clearly excelled the older on the tests requiring immediate problem-solving ability, whereas the intergroup differences were less pronounced on tests more heavily dependent upon previously accumulated experience' (Fitzhugh, Fitzhugh, and Reitan, 1964).

The relationship between the allied factors of education and intelligence and the effects of neurological disorders have received little attention. It has often been hypothesized that a person's ability to withstand intellectual deterioration after brain impairment might be positively related to these two factors. One of the few direct attempts to test this hypothesis was carried out by Weinstein and Teuber (1957) who found no relationship between education and scores on a general intelligence test and the magnitude of loss on the same test (The Army General Classification Test) after injury.

Finally, there is a common assumption that the effects of brain impairment are constant from person to person. The fact that different individuals have been shown to employ different modalities and methods in the acquisition of skills argues for a degree of idiosyncratic brain organization. If this is so, there may well be quite different effects due to these individual differences. On the one hand two individuals with lesions in different locations may show similar disturbances while two individuals with lesions in the same location may show quite different effects. This will be most marked in those tasks of some complexity, such as reproducing block designs, where there are a number of alternative routes to the goal.

Even less is known about the effects of personality and reaction to brain damage. Now that the uniform effects of brain lesions are becoming better understood these individual differences might well be studied since they may well have important implications for the management and rehabilitation of the patient.

Types of group studied

Possibly the most serious drawback to early studies was the failure to use carefully selected groups of known characteristics. Results derived from heterogeneous collections of patients made it difficult to further knowledge of specific brain-behaviour relationships. As remarked elsewhere this was associated with the uncritically accepted assumption of the unitary effects of brain damage.

Even where specific groups were selected the experimental design was not always appropriate to the question being asked. Reitan (1966) discussing the question of frontal lobe function points out how numerous studies followed Rylander's design of comparing a frontal damaged group with a control group and then assuming that the differences reflected changes or functions specific to the frontal lobes. A better comparison would have resulted from comparison of frontal patients with patients having lesions elsewhere in the brain. The more powerful paradigm of 'double dissociation' of function has seldom been employed.

There has also been a tendency to generalize too widely, e.g. the Halstead-Reitan battery has generally been shown to distinguish well between groups of brain damaged subjects and neurotic or normal control groups. However the inclusion of schizophrenic patients greatly reduces or even removes its discriminating power (Watson *et al.*, 1968; Klonoff, Fibiger, and Hutton, 1970; Lacks *et al.*, 1970; Donnelly *et al.*, 1972).

Test administration and interpretation

Every effort should be made to reduce the variance produced by unstandardized and subjective methods of administration and scoring. The test instructions themselves are a powerful factor in developing in the subject a particular 'set' to the task at hand. This may either facilitate or inhibit the patient's performance as shown by Lodge (1966). Rate of presentation also plays a part. Experiments by Birch, Belmont, and Karp (1964, 1965b, 1967) suggest that there may be a prolongation of inhibition in many brain damaged patients and that decrement in function may be produced where sequential material is presented too quickly. This seems to be particularly relevant to the assessment of memory and learning and supports the findings for an interference effect in certain amnesic disorders (Ch. 5). The discovery of cases of 'latent' aphasia, described below, also is a warning that particular care should be taken in checking the patient's ability to comprehend the instructions *fully*. Too often the assumption of adequate comprehension is made on the grounds of a brief interview which requires little precision of language.

Test selection

It must be emphasized that the following selection of tests in no way constitutes a 'battery'. It does represent tests which might prove useful in delineating the patient's areas of difficulty as well as providing diagnostic information in many instances. Tests should be selected which in the light of the patient's history, neurological examination and current neuropsychological knowledge maximize the opportunities for emergence of significant behavioural indicators. Alternative tests will suggest themselves to different workers.

1.   General examination (intelligence, memory, comprehension). Wechsler Adult Intelligence Scale (or selected short form) (Duke, 1967).
Wechsler Memory Scale.
Delayed Memory Tasks.
Aphasia Screening Test (Russell *et al.*, 1970).
Token Test (De Renzi and Vignolo, 1962).

2.   Tests which may produce information with regional significance.
A   Frontal.
 (i) Abstraction, conceptual shift.
      Colour-Form Sorting Test (Goldstein and Scheerer,1941)
      Milan Sorting Test (De Renzi *et al.*, 1966)
      Halstead Category Test (Halstead, 1947)
      Wisconsin Card Sorting Test (Grant and Berg, 1948)
 (ii) Planning, regulating, checking programmes of action.
      Porteus Maze Test (Porteus, 1965)
      Trail Making Test (Reitan, 1966b)
      Complex Figure of Rey (Rey, 1959; Osterreith, 1944)
      Arithmetical problem solving
(iii) Verbal behaviour and verbal regulation of behaviour (Christensen, 1975)
      Verbal Fluency Test (Benton, 1967b)

B   Temporal.
(i)   Material or modality specific memory tasks.
      Visual.
         Rey Figure (Rey, 1959).
         Benton Visual Retention Test (Benton, 1955).
         Recurring Nonsense Figures (Kimura, 1963)
         Nonverbal Sequential Memory test from the Illinois
            Test of Psycholinguistic Abilities
         Facial Recognition.

(ii)   Amnesic syndrome tests (Lhermitte and Signoret, 1972)
       Maze Learning Task (Milner, 1965)
(iii) Auditory perceptual tests.
       Seashore Rhythm Test (from Halstead-Reitan battery)
       Speech Sounds Perception Test (from Halstead-Reitan battery)
       Environmental Sounds Test (Faglioni *et al.*, 1969)
       Austin Meaningless Sounds Test
C.   Parietal.
(i)   Constructional praxis.
       Benton V.R.T. (Copying)
       Rey Figure
       WAIS Block Design and Object Assembly
       Fairfield Block Substitution Test (Grassi, 1947)
       Three dimensional Praxis Test (Benton and Fogel, 1962)
       Halstead-Reitan Tactual Performance Test
(ii)   Quasi-spatial synthesis (Christensen, 1975).
       (a) logico-grammatical
       (b) mathematical
(iii) Cross modal association tests.
(iv)   Spatial.
       The following may supplement sundry 'spatial' tests above.
       Stick Test (Benson and Barton, 1970)
       Pool Reflection Test (Cattell, 1944)
       Money's Standardization Road Map Test (Butters *et al.*, 1972)
D.   Occipital
       Colour naming
       Colour-form association (De Renzi *et al.*, 1972)
       Visual irreminiscence
3.   Neurological tests
       Finger Tapping Test (Halstead-Reitan battery)
       Motor Impersistence
       Finger recognition (Benton, 1959)
       Right-left orientation (Benton, 1959)
       Double simultaneous stimulation
4.   Miscellaneous
       Symbol-Digit-Modalities Test (Smith, 1973)
       Continuous Performance Test (Rosvold *et al.*, 1956; Schein, 1962)
       Reaction times tests (Pillon, 1973)
       Queensland Test (McElwain and Kearney, 1970)
5.   Language
Comprehensive examination for aphasia (Spreen and Benton, 1969).
Notes: The references after certain tests contain either original descriptions or key articles.

   Austin Meaningless Sounds Test consists of pairs of either similar or dissimilar English words rendered meaningless by being played backwards. The patient must discriminate similarity or difference.

The Queensland Test consists of five 'performance' tasks which can be given by demonstration without verbal instructions and is useful in situations of reduced communication, e.g. in cases of impaired comprehension or with patients who do not speak the native language.

The tests have been ordered in a way which follows the 'localizationist' position or functional system approach. The material could be arranged just as well according to psychological functions such as memory, perception, intelligence, praxis, language and attention (Benton, 1967).

Additional topics related to assessment

The localizationist format of the text has meant that some important topics appear to have been overlooked. In the case of language this meant a serious omission which is partly rectified here. The other topics receive a little extra emphasis related to assessment. It is hoped that these will begin to show the relatedness of material presented earlier in the text. Space precludes more extensive treatment and a companion volume is in preparation.

Language

As Luria (1972) points out there have been three stages in the history of aphasiology: (1) the 'classical' period characterized by the search for localized language centres; (2) the neuropsychological stage characterized by the attempt 'to establish the factors primarily disturbed as a result of local brain lesions' in an endeavour to understand the basic mechanisms of language, and (3) the beginning study of neurodynamic changes associated with brain lesions which may contribute to disorders of language as well as to disorders of other psychological functions. One example of this third stage of study is the recognition that a dynamic change in the control of inhibition may help to explain difficulties such as those seen with attempts at word finding in aphasic patients. In order to select the correct word it is necessary to be highly selective which seems to imply inhibition of competing associations (or response tendencies) which arise during the course of the search. Since these associations may be on the basis of phonetic, structural, or semantic relationships a disturbance in the dynamics of control of inhibitions will lead to a bewildering array of seemingly different types of responses.

The third of these stages is just beginning though there is still a great need for continuing study of the neuropsychological approach in parallel with neurodynamic studies.

Neurological models of language. Still the most widely accepted model for the basis of language is the classical one stemming from the nineteenth century studies begun by Broca and Wernicke. The modern exposition of this position is seen best in the works of Geschwind (Cohen and Wartofsky, 1974). A number of cortical centres, each having a special role in language, are united together by fibre pathways so that disturbances of language are to be conceived of as due to damage to the 'centres' themselves or to a break in the connections between them. Although the disconnection model may be a useful explanatory device in some situations it does not appear to be backed by compelling evidence in the oft cited examples of conduction aphasia (see below). Even putting this difficulty aside the model as outlined by Geschwind (1969, 1970) is far too simple to cope with the complex disturbances subsumed under the term aphasia. There appears to be too great an emphasis on phonemic or phonological disintegration in such a model and insufficient consideration given to the basis of the syntactic or semantic elements of language. A more ambitious model which attempts to cope with this deficiency is that of Whitaker (1971). Here what Whitaker terms the central language system has two major anatomical organizations, one subserving the phonological and the other the syntactic/semantic components of language (Fig. 9.2). The phonological aspect of language has as its substratum

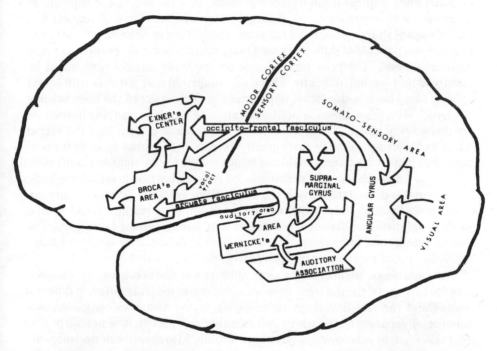

Fig. 9.2 Model of language representation in the brain, Figure 8, p. 62. H.A. Whitaker, (1972) *On the Representation of Language in the Human Brain*. Linguistic Research Inc.

'Heschl's gyrus, some of Wernicke's area, the arcute fasciculus, Broca's area and perhaps the vocal tract area of the motor cortex.' The basis of the syntactic/ semantic component lies in 'part of Wernicke's area, the auditory association cortex, the supramarginal gyrus (and) part of the angular gyrus.' These zones are connected to the frontal language areas and receive input from visual and tactile association areas. Though the obvious anatomical areas related to language dysfunction have been incorporated there are serious drawbacks in Whitaker's attempts to apply the model though some of these may stem from the grammatical model used. Caplan and Marshall (1975) have provided a useful review of this model.

They point out that this model would be supported if cases of intact phonology with disruption of syntactic/semantic aspects of language could be found. They point out that the clinical literature does not appear to describe even one such case. The model also is unable in its present form to explain known facts of aphasia. It is possible on the other hand that a two-step mechanism in the form of separate phonological and semantic structures in neural representation as suggested by the cases of Rinnert and Whitaker (1973) and Yamadori and Albert (1973) could be incorporated into such a model.

Functional relationships of aphasia with other disorders. Just over a decade ago Weinstein (1965) pointed to the need for study of apparently non-language deficits associated with aphasia as well as the study of residual abilities in aphasic patients. Both types of study should help to establish whether certain aphasic symptoms are 'a direct result of cerebral insult, or a secondary consequence of other forms of impairment. . .' Weinstein reviewed the work of himself and his colleagues showing the more frequent association in aphasic patients than non-aphasic patients of difficulties on a body schema test and several seemingly non-verbal tests. The poor performance on the body schema tests might be construed as a 'verbal' difficulty. One study suggested that patients with severe aphasia often have 'a significant impairment of that aspect of the body schema concerned with the expression or identification of words identifying his own or another's body parts.' The experimental design made it clear that the verbal difficulty with naming body parts greatly exceeded the verbal identification of other inanimate objects and could not be accounted for by right-left confusion.

While a body schema test deficit can be seen as part of a verbal-symbolic disruption it is difficult to see how the other failures of aphasic patients on non-verbal tasks such as hidden figures or locomotor map reading could have a similar explanation. Weinstein points out that failure cannot be construed as due to 'intellectual impairment' since intellectual deficit after cerebral lesions can either occur together or independently.

The question of intellectual status in aphasia has been reviewed by Zangwill (1969). In view of the different types of intelligence measures used in different studies and the fact that these are often aggregate measures composed of a number of separate tests each of considerable complexity it is not surprising that no constant relationships have been found. Moreover such measures are often related to heterogeneous collections of patients suffering from 'aphasia'. It will probably be more fruitful to at least look at the relationship between supposedly non-language tasks and sub-groups of aphasic patients with relatively pure symptoms or groups of symptoms. Clinical experience warns us that such cases are rare but careful study would be more productive than the large group studies where so many variables are confounded. Some non-verbal tests of intelligence such as Raven's Coloured Progressive Matrices appear to be performed poorly by patients with either left or right hemisphere (posterior) lesions but for different reasons, Basso *et al.* (1973). Failure of patients with right posterior lesions appeared to be associated with disruption of visual processing. The poor performance of aphasic patients on the other hand showed no relationship with visual field defects. Basso *et al.*, consider that the left posterior area 'is involved in the performance of several different intellectual tasks, verbal as well as non-verbal. The view may be advanced that this region subserves a superordinate, intellectual ability, sharing many of the characteristics attributed to the 'g' factor by psychologists.' Such a general hypothesis needs more support. The frequently reported poor performance of aphasic patients on non-verbal tasks may be in no small part due to an associated constructional apraxia (Alajouanine and Lhermitte, 1964).

Closely related to intellectual status is the question of abstract or conceptual difficulties in aphasia. Once again difficulties arise because of the use of a variety of tasks in heterogeneous collections of patients. Some early studies reported loss of abstraction (e.g. Goldstein, 1948) while others did not (Bauer and Beck. 1954). More recently the Milan group have confirmed the findings of Goldstein using a modified and extended version of the Weigl Colour Form Sorting Test (De Renzi *et al.*, 1966). Groups of non-aphasic patients with both left and right sided lesions were not different from controls whereas the mean score for the aphasic group was only about one half of that of the control group. Such findings support the general conclusion reached elsewhere that this type of test is sensitive to left hemisphere lesions but even more so in the presence of aphasia. These authors proffer two hypotheses, (1) that the deficit in abstract thinking is due to a disruption of 'inner language', and (2) that 'the same areas subserving linguistic activities in the left hemisphere are also specialized in carrying out tasks of a symbolic nature.' It is not surprising that when such gross conceptions of localization are considered that there should be an overlap in function.

The complex nature of the interaction between conceptual behaviour, perception and language may be gauged from a sample of recent experiments to do with colour. Failure on the colour sorting test using the Holmgren skeins had been thought by Goldstein to represent a difficulty in abstract thinking while other felt that failure reflected a difficulty in hue discrimination. De Renzi *et al.* (1972b) tested patients grouped according to laterality, presence or absence of aphasia, and presence or absence of visual field defect. Three groups performed poorly, namely right sided lesions with field defects and left sided lesion with and without field defects.

It was clear that the right hemisphere group's failure was associated with poor hue discrimination but the reason for the aphasics' failure was unclear. In a second study De Renzi *et al.* (1972a) asked patients and control subjects to select coloured pencils and then to colour appropriately outline drawings of objects. The objects selected had characteristic colours either by nature or convention (cherries, national flag etc.). Patients with aphasia were more significantly impaired on this task of associating colour to object than any other group. When these patients' performance on other tasks was examined the poor performance on the colour association task was seen to be related to tasks requiring a certain degree of conceptualization but not to other perceptual tasks.

These difficulties with colour extend to naming. Nehemkis and Lewisohn (1973) found that both aphasic and non-aphasic left hemisphere patients were slower to name colours than to read words but the difficulty was greatly accentuated by the presence of aphasia. Similarly, Wyke and Holgate, 1973 found that aphasic patients had more difficulty in naming coloured drawings of objects than naming coloured tokens or uncoloured drawings of objects alone. More details are available in the individual experiments which would support Weinstein's contention mentioned above that study of associated deficits may give us further insight into the nature of aphasia and its relation to perceptual, conceptual and other aspects of functioning.

Latent or minimal dysphasia. There appears to be a need to develop tests which are highly sensitive to the more subtle forms of expressive and receptive language difficulty. These are necessary for the early diagnosis of incipient dysphasia and in the later stages of recovery from aphasia where minor difficulties may readily be overlooked if only the usual clinical measures requiring little in the way of precision are used.

Critchley (1972) points out that one of the common areas in which 'minimal dysphasia' shows itself is in alteration in verbal production. More commonly this is seen in the form of underproduction both in spoken and written language. Patients may respond to direct questions but do not take part in an interchange. Critchley remarks, 'he seems reluctant to embark upon the seas of conversation.' Luria and others have commented on this verbal adynamia which appears to be more characteristic of left frontal lesions than lesions elsewhere in the left hemisphere. On the other hand, the patient may produce more language than usual, an 'aggressive loquacity' which Critchley hypothesizes the incipient aphasic unconsciously uses to prevent or deter the interlocutor from introducing material which the patient may be unable to handle.

The significance of such changes in production will often be difficult in the absence of any estimate of premorbid performance though the gathering of group data in the 'psychometric' way suggested by Benton (1967) (see below) would go some way towards overcoming this difficulty.

Numerous qualitative changes may also be seen in cases of minimal dysphasia. Some of these may be specific to language but some appear to be reflections in language of more general difficulties for example those of frontal lobe involvement.

A case in point might be the provision of redundant material when the patient is asked to define a word or answer a question. This Critchley (op. cit.) terms 'verbiage which is low in reference—function though not wholly beside the point', (p.224). It is possibly an example of the general difficulty which the frontal patient has of inhibiting response tendencies especially those which are of nearly equal strength (see Ch. 4).

A quite distinct kind of difficulty which is often considered in the context of latent or minimal dysphasia is that which has been termed by Luria in numerous publications 'the verbal regulation of behaviour'. These difficulties can be elicited best by the clinical tests which have been developed by Luria and described by Christensen (1975).

Perhaps no single test has been as helpful as the recently developed Token Test.

The token test. This test was designed for 'those aphasic patients in whom aphasic disorders seem very slight or altogether lacking during normal conversation. . .' (De Renzi and Vignolo 1962). It seems well suited to such cases of minimal or latent aphasia.

The test consists of a number of instructions which the patient is asked to carry out using coloured tokens of two shapes (round and square), two sizes and five colours. The test begins with the simplest instructions ('Show me a red one', 'Show me a square one') and moves to compound instructions involving two and three attributes ('Touch the small green circle') then more complex instructions involving very often relational terms. These later items include: 30 Put the white circle in front of the blue square; 33 Put the green square beside the red circle; 35 Put the red circle between the yellow square and the green square; 36 Touch all the circles except the green one. The major aspects of the test are (1) comprehension and (2) abstraction. It is difficult to separate these two features. '. .here we have a number of messages, sufficiently elementary from a conceptual standpoint, short and easy to remember. . . which, however, make two kinds of demands upon the comprehension of the patient: one arises out of the difficulty of identifying a particular token specified by three independent features and the other from that of grasping the semantic complications introduced by the 'small instruments of language' (op. cit.). In this early study, 13 supposedly pure motor aphasics and 6 recovered receptive aphasics without any conversational difficulty were shown by the test to have clear evidence of disturbance of speech comprehension. This sensitivity to any form of aphasia has been confirmed by other workers (Orgass and Poeck, 1966; Hartje, et al., 1973)

The Token Test is performed more poorly not only by aphasic patients compared with non-aphasics but in a comparison of non-aphasic patients with lesions of either hemisphere, those with left hemisphere lesions performed significantly worse than those with right lesions (Boller and Vignolo, 1966). These authors use the term 'latent sensory aphasia' for this difficulty and consider it to be largely independent of general intellectual impairment. Boller (1968) attempted to produce comparable tests of latent *expressive* aphasia without success. He felt that to be successful such a test would have to take into consideration the qualitative alterations of expression as well as the quality of material evoked by the patient on request in fluency or word production tests.

The attractiveness of the test has been increased by the development of a satisfactory short form of only 16 items by Spellacy and Spreen (1969) although the full test itself can be administered in a relatively short time.

A somewhat unexpected finding was reported by Swisher and Sarno (1969) where a group of non-aphasic patients with right hemisphere lesions performed more poorly than normal controls on the later sections of the test. Though a number of reasons were suggested for this difference its significance is uncertain.

In general, results with the Token Test seem to indicate that statements suggesting that comprehension of language is rarely disturbed after lesions of the frontal speech areas can only be accepted if a gross clinical criterion is accepted.

Since performance on the Token Test obviously involves a number of factors, experiments such as that of Smith (1974) will help to clarify the nature of the difficulties in certain groups or individuals. Smith noted that aphasic patients particularly those of Broca's type have been described as tending to use few words of any kind and that they were 'particularly disinclined to use the small function words of language such as prepositions.' While they had difficulty in arranging objects in relation to each other on spoken directions they were able to put word cards into systematic order as parts of speech to make statements which approximated the conventional rules of language.

Comprehension. The simple equation of defects of comprehension only with Wernicke's area should be dispelled. Hécaen and Consoli (1973) point out that Dejerine had claimed that lesions of Broca's area sometimes led to an effect on all modalities of language. While they were able to read the words patients often had difficulty in understanding the meaning of written phrases. Some patients sometimes has difficulty also with understanding longer phrases presented orally. Hécaen and Consoli confirmed both these findings in a considerable number of their subjects. They also remind us that early neurologists such as Pierre Marie anticipated the recent finding of Zangwill (1972) of lack of aphasia in two cases of tumour excision involving Broca's area.

Repetition. Brown (1975b) mentions how entrenched the notion has become that the basis of repetition difficulties is due to preferential damage to a pathway connecting the anterior and posterior speech areas. Among the possible anatomical pathways the arcuate fasciculus has been most strongly advocated (Geschwind, 1969, 1970) and Geschwind's view is widely accepted. Brown points out that repetition is not a special function of language but merely a method of testing and that in any given patient repetition may show any of the major qualitative changes in language seen in aphasic patients in general, e.g. 'anomic errors, errors related to phrase length (possibly to verbal memory), verbal or semantic paraphasia, literal or phonemic paraphasia, dysarthria and echolalia.' Brown's own anatomical studies (1975a) do not support the classical view of conduction aphasia. Likewise Luria (1972) in seeking to explain the retention of the term 'conduction aphasia' points out 'that not one case has been carefully described of a patient who, while unable to repeat words, yet retained his spontaneous speech.' Luria considers this acceptance due in part to the fact that 'data which accord with accepted notions remain in memory while contradictory facts are neglected' as well as the fact that many workers cling (sometimes unconsciously) to the outmoded concept of strict localization of function.

Experimental studies of a small number of patients with 'disproportionate impairment of the ability to repeat verbal stimuli' have been carried out by Warrington and her colleagues (Warrington and Shallice, 1969; Shallice and Warrington, 1970; Warrington, Logue and Pratt, 1971). These patients suffered from a selective impairment of auditory verbal short term memory both auditory and visual long term memory being satisfactory. The area implicated appeared to be the left supramarginal and angular gyrus region. Warrington suggests that the use of tasks differentially loaded with short term and long term components might lead to the discovery of a subgroup of patients whose repetition difficulties are on the basis of defective short term memory. A latter study (Shallice and Warrington 1974) showed two of these patients to have a striking dissociation between verbal and nonverbal material in short term memory. An alternative explanation has been put forward by Strub and Gardner (1974) based on the examination of a case similar to those of Warrington. Their analysis suggested the disorder might be better viewed as a linguistic rather than a mnestic disorder in which the patient has difficulty in the processing and ordering of phonemes. Either explanation would need to be considered by an adequate neurological model.

Naming. Disorders of naming are met with very frequently in aphasia of all types though its prominence in some cases has appeared to justify a separate category of nominal or amnesic aphasia. The lesions in these latter cases appear to occur most frequently in the mid-temporal region.

Luria (1972) has shown that naming is a complex psychological function which may be disturbed by lesions in a number of separate sites. 'Among the factors which predispose to anomia are defective phonematic perception or articulatory control, impaired visual perception and—most important of all— disorganization of the central processes of word choice.' Thus the significance of anomia as of any other symptom depends on careful neuropsychological dissection of the possible contributing factors along the lines described by Luria in numerous publications (Luria, 1965, 1973b). Such an analysis by Rochford (1971) revealed that the naming errors found in demented patients occurred largely on the basis of visual recognition difficulties so that performance was improved with the provision of recognition cues. Patients with anomia associated with dysphasia showed no such improvement. Continued neuropsychological analysis of this type should clarify the nature of anomia.

Test construction in aphasia. In 1967 Benton made a plea for a 'universal' or international aphasia examination. This exercise has continued with the parallel work of Spreen, Benton and the Milan group of workers. The Spreen-Benton Aphasia Examination represents an important step in the development and use of a first English language version of such a test. Benton lists the requirements which would need to be published in a usable form if such an examination were to fulfil its major contribution as a means of effective communication between those concerned with the study of communication problems. The major requirements would be (1) standardization information; (2) explicit description of testing procedures; (3) exact scoring criteria; (4) detailed interpretation guides, and (5) evidence of a high degree of clinical utility. Benton urges the adoption of the pragmatic approach which proved so useful in the development of tests of intelligence such as the Wechsler scales which have been so widely used. Psychologists will anticipate that such an undertaking on an international scale would be a very large undertaking indeed but this would be offset by the advantages of possessing for the first time the means for a direct comparison of the findings of widespread groups of researchers. The Spreen-Benton examination possesses the distinct advantage of allowing the examiner to construct a profile of directly comparable percentile scores which are corrected for age and educational level. Separate profiles are available based on (a) normal adults and (b) a reference group of aphasic patients. Other reference group information is being prepared, e.g. for normal aged patients. This aphasia examination also provides explicitly for the administration of tests 'designed to detect the presence of visual or tactile deficits which might affect performance on the language tests.' These tests are given whenever the patient's performance is poor on tests such as visual naming, reading or tactile naming. Benton concludes that not only may new facts about aphasia emerge 'but it may be anticipated that the very existence of an examination based on rigorous scientific criteria would have the effect of raising the quality of aphasia research throughout the world.'

Other workers have suggested that the assessment of aphasia might be improved if refined statistical weighting procedures such as multiple discriminant function analysis were applied to the data from carefully defined groups. There is also a need to expand the traditional methods of examination if we are to gain more insight into aphasia. By employing novel methods Hatfield and Zangwill (1974) have been able to show the ideational processes of an aphasic patient may be intact despite severe disorders of spoken or written language. One patient with marked expressive aphasia was both able to represent a given short story through a series of drawings and spontaneously describe current happenings and possible future happenings in his drawings.

Finally, it should be remembered that an adequate theory of language should have some provision for dealing with what Borkowski (1967) has called the 'extraverbal component of language'.

Dementia

Assessment of the presence and degree of dementia is one of the most frequent tasks asked of clinical psychologists. Despite the importance of the problem, so far there have been very few well designed studies which have attempted to quantify specific defects in dementia. One of the first requirements will be a systematic serial examination of those cases in which early detection of a specific type of process can be made. In speaking of progressive neurological diseases in general Smith (1975) commented. . .'it is reasonable to assume that the specific morbid anatomy of the progressive neurological diseases is reflected in relatively discrete and characteristic patterns of initial or later emerging psychological as well as sensory and motor disturbances.' This opinion is shared by Perez *et al.* (1975). 'It is our hypothesis that different diseases produce different quantitative scores on currently designed multiple tests of intellectual and cognitive measures.' These investigators found that a group of patients with neuronal degeneration (Alzheimer's dementia, see below) were consistently and significantly poorer on the WAIS (Wechsler Adult Intelligence Scale) than either of two groups with dementia associated with vascular disorders. While this type of study should be extended, all that has been said with regard to the drawbacks of psychometric approaches should be borne in mind if studies of dementia are not to repeat the mistakes of the early studies of 'brain damage' reviewed in the first part of this chapter. The use of standardized tests made up of a number of subtests each of multifactorial composition is likely to produce little of value unless accompanied by (or qualified by) neuropsychological dissection of the reasons for failure. Certainly examination of the dementing patient should include as complete a documentation of psychological function as possible, with quantitative measures based on age norms being used wherever possible.

The very term dementia itself presents problems. Some writers (Horenstein, 1971) use the term to include both localized as well as widespread conditions. Others define it in terms of 'global impairment of intellect, memory and personality' (Roth and Myers, 1975). With the increasing application of neuropsychological assessment it should now be possible to recognize the nature and extent of localized lesions even in the early stages. Infarction in the territories of relatively major cerebral vessels could presumably soon be brought into this category with adequate research. Though the effects on the motor and sensory systems and, to a lesser extent the language system, are adequately described in most neurological texts the accompanying alterations in the higher functions are only now being elucidated in any detail. Neuropsychological examination may complement other examinations in making 'anatomical sense' of the effects of the lesion. This should aid not so much in diagnosis but in understanding the patient as a whole. A typical case would be ischaemia in the territory of the posterior cerebral arteries. Here recovery after a period of confusion and visual difficulty may leave the patient disoriented and suffering from apparent dementia. Psychological examination usually reveals a pervasive amnesic syndrome with relative preservation of intellect on standard intellectual tests (e.g. Lhermitte and Beauvois, 1973). These cases often proceed to dement probably because of the occurrence of multiple infarcts (Hachinski, Lassen and Marshall, 1974). Lhermitte, Gautier and Derouesné (1970) believe that most of these infarcts are due to thromboembolism from the heart and extracranial circulation and 'in only a small minority of cases are cerebral softenings caused by *in situ* thrombosis of cerebral vessels.' This argues for intensive investigation and treatment of these extracerebral factors in all suspected cases of dementia.

Although the three major features of dementia (deficits of memory, intellect, and personality) interact with each other it may be helpful to outline typical changes separately.

Memory. By far the most common finding in suspect cases of early dementia is the selective impairment in recent memory, i.e. reduction in the ability to register ongoing events or to learn new material. In the early stages and almost as a general rule and seemingly independent of the aetiology, the memory disorder has much of the character of the amnesic syndrome with relative preservation of immediate memory as measured for example by the ability to repeat six or seven digits forwards. As the disorder progresses this short term memory ability decreases and by the time this is evident, signs of more widespread intellectual deterioration are present. One of the most sensitive early tests is paired verbal associate learning the patient being able to repeat most of the verbal associations based on long stored information but is completely unable to learn any novel verbal associations presented to him. Several recent studies (Brooks, 1972; Lewisohn *et al.*, 1972; Bahrach and Mintz, 1974; Kljajic, 1975) have supported the sensititivy of this verbal learning task to cerebral involvement regardless of the site of injury. Separate age norms on this kind of task (e.g. the Paired Associates of the Wechsler Memory Scale) would be of great value in this regard. In our experience one of the important 'rules-of-thumb' in detecting early dementia is a psychometric difference between the intelligence and memory quotients bearing in mind, of course, the numerous causes of memory difficulty mentioned in earlier chapters.

The amnesia of presenile dementia. On the basis of evidence of pathological changes in the hippocampal region in patients with presenile dementia, Corsellis (1970) has argued that the severe disorder of recent memory exhibited by these patients may be due to the hippocampal lesions since there is now a good deal of evidence that bilateral damage of these structures produces the amnesic syndrome. Miller (1971, 1973) has specifically examined this hypothesis and has demonstrated that the memory disorder of the patient with presenile dementia is qualitatively different from that of the typical amnesic syndrome. He feels that, while hippocampal lesions may play a part in the aetiology of presenile amnesia, they cannot provide the whole explanation. He has elsewhere demonstrated (Miller, 1972b) that difficulty in adequate coding of incoming material in short term memory might also play a part in the memory difficulty of the demented patient and suggests that other factors such as impaired attention and retrieval are likely to be involved (Miller, 1973).

Intellect. In the area of intellectual behaviour the frontal lobe functions seem the first to falter. Thus the tests summarized at the end of the previous section, and discussed in detail in Chapter 4 will bring these to the fore. It is as true of the usual case of early dementia as of tumours and other localized lesions of the frontal lobes that the patient may appear essentially normal until appropriate tests are applied. These tests are those which require flexibility of operations, the planning, execution and evaluation of programmes of action. Problem solving in the sense of applying stored information to new situations is poor and marked by the use of stereotypes. There is a poverty of ideation and a failure to make an adequate preliminary investigation of a situation. Another early change is difficulty with abstract thinking and the very simple Colour-Form Sorting Test will usually bring this to the fore within a few minutes.

As the patient deteriorates the intellectual deficit becomes obvious and other features, such as delusions, may be added. Roth and Myers (1975) comment: 'His inability to grasp what is happening leads to false ideas, for instance, that he has been robbed. These ideas are technically delusions because they are held in the face of evidence of their falsehood but not, as in schizophrenia, because the evidence of falsehood is rejected, *but because this evidence is not understood'*.

It is because of the frequent encounter with these mnestic and 'frontal' intellectual disorders in many patients whose dementia is subsequently demonstrated to have varied aetiological bases that the present author is less sanguine than some about finding separate characteristic patterns for different forms of dementia but this is not to lessen the importance of looking for such systematic relationships.

Personality. The personality changes seen with dementing processes are protean. Some of these changes may be seen as responses to the patient's sensing of his own intellectual, and often physical disintegration. Other changes such as loss of the control of inhibition may be a more direct result of cerebral damage, e.g. wasting of the frontal lobes. In some cases of dementia personality changes of the frontal type may be present before the changes in memory and intellect are evident. On neurosychological examination these cases, especially when they appear in middle age, raise the differential diagnosis of frontal tumour.

Detailed descriptions of the many changes in personality are given in standard textbooks of psychiatry. No systematic attempts have been made to relate particular forms of affective change to different types of dementia although occasional references are made to the more frequent presence of certain symptoms with one type of dementia than with others, e.g., the common occurrence of pathological laughing or crying in multi-infarct dementia and its relative absence in Alzheimer's disease.

Whatever the nature of the personality changes the intelligent management of the patient may well rest on an adequate appraisal of them and their interaction with the intellectual deficits.

Pseudo-dementia. Any condition which causes withdrawal and psychomotor retardation may readily masquerade as dementia. If the patient is difficult to test the distinction may have to rest to a large extent upon the history. Depression in elderly patients is probably the condition most frequently confused with dementia. Patient examination will often reveal evidence of preservation of intellect. Certainly if the patient can exhibit evidence of the ability to learn new material the probability of dementia is greatly lessened by this fact alone. Miller (1973) mentions how the presence of marked recent memory disorder in 'presenile' dementia has long been exploited by clinical psychologists in the differential diagnosis between dementia and functional psychiatric disorder. The literature contains many cases originally diagnosed as dementia which have responded well to drug treatment, electroconvulsive treatment and other forms of therapy.

Whether a true dementia or pseudodementia exists one must agree with Williams (1965) that the measurement of intellectual impairment in these cases 'though often of great clinical interest, is almost invariably difficult.' It is of paramount importance to be familiar with the assessment of older age groups (see Williams, 1970).

The relationships between depression, dementia and pseudodementia have been reviewed recently by Post (1975).

While there is no intention of dealing extensively with this topic the fact that numerous sources still overemphasize the role of cerebral arteriosclerosis in the production of dementia warrants a note. Recent evidence would seem to suggest that there are two major types of pathology likely to be frequently associated with dementia (1) vascular disturbances in the form of thromboembolism aggravated in some instances by stenosis in parts of the cerebral circulation and (2) neuronal degeneration. This second common form of 'senile' dementia does not appear to be related in any way to arteriosclerosis. With increasing age the two conditions may be seen together though one form usually predominates.

In the vascular group it seems that multiple infarcts need to occur before dementia is caused, dementia being singularly uncommon after single vascular accidents . Roth and Myers (1975) consider it unwise to diagnose dementia on the basis of the presence of arteriosclerosis alone without the evidence of one or more strokes. Since the evidence of 'minor strokes' may often cause episodic changes of higher psychological functions without sensory, motor or other more obvious symptoms being present, history taking should be very careful in this regard. It would also be ideal if all patients with 'transient ischaemic attacks' were to undergo neuropsychological examination at the time. In our experience higher order disturbances, particularly memory disorders, are found in a high proportion of these cases. In this way the development of multiple infarct dementia would become clearer.

With regard to the other and more common type of pathology, i.e. neuronal degeneration, many recent writers agree that Alzheimer's disease of the presenium and one class of senile dementia are one and the same condition. The clinical findings and pathological findings are identical (Brain and Walton, 1969; Hackinski *et al.*, 1974; Corsellis, 1975; Perez *et al.*, 1975). The cerebral atrophy affects the frontal and temporal lobes maximally being less marked in posterior regions. This is apparent in the neuropsychological examination. It comes almost as a surprise that patients with profound personality changes, marked memory disorder and great difficulty with auditory comprehension are able to read single words, name pictures of objects and carry out other tasks which are largely dependent upon the integrity of the posterior cortical areas.

Head injuries

It might appear at first sight that the largely 'localizationist' approach throughout the present text might be inapplicable to conditions of widespread damage or in cases where it has been difficult to establish the extent of the neurological damage. This is far from the case.

Among the most frequently reported changes after head injury are alterations in personality and lessening of the ability to abstract or manipulate concepts. Coupled with these may be disorders of attention and a variety of praxognosic and language defects. Some writers bring these commonly occurring symptoms together as a syndrome (Ford, 1976).

The long term effects of head injuries are more fruitfully considered as damage to specific brain systems rather than under the global term 'dementia' or 'head injury syndrome'. This is not to say that cerebral injury in many cases of closed head injury is not widespread but, that a thorough neuropsychological examination is likely to bring to light information crucial in the management and rehabilitation of such patients.

Parker comments 'It is the borderline case which presents the greatest problem. When clinical assessment still leaves a doubt about the possibility of early dementia the psychologists' findings usually come to the same indefinite conclusion.' (Parker, 1969). This author mentions the case of a 15 year old boy assessed before a severe head injury on the Wechsler Intelligence Scale for children at 113 I.Q. After a severe head injury which rendered him unconscious for five weeks his WISC I.Q. was 109. This sort of finding is often taken to mean that there is no measurable degree of intellectual impairment. However this is so only if one equates intelligence with the results of these standardized aggregate measures which depend to such a large degree on stored information and well established skills. Further examination of such cases often reveals characteristic difficulties on tasks of new learning or problem solving. The fact is not that no impairment is present but that inappropriate means are often used to assess it. Prime among the long term changes after head injury are those associated with frontal lobe damage. As mentioned in Chapter 4 the cognitive changes appear to be more closely associated with the dorsolateral cortex, the changes in impulse control and other personality changes being associated with the basomedial frontal cortex. In head injuries either or both sets of changes may be seen though basal injury is usually much more pronounced.

Recovery of function after brain injury. There has been relatively little study devoted as yet to the recovery of intellectual and emotional function after brain injury. Exceptions such as the prolonged and extensive work of Teuber (1975) give an excellent picture of the natural history of recovery over periods up to 30 years. Other workers such as Bond (1975) are examining the relationships between cognitive and physical difficulties after head injury to adjustment to daily living. Factors arising from these studies need to be widely promulgated since rehabilitation services err most frequently in concentrating heavily on physical disabilities with very little attention being paid to intellectual and emotional handicaps. This may stem from the assumption that while physical handicaps may be improved by therapy the psychological handicaps may not. The various forms of psychological therapy including 'behaviour modification' techniques should be evaluated at this stage. Used against a background of accurate neuropsychological assessment they should prove more effective than arbitrary rules. Studies documenting cognitive recovery such as Mandleberg and Brooks (1975) need extending to all areas of neuropsychological function. Quantitative appraisal of 'emotional' changes presents more difficulty but no more so than in other areas of personality disorder.

Memory disorders

Systematic memory examination is apt to be rewarding in a high proportion of cases. In our experience it forms the most useful first step in neuropsychological assessment. While there is a wide range of tests many have the disadvantage of lacking suitable age norms.

Wechsler Memory Scale. This scale consists of seven separate subtests and despite its apparent deficiencies is useful in clinical practice though it usually needs to be supplemented by other measures. Not the least of its advantages is the fact that it was normed against the Wechsler-Bellevue Intelligence Scale. Fields (1971) has demonstrated a WAIS-WMS correlation of 0.83 and suggests that clinicians may thus expect a reasonably accurate estimate of the I.Q. from the brief memory scale. On the other hand the high correlation in normal subjects makes a large I.Q.–M.Q. difference very suggestive of a memory disorder.

However, because of the global nature of these two aggregate measures and perhaps because they both share a common factor, not all patients with a memory disturbance will show an I.Q.–M.Q. difference. However, *where it does occur*, it always appears to have diagnostic significance.

Some studies have cast doubt on the validity of the Wechsler Memory Scale as a test of memory as such. Eysenck and Halstead (1945) had shown a high correlation between fifteen popular memory tasks (including the bulk of the WMS) and an intelligence test (the Progressive Matrices 1938). They felt that it was misleading to accept scores on such tests as estimates of memory ability. Others like Parker (1957) have found no difference in M.Q. between groups where it could be assumed that a difference in memory ability was to be expected. The use of the WMS as a test of 'brain damage' (Howard, 1950, 1954, 1966) is subject to the same criticisms as other measures based on a unitary conception of cerebral impairment.

Of the separate subtests on the WMS the most frequent deficits seem to be on associate learning, visual reproduction, and logical memory (prose passages) in that order. Zangwill (1943) had commented quite early that the learning of simple test material like verbal paired associates was 'virtually impossible in cases of marked organic memory disturbance. . .' Cohen (1950) was unable to confirm this on the WMS. The fact that others (e.g. Brooks, 1972) have found such differences suggests that group-composition may play a part.

The most frequent difficulty on the WMS with organic patients in general seems to be poor performance on the paired associates. If there is a marked discrepancy between the old and new associations an organic deficit may be suspected. In the amnesic syndrome this is usually accompanied by poor performance on the visual reproduction, especially card 3, good performance on digit span and relatively poor performance on logical memory (prose), the remaining four subtests being well performed. In the case of dementia poor performance on the three more sensitive tests is also accompanied by a fall off in the other subtests so that the overall memory quotient tends to be depressed.

Even the very brief items on current information and orientation may raise the question of cerebral impairment. It is important to use standard measures since it has been shown that even such simple tests may detect patients who have not appeared temporally disoriented on clinical examination (Benton, van Allen and Fogel, 1964; Levin and Benton, 1975).

Finally lateralized lesions may first reveal themselves in differential performance such as poor performance on visual reproduction with other tests begin performed adequately or well. Any such performance should be systematically investigated with more extensive procedures, e.g. the Benton Visual Retention Test. The very brevity of the examination means that some material-specific memory deficits may be readily overlooked.

Frontal amnesia. While there is some general agreement about the selective memory impairment with temporal lesions the position of the frontal lobes with regard to memory seems less clear. Some have reported no loss either on conventional or special tests (Hebb, 1945; Ghent, Mishkin and Teuber, 1962; Milner, 1968; Butters *et al.*, 1970) while others have reported clear-cut memory losses (Prisko, 1963; Talland, Sweet and Ballantine, 1967). The difference is in part due to the nature of tests given and their manner of application. Barbizet (1970) agrees with Luria (1966) that the difficulty is one of inability to achieve voluntary memorization and this increases with the complexity of the material. The apparent conflict seems to lie partly in the definition of memory and learning which is accepted. The following quotations from Barbizet suggest an explanation that would account for the findings of most studies. In some cases 'the examiner can, by taking the place of the faulty frontal lobes of his patient, force him with constant repetition to learn a list of words or a short text, which he will retain quite well.' The fact that the patient cannot do this for himself suggests a loss of the 'strategies of learning.' At other times frontal patients act as though they have lost the 'strategies of recall' which enable them to utilize information which they have already stored. 'The evidence seems to suggest that frontal lesions suppress the programs that govern the execution of the mental strategies that bring recall and memorization into play during the operation of any new task, whether it be the resolution of a problem or the learning of a piece of poetry' (Barbizet, 1970, p.87). In similar vein, Luria (1973b) considers that patients with frontal lesions do not suffer from 'primary disturbances of memory' but rather from a more subtle disturbance of mnestic activity, both of learning and recall, due to disturbance in 'retention' of a complex and consecutive programme for the intellectual act.' Further evidence of this is provided by both authors. We have found that the plateau of learning described by Luria for learning of a long series of words is brought out in most dramatic form on the electric maze described earlier. Having reached a certain degree of mastery the patient is often completely unable to improve his performance despite a large number of trials. This failure to benefit from experience requires a more extended task than is usually present in most clinical tests and we have found the electrical maze of particular value in assessing the degree of this frontal deficit particularly in intelligent subjects.

Affective amnesia. Various forms of forgetting are associated with sundry psychological disturbances often loosely referred to as functional states. It may be difficult at times to distinguish between these affective forgettings and those caused by organic cerebral conditions. Apart from the presence of positive psychiatric signs certain rules appear to be of value. Since early dementia, the amnesic syndrome, and cortical amnesia (material specific) have fairly characteristic pictures, the functional disorders may be suspected where the pattern of performance on memory tasks does not conform to one of these. In hysterical states including the Ganser syndrome the patient frequently offers a pattern of loss which is in keeping with his unconscious or partly conscious enactment of the role of a patient with memory disorder. This never seems to possess the characteristic difference between learning old logical verbal associations and novel ones. Neurotic patients almost always learn some of each and may repeat incorrect but logical associations on even the easiest items. Neurotic patients, also, do not usually present the marked difference between good immediate span and poor recent memory so typical of all organic conditions which affect the hippocampal and mamillo-thalamic regions.

Delayed recall. This is probably used insufficiently or at least is not often objectively studied. If preliminary memory examination forms the first part of the neuropsychological examination then delayed recall can often be introduced at the end of the session. This will bring to light many early cases where recall almost immediately after presentation, as in the WMS, may have produced little or no evidence. The addition of a visual test such as the Rey Figure to the WMS means that delayed recall for both audio verbal and visual material can be done with economy of time. Brooks (1972) has tested such a procedure by computing a forgetting score based on the difference between immediate and delayed recall scores. His results suggest that not only do patients with organic memory disturbances acquire less information than normals initially but they lose proportionately more of it over time. Unfortunately, many studies in the literature present retention scores without registration data making it difficult to ascertain how much forgetting took place on a given task.

Remote memory. In 1904, Ribot described the loss of memory in dementia as affecting recent memory most severely with less and less effect for memories which were increasingly remote in time, with childhood memories being best preserved. This observation has been dignified by the term Ribot's Law and has continued to appear in textbooks even in recent years. There is now ample clinical and experimental evidence to suggest that this law should be repealed. Using the questionnaire technique for studying memory of remote events as well as the memory for well known faces Sanders and Warrington (1974) have shown that in amnesic patients there is no evidence to support a relative sparing of remote over recent events. The same holds true for groups of normal ageing subjects (Warrington and Sanders, 1971; Squire, 1974). The latter author has also demonstrated that the effect is not affected by length of education, highly educated subjects showing similar results to those of average education.

A detailed systematic examination of memory covers a very wide area of brain function. A framework for such an examination is shown below. Tests to cover the various contingencies should be available in the clinic. Different workers will have preference for certain tests. It should be stressed that deficits in certain areas are likely to be missed unless they are looked for with appropriate measures. However, in day-to-day clinical practice a more restricted sampling will usually suffice.

Table 9.2 Restricted sampling

SENSE MODALITY	TYPE OF MATERIAL	MODE OF TESTING	TIME LAPSE
Visual	Verbal versus	Registration	Immediate
Auditory	nonverbal	Recognition	Delayed
Tactile	Meaningful versus	(matching-to-sample;	Remote
	meaningless	recurring items)	

Case No. 1

A 55 year old woman was admitted with a history of several weeks patchy memory loss of relatively sudden onset. On admission she appeared correctly oriented for time and place and gave a history of treatment over some years for hypertension. It was suspected that her cerebral circulation might be at fault and angiography was carried out among other investigations but nothing of abnormal nature was demonstrated.

A routine psychological examination gave her a Verbal I.Q. of 99 and a Performance I.Q. of only 76 with a Memory Quotient of 77. At first the very marked discrepancy between the verbal and performance intelligence measures suggested the possibility of a localized lesion, possibly in the right hemisphere. Examination of the contents of the memory scale showed some confusion of temporal orientation, perfect performance on mental control, a normal performance on digits forward (7) and backwards (4) with virtually no recall of the logical prose passages, visual reproduction or the new associations on the paired-associate learning task. The old associations were recalled without much difficulty. Thus the memory difficulty approximated a recent memory disorder of organic origin which raised the possibility of an early dementing process. Further examination revealed that the patient also had difficulty with verbal reasoning and abstraction. She also had difficulty with naming and with comprehension of written language and it became apparent that, although mild, there was some evidence of a euphoria which fluctuated and was replaced by periods of indifference. The patient obtained an I.Q. of only 74 on the Porteus Maze Test and this collection of signs was thought to be indicative of a presenile dementia with maximum impact on the frontal and temporal regions. There were no other signs of note.

Confirmation came shortly afterwards on air encephalography. This demonstrated some dilatation of the ventricular system with quite marked widening of the sulci consistent with a diagnosis of presenile dementia.

This association of recent memory loss with fall off in frontal lobe functions together with relative preservation of well established memories and skills seems quite typical of the early cases of presenile dementia which we have seen. It is noteworthy that the immediate memory is well preserved in such cases.

Case No. 2

A.B. a nineteen year old girl sustained multiple injuries when struck by a car while crossing the road. She was unconscious on admission to hospital and suffered a lumbar spinal fracture and fractured pelvis. There was no skull fracture. Over three weeks her conscious state improved slowly. In the early stages of this recovery a profound right hemiplegia was noted which improved; but three months after unjury she still had marked weakness and clumsiness of the right side. Nine months after the injury she had further improved and returned to work as a laboratory assistant but her work was felt to be below par. She herself believed that her intellectual abilities were back to their previous level. Like most patients with severe head injury she had suffered from a memory disorder but on gross clinical examination this appeared to have cleared.

Just one year after the injury A.B. was tested by a psychologist who performed an intelligence and personality examination—WAIS, Verbal I.Q. 113, Performance I.Q.97, Wechsler Memory Quotient 94. A number of 'organic' signs were noted but there was no suggestion by the psychologist that any of the changes were due to brain injury. He was aware of an apparent fall-off from what had been a very good scholastic record but felt that her poor performances could be accounted for by psychodynamic factors revealed in the personality examination. By this time the patient had been given a less exacting job at work and was having difficulty in learning material which she had handled easily before her injury. Her neurologist noted among other things that there was a marked difference between her present performance in arithmetic and her previously very good performance in mathematics at night school just before her accident and sought a neuropsychological assesment.

At this examination the patient was mildly uninhibited but not distractible. She was below her anticipated level on new verbal learning. Her maze learning was good though marred on a few occasions by the disregard of instructions despite her ability to repeat these almost perfectly. On the Word Fluency she was very much reduced in output, produced several perseverations and one puerile joke on the 'F' list,…fish, fat, *fin* (joke, I mean thin), fish, flake. This performance was in marked contrast to her ability to produce a large number of appropriate responses to the logical category of animals and was thought to reflect left frontal lobe damage.

Even more striking was her inability to solve arithmetical problems of the discursive variety described by Luria. Here she failed to make adequate preliminary analysis of the problems, acted impulsively on well tried but irrelevant hypotheses and was unable to utulitze feedback from her own working to reach the solution.

Further studies on follow-up have confirmed the suspicion raised at the second testing that the patient had sustained frontal injury with major accent on the left side. Two years later there is no improvement in her condition and the patient is being directed to retraining as it is now clear that she would be unable to succeed with her ambition to continue tertiary education.

The case is presented as a typical result of head injury which was not appreciated because of lack of appropriate examination. It is felt that some of the depressive self-concern shown in the Rorschach and other tests given by the first psychologists is a natural expression of the patient's sensing of her intellectual deficit and personality change.

Case No.3

A 55 year old man presented with an episode of slurred speech and weakness in his left hand which had commenced while he was at work on the morning of his admission. In the week before he had noticed an intermittent appearance of a filminess in front of his left eye which he described as being like 'white lace'. He was a rather drowsy, overweight man but fully conscious.

He had slurred speech and a left-sided slight facial weakness of the upper motor neurone type. His blood pressure was elevated to 190/120. Physical examination revealed cardiac enlargement and considerable smooth firm enlargement of the liver. Central nervous system examination showed that the slurred speech was not accompanied by any form of dysphasia. As well as the facial weakness there was a slightly decreased power down his left side with decreased coordination in the left upper limb.

He was treated with antihypertensive therapy. His neurological signs had all disappeared the day after his admission. His speech remained somewhat slurred but a careful history taking revealed that this difficulty had been with him most of his life. Among the radiological investigations carotid angiography showed a stenosis in the cavernous portion of the left internal carotid artery. The patient improved somewhat on treatment and was discharged eleven days after his admission.

He was next referred for neuropsychological examination by his general practitioner with a history of impaired intellectual functioning since his transient ischaemic episode. Memory examination showed a Wechsler Memory Quotient of 100, but this was thought to be well below his premorbid level as he had been the managing director of a large flourishing business which he had himself developed. The subtests revealed excellent immediate memory (8 digits forward and 7 backward), good orientation and mental control but a logical memory for prose somewhat below what one would have expected of him. He showed complete inability to retain new information on both the visual reproduction and paired associate tests. Questioning revealed that this man was in fact a very heavy drinker and it was assumed that the recent memory disorder was of the Korsakoff variety. Further routine investigation showed that there was a marked discrepancy between his verbal and performance scores with a very pronounced constructional apraxia. He managed only a scale score of 3 on the Block Design test and zero on the Object Assembly subtest. In the latter his constructions made no sense at all. His local practitioner was advised that he was suffering from a combination of a vascular episode affecting the right hemisphere and was compounded by the effects of alcoholism. It was pointed out that he was not at the moment considered to be a case of dementia. Cessation of alcohol was strongly advocated.

Case No. 4

A 26 year old woman was referred by the psychological service of a government employment agency because she had failed in a number of job situations. They were aware of the history of a head injury some 12 years before when the patient was thrown from her horse. However, she had apparently completed her eleventh year of schooling without difficulty and their examination with the WAIS gave her a Verbal Intelligence Quotient of 135, and there was neither history nor present evidence of personality disorder.

History taking on this referral showed that after leaving high school she had attended a practical course in home management but failed miserably. She subsequently tried a business course but failed here also. She then spent some time looking after her father on his property but, from her own account, was unsuccessful here also and later went on a tour of the world, her family being well to do.

During this interview the psychologist remembered that he had interviewed this patient two years before when she was having difficulty with her ward duties after she had enrolled as a trainee nurse and had successfully completed the two month period of preliminary academic training. The nature of her difficulties was not apparent and she was dismissed from the hospital before psychological examination could be arranged. Later she entered the clerical division of the state public service but her services were terminated after four months despite the fact that her duties were restricted to routine filing and similar chores.

Neuropsychological examination began with the Wechsler Memory Scale. The Memory Quotient was 106 and there was not the slightest sign of difficulty on any of the subtests. The patient expressed some perplexity about her failures at work and apart from being a little talkative concentrated well. Because of the story of an earlier head injury and her subsequent poor occupational record despite a high 'test' Intelligence she was given the Austin Maze Test. On this task she showed the qualitative features described by Milner, and by Walsh (Ch.4) and, despite frequent verbalizations showing that she realized where her most frequent errors occurred, she was totally unable to eradicate them. The problem given to her on the maze was one which we have found that adults of average intelligence can score an errorless trial after ten or fewer attempts. Her 15 trials gave the following errors:48, 33, 60, 48, 24, 18, 15, 9, 14, 17, 11, 16, 58, 16, 36. The test was then discontinued. Throughout the test she continued to disregard the instructions despite warnings and despite repeated correct verbalizations of her own about the rules.

This patient revealed in a very clear form the curious dissociation between knowing and doing and the failure to benefit from feedback from her own errors (failure of error utulization). Other tests confirmed this. The case highlights the somewhat subtle but pervasive effects of what one presumes is bilateral frontal lobe damage. It also highlights the damage of using an 'I.Q. level' as the basis for prediction of rehabilitation in case of head injury.

As a postscript, retrospective examination of the situation showed that the 'curious dissociation' was at the basis of her difficulties. Despite clear verbal statements of what she had to do in certain job situations she often carried out acts which were quite at variance with her words and were on many occasions unacceptable and oft-times risky.

Case No. 5

A 55 year old man was admitted after an episode of collapse due to weakness of his right leg of sudden onset lasting a few hours two days prior to his admission. He had suffered at the time from mild headaches. There was no dizziness, irritability or vomiting accompanying the attack nor any sensory changes. He had a thirty year history of migraine.

On examination he showed sensory inattention for the left side of his body and the left half visual field but clinical neurological examination revealed no other abnormality.

Angiography showed that the right internal carotid artery was completely obstructed at its origin. This patient improved over a few days and appeared perfectly normal and was referred for neuropsychological examination prior to his discharge.

This examination showed that this man had the finest example of constructional apraxia that the author had seen, demonstrating the well known fact of the silence of this condition. There was also a mild but quite noticeable material specific memory loss for visual material. Other intellectual and mnestic functions were normal.

The Verbal Intelligence Quotient was 105, Performance Intelligence Quotient 86, the difference being due solely to the constructional apraxia. His memory quotient was 103 and the average intelligence measures were in keeping with his educational and occupational backgrounds. The patient had failed to pass the examination held at the end of his eight years primary schooling. He was discharged to be followed in outpatient department. There have been no further episodes since his admission eight months ago and he is coping well with his work.

Case No. 6

A 37 year old man was referred for examination following a near successful attempt at suicide by carbon monoxide poisoning the man having attached a hose to the exhaust of his car which he then led back into the interior. On physical recovery it was noted that the patient was having difficulty with his memory and that his recall of ongoing events lasted only for 3 to 4 minutes.

On examination with the Naylor-Harwood Adult Intelligence Scale (the Australian equivalent of the WAIS) he showed a verbal intelligence quotient of 97 with a performance quotient of 99 in keeping with his occupation as a fireman with only eight years of prior education. There was nothing at all in any of these performances to suggest cerebral impairment. However examination with the Wechsler Memory Scale showed a quotient of only 67 with a classical picture of axial amnesia. He showed very poor recall of logical prose with no evidence of confabulation. He managed 7 digits forward and 5 backward and he managed in the three trials of the associate learning to retain 5 of the familiar associations but was unable to retain any of the new associations. Moreover his visual memory was exceedingly poor making only 2 of the possible 13 points and his description of his difficulty accorded well with the description given of the amnesic syndrome. Because of the severity of the amnesia and the evidence on the difference between the hippocampal versus the mamillo-thalamic forms described earlier, he was given the various tests of Lhermitte and Signoret. On these he presented most of the features of the hippocampal group with pure forgetting and lack of confusion errors. He showed no associated features of the frontal type that are often seen with the alcoholic Korsakoff patient. This case is included as it is difficult to understand how a generalized toxic agent can have such a specific effect, presumably on the axial structures.

Case No. 7

A nineteen year old male was admitted late in 1969 having had two episodes suggestive of temporal lobe epilepsy a week before his admission. There was no previous history of major head injury.

On admission central nervous system examination was normal. The following investigations were also normal—skull x-Ray, CSF examination, air encephalogram, and radioisotopic brain scan. EEG showed some suspicious activity in the right temporal region on overbreathing. This was repeated over the next two weeks and bilateral abnormality was brought out with overbreathing but once again the right anterior temporal region predominated. It was felt that no clear focal abnormality had been demonstrated and the patient was discharged on anticonvulsant therapy two weeks after admission.

The patient was reviewed from time to time. March 1970. No further fits. EEG:'…trace much the same as before … but no indication of any focal or paroxysmal abnormality.' After a further period without fits he was discharged to the care of his general practitioner. April 1974. Patient admitted complaining of headache and vomiting. Muscle tone, power, sensation and cranial nerve functions were normal but there were signs of raised intracranial pressure. An echogram carried out in the casualty department revealed no shift. A few days later a brain scan was reported as showing 'a doubtful area of increased uptake in the *left anterior temporal region,* which could be consistent with a space occupying lesion.'

An angiogram at this time carried out by catheterization included the following comments—'… no definite abnormality could be seen in the right or left intracerebral carotid artery runs. The anterior cerebral arteries in the AP projection are slightly displaced to the left, but this is most likely accounted for by the degree of rotation of the head to the left … the basilar artery was lying very close to the clivus (bony base) suggesting the possibility of a space-occupying lesion in the posterior fossa causing the basilar artery to be displaced anteriorly…'

Air encephalogram was abandoned for technical reasons but the normal position and dimensions of the fourth ventricle seemed to exclude a posterior fossa tumour. Ventriculogram showed a small right ventricle and a rather large left ventricle.

On 2nd May 1974 no cause had yet been found and a brain biopsy in the parietal regions had proved negative. About this time a possible infective basis for the disorder was considered because the patient developed a fever and a number of pustules scattered over his body; but investigation was once again unhelpful.

EEG on 24th April 1974 reported '... No focalization is seen here, although in the parasagittal runs, some emphasis of delta can be seen in the *left anterior temporal* region. The previous reports mentioned the *right* anterior temporal region, but certainly this cannot be confirmed on this record'.

Neuropsychological examination in 1974 was suggestive of gross intellectual deficit as seen with expanding lesions. There was a marked discrepancy between the WAIS Verbal I.Q. (92) and Performance I.Q. (69). The Digit-Symbol Substitution and Block Design subtests were the most poorly performed. The Wechsler Memory Quotient was only 61 with many of the principal features of the amnesic syndrome. Visual recall was also poor on the Benton Visual Retention Test. The constructional apraxia was marked with planning difficulties but no constructional deviation. The patient's language functions were well preserved. Further examination was contemplated and a report was written stating that the preliminary findings were suggestive of a deeply placed lesion in the right hemisphere affecting the anterior portion of that hemisphere. (The report was made 'blind' on the basis of a graduate student's examination).

Following this report a right frontal craniotomy was made and a tumour mass was found deep in the right frontotemporal region extending to the midline. The tumour proved to be an astrocytoma.

This case, while incompletely examined from the neuropsychological point of view, is presented to demonstrate the assistance which may be made in difficult cases with equivocal or conflicting neurological signs.

Case No.8

A 56 year old housewife was admitted in July, 1972, with a history of blackouts consisting of a period of detachment from reality with staring eyes and lack of awareness of her whereabouts. There had been a 15 year history of such attacks. On closer questioning most of the absences appeared to last about 2 minutes after which the patient would continue with whatever she was doing or saying. There was also a history about 15 years before of a head injury without loss of consciousness but followed by severe headache for about a week suggesting possible cerebral contusion and traumatic haemorrhage. The blow struck her on the right temple.

Electroencephalographic examinations seemed to strongly implicate the left temporal region and, as the patient was not completely controlled on drug medication, she was considered for temporal lobectomy. There was no indication of abnormality on the right side in the EEG.

The neuropsychologist was approached to answer the following question 'Does this patient have an amnesia to which she is not entitled?' This pithy referral suggests that in line with the prior history and investigations one would not be surprised to note changes referrable to the left temporal region such as a decrease in verbal memory capacity as discussed in Chapter 5. However before proceeding with temporal lobectomy the neurologist wished to be assured that there was no indication of difficulty implicating the right side for fear of producing a pervasive amnesic syndrome.

On examination the patient appeared to have a verbal intelligence quotient (97) in keeping with her educational and occupational background and her memory quotient was also 97. The components of the Wechsler Memory Scale showed a good performance on logical prose material and short term memory represented by 7 digits forward but poor performance on the difficult associations of the associate learning task.

This latter difficulty might well be in keeping with a long standing focus in the left temporal lobe. However, visual reproduction was exceedingly poor and this raised the question of possible pathology on the right side. At this examination there was only time to perform two of the subtests on the Wechsler Performance Scale. These were the Object Assembly and Block Design subtests and they were well below the average of her verbal scale. The neurologists were advised that there were such indications and at this stage the patient was under investigation with intracerebral electrodes. In a period of confusion following the implantation the patient managed to remove one of the wires which was subsequently replaced. Readings taken from the electrodes consistently implicated the left temporal region and preparations were in hand for temporal lobectomy when the patient died suddenly several weeks after the implantation of the electrodes of a massive pulmonary embolism.

At autopsy the region of the left hippocampus appeared normal but in coronal sections there was considerably atrophy of Ammon's Horn and the hippocampus in the *right* cerebral hemisphere. This was thought to be of long standing possibly associated with the earlier injury.

This case is presented to demonstrate that indications may have already been present in the neuropsychological examination which would have counterindicated temporal lobectomy and, in the light of recent experience, it suggested that more extensive neuropsychological examination would have been indicated prior to proceeding with resection. One can only surmise that removal of the left temporal lobe in the presence of atrophy in the right hippocampus would probably have produced an amnesic syndrome of marked severity.

Case No. 9

A man aged 41 was diagnosed as having mumps three months previously. This had been complicated by mumps orchitis, probable pancreatitis and encephalitis which was associated with a one month history of episodic headaches, confusion, general malaise and listlessness. There was no nausea, vomiting or photophobia with the headache, but patient had increased difficulty with working with figures which alarmed him especially as he was a mathematics teacher at the tertiary level.

He had numerous complaints and was seen by the psychiatrist who felt that he was a very obsessional individual.

On neuropsychological examination he gave an intensely detailed description of his symptoms and prominent among his complaints was that of poor memory. He was depressed after his severe illness and very concerned about his headaches and memory disorder. His verbal intelligence quotient was 136, performance intelligence quotient 108, memory quotient 104. The marked discrepancy between his memory and his verbal intelligence quotient led us to examine his memory functions more closely and on the Wechsler Memory Scale, the Benton Visual Retention Test and the tests of Lhermitte, and Signoret he gave a quite typical picture of hippocampal amnesia with very rapid forgetting, material being retained only for a few minutes.

It was considered that this patient was suffering from the effects of encephalitic memory disturbance and although his performance measures were less than one would have expected it was felt that these were depressed by his debilitating illness at this stage since he showed no qualitative features suggestive of visuospatial or visuoconstructive deficits. He was also able to complete the Porteus Mazes without the slightest difficulty.

This case is presented because at the time of his referral it was considered by his physicians that the patient's complaints were definitely of a functional nature and he was referred more or less to rule out the possibility of an organic deficit. Apart from the test findings already mentioned the patient gave a text book description of the day to day difficulties of a patient with axial amnesia of moderate severity. The patient's physical condition improved with the passage of time and his memory deficit has lessened over the ensuing two years but still shows evidence of more rapid forgetting than was previously the case. He is still incapacitated by his obsessional neurosis.

Case No. 10

A 58 year old woman was admitted to the Neurology Department from a private hospital for increasing confusion. She had been under treatment for two months for alcoholism. She was quite an unreliable historian and denied excessive alcoholic intake, but she did admit to increasing forgetfulness and confusion in recent times.

On examination she was a dishevelled, elderly lady who was reasonably oriented in place and time but she had poor distant and recent memory and was unable to perform simple mental functions such as serial subtraction. Clinical neurological examination was essentially normal except that her gait was rather unsteady. The only other finding of note was a mild degree of liver swelling.

Neuropsychological examination was commenced on the day after admission and the picture she presented was a rather complex one. There was a very marked difference between her verbal and her performance measures on the Wechsler Adult Intelligence Scale, Verbal 107, Performance 76. Her memory quotient on the Wechsler Memory Scale was 89. She had difficulty with reproduction of the logical prose passages with a clear confabulation on slight pressure to get her to recall more of the material. Her nonverbal memory was particularly poor, and this was confirmed with further testing using the Benton Visual Retention Test.

Qualitative features on the Wechsler Performance subtests showed a marked constructional apraxia apparent in the object assembly and block design subjects. There was no evidence of any inattention or other signs of parietal lobe disturbance in her drawings or constructions. Given the Goldstein version of the block design test the patient demonstrated that she was able to benefit from partial plans as provided in the structured versions of the problems, indicating that the difficulty was likely to be due to frontal lobe dysfunction rather than to disruption of spatial coordinates from a posterior lesion. The visual memory and visual constructive performances were in marked contrast to her completely normal set of performances of the verbal subtests and this suggested that she might harbour a lesion in the right hemisphere.

Despite the poor performance overall on the memory scale it was noted that she was able to learn new associations scoring 9 out of 10 on the first trial of the associate learning task. This suggested that this was probably not a simple case of alcoholic memory disorder and the discrepancy between the visual reproduction on the WMS and the Benton VRT on the one hand and the relative ease of recall for new verbal associations raised the possibility of a material specific memory defect over and above any difficulties arising on the basis of alcohol.

Because of the possibility of a lesion in the right temporal region auditory perceptual tests in the form of the speech sounds perception test and an auditory rhythm test were given but these showed no gross impairment. Auditory short term memory was normal.

The findings were considered to be in keeping with a lesion of the right temporal region with effects on the frontal lobe and it was felt that the total picture was clouded by the effects of her alcoholism.

The question was resolved by further neurological investigation, left carotid angiography showing a displacement of the internal cerebral vein toward the left possibly suggestive of a mass in the right temporal region and a brain scan showed increased uptake in the right midtemporal region consistent with a tumour.

At operation a firm mass was found deep in the anterior part of the temporal lobe and this proved to be an astrocytoma. The mass was removed with minimal difficulty and the patient did remarkably well postoperatively.

Case No. 11

A fifty year old business manager was admitted in May 1974 with the story of abrupt onset of difficulty with recent memory. This had occurred some days before and was accompanied by bilateral frontal headaches constant in nature and lasting three to four hours from late morning to early afternoon. He had experienced a similar episode of headache and dysmnesia some five years before this in which he forgot things he had been told several days before. This had apparently resolved spontaneously and was not investigated. He had been in good health since but was described as having an anxious personality.

Physical examination was essentially normal apart from moderate hypertension. Neurological examination revealed no localizing signs but reflexes were all hyperactive and a mild pouting response was elicited. The patient was somewhat vague, very sluggish and taciturn though he responded correctly and appropriately to direct questioning. He volunteered nothing.

Neuropsychological examination the day after admission confirmed his recent memory loss which had all the characteristics of the amnesic syndrome. Relevant test findings—Verbal I.Q. 104; Performance I.Q., 99; Memory Quotient 70. His immediate memory was good (8 digits forwards, 4 or 5 backward). His visual reproduction score was only 2 (maximum 14) and while he learned all the old verbal associations he was unable to retain even one new association.

At this stage it was considered that he had an alcoholic basis for his amnesia. Several facts appear to be against this. Firstly a more careful history taking from his wife confirmed the sudden onset and his competence just prior to this. She also confirmed that his drinking was less than extravagant and she appeared to be a reliable witness. Subsequent neuropsychological examinations have confirmed the static and severe nature of the amnesia but has never revealed any of the frontal lobe features so frequently seen in alcoholic cases though the stable nature of the condition has allowed extensive testing.

Neurological examinations have continued to be unproductive. It is now thought that this 'axial' amnesia has occurred on a vascular basis and the accompaniment of a severe and lasting adynamia and impotence shows a similarity to the amnesia seen after anterior communicating artery aneurysms probably associated with spasm of the anterior cerebral arteries. Despite the profound adynamia the patient's reaction time remains normal.

References

Ackerly, S.S. & Benton, A.L. (1948) Report of a case of bilateral frontal lobe defect. *Research Publications, Association for Research in Nervous and Mental Diseases,* 27, 479-504.

Adams, R.D., Collins, G.H. & Victor, M. (1962) Troubles de la memoire et de l'apprentissage chez l'homme. In Paris: Centre National de la Recherche Scientifique. *Physiologie de l'hippocampe,* 273-296.

Aimard, G., Devic, M., Lebel, M., Trouillas, P. & Boisson, D. (1975) Pure (dynamic?) agraphia of frontal origin. *Revue Neurologique,* 131, 505-512.

Ajax, E.T. (1967) Dyslexia without agraphia. *Archives of Neurology,* 17, 645-652

Ajuriaguerra, J. de & Hécaen, H. (1951) La restauration fonctionnellé aprés lobectomie occipitale. *Journal de Psychologie normale et pathologique,* 44, 510-546.

Ajuriaguerra, J. de & Hécaen, H. (1960) *Le Cortex Cerebral.* Paris: Masson.

Akelaitis, A.J. (1940) A study of gnosis, praxis and language following partial and complete section of the corpus callosum. *Transactions of the American Neurological Association,* 66, 182-185.

Akelaitis, A.J. (1941a) Psychobiological studies following section of the corpus callosum. *American Journal of Psychiatry,* 97, 1147-1157.

Akelaitis, A.J. (1941b) Studies on the corpus callosum. VIII. *American Journal of Psychiatry,* 98, 409-414.

Akelaitis, A.J. (1941c) Studies on the corpus callosum. II. *Archives of Neurology and Psychiatry,* 45, 788.

Akelaitis, A.J. (1942a) Studies on the corpus callosum. V. *Archives of Neurology and Psychiatry,* 47, 971-1008.

Akelaitis, A.J. (1942b) Studies on the corpus callosum. VI. Orientation (temporal-spatial gnosis) following section of the corpus callosum. *Archives of Neurology and Psychiatry,* 48, 914-937.

Akelaitis, A.J. (1943) Studies on the corpus callosum. VII. Studies of language functions (tactile and visual lexia and graphia) unilaterally following sections of the corpus callosum. *Journal of Neuropathology and Experimental Neurology,* 2, 226-262.

Akelaitis, A.J., Risteen, W.A. & Van Wagenen, W.P. (1941) A contribution to the study of dyspraxia and apraxia following partial and complete section of the corpus callosum. *Transactions of the American Neurological Association,* 67, 75-78.

Akelaitis, A.J., Risteen, W.A. & Van Wagenen, W.P. (1942) Studies on the corpus callosum. III. A contribution to the study of dyspraxia and apraxia following partial and complete section of the corpus callosum. *Archives of Neurology and Psychiatry,* 48, 914-937.

Akelaitis, A.J., Risteen, W.A. & Van Wagenen, W.P. (1943) Studies on the corpus callosum. IX. Relation of the grasp reflex to section of the corpus callosum. *Archives of Neurology and Psychiatry,* 49, 820-825.

Alajouanine, T. (1960) *Les Grandes Activités du Lobe Occipital.* Paris: Masson.

Alajouanine, T., Castaigne, P. & De Ribaucourt-Ducarne, B. (1960) Valeur clinique de certains tests perceptifs et perceptivo-moteurs. In *Les Grandes Activités du Lobe Occipital,* ed. Alajouanine, T. Paris: Masson.

Alajouanine, T., Lhermitte, F. & De Ribaucourt-Ducarne, B. (1960) Les alexies agnosiques et aphasiques. In *Les Grandes Activitiés du Lobe Occipital,* ed. Alajouanine, T. Paris: Masson.

Alajouanine, T. & Lhermitte, F. (1957) Des anosognosies électives. *Encephale,* 46, 505-519.

Alajouanine, T. & Lhermitte, F. (1964) Nonverbal communication in aphasia. In *Disorders of Language,* eds. De Reuck, A.V.S. & O'Connor, M. London: Churchill.

Albert, M.L., Feldman, R.G. & Willis, A.L. (1974) The 'subcortical dementia' of progressive supranuclear palsy. *Journal of Neurology, Neurosurgery and Psychiatry,* 37, 121-130.

Albert, M.L., Reches, A. & Silverberg, R. (1975) Associative visual agnosia without alexia. *Neurology,* 25, 322-326.

Albert, M.L. Yamadori, A., Gardner, H. & Howes, D. (1973) Comprehension in alexia. Brain. *Brain,* 96, 317-328.

Allen, J.M. (1930) Clinical study of tumours involving the occipital lobes. *Brain,* 53, 194-243.

Allen, R.M. (1948) The test performance of the brain diseased. *Journal of Clinical Psychology*, **4**, 218-284.

Allen, R.M. (1949) A comparison of the test performance of the brain injured and the brain diseased. *American Journal of Psychiatry*, **106**, 195-198.

Allison, R.S. (1962) *The Senile Brain: A clinical study*. London: Edward Arnold Ltd.

Allison, R.S. (1966) Perseveration as a sign of diffuse and focal brain damage. *British Medical Journal*, **2**, 1095-1101.

Allison, R.S. & Hurwitz, L.J. (1967) On perseveration in aphasics. *Brain*, **90**, 429-448.

Alpers, B.J. & Mancall, E.L. (1971) *Essentials of the Neurological Examination*. Philadelphia: Davis.

Anastasi, A. (1976) *Psychological Testing*. 4th Edition. New York: Macmillan.

Angelergues, R. (1969) Memory disorders in neurological disease. In *Handbook of Clinical Neurology*, eds. Vinken, P.J. & Bruyun, G.W. Vol. 3, Ch. 16. Amsterdam: New-Holland.

Appelbaum, S.A. (1960) Automatic and selective processes in the word associations of brain-damaged and normal subjects. *Journal of Personality*, **28**, 64-72.

Arnot, R.E. (1949) Clinical indications for prefrontal lobotomy. *Journal of Nervous and Mental Disease*, **109**, 267-269.

Arrigoni, G. & De Renzi, E. (1964) Constructional apraxia and hemispheric locus of lesion. *Cortex*, **1**, 170-197.

Assal, G. (1974) Troubles de la reception auditive du langage lors de lesions du cortex cerebral. *Neuropsychologia*, **12**, 399-401.

Austin, G.M. & Grant, F.C. (1955) Observations following total hemispherectomy]n man. *Surgery*, **38**, 239.

Babcock, H. (1930) An experiment in the measurement of mental deterioration. *Archives of Psychology*, **117**, 105.

Babinski, J. (1914) Contribution a l'étude des troubles mentaux dans l'hémiplégié organique cérébrale. *Revue Neurologique*. **1**, 845-848.

Bachrach, H. & Mintz, J. (1974) The Wechsler Memory Scale as a tool for the detection of mild cerebral dysfunction. *Journal of Clinical Psychology*, **30**, 58-60.

Baddeley, A.D. & Warrington, E.K. (1970) Amnesia and the distinction between long- and short-term memory. *Journal of Verbal Learning and Verbal Behaviour*, **9**, 176-189.

Baddeley, A.D. & Warrington, E.K. (1973) Memory coding and amnesia. *Neuropsychologia*, **11**, 159-165.

Baer, D.J. (1964) Factors in perception and rigidity. *Perceptual and Motor Skills*, **19**, 563-570.

Baldwin, M. (1956) Modifications psychiques survenant apres lobectomie temporal subtotale. *Neurochirurgie*, **2**, 152-167.

Balthazar, E.E. & Morrison, D.H. (1961) The use of Wechsler Intelligence Scales as diagnostic indicators of predominantly left-right and indeterminate unilateral brain damage. *Journal of Clinical Psychology*, **17**, 161-165.

Barbizet, J. (1970) *Human Memory and its Pathology*. San Francisco: Freeman.

Barbizet, J. Devic, J.M. & Duizabo, P. (1967) Etude d'un cas d' encéphalite amnesiante d'origine hérpetique. *Société medicale des hopitaux de Paris*, **118**, 1123-1132.

Barron, F. (1953) An ego strength scale which predicts response to therapy. *Journal of Consulting Psychology*, **17**, 327-333.

Basso, A., De Renzi, E., Faglioni, P. Scotti, G. & Spinnler, H. (1973) Neuropsychological evidence for the existence of cerebral areas critical to the performance of intelligence tasks. *Brain*, **96**, 715-728.

Battersby, W.S. (1951) The regional gradient of critical flicker frequency after frontal or occipital injury. *Journal of Experimental Psychology*, **42**, 59-68.

Battersby, W.S. (1956) Neuropsychology of higher processes: cerebral damage and visual perception. In *Progress in Clinical Psychology*. New York: Grune & Stratton.

Battersby, W.S., Bender, M.B. Pollack, M. & Kahn, R.L. (1956) Unilateral "spatial agnosia" ("inattention") in patients with cerebral lesions. *Brain*, **79**, 68-93.

Battersby, W.S. Krieger, H.P. & Bender, M.B. (1955) Visual and tactile discriminative learning in patients with cerebral tumours. *American Journal of Psychiatry*, **68**, 562-574.

Battersby, W.S., Krieger, H.P., Pollack, M. & Bender, M.B. (1953) Figure ground discrimination and the abstract attitude in patients with cerebral tumours. *Archives of Neurology and Psychiatry*, **70**, 703-712.

Battersby, W.S. Teuber, H.L. & Bender, M.B. (1953) Problem solving behaviour in men with frontal or occipital brain injuries. *Journal of Psychology*, **35**, 329-351.

Bauer, R. & Beck, D. (1954) Intellect after cerebro-vascular accident. *Journal of Nervous and Mental Disease*, **120**, 379-384.

Bay, E. (1953) Disturbances of visual perception and their examination. *Blain*, **76**, 515-550.

Beck, E. & Corsellis, J.A. (1963) Das Fornixsystem des Menschen im Lichte anatomischer und pathologischer Untersuchungen. *Zentralblatt fur die gesamte Neurologie und Psychiatrie*, **173**, 220-221.

Beckner, M. (1959) *The Biological Way of Thought*. New York: University Press.

Belmont, L. & Birch, H. (1960) The relation of time of life to behavioural consequences in brain damage: 1. The performance of brain-injured adults on the marble board test. *Journal of Nervous and Mental Disease*, **131**, 91-97.

Belmont, I., Karp, E. & Birch, H.G. (1971) Hemispheric incoordination in hemiplegia. *Brain*, **94**, 337-348.

Bender, M.B. (1952) *Disorders in Perception*. Springfield, Illinois: Thomas.

Bender, M.B. & Diamond, S.P. (1970) Disorders in perception of space due to lesions of the nervous system. *Research Publication, Association for Research in Nervous and Mental Disease*, **48**, 176-185.

Bender, M.B. & Feldman, M. (1965) The so-called "visual agnosias". *Proceedings 8th International Congress of Neurology (Vienna)*, **3**, 153-156.

Bender, M.B. & Kanzer, M.M. (1941) Dynamics of homonymous hemianopsias and preservation of central vision. *Archives of Neurology and Psychiatry*, **45**, 481-485.

Bender, M.B. & Teuber, H.L. (1947) Spatial organization of visual perception following injury to the brain. *Archives of Neurology and Psychiatry*, **58**, 721-739.

Bender, M.B. & Teuber, H.L. (1948) Spatial organization of visual perception following injury to the brain. *Archives of Neurology and Psychiatry*, **59**, 39-62.

Benson, D.F. & Barton, M.I. (1970) Disturbances in constructional ability. *Cortex*, **6**, 19-46.

Benson, D.F., Marsden, C.D. & Meadows, J.C. (1974) The amnesic syndrome of posterior cerebral artery occlusion. *Acta Neurologica Scandanavica*, **50**, 133-145.

Benson, D.G. Segarra, J. & Albert, M.L.,(1974) Visual agnosia—prosopagnosia. *Archives of Neurology*, **30**, 307-310.

Benton, A.L. (1950) A multiple choice type of the Visual Retention Test. *Archives of Neurology and Psychiatry*, **64**, 699-707.

Benton, A.L. (1955) *The Visual Retention Test*. New York: The Psychological Corporation.

Benton, A.L. (1959) *Right-left Discrimination and Finger Localization*. New York: Hoeber.

Benton, A.L. (1961) The fiction of the "Gerstmann syndrome". *Journal of Neurology, Neurosurgery, and Psychiatry*, **24**, 176-181.

Benton, A.L. (1962) The visual retention test as a constructional praxis task. *Confinia Neurologica*, **22**, 141-155.

Benton, A.L. (1965) The problem of cerebral dominance. *Canadian Psychologist*, **6**, 332-348.

Benton, A.L. (1967a) Constructional apraxia and the minor hemisphere. *Confinia Neurologica*, **29**, 1-16.

Benton, A.L. (1967b) Problems of test construction in the field of aphasia. *Cortex*, **3**, 32-58.

Benton, A.L. (1967c) Psychological tests for brain damage. In *Comprehensive Textbook of Psychiatry*, eds. Freedman, A.M. & Kaplan, H.I. Baltimore: Williams and Wilkins.

Benton, A.L. (1968) Differential behavioral effects of frontal lobe disease. *Neuropsychologia*, **6**, 53-60.

Benton, A.L. (1969a) Constructional apraxia; some unanswered questions. In *Contributions to Clinical Neuropsychology*, ed. Benton, A.L. Ch. 5. Chicago: Aldine.

Benton, A.L. (1969b) ed. *Contributions to Clinical Neuropsychology*. Chicago: Aldine.

Benton, A.L. (1969c) Disorders of spatial orientation. In *Handbook of Clinical Neurology*, eds. Vinken, P.J. & Bruyn, G.W. Vol. 3, Ch. 12. Amsterdam: North Holland.

Benton, A.L. (1972) The 'minor' hemisphere. *Journal of the History of Medicine and Allied Sciences*, **27**, 5-14.

Benton, A.L. (July, 1975) In editorial—On cerebral localization and dominance. *Bulletin of the International Neuropsychology Society*.

Benton, A., Elithorn, A., Fogel, M. & Kerr, M. (1963) A perceptual maze test sensitive to brain damage. *Journal of Neurology, Neurosurgery, and Psychiatry*, **26**, 540-544.

Benton, A.L. & Fogel, M.L. (1962) Three dimensional constructional praxis. *Archives of Neurology*, **7**, 347-354.

Benton, A.L. & Hécaen, H. (1970) Stereoscopic vision in patients with uniiateral cerebral disease. *Neurology*, **20**, 1084-1088.

Benton, A.L. & Joynt, R.J. (1959) Reaction time in unilateral cerebral disease. *Confinia Neurologica*, **19**, 247-256.

Benton, A.L., Levin, H.S. & Van Allen, M.W. (1974) Geographic orientation in patients with unilateral cerebral disease. *Neuropsychologia*, **12**, 183-191.

Benton, A.L. & Van Allen, M.W. (1968) Impairment in facial recognition in patients with cerebral disease. *Cortex*, **4**, 344-358.

Benton, A.L. & Van Allen, M.W. (1972a) Aspects of neuropsychological assessment in patients with cerebral disease. In *Aging and the Brain*, ed. Gaitz, C.M. New York: Plenum.

Benton, A.L. & Van Allen, M.W. (1972b) Prosopagnosia and facial discrimination. *Journal of Neurological Science*, **15**, 167-172.

Benton, A.L. Van Allen, M.W. & Fogel, M.L. (1964) Temporal orientation in cerebral disease. *Journal of Nervous and Mental Disease*, **139**, 110-119.

Ben-Yishay, Y., Diller, L., Mandelberg, I., Gordon, W. & Gerstman, L.J. (1971) Similarities and differences in Block Design performance between older normal and brain-injured persons: A task analysis. *Journal of Abnormal Psychology*, **78**, 17-25.

Bergman, P.S. (1957) Cerebral blindness. *Archives of Neurology and Psychiatry*, **78**, 568-584.

Berlin, C.I., Lowe-Bell, S.S., Jannetta, P.J. & Kline, D.G. (1972) Central auditory deficits after temporal lobectomy. *Archives of Otolarngology*, **96**, 4-10.

Beyn, E.S. & Knyazeva, G.R. (1962) The problem of prosopagnosia. *Journal of Neurology, Neurosurgery and Psychiatry*, **25**, 154-158.

Bickford, R.G., Mulder, D.W. Dodge, H.W. Svien, H.J. & Rome, H.P. (1958) Changes in memory function produced by electrical stimulation of the temporal lobe in man. *Research Publications, Association for Research in Nervous and Mental Disease*, **36**, 227-243.

Birch, W. (1975) Assessment of the presence and laterality of brain damage in adults. Unpublished Master's thesis, University of Melbourne, Australia.

Birch, H.G., Belmont, I. & Karp, E. (1964) The relation of single stimulus threshold to extinction in double simultaneous stimulation. *Cortex*, **1**, 19-39.

Birch, H.G. Belmont, I. & Karp, E. (1965b) The prolongation of inhibition in brain damaged patients. *Cortex*, **1**, 397-409.

Birch, H.G., Belmont, I. & Karp, E. (1967) Delayed processing and extinction following cerebral damage. *Brain*, **90**, 113-130.

Birkmayer, W. (1951) *Hirnverletzungen Mechanismus, Spaetkomplikationen Funktions Wandel.* Vienna: Springer.

Black, F.W. (1974) Cogitive effects of unilateral brain lesions secondary to penetrating missile wounds. *Perceptual and Motor Skills*, **38**, 387-391.

Black, F.W. (1976) Cognitive deficits in patients with unilateral war-related frontal lobe lesions. *Journal of Clinical Psychology*, **32**, 366-372.

Blakemore, C.B. (1969) Psychological effects of temporal lobe lesions in man. In Current Problems in Neuropsychiatry: schizophrenia, epilepsy, the temporal lobe, ed. Herrington, R.N. *British Journal of Psychiatry*, Special Publication No. 4, Ch. 10, 60-69.

Blakemore, C.B., Ettlinger, G.& Falconer, M.A.(1966)Cognitive abilities in relation to frequency of seizures and neuropathology of the temporal lobes in man. *Journal of Neurology, Neurosurgery and Psychiatry*, **29**, 268-272.

Blakemore, C.B. & Falconer, M.A. (1967) Long-term effects of anterior temporal lobectomy on certain cognitive functions. *Journal of Neurology, Neurosurgery, and Psychiatry*, **30**. 364-367.

Blum, J.S., Chow, K.L. & Pribram, K.H. (1950) A behavioural analysis of the organization of the parieto- temporo-preoccipital cortex. *Journal of Comparative Neurology*, **93**, 53-100.

Blume, W.T., Grabow, J.D., Darley, F.L. & Aranson, A.E. (1973) Intracarotid amobarbital test of language and memory before temporal lobectomy for seizure control. *Neurology*, **23**, 812-819.

Bodamer, J. (1947) Die prosop-Agnosie. *Archiv Fuer Psychiatrie und Nervenkrankheiten Vereinigt Mit Zietschrift Fuer Die Gesamte Neurologie und Psychiatrie*, **179**, 6-53.

Bogen, J.E. (1969a) The other side of the brain I: Dysgraphia and dyscopia following cerebral commissurotomy. *Bulletin of the Los Angeles Neurological Societies*, **34**, 73-105.

Bogen, J.E. (1969b) The other side of the brain II: An appositional mind. *Bulletin of the Los Angeles Neurological Societies*, **34**, 135-162.

Bogen, J.E.(1969c) The other side of the brain III: The corpus callosum and creativity. *Bulletin of the Los Angeles Neurological Societies*, **34**, 191-220.

Bogen, J.E. & Gazzaniga, M.S. (1965) Cerebral commisurotomy in man: minor hemisphere dominance for certain visuospatial functions. *Journal of Neurosurgery*, **23**, 394-399.

Bogen, J.E. & Gorden, H.W.(1971) Musical test for functional lateralization with intracarotid amobarbital. *Nature*, **230**, 524-525.

Boller, F. (1968) Latent aphasia: Right and left "non aphasic" brain-damaged patients compared. *Cortex*, **4**, 245-256.

Boller, F. & De Renzi, E. (1967) Relationship between visual memory defects and hemispheric locus of lesion. *Neurology*, **17**, 1052-1058.

Boller, R. & Vignolo, L.A. (1966) Latent sensory aphasia in hemisphere-damaged patients: An experimental study with the Token Test. *Brain*, **89**, 815-830.

Bond, M.R. (1975) Assessment of the psychosocial outcome after severe head injury. Ciba Foundation Symposium 34 (new series) pp.141-157. Amsterdam: Elsevier.

Bonkowski, R.J. (1967) Verbal and extraverbal components of language as related to lateralized brain damage. *Journal of Speech and Hearing Research*, **10**, 558-564.

Boring, E.G. (1929) *A History of Experimental Psychology*. New York Appleton-Century-Crofts.

Borkowski, J.G., Benton, A.L. & Spreen, 0. (1967) Word fluency and brain damage. *Neuropsychologia*, **5**, 135-140.

Bornstein, B. (1965) Prosopagnosia. *Proceedings of the 8th International Congress of Neurology (Vienna)*, **3**, 157-160.

Bornstein, B. (1963) Prosopagnosia. In *Problems of Dynamic Neurology*, ed. Halpern, L. Jerusalem: Hadassah Medical Organization.

Bornstein, B. & Kidron, D.P. (1959) Prosopagnosia. *Journal of Neurology, Neurosurgery, and Psychaitry*, **22**, 124-131.

Boudin, G., Barbizet, J., Derouesné, C. & Van Amerogen, P. (1967) Cécité corticale et probléme des "amnesies occipitales". *Revue Neurologique*, **116**, 89-97.

Boudin, G., Brion, S., Pepin, B. & Barbizet, J. (1968) Syndrome de Korsakoff d'etiologie arteriopathique. *Revue Neurologique*, **119**, 341-348.

Bourne, L.E. (1966) *Human Conceptual Behaviour*. Boston: Allyn & Bacon.

Bowman, K.M. & Engle, B. (1960) Review of psychiatric progress: geriatrics. *American Journal of Psychiatry*, **116**, 629-630.

Bowsher, D. (1970) *Introduction to the Anatomy and Physiology of the Nervous System*. Second Edition. Oxford: Blackwell.

Boyle, G. (1975) Shortened Halstead Category Test. *Australian Psychologist*, **10**, 81-84.

Bradley, K.C., Dax, E.C. & Walsh, K.W. (Frebruary 1, 1958) Modified leucotomy: Report of 100 cases. *Medical Journal of Australia*, 133-138.

Brain, R. (1941) Visual disorientation with special reference to lesions of the right hemisphere. *Brain*, **64**, 244-272.

Brain, Lord & Walton, J.W. (1969) *Brain's Diseases of the Nervous System*. Seventh Edition. London: Oxford University Press.

Brain, W.R. (1945) Speech and handedness. *Lancet*, **2**. 837-842.

Branch, C., Milner, B. & Rasmussen, T. (1964) Intracarotid sodium amytal for the lateralization of cerebral speech dominance. *Journal of Neurosurgery*, **21**, 399-405.

Brazier, M.A.B. (1968) *The Electrical Activity of the Nervous System*. Third Edition. London: Pitman Medical Publishing Co.

Breasted, J.H. (1930) *The Edwin Smith Surgical Papyrus*. Chicago: University of Chicago Press.

Breschi, F., D'angelo, A. & Pluchino, F. (1970) Résultat a distance de l'hémispherectomie dans 13 cas d'hemiatrophie cérébrale infantile épiliptogene. *Neurochirugie*, **16**, 397-411.

Brewer, W.F. (1969) Visual memory, verbal encoding and hemispheric localization. *Cortex*, **5**, 145-151.

Brierley, J. (1966) The neuropathology of amnesic states. In *Amnesia*, eds. Whitty, C.W.M. & Zangwill, 0. London: Butterworths.

Brion, S. & Jedynak, C.P. (1972) troubles du transfert interhemispherique. Le signe de la main étrangère. *Revue Neurologique*, **126**, 257-266.

Brodmann, K. (1909) *Vergleichende Lokalisationslehre der Grosshirnrinde*. Leipzig: Barth.

Brooks, N. (1972) Memory and head injury. *Journal of Nervous and Mental Disease*, **155**, 350-355.

Brown, J.W. (1975a) On the neural organization of language: cortical and thalamic relationships. *Brain and Langauge*, **2**, 18-30.

Brown, J.W. (1975b) The problem of repetition: A study of "conduction" aphasia and the "isolation" syndrome. *Cortex*, **11**, 37-52.

Bruell, J.H. & Albee, G.W. (1962) Higher intellectual functions in a patient with hemispherectomy for tumours. *Journal of Consulting Psychology*, **26**, 90-98.

Bryan, E. & Brown, M.A. (1957) A method for differential diagnosis of brain damage in adolescents. *Journal of Nervous and Mental Disease*, **125**, 69-72.

Bryden, M.P. (1965) Tachistoscopic recognition, handedness, and cerebral dominance. *Neuropsychologia*, **3**. 1-8.

Bryden, M.P. (1973) Perceptual asymmetry in vision: relation to handedness, eyedness, and speech lateralization. *Cortex*, **9**, 419-435.

Bryden, M.P. & Rainey, C.A. (1963) Left-right differences in tachistoscopic recognition. *Journal of Experimental Psychology*, **66**, 568-571.

Bryden, M.P. & Zurif, E.B. (1970) Dichotic listening performance in a case of agenesis of the corpus callosum. *Neuropsychologia*, **8**, 371-377.

Buss, A.H. (1952) Some determinants of rigidity in discrimination reversal learning. *Journal of Experimental Psychology*, **44**, 222-227.

Butler, S.R. & Norrsell, W. (1968) Vocalization possibly initiated by the minor hemisphere. *Nature*, **220**, 793-794.

Butters, N. & Barton, M. (1970) Effect of parietal lobe damage on the performance of reversible operations in space. *Neuropsychologia*, **8**, 205-214.

Butters, N., Barton, M. & Brody, B.A. (1970) Role of the right parietal lobe in the mediation of cross-modal associations and reversible operations in space. *Cortex*, **6**, 174-190.

Butters, N. & Brody, B.A. (1968) The role of the left parietal lobe in the mediation of intra- and cross-modal associations. *Cortex*, **4**, 328-343.

Butters, N. & Cermak, L.S. (1974) Some comments on Warrington and Baddeley's report of normal short-term memory in amnesic patients. *Neuropsychologia*, **12**, 283-285.

Butters, N., Lewis, R., Cermak, L.S. & Goodglass, H. (1973) Material-specific memory deficits in alcoholic Korsakoff patients. *Neuropsychologia*, **11**, 291-299.

Butters, N., Samuels, I., Goodglass, H. & Brody, B. (1970a) Short-term visual auditory memory disorders after parietal and frontal lobe damage. *Cortex*, **6**, 440-459.

Butters, N., Samuels, I., Goodglass, H. & Brody, B. (1970b) Short-term visual memory and learning deficits in brain damaged patients. *Procedings of the 78th Annual Convention of the American Psychological Association*, **5**, 227-228.

Butters, N. Soeldner. C. & Fedio, P. (1972) Comparison of parietal and frontal lobe spatial deficits in man: extra-personal vs personal (egocentric) space. *Perceptual and Motor Skills*, **34**, 27-34.

Cairns, H. & Davidson, M.A. (1951) Hemispherectomy in the treatment of infantile himiplegia. *Lancet*, **ii**, 411-415.

Caplan, D., Holmes, J.M. & Marshall, V.C. (1974) Word classes and hemispheric specialization. *Neuropsychologia*, 331-337.

Caplan, D. & Marshall, J.C. (1975) Generative grammar and aphasic disorders: A theory of language representation in the human brain. *Foundations of Language*, **12**, 583-596.

Carmichael, A.E. (1966) The current status of hemispherectomy for infantile hemiplegia. *Clinical Proceedings of the Children's Hospital D.C.*, **22**, 285-293.

Carmon, A. & Nachson, I.(1971) Effect of unilateral brain damage on perception of temporal order *Cortex*, **7**, 410-418.

Carmon, A.(1971) Sequenced motor performance in patients with unilateral cerebral lesions. *Neuropsychologia*, **9**, 445-449.

Carmon, A. & Bechtoldt, H.P. (1969) Dominance of the right cerebral hemisphere for stereopsis. *Neuropsychologia*, **7**, 29-39.

Carpenter, M.B. (1972) *Core Text of Neuroanatomy*. Baltimore: The Williams and Wilkins Company.

Cattell, R.B. (1944) *A Culture-free Test*. New York: The Psychological Corporation.

Cattell, R.B., Dubin, S.S. & Saunders, D.K.(1954) Verification of hypothesized factors in one hundred and fifteen objective personality tests. *Psychometrika*, **19**, 209-230.

Cattell, R.B. & Tiner, L.B. (1949) The varieties of structural rigidity. *Journal of Personality*, **17**, 321-341.

Cermak, L.S. & Butters, N. (1972) The role of interference and encoding in the short-term memory deficits of Korsakoff patients. *Neuropsychologia*, **10**, 89-95.

Cermak, L.C., Butters, N. & Gerrein, J. (1973) The extent of verbal encoding ability of Korsakoff patients. *Neuropsychologia*, **11**, 85-94.

Cermak, L.S., Butters, N. & Goodglass, H. (1971) The extent of memory loss in Korsakoff patients. *Neuropsychologia*, **9**, 307-315.

Chapman, L.F. & Wolff, H.F. (1959) The cerebral hemispheres and the highest integrative functions of man. *Archives of Neurology*, **1**, 357-424.

Chédru, F., Leblanc, M. & Lhermitte, F. (1973) Visual searching in normal and brain-damaged subjects (contribution to the study of unilateral inattention). *Cortex*, **9**, 94-111.

Cherlow, D.G. & Serafetinides, E.A. (1976) Speech and memory assessment in psychomotor epileptics. *Cortex*, **12**, 21-26.

Chesher, E.D. (1936) Some observations concerning the relation of handedness to the language mechanism. *Bulletin of the Neurological Institute of New York*, **4**, 556-562.

Chown, S.H. (1959) Rigidity—a flexible concept. *Psychological Bulletin*, **56**, 195-223.

Christensen, A.L. (1975) *Luria's Neuropsychological Investigation*. Copenhagen: Munksgaard.

Clarke, E. & Dewhurst, K. (1972) *An Illustrated History of Brain Function*. Oxford: Sandford.

Clarke, E. & O'Malley, C.D. (1968) *The Human Brain and Spinal Cord*. Berkeley: University of California Press.

Cogan, D.G. (1960) Hemianopia and associated symptoms due to parieto-temporal lobe lesions. *American Journal of Ophthalmology*, **50**, 1056-1066.

Cogan, D.G. (1966) *Neurology of the Visual System*. Springfield, Illinois: Thomas.

Cohen, J. (1950) Wechsler Memory Scale performances of psychoneurotic, organic and schizophrenic groups. *Journal of Consulting Psychology*, **14**, 371-375.

Cohen, J. (1952) A factor analytically based rationale for the Wechsler-Bellevue. *Journal of Consulting Psychology*, **16**, 272-277.

Cohen, L. (1959) Perception of reversible figures after brain injury. *Archives of Neurology and Psychiatry*, **81**, 765-775.

Cohen, R.S. & Wartofsky, M.W. (eds.) (1974) *Boston Studies in the Philosophy of Science*, Vol. XVI. Norman Geschwind. Selected Papers on Language and the Brain. Dordrecht, Holland: Reidel.

Conrad, K. (1949) Ueber aphasische Sprachstochungen bei hirnverletzten Linkshaendeia. *Nervenarzt*, **20**, 148-154.

Corkin, S.H. (1964) Somesthetic function after cerebral damage in man. Unpublished doctoral thesis, McGill University.

Corkin, S. (1965) Tactually-guided image learning in man: Effect of unilateral cortical excisions and bilateral hippocampal lesions. *Neuropsychologia*, **3**, 339-351.

Corkin, S. (1968) Acquisition of motor skill after bilateral medial temporal-lobe excision. *Neuropsychologia*, **6**, 255.

Corkin, S., Milner, B. & Rasmussen, T. (1964) Effects of different cortical excisions on sensory thresholds in man. *Transactions of the American Neurological Association*, **89**, 112-116.

Corsellis, J.A.N. (1970) The limbic areas in Alzheimer's disease and in other conditions associated with dementia. In *Alzheimer's Disease and Related Conditions*, eds. Wolstenholme, G.E.W. & O'Connor, M. London: Chruchill.

Corsellis, J.A.N. (1975) The pathology of dementia. *British Journal of Psychiatry*, Special Publication No. 9, 110-118.

Costa, L. & Vaughan, H. (1962) Performance of patients with lateralized cerebral lesions I: Verbal and perceptual tests. *Journal of Nervous and Mental Disease*, **134**, 162-168.

Costa, L.D., Vaughan, G. Jr., Horwitz, M. & Ritter, W. (1969) Patterns of behavioral deficit associated with visual spatial neglect. *Cortex*, **5**, 242-263.

Courville, C.B. (1942) Coup-contrecoup mechanism of cranio-cerebral injuries: Some observations. *Archives of Surgery*, **55**, 19-43.

Courville, C.B. (1945) *Pathology of the Nervous System*. Second Edition. Mountain View, California: Pacific Press.

Critchley, M. (1949) The phenomenon of tactile inattention with special reference to parietal lesions. *Brain*, **72**, 538-561.

Critchley, M. (1953) *The Patietal Lobes*. London: Arnold.

Critchley, M. (1964) The problem of visual agnosia. *Journal of Neurological Science (Amst.)*, **1**, 274-290.

Critchley, M. (1965) Acquired anomalies of colour. *Brain*, **88**, 711-724.

Critchley, M. (1966) The enigma of Gerstmann's syndrome. *Brain*, **89**, 183-198.

Critchley, M. (1972) Communication: Recognition of its minimal impairment. In *Scientific Foundations of Neurology*, eds. Critchley, M., O'Leary, J.L. & Jennett, B. Ch. 8. London: Heinemann.

Crockett, H.G. & Estridge, N.M. (1951) Cerebral Hemispherectomy. *Bulletin of the Los Angeles Neurological Society*, **16**, 71-87.

Crown, S. (1952) An experimental study of psychological changes following prefrontal lobotomy. *Journal of General Psychology*, **47**, 3-41.

Cumming, W.J.K., Hurwitz, L.J. & Perl, N. (1969) A study of a patient who had alexia without agraphia. *Journal of Neurology, Neurosurgery and Psychiatry*, **33**, 34-39.

Curry, F.K.W. (1967) A comparison of left-handed and right-handed subjects on verbal and non-verbal dichotic listening tasks. *Cortex*, **3**, 343-352.

Curry, F.K.W. (1968) A comparison of the performance of a right hemispherectomised subject and twenty-four normals on four dichotic listening tasks. *Cortex*, **4**, 144-153.

Damasio, A.R., Lima, A. & Damasio, H. (1975) Nervous function after right hemispherectomy. *Neurology*, **25**, 89-93.

Dana, C.L. (1915) *Textbook of Nervous Diseases*. Eighth Edition. New York: Wood.

Dandy, W.E. (1928) Removal of right cerebral hemisphere for certain tumours with hemiplegia. *J.A.M.A.*, **90**, 823-825.

Dandy. W.E. (1933) Physiological studies following extirpation of the right cerebral hemisphere in man. *Johns Hopkins Hospital Bulletin,* 53, 31-51.

Darwin, C.J. (1971) Ear difference in the recall of fricatives or vowels. *Quarterly Journal of Experimental Psychology,* 23, 46-62.

Davson, H. (1967) *Pysiology of the Cerebrospinal Fluid.* Boston: Little, Brown & Company.

Dee, H.L. (1970) Visuoconstructive and visuoperceptive deficit in patients with unilateral cerebral lesions. *Neuropsychologia,* 8, 305-314.

Dee, H.L. & Fontenot, D.J. (1973) Cerebral dominance and lateral differences in perception and memory. *Neuropsychologia,* 11, 167-173.

De Jong, R.N. (1973) The neurologic aspects of dementia. *Transactions of the American Neurological Association,* 98, 109-113.

De Jong, R.N., Itabashi, H.H. & Olson, J.R. (1968) "Pure" memory loss with hippocampal lesions: a case report. *Transactions of the American Neurological Association,* 93, 31-34.

De Jong, R.N., Itabashi, H.H. & Olson, J.R. (1969) Memory loss due to hippocampal lesions. Report of a case. *Archives of Neurology,* 20, 399-348.

Delay, J. (1942) *Les Dissolutions de la Memoire.* Paris: Presses Universitaires de France.

Denny-Brown, D. & Chambers, R.A. (1958) The parietal lobe and behaviour. *Research Publications Association for Research in Nervous and Mental Disease,* 36, 35-117.

Denny-Brown, D., Meyer, J.S. & Horenstein, S. (1952) The significance of perceptual rivalry resulting from parietal lesions. *Brain,* 75, 433-471.

De Renzi, E. & Faglioni, P. (1962) Il disorientamento spaziale da lesione cerebrale. *Sistema Nervoso,* 14, 409-436.

De Renzi, E. & Faglioni, P. (1965) The comparative efficiency of intelligence and vigilance tests in detecting hemispheric cerebral damage. *Cortex,* 1, 410-433.

De Renzi, E. & Faglioni, P. (1967) The relationship between visuo-spatial impairment and constructional apraxia. *Cortex,* 3, 327-342.

De Renzi, E., Faglioni, P., Savoiardo, M. & Vignolo, L.A. (1966) The influence of aphasia and of hemispheric side of the cerebral lesion on abstract thinking. *Cortex,* 2, 399-420.

De Renzi, E., Faglioni, P. & Scotti, G. (1969) Impairment of memory for position following brain damage. *Cortex,* 5, 274-284.

De Renzi, E., Faglioni, P. & Scotti, G. (1970) Hemispheric contribution to exploration of space through the visual and tactile modality. *Cortex,* 6, 191-203.

De Renzi, E., Faglioni, P. & Scotti, G. (1971) Judgment of spatial orientation in patients with focal brain damage. *Journal of Neurology, Neurosurgery and Psychiatry,* 34, 489-495.

De Renzi, E., Faglioni, P., Scotti, G. & Spinnler, H. (1972a) Impairment in associating colour to form, concomitant with aphasia. *Brain,* 95, 293-304.

De Renzi, E., Faglioni, P., Scotti, G. & Spinnler, H. (1972b) Impairment of color sorting behavior after hemispheric damage: an experimental study with the Holmgren Skein Test. *Cortex,* 8, 147-163.

De Renzi, E., Faglioni, P. & Spinnler, H. (1968) The performance of patients with unilateral brain damage on face recognition tasks. *Cortex,* 4, 17-34.

De Renzi, E. & Scotti, G. (1969) The influence of spatial disorders in impairing tactile recognition of shapes. *Cortex,* 5, 53-62.

De Renzi, E., Scotti, G. & Spinnler, H. (1969) Perceptual and associative disorders of visual recognition. *Neurology,* 19, 634-642.

De Renzi, E. & Spinnler, H. (1966a) The influence of verbal and non-verbal defects on visual memory tasks. *Cortex,* 2, 322-335.

De Renzi, E. & Spinnler, H. (1966b) Facial recognition in brain-damaged patients. *Neurology,* 16, 145-152.

De Renzi, E. & Spinnler, H. (1967) Impaired performance on color tasks in patients with hemispheric damage. *Cortex,* 3, 194-217.

De Renzi, E. & Vignolo, L.A. (1962) The Token Test; a sensitive test to detect receptive disturbances in aphasics. *Brain,* 85, 665-678.

De Renzi, E. & Vignolo, L.A. (1966) Abstract thinking in brain-damaged patients. *Cortex,* 2, 399-420.

De Romanis, F. & Benfatto, B. (1973) Presentazione e discussione di quattro casi di prosopagnosia. *Rivista di Neurologia,* 43, 111-132.

Derouesné, C. (1973) Le syndrome "pré-moteur". *Revue Neurologique,* 128, 353-363.

Dew, H.R. (1922) Tumours of the brain: their pathology and treatment: an analysis of 85 cases. *Medical Journal of Australia,* 1, 515-521.

Dimond, S.J. (1972) *The Double Brain.* London: Churchill Livingstone.

Dimond, S.J. & Beaumont, J.G. (eds.) (1974) *Hemisphere Function in the Human Brain*. London: Elek Science.

Dimsdale, H., Logue, V. & Piercy, M. (1964) A case of persisting impairment of recent memory following right temporal lobectomy. *Neuropsychologia*, **1**, 287-298.

Doehring, D.G. & Bartholomeus, B.N. (1971) Laterality effects in voice recognition. *Neuropsychologia*, **9**, 425-430.

Donnelly, E.F., Dent, J.K., Murphy, D.L. & Mignone, R.J. (1972) Comparison of temporal lobe epileptics and affective disorders on the Halstead-Reitan test battery. *Journal of Clinical Psychology*, **28**, 61-62.

Dorff, J.E., Mirsky, A.F. & Mishkin, M. (1965) Effects of unilateral temporal lobe removals on tachistoscopic recognition in the left and right visual fields. *Neuropsychologia*, **3**, 39-51.

Drachman, D.A. & Arbit, J. (1966) Memory and the hippocampal complex. *Archives of Neurology*, **15**, 52-61.

Drewe, E.A. (1974) The effect of type and area of brain lesion on Wisconsin Card Sorting Test performance. *Cortex*, **10**, 159-170.

Drewe, E.A. (1975a) Go-No-Go learning after frontal lobe lesions in humans. *Cortex*, **11**, 8-16.

Drewe E.A. (1975b) An experimental investigation of Luria's theory on the effects of frontal lobe lesions in man. *Neuropsychologia*, **13**, 421-429.

Duensing, F. (1954) Zur Frage der optisch-raumlichen Agnosie. *Archiv fur Psychiatrie und Nervenkrankheiten*, **192**, 185-206.

Duke, R.B. (1967) Intellectual evaluation of brain-damaged patients with a WAIS short form. *Psychological Reports*, **20**, 858.

Durnford, M. & Kimura, D. (1971) Right hemisphere specialization for depth perception reflected in visual field differences. *Nature*, **231**, 394-395.

Efron, R.(1963) Temporal perception, aphasia, an déjà vu. *Brain*, **86**, 403-424.

Ehrenberg, R. & Gullingrud, M.J.O. (1955) Electroconvulsive therapy in elderly patients. *American Journal of Psychiatry*, **111**, 734-747.

Elithorn, A. (1955) A preliminary report on a perceptual maze test sensitive to brain damage. *Journal of Neurology, Neurosurgery and Psychiatry*, **18**, 287-292.

Elithorn, A.(1965) Psychological tests. An objective approach to the problem of task difficulty. *Acta Neurologia Scandinavica*, Supplementum 13, Part 2, 661-667.

Elithorn, A., Kerr, M. & Jones, D. (1963) A binary perceptual maze. *American Journal of Psychology*, **76**, 506-508.

Ettlinger, E.G. (ed.) (1965) *Functions of the Corpus Callosum*. London: Churchill.

Ettlinger, G., Blakemore, C.B., Milner, A.D. & Wilson, J. (1972) Agenesis of the corpus callosum: a behavioural investigation. *Brain*, **95**, 327-346.

Ettlinger, G., Blakemore, C.B., Milner, A.D. & Wilson, J. (1974) Agenesis of the corpus callosum: A further behavioural investigation. *Brain*, **97**, 225-234.

Ettlinger, G., Warrington, E. & Zangwill, O.L. (1957) A further study of visual-spatial agnosia. *Brain*, **80**, 335-361.

Evans, J.P. (1935) A study of the sensory defects resulting from excision of the cerebral substance in humans. *Research Publications, Association for Research in Nervous and Mental Disease*, **15**, 331-370.

Eysenck, H.J. & Halstead, H. (1945) The memory function, I. A factorial study of fifteen clinical tests. *American Journal of Psychiatry*, **102**, 174-179.

Fabbri, W. (1956) Leucotomia transorbitaria di Fiamberti e rispetto della personalita individuale nei rilievi psicometrici con il test di Porteus. *Note e Rivista di Psichiatria*, 311-332.

Faglioni, P., Scotti, G. & Spinnler, H. (1968) Impaired recognition of written letters following unilateral hemispheric damage. *Cortex*, **5**, 120-133.

Faglioni, P., Scotti, G. & Spinnler, H. (1970) Colouring drawings impairment following unilateral brain damage. *Brain Research*, **24**, 546.

Faglioni, P., Scotti, G. & Spinnler, H. (1971) The performance of brain-damaged patients in spatial localization of visual and tactile stimuli. *Brain*, **94**, 443-454.

Faglioni, P., Spinnler, H. & Vignolo, L.A. (1969) Contrasting behavior of right and left hemisphere damaged patients on a discriminative and a semantic task of auditory recognition. *Cortex*, **5**, 366-389.

Falconer, M.A. & Wilson, J.L. (1958) Visual changes following anterior temporal lobectomy: their significance in relation to "Meyer's loop" of the optic radiation. *Brain*, **81**, 1-14.

Feather, N.T. (1966) Effects of prior success and failure on expectations of success and subsequent performance. *Journal of Personality and Social Psychology*, **3**, 287-298.

Feindel, W. (1974) Temporal lobe seizures. In *Handbook of Clinical Neurology*, eds. Vinken, P.J. & Bruyn, G.W. Vol. 15, Ch. 5. Amsterdam: North-Holland.

Feuchtwanger, E. (1923) Die Funktionen des Stirnhirnes, ihre Pathologie und Psychologie. Berlin: Springer.

Field, J.G. (1960) Two types of tables for use with Wechsler's intelligence scales. *Journal of Clinical Psychology*, **16**, 3-7.

Fileds, F.R. (1971) Relative effects of brain damage on the Wechsler Memory and Intelligence Quotients. *Diseases of the Nervous System*, **32**, 673-675.

Fisher, G.M. (1960) A corrected table for determining the significance of the difference between verbal and performance IQ's on the WAIS and Wechsler-Bellevue. *Journal of Clinical Psychology*, **16**, 7-9.

Fisher, M. (1956) Left hemiplegia and motor impersistence. *Journal of Nervous and Mental Disease*, **123**, 201-218.

Fisher, S. (1949) An overview of trends in research dealing with personality rigidity. *Journal of Personality*, **17**, 342-351.

Fitzhugh, K.B. & Fitzhugh, L.C. (1964) WAIS results for subjects with longstanding chronic, lateralized and diffuse cerebral dysfunction. *Perceptual and Motor Skill*, **19**, 735-739.

Fitzhugh, K.B., Fitzhugh, L.C. & Reitan, R.M. (1961) Psychological deficits in relationship to acuteness of brain dysfunction. *Journal of Consulting Psychology*, **25**, 61-66.

Fitzhugh, K.B., Fitzhugh, L.C. & Reitan, R.M. (1962a) Wechsler-Bellevue comparisons in groups with "chronic" and "current" lateralized and diffuse brain lesions. *Journal of Consulting Psychology*, **26**, 306-310.

Fitzhugh, K.B., Fitzhugh, L.C. & Reitan, R.M. (1962b) Relation of acuteness of organic brain dysfunction to Trail Making Test performances. *Perceptual and Motor Skills*, **15**, 399-403.

Fitzhugh, K.B., Fitzhugh, L.C. & Reitan, R.M. (1963) Effects of "chronic" and "current" lateralized and non-lateralized cerebral lesions upon Trail Making Test performances. *Journal of Nervous and Mental Disease*, **137**, 82-87.

Fitzhugh, K.B., Fitzhugh, L.C. & Reitan, R.M. (1964) Influence of age upon measures of problem solving and experiential background in subjects with longstanding cerebral dysfunction. *Journal of Gerontology*, **19**, 132-134.

Fleming, G.W.T.H. (1942) Some preliminary remarks on prefrontal leucotomy. *Journal of Mental Science*, **88**, 282-284.

Fleminger, J.J., de Horne, D.J. & Nott, P.N. (1970) Unilateral electroconvulsive therapy and cerebral dominance: effect of right- and left-sided electrode placement on verbal memory. *Journal of Neurology, Neurosurgery, and Psychiatry*, **23**, 408-411.

Foerster, O. (1936) Cited in Gloning, Gloning and Hoff (1968) p.34.

Fogel, M.L. (1962) The Intelligence Quotient as an index of brain damage. *American Journal of Orthopsychiatry*, **32**, 338-339.

Fogel, M.L. (1964) The Intelligence Quotient as an index of brain damage. *American Journal of Orthopsychiatry*, **34**, 555-562.

Folstein, M.F., Folstein, S.E. & McHugh, P.R. (1975) "Mini-mental state" A practical method for grading the cognitive state of patients for the clinician. *Journal of Psychiatric Research*, **12**, 189-198.

Fontenot, D.J. & Benton, A.L. (1971) Tactile perception of direction in relation to hemispheric locus of lesion. *Neuropsychologia*, **9**, 83-88.

Ford, B. (1976) Head injuries—What happens to survivors. *Medical Journal of Australia*, **1**, 603-605.

Forgus, R.H. (1966) *Perception*. New York: McGraw-Hill.

Frederiks, J.A.M. (1969) Disorders of the Body Schema. In *Handbook of Clinical Neurology*, eds. Vinken, P.J. & Bruyn, G.W. Vol. 4, Ch. 11. Amsterdam: North-Holland.

Freeman, W. (1953a) Level of achievement after lobotomy: a study of 1000 cases. *American Journal of Psychiatry*, **110**, 269-276.

Freeman, W. (1953b) Hazards of lobotomy: report on 2000 operations. A.M.A. *Archives of Neurology and Psychiatry*, Chicago, **69**, 640-643.

Freeman, W. & Watts, J.W. (1942) *Psychocurgery*. Springfield, Illinois: Thomas.

Freeman, W., & Watts, J.W. (1948) The thalamic projection to the frontal lobe. *Research Publications, Association for Research in Nervous and Mental Disease*, **27**, 200-209.

Freeman, W. & Watts, J.W. (1950) *Psychosurgery*. Second Edition. Springfield, Illinois: Thomas.

French, L.A., Johnson, D.R. & Adkins, G.A. (1966) Cerebral hemispherectomy for intractable seizures. A long-term follow-up. *The Journal—Lancet*, **81**, 58-65.

Freud, S. (1953) *Zur Auffassung der Aphasien* 1891). New York: International Universities Press Inc.

Fryer, D.G. & Rich, M.P. (1960) Denial of illness in relation to intellectual functions. *Journal of Nervous and Mental Disease*, **131**, 523-527.

Fuchs, W. (1938) Pseudo-fovea. In *A Source Book of Gestalt Psychology*, ed. Ellis, W.D. London: Kegan Paul.

Fuller, G.B. & Laird, J.J. (1963) The Minnesota Percepto-Diagnostic Test. *Journal of Clinical Psychology*, **19**, 3-34.

Fuller, G.B. (1967) *Revised Minnesota Percepto-Diagnostic Test.* New York: Psychological Corporation.

Gaffan, D. (1972) Loss of recognition memory in rats with lesions of the fornix. *Neuropsychologia* **10**, 327-341.

Gainotti, G. (1972) Emotional behaviour and hemispheric side of lesion. *Cortex*, **8**, 41-55.

Gainotti, G., Messerli, P. & Tissot, R.(1972a) Troubles du dessin et lésions hémisphériques rétrorolandiques unilatérales gauches et droites. *Encephale*, **61**, 245-264.

Gainotti, G., Messerli, P. & Tissot, R. (1972b) Qualitative analysis of unilateral spatial neglect in relation to laterality of cerebral lesions. *Journal of Neurology, Neurosurgery and Psychiatry*, **35**, 545-550.

Gainotti, G. & Tiacci, C. (1970) Patterns of drawing disability in right and left hemispheric patients. *Neuropsychologia*, **8**, 379-384.

Gal, P. (1959) Mental disorders of advanced years. *Geriatrics*, **14**, 224.

Gallinek, A. (1948) The nature of affective and paranoid disorders during the senium in the light of electric convulsive therapy. *Journal of Nervous and Mental Disease*, **108**, 293-303.

Gardner, W.J., Karnosh, L.J., McClure, C.C. & Gardner, A.K. (1955) Residual function following hemispherectomy for tumour and for infantile hemiplegia. *Brain*, **78**, 487-502.

Garron, D.C. & Chiefetz, D.I. (1965) Comment on "Bender Gestalt discernment of organic pathology". *Psychological Bulletin*, **63**, 197-200.

Gassel, M.M. (1969) Occipital lobe syndromes (excluding hemianopia). In *Handbook of Neurology*, eds. Vinken, P.J. & Bruyn, G.W. Vol. 2, Ch. 20. Amsterdam: New Holland.

Gassel, M.M. & Williams, D. (1963) Visual function in patients with homonymous hemianopia. Part III. The completion phenomenon; insight and attitude to the defect; and visual functional efficiency. *Brain*, **86**, 229-260.

Gastaut, H. (1970) Clinical and electroencephalographical classification of epileptic seizures. *Epilepsia*, **11**, 102-113.

Gastaut, H. & Broughton, R.(1972) *Epileptic Seizures. Clinical and Electrographic Features, Diagnosis and Treatment.* Springfield, Illinois: Thomas.

Gastaut, H., Jasper, H.H., Bancaud, J. & Waltregny, A. (1969) *The Physiopathogenesis of the Epilepsies.* Springfield: Thomas.

Gazzaniga, M.S. (1970) *The Bisected Brain.* New York: Appleton-Century-Crofts.

Gazzaniga, M.S. (1972) One brain-Two minds? *American Scientists*, **60**, 311-317.

Gazzaniga, M.S., Bogen, J.E. & Sperry, R.W. (1962) Some functional effects of sectioning the cerebral commissures in man. *Proceedings of the National Academy of Science*, **48**, 1765-1769.

Gazzaniga, M.S., Bogen, J.E. & Sperry, R.W. (1965) Observations on visual perception after disconnexion of the cerebral hemispheres in man. *Brain*, **88**, 221-236.

Gazzaniga, M.S., Glass, A.V., Sarno, M.T. & Posner, J.B. (1973) Pure word deafness and hemispheric dynamics: a case history. *Cortex*, **9**, 136-143.

Geldard, F.A. (1972) *The Human Senses.* Second Edition. New York: Wiley.

Gerboth, R. (1950) A study of the two forms of the Wechsler-Bellevue Intelligence Scale. *Journal of Consulting Psychology*, **14**, 365-370.

Gerstmann, J. (1930) Zur Symptomatologie der Hirnlasionen im Ubergangsgebiet der unteren Parietalund mittleren Occipitalwindung. (Das Syndrom: Fingeragnosie, Rechts-Links-Storung, Agraphie, Akalkulie.) *Nervenarzt*, **3**, 691-695.

Gerstmann, J. (1957) Some notes on the Gerstmann syndrome. *Neurology*, **7**, 866-869.

Geschwind, N. (1962) The anatomy of acquired disorders of reading. In *Reading Disability*, ed. Money, J. Baltimore: Johns Hopkins Press.

Geschwind, N. (1965a) Alexia and colour-naming disturbance. In *Functions of the Corpus Callosum*, ed. Ettlinger, G. London: Churchill.

Geschwind, N. (1965b) Disconnection syndromes in animals and man. Part I. *Brain*, **88**, 237-294.

Geschwind, N. (1965c) Disconnection syndromes in animals and man. Part II. *Brain*, **88**, 585-644.

Geschwind, N. (1966) Carl Wernicke, the Breslau School, and the History of Aphasia. In *Brain Function: Speech, Language and Communication*, ed. Carterette, E.C. Berkeley and Los Angeles, California: University of California Press.

Geschwind, N. (1967) Brain mechanisms suggested by studies of hemispheric connections. In *Brain Mechanisms Underlying Speech and Language*, ed. Darley, F.L. New York: Grune and Stratton.

Geschwind, N. (1969) Problems in the anatomical understanding of the aphasias. In *Contributions to Clinical Neuropsychology*, ed. Benton, A.L. Ch. 4. Chicago: Aldine Publishing Company.

Geschwind, N. (1970) The organization of language and the brain. *Science*, **170**, 940-944.

Geschwind, N. & Fusillo, M. (1966) Color naming defects in association with alexia. *Archives of Neurology*, **15**, 137-146.

Geschwind, N. & Kaplan, E. (1962) A human cerebral deconnection syndrome. *Neurology*, **12**, 675-685.

Gibson, J.A. (1967) *A Guide to the Nervous System*. Second Edition. London: Faber and Faber.

Gibson, W.C. (1962) Pioneers of localization of function in the brain. *Journal of the American Medical Association*, **180**, 944-951.

Gibson, W.C. (1969) The early history of localization in the nervous system. In *Handbook of Clinical Neurology*, eds. Vinken, P.J. & Bruyn, G.E. Vol. 2, Ch. 2. Amsterdam: North-Holland.

Ghent, L., Mishkin, M. & Teuber, H.L. (1962) Short-term memory after frontal lobe injury in man. *Journal of Comparative and Physiological Psychology*, **55**, 705-709.

Gilliatt, R.W. & Pratt, R.T.C. (1952) Disorders of perception and and performance in a case of right-sided cerebral thrombosis. *Journal of Neurology, Neurosurgery, and Psychiatry*, **15**, 264-271.

Girgis, M. (1971) The orbital surface of the frontal lobe of the brain. *Acta- Psychiatrica Scandanavica, Supplementum*, **222**, 1-58.

Gleason, W.J. (1953) Rigidity and negative transfer effects in patients with cerebral damage. Unpublished doctoral dissertation, Northwestern University.

Glees, P. & Griffith, H.B. (1952) Bilateral destruction of the hippocampus (cornu ammonis) in case of dementia. *Monatsschrift fur Psychiatrie und Neurologie*, **123**, 193-204.

Glickstein, M. (1965) Neurophysiology of learning and memory. In *Medical Physiology and Biophysics*, eds. Ruch, T.C. & Patton, H.D. 19th Edition. Ch. 24. pp.480-493. Philadelphia: Saunders.

Gloning, K. (1965) *Die zerebral bedingten Storungen des raumlichen Sehens und des Raumerlebens*. Wien: Maudrich Verlag.

Gloning, I., Gloning, K. & Hoff, H. (1968) *Neuropsychological Symptoms in Lesions of the Occipital Lobe and Adjacent Areas*. Paris: Gauthier-Villars.

Gloning, I., Gloning, K., Hoff, H. & Tschabitsher, H. (1966) Zur prosopagnosie. *Neuropsychologia*, **4**, 113-131.

Gloning, I., Gloning, K., Jellinger, K. & Quatember, R. (1970) *Neuropsychologia*, **8**, 199-204.

Gloning, K., Haub, G. & Quatember, R. (1967) Standardisierung einer Untersuchungsmethode der sogenannten "Prosopagnosie". *Neuropsychologia*, **5**, 99.

Gloning, K. & Hoff, H. (1969) Cerebral localization of disorders of higher nervous activity. In *Handbook of Clinical Neurology*, eds. Vinken, P.J. & Gruyn, G.W. Vol. 2, Ch. 3. Amsterdam: North Holland.

Glowinski, H. (1973) Cognitive deficits in temporal lobe epilepsy: An investigation of memory functioning. *Journal of Nervous and Mental Disease*, **157**, 129-137.

Goldstein, G., Neuringer, C. & Olson, J. (1968) Impairment of abstract reasoning in the brain-damaged: Qualitative or quantitative? *Cortex*, **4**, 372-388.

Goldstein, G. & Shelly, C.H. (1973) Univariate vs. Multivariate analysis in neuropsychological test assessment of lateralized brain damage. *Cortex*, **9**, 204-216.

Goldstein, K. (1927) Die localisation in der grosshirnrinde. In *Handbuch der Normalen und Pathologischen Physiologie*, eds. Bethe, A. & Fisher, E. Berlin: Springer.

Goldstein, K. (1936a) The significance of the frontal lobes for mental performance. *Journal of Neurology and Psychopathology*, **17**, 27-40.

Goldstein, K. (1936b) The modification of behavior consequent to cerebral lesions. *Psychiatric Quarterly*, **10**, 586-610.

Goldstein, K. (1939a) Clinical and theoretical aspects of lesions of the frontal lobes. *Archives of Neurology and Psychiatry*, **41**, 865-867.

Goldstein, K. (1939b) *The Organism*. New York: American Book.

Goldstein, K. (1940) *Human Nature*. Cambridge, Mass.: Harvard University Press.

Goldstein, K. (1942a) *After Effects of Brain Injuries in War*. New York: Grune and Stratton.

Goldstein, K. (1942b) The two ways of adjustment of the organism to central defects. *Journal of the Mount Sinai Hospital*, **9**, 504-513.

Goldstein, K. (1943) Brain concussion: Evaluation of the after effects by special tests. *Diseases of the Nervous System*, **4**, 3-12.

Goldstein, K. (1944) Mental changes due to frontal lobe-damage. *Journal of Psychology*, **17**, 187-208.

Goldstein, K. (1948) *Language and Language Disturbance.* New York: Grune and Stratton.

Goldstein, K. (1959) Functional disturbances in brain damage. In *American Handbook of Psychiatry*, ed. Arieti, S. Vol. 1, Ch. 39. New York: Basic Books.

Goldstein, K. & Gelb, A. (1918) Psychologische Analysen Hirnpathologischer Falle auf Grund von Untersuchungen Hirnverletzer. *Zeitschrift fur die gesamte Neurologie und Psychiatrie*, **41**, 1.

Goldstein, K. & Scheerer, M. (1941) Abstract and concrete behaviour: An experimental study with special tests. *Psychological Monographs*, **43**, 1-151.

Goldstein, M.N. & Joynt, R.J. (1969) Long-term follow-up of a callosal-sectioned patient. *Archives of Neurology*, **20**, 96-102.

Goldstein, S.G., Kleinknecht, R.A. & Deysach, R.E. (1973) Effect of experience and amount of information on identification of cerebral impairment. *Journal of Consulting and Clinical Psychology*, **41**, 30-34.

Goldstein, S.G., Kleinknecht, R.A. & Gallow, A.E. (1970) Neuropsychological changes associated with carotid endarterectomy. *Cortex*, **6**, 308-322.

Gollin, E.S. (1960) Development studies of visual recognition of incomplete objects. *Perceptual and Motor Skills*, **11**, 289-298.

Goodglass, H. (1967) Binaural digit presentation and early lateral brain damage. *Cortex*, **3**, 295-306.

Goodglass, H. & Peck, E.A. (1972) Dichotic ear order effects in Korsakoff and normal subjects. *Neuropsychologia*, **10**, 211-217.

Gordon, N.G. (1972) The Trail Making Test in neuropsychological diagnosis. *Journal of Clinical Psychology*, **28**, 167-169.

Gott, P.S. (1973) Cognitive abilities following right and left hemispherectomy. *Cortex*, **9**, 266-274.

Graham, F.K. & Kendall, B.S. (1960) Memory-for-Designs Test: Revised general manual. *Perceptual and Motor Skills*, **11**, 147-188.

Graña, F., Rocca, E.D. & Graña, L. (1954) *Las Trepanaciones Craneanas en el Peru en la época pre-Hispanica.* Lima, Peru: Santa Maria.

Grant, A.D. & Berg, E.A. (1948) A behavioural analysis of degree of reinforcement and ease of shifting to new responses in a Weigl-type card sorting. *Journal of Experimental Psychology*, **38**, 404-411.

Grassi, J.R. (1947) The Fairfield Block Substitution Test for measuring intellectual impairment. *Psychiatric Quarterly*, **21**, 474-489.

Grassi, J.R. (1950) Impairment of abstract behaviour following bilateral prefrontal lobotomy. *Psychiatric Quarterly*, **24**, 74-88.

Greenblatt, M., Arnold, R. & Solomon, H.C. (1950) *Studies in Lobotomy.* New York: Grune & Stratton.

Gregson, R.A.M. & Taylor, G.M. (1975) *An Administrative Manual for the Patterned Cognitive Impairment Test Battery.* New Zealand: University of Canterbury.

Grunthal, E. (1947) Uber das Klinische Bild nach unschriebenem beiderseitige Ausfall der Ammonshornrinde. *Monatsschrift fur Psychiatrie und Neurologie*, **113**, 1-16.

Guertin, W.H., Ladd, C.E., Frank, G.H., Rabbin, A.I. & Heister, D.S. (1966) Research with the Wechsler Intelligence Scales for Adults. *Psychological Bulletin*, **66**, 385-409.

Guthrie, T.C. & Grossman, E.M. (1952) A study of the syndrome of denial. *Archives of Neurology and Psychiatry*, **68**, 362-371.

Haase, G.R. (1971a) Diseases presenting as dementia. *Contemporary Neurology Series*, **9**, 163-207.

Haase, G.R. (1971b) Diseases presenting as dementia. In *Dementia*, ed. Wells, C.E. Oxford: Blackwell.

Hachinski, V.C., Lassen, N.A. & Marshall, J. (1974) Multi-infarct dementia. A cause of mental deterioration in the elderly. *Lancet*, **2**, 207-210.

Hall, P. (1963) Korsakov's syndrome following herpes zoster encephalitis. *Lancet*, **1**, 752-753.

Hall, P. (1965) Subacute viral encephalitis amnesia. *Lancet*, **2**, 1077.

Halstead, W.C. (1947) *Brain and Intelligance.* Chicago: University of Chicago Press.

Halstead, W.C. (1958) Some behavioural aspects of partial temporal lobectomy in man. *Research Publications, Association for Research in Nervous and Mental Disease*, **36**, 478-490.

Halstead, W.C. (1959) The statics and the dynamics. In *Reflexes to Intelligence*, eds. Beck, S.J. & Molish, H.B. Glencoe, Illinois: The Free Press.

Hamlin, R.M. (1970) Intellectual function 14 years after frontal lobe surgery. *Cortex*, **6**, 299-307.

Handfield-Jones, R.M. & Porritt, A.E. (1949) *The Essentials of Modern Surgery.* Edinburgh: Livingstone.

Hanfmann, E., Rickers-Ovsiankina, M. & Goldstein, K. (1944) Case Lanuti: extreme concretization of behaviour due to damage of the brain cortex. *Psychological Monographs*, **57**, No. 4, Whole No. 264.

Hartje, W., Kerschensteiner, M., Poeck, K. & Orgass, B. (1973) A cross-validation study on the Token Test. *Neuropsychologia*, **11**, 119-121.

Harvey, O.J., Hunt, D.E. & Schroeder, D.M. (1961) *Conceptual Systems and Personality Organization*. New York: Wiley.

Hatfield, F.M. & Zangwill, O.L. (1974) Ideation in aphasia: The Picture-Story method. *Neuropsychologia*, **12**, 389-393.

Head, H. (1920) *Studies in Neurology*. Oxford: Oxford University Press.

Heathfield, K.W.G., Croft, P.B. & Swash, M. (1973) The syndrome of transient global amnesia. *Brain*, **96**, 729-736.

Hebb, D.O. (1939a) Intelligence in man after large removals of cerebral tissue: report of four left frontal lobe cases. *Journal of General Psychology*, **21**, 73-87.

Hebb, D.O. (1939b) Intelligence in man after large removals of cerebral tissue: defects following right temporal lobectomy. *Journal of General Psychology*, **21**, 437-446.

Hebb, D.O. (1941) Human intelligence after removal of cerebral tissue from the right frontal lobe. *Journal of General Psychology*, **25**, 257-265.

Hebb, D.O. (1942) The effect of early and late brain injury upon test scores and the nature of normal adult intelligence. *Proceedings of the American Philosophical Society*, **85**, 275-292.

Hebb, D.O. (1945) Man's frontal lobes; a critical review. *Archives of Neurology and Psychiatry*, **54**, 10-24.

Hebb, D.O. (1949) *The Organization of Behavior*. New York: Wiley.

Hebb, D.O. & Penfield, W. (1940) Human behavior after extensive bilateral removal from the frontal lobes. *Archives of Neurology and Psychiatry*, **44**, 421-438.

Hécaen, H. (1962) Clinical symptomatology in right and left hemispheric lesions. In *Interhemispheric Relations and Cerebral Dominance*, ed. Mountcastle, V.B. Ch. 10. Baltimore, Johns Hopkins Press.

Hécaen, H. (1964) Mental symptoms associated with tumors of the frontal lobe. In *The Frontal Granular Cortex and Behaviour*, eds. Warren, J.M. & Akert, K. Ch. 16. New York: McGraw Hill.

Hécaen, H. (1969) Aphasic, apraxic and agnosic syndromes in right and left hemisphere lesions. In *Handbook of Clinical Neurology*, eds. Vinken, P.J. & Bruyn, G.W. Vol. 4, Ch. 15. Amsterdam: North-Holland.

Hécaen, H., Ajuriaguerra, J. de, & Massonet, J. (1951) Les troubles visuo-constructifs par lésion pariéto-occipitale droite. *Encéphale*, **40**, 122-179.

Hécaen, H. & Ajuriaguerra, J. de. (1952) *Méconnaissances et hallucinations corporelles*. Paris: Masson.

Hécaen, H. & Angelergues, R. (1961) Etude anatomo-clinique de 280 cas de lésions rétro-rolandiques unilatérales des hémispherès cérébraux. *Encephale*, **6**, 533-562.

Hécaen, H. & Angelergues, R. (1962) Agnosia for faces (prosopagnosia). *Archives of Neurology*, **7**, 92-100.

Hécaen, H., Angelergues, R. & Douzenis, J.A. (1963) Les agraphies. *Neuropsychologia*, **1**, 179-208.

Hécaen, H. & Consoli, S. (1973) Analysis of language disorders in lesions of Broca's area. *Neuropsychologia*, **11**, 377-388.

Hécaen, H., Penfield, W., Bertrand, C. & Malmo, R. (1956) The syndrome of apractognosia due to lesions of the minor cerebral hemisphere. *Archives of Neurology and Psychiatry*, **75**, 400-434.

Hécaen, H. & Sauguet, J. (1972) Cerebral dominance in left-handed subjects. *Cortex*, **8**, 19-48.

Heilbrun, A.B. (1956) Psychological test performance as a function of lateralization of cerebral lesion. *Journal of Comparative and Physiological Psychology*, **49**, 10-14.

Heilbrun, A.B. (1962) Issues in the assessment of organic brain damage. *Psychological Reports*, **10**, 511-515.

Heilman, K.M. & Valenstein, E. (1972a) Auditory neglect in man. *Archives of Neurology*, **26**, 32-35.

Heilman, K.M. & Valenstein, E. (1972b) Frontal lobe neglect in man. *Neurology*, **22**, 660-664.

Heilman, K.M., Watson, R.T. & Schulman, H.M. (1974) A unilateral memory defect. *Journal of Neurology, Neurosurgery, and Psychiatry*, **37**, 790-793.

Heimburger, R.F., Demeyer, W. & Reitan, R.M. (1964) Implications of Gerstmann's syndrome. *Journal of Neurology, Neurosurgery and Psychiatry*, **27**, 52-57.

Heron, A. & Chown, S. (1967) *Age and Function*. London: Churchill.

Heron, W. (1957) Perception as a function of retinal locus and attention. *American Journal of Psychology*, **70**, 38-48.

Herrick, C.J. (1963) *Brains in Rats and Men*. (Reprinted from 1926). Chicago: University of Chicago.

Hewson, L. (1949) The Wechsler-Bellevue Scale and the substitution test as aids in neuropsychiatric diagnosis. *Journal of Nervous and Mental Disease*, **109**, 158-183.

Hillbom, E. (1960) After effects of brain injuries. *Acta Psychiatrica et Neurologica Scandanavica*, 35, Suppl. 142.

Hilliard, R.D. (1973) Hemispheric laterality effects on a facial recognition task in normal subjects. - *Cortex*, 9, 246-258.

Hillier, W.F. (1954) Total left cerebral hemispherectomy for malignant glioma. *Neurology*, 4, 718-721.

Hines, D. & Satz, P. (1971) Superiority of right visual half-fields in right handers for recall of digits presented at varying rates. *Neuropsychologia*, 9, 21-25.

Hohne, H.H. & Walsh, K.W. (1970) *Surgical Modification of the Personality*. Mental Health Authority, Victoria, Special Publications No. 2 Melbourne: Victorian Government Printer.

Holbourn A.H.S. (1943) Mechanics of head injuries. *Lancet*, 2, 438-441.

Holmes, G. (1918) Disturbances of visual orientation. *British Journal of Ophthalmology*, 2, 449-469.

Holmes, G. (1927) Disorders of sensation produced by cortical lesions. *Brain*, 1, 413-428.

Holt, R.R. (ed.) (1968) *Diagnostic Psychological Testing* by Rapaport, D., Gill, M.M. & Schafer, R. New York: International Universities Press.

Horenstein, S. (1971) The clinical use of psychological testing in dementia. *Contemporary Neurology Series*, 9, 61-80.

Howard, A.R. (1950) Diagnostic value of the Wechsler Memory Scale with selected groups of institutionalized patients. *Journal of Consulting Psychology*, 14, 376-380.

Howard, A.R. (1954) Further validation studies of the Wechsler Memory Scale. *Journal of Clinical Psychology*, 10, 164-167.

Howard, A.R. (1966) A fifteen-year follow-up with the Wechsler Memory Scale. *Journal of Consulting Psychology*, 30, 175-176.

Howes, D. (1962) An approach to the quantitative analysis of word blindness. In *Reading Disability: progress and research in dyslexia*, ed. Money, J. Baltimore: Johns Hopkins Press.

Howes, D. & Boller, F. (1975) Simple reaction time: evidence for focal impairment from lesion of the right hemisphere. *Brain*, 98, 317-322.

Hughes, C.P., Myers, F.K., Smith, K. & Torack, R.M. (1973) Nosologic problems in dementia. *Neurology*, 23, 344-351.

Hurwitz, L.J. & Adams, G.F. (1972) Rehabilitation of hemiplegia: indices of assessment and prognosis. *British Medical Journal*, 1, 94-98.

Inglis, J. (1970) Shock, surgery, and cerebral asymmetry. *British Journal of Psychiatry*, 117, 143-148.

Inglis, J. & Sykes, D.H. (1967) Some sources of variation in dichotic listening in children. *Journal of Experimental Child Psychology*, 5. 480-488.

Jackson, J.H. (1890) Case of tumour of the right temporosphenoidal lobe bearing on the localization of the sense of smell and on the interpretation of a particular variety of epilepsy. *Brain*, 12, 346-357.

Jackson, J.H. (1958) *Selected Writings of John Hughlings Jackson*, ed. Taylor, J. New York: Basic Books.

Jasper, H.H. (1958) Functional subdivisions of the temporal region in relation to seizure patterns and subcortical connections. In *Temporal Lobe Epilepsy*, eds. Baldwin, M. & Bailey, P. Springfield, Illinois: Thomas.

Jastak, J. (1953) Ranking Bellevue subtest scores for diagnostic purposes. *Journal of Consulting Psychology*, 17, 403-410.

Jeeves, M.A. (1965a) Psychological studies of three cases of congenital agenesis of the corpus callosum. In *Functions of the Corpus Callosum*, ed. Ettlinger, E.G. London: Churchill.

Jeeves, M.A. (1965b) Agenesis of the corpus callosum: physiopathological and clinical aspects. *Proceedings of the Australian Association of Neurology*, 3, 41-48.

Jefferson, G. (1937) Removal of right or left frontal lobes in man. *British Medical Journal*, 2, 199-206.

Jewesbury, E.C.O. (1969) Parietal lobe syndromes. In *Handbook of Clinical Neurology*, eds. Vinken, P.J. & Bruyn, G.W. Vol. 2, Ch. 21. Amsterdam: North Holland.

Johnson, G., Parsons, O.A., Holloway, F.A. & Bruhn, P. (1973) Intradimensional reversal shift performance in brain-damaged and chronic alcoholic patients. *Journal of Consulting and Clinical Psychology*, 40, 253-258.

Jones, M.K. (1974) Imagery as a mnemonic aid after left temporal lobectomy: Contrast between material-specific and generalized memory disorders. *Neuropsychologia*, 12, 21-30.

Joynt, R.J. & Goldstein, M.N. (1975) Minor Cerebral Hemisphere. In *Advances in Neurology*, ed. Friedlander, W.J. Vol. 7. New York: Raven Press.

Julesz, B. (1964) Binocular depth perception without familiarity cues. *Science*, 145, 356-363.

Kaplan, H.A. & Ford, D.H. (1966) *The Brain Vascular System*. Amsterdam: Elsevier.

Kastenbaum, R. (1965) Wine and fellowship in ageing: an exploratory action program. *Journal of Human Relations*, **13**, 266-277.

Kauffman, I. (1963) Some aspects of brain damage as related to Einstellung. *Journal of Neuropsychiatry*, **4**, 143-148.

Kilpatrick, D.G. (1970 The Halstead Category Test of brain dysfunction: Feasibility of a short form. *Perceptual and Motor Skills*, **30**, 577-578.

Kimble, D.P. (1963) *Physiological Psychology*. Reading, Massachusetts.

Kimura, D. (1961a) Some effects of temporal lobe damage on auditory perception. *Canadian Journal of Psychology*, **15**, 156-165.

Kimura, D. (1961b) Cerebral dominance and the perception of verbal stimuli. *Canadian Journal of Psychology*, **15**, 166-171.

Kimura, D. (1963) Right temporal lobe damage: perception of unfamiliar stimuli after damage. *Archives of Neurology*, **8**, 264-271.

Kimura, D. (1964) Left-right differences in the perception of melodies. *Quarterly Journal of Experimen)al Psychology*, **16**, 355-358.

Kimura, D.(1966) Dual functional asymmetry of the brain in visual perception. *Neuropsychologia*, **4**, 275-285.

Kimura, D. (1967) Functional asymmetry of the brain in dichotic listening. *Cortex*, **3**, 163-178.

Kimura, D. (1969) Spatial localization in left and right visual fields. *Canadian Journal of Psychology*, **23**, 445-448.

Kimura, D. (1973) The asymmetry of the human brain. *Scientific American*, **228**, 70-80.

Kimura, D. & Durnford, M. (1974) Normal studies on the function of the right hemisphere in vision. In *Hemisphere Functions in the human Brain*, eds. Dimond, S.J. & Beaumont, J.G. Ch. 3. London: Paul Elek (Scientific Books) Ltd.

King, E. (1967) The nature of visual field defects. *Brain*, **90**, 647-668.

Kinsbourne, M. (1971) Cognitive Deficit: Experimental Analysis. In *Psychobiology*, ed. McGaugh, J.L. Ch. 7. New York: Academic Press.

Kinsbourne, M. (1972) Contrasting patterns of memory span decrement in ageing and aphasia. *Journal of Neurology, Neurosurgery and Psychiatry*, **35**, 192-195.

Kinsbourne, M. & Smith, W.L. (1974) *Hemisphere Disconnection and Cerebral Function*. Springfield, Illinois: Thomas.

Kinsbourne, M. & Warrington, E.K. (1962) A study of finger agnosia. *Brain*, **85**, 47-66.

Kinsbourne, M. & Warrington, E.K. (1963) The localizing significance of limited simultaneous visual form perception. *Brain*, **86**, 697-702.

Kinsbourne, M. & Warrington, E.K. (1964) Observations on colour agnosia. *Journal of Neurology, Neurosurgery and Psychiatry*, **27**, 296-299.

Kisker, G.W. (1944) Abstract and categorical behaviour following therapeutic brain surgery. *Psychosomatic Medicine*, **6**, 146-150.

Kleist, K. (1934) *Gehirnpathologie*. Leipzig: Barth.

Kljajic, I. (1975) Wechsler Memory Scale indices of brain pathology. *Journal of Clinical Psychology*, **31**, 698-701.

Klonoff, H., Fibiger, C.H. & Hutton, G.H. (1970) Neuropsychological patterns in chronic schizophrenia. *Journal of Nervous and Mental Disease*, **150**, 291-300.

Kløve, H. & Fitzhugh, K.B. (1962) The relationship of differential EEG patterns to the distribution of Wechsler-Bellevue scores in a chronic epileptic population. *Journal of Clinical Psychology*, **18**, 334-337.

Kløve, H., Grabow, J.D. & Trites, R.L. (1969) Evaluation of memory functions with intracarotid sodium amytal. *Transactions of the American Neurological Association*, **94**, 76-80.

Kløve, H. & Reitan, R.M. (1958) The effects of dysphasia and spatial distortion on Wechsler-Bellevue results. *Archives of Neurology and Psychiatry*, **80**, 708-713.

Kløve, H., Trites, R.L. & Grabow, J.D. (1970) Intracarotid sodium amytal for evaluating memory function. *Electro-encephalography and Clinical Neurophysiology*, **28**, 418-419.

Knight, G. (1965) Stereotactic tractotomy in the surgical treatment of mental illness. *Journal of Neurology, Neurosurgery and Psychiatry*, **28**, 304-310.

Knight, G. (1972) Psychosurgery Today. *Proceedings of the Royal Society of Medicine*, **65**, 1099-1108.

Knight, G.C. & Tredgold, R.F. (1955) Orbital leucotomy. A review of 52 cases. *Lancet*, **1**, 981-985.

Knox, C. & Kimura, D. (1970) Cerebral processing of non-verbal sounds in boys and girls. *Neuropsychologia*, **8**, 227-237.

Konow, A. & Pribram, K.H. (1970) Error recognition and utilization produced by injury to the frontal cortex in man. *Neuropsychologia*, **8**, 489-491.

Korman, M. & Blumberg, S. (1963) Comparative efficiency of some tests of cerebral damage. *Journal of Consulting Psychology*, **27**, 303-309.

Kotzmann, M. (1972) Tactile discrimination of three-dimensional form in brain-damaged subjects. Unpublished thesis. University of Melbourne.

Krieg, W.J.S. (1963) *Connections of the Cerebral Cortex*. Evanston, Illinois: Brain Books.

Kroll, M.B. & Stolbun, D. (1933) Was ist konstructive Apraxie? *Zeitschrift fur die gesamte Neurologie und Psychiatrie*, **148**, 142-158.

Krynauw, R.A. (1950a) Infantile hemplegia treated by removing one cerebral hemisphere. *Journal of Neurology, Neurosurgery and Psychiatry*, **13**, 243-267.

Lacks, P.B. Colbert, J., Harrow, M. & Levine, J. (1970) Further evidence concerning the diagnostic accuracy of the Halstead organic test battery. *Journal of Clinical Psychology*, **26**, 480-481.

Laitinen, L.V. & Livingston, K.E. (eds.) (1973) *Surgical Approaches in Psychiatry*. Lancaster: Medical and Technical Publishing Company.

Landis, C., Zubin, J. & Mettler, F.A. (1950) The functions of the human frontal lobe. *Journal of Psychology*, **30**, 123-138.

Lansdell, H. (1962a) A sex difference in effect of temporal lobe neurosurgery on design preference. *Nature*, **194**, 852-854.

Lansdell, H. (1962b) Laterality of verbal intelligence in the brain. *Science*, **135**, 922-923.

Lansdell, H. (1968) The use of factor scores from the Wechsler-Bellevue Scale of Intelligence in assessing patients with temporal lobe removals. *Cortex*, **4**, 257-268.

Lashley, K.S. (1941) Patterns of cerebral integration indicated by the scotomas of migraine. *Archives of Neurology and Psychiatry*, **46**, 331-339.

Lashley, K.S. & Clark, G. (1946) The cytoarchitecture of the cerebral cortex of Ateles. *Journal of Comparative Neurology*, **85**, 223-306.

Lawson, I.R. (1962) Visual-spatial neglect in lesions of the right cerebral hemisphere: a study in recovery. *Neurology*, **12**, 23-33.

Lehtonen, R. (1973) Learning, memory and intellectual performance in a chronic state of amnesic syndrome. *Acta Neurologica Scandanavica*, Supplement 54, 107-143.

Leiscester, J., Sidman, M., Stoddard, L.T. & Mohr, J.P. (1969) Some determinants of visual neglect. *Journal of Neurology, Neurosurgery and Psychiatry*, **32**, 580-587.

Lehman, P., Loiseau, P. & Cohadson, F.(1963) Sur deux cas d'encéphalite rapellant cliniquement les encéphalites nécrosantes temporales mais d'évolution favourable. *Revue Neurologique*, **108**, 798-806.

Lennox, W.G. & Lennox, M.A. (1960) *Epilepsy and Related Disorders*. Boston: Little Brown and Company.

Le Vere, T.E. (1975) Neural stability, sparing, and behavioral recovery following brain damage. *Psychological Review*, **82**, 344-358.

Levin, H.S. & Benton, A.L. (1975) Temporal orientation in patients with brain disease. *Applied Neurophysiology*, **38**, 56-60.

Levy, J. (1974a) Psychobiological implications of bilateral asymmetry. In *Hemisphere Function in the Human Brain*, eds. Dimond, S.J. & Beaumont, J.G. Ch. 6. London: Elek Science.

Levy, J. (1974b) Cerebral asymmetries as manifested in split-brain man. In *Hemispheric Disconnection and Cerebral Function*, eds. Kinsbourne, M. & Lynn Smith, W. Ch. 9. Springfield, Illinois: Thomas.

Levy, J., Nebes, R.D. & Sperry, R.W. (1971) Expressive language in the surgically separated minor hemisphere. *Cortex*, **7**, 49-58.

Levy, J., Trevarthen, C.B. & Sperry, R.W. (1972) Perception of bilateral chimeric figures following hemispheric deconnection. *Brain*, **95**, 61-78.

Levy-Agresti, J. & Sperry, R.W. (1968) Differential perceptual capacities in major and minor hemispheres. *Proceedings of the National Academy of Science*, **61**, 1151.

Lewinsohon, P.M. (1971) Assessment of clinical (diagnostic) skill: Illustration of a quantitative approach. *Professional Psychology*, **2**, 303-304.

Lewinsohn, P.M., Zieler, R.E., Libet, J., Eyeberg, S. & Nielson, G. (1972) Short-term memory: A comparison between frontal and non-frontal right- and left-hemisphere brain-damaged patients. *Journal of Comparative Physiological Psychology*, **81**, 248-255.

Lewis, N.D.C., Landis, C. & King, H.E. (1956) *Studies in Topectomy*. New York: Grune and Stratton.

Ley, P. (1970) Acute psychiatric patients. In *The Psychological Assessment of Mental and Physical Handicaps*, ed. Mittler, P. Ch. 7. London: Tavistock Publications.

Lhermitte, F. (1951) *Les Hallucinations*. Paris: Doin.

Lhermitte, F. & Beauvois, M.F. (1973) A visual-speech disconnexion syndrome. *Brain*, **96**, 695-714.

Lhermitte, F., Chain, F. & Aron, D. (1965) 10 cas d'agnosie des couleurs. *Proceedings of the 8th International Congress of Neurology, Vienna,* **3,** 217-221.

Lhermitte, F., Derouesné, J. & Signoret, J.L. (1972) Analyse neuropsychologique du syndrome frontal. *Revue Neurologique,* **127,** 415-440.

Lhermitte, F., Gautier, J.C. & Derouesné, C. (1960) Nature of occlusions of the middle cerebral artery. *Neurology,* **20,** 82-88.

Lhermitte, F. & Signoret, J.L. (1972) Analyse neuropsychologique et differenciation des syndromes amnesique. *Revue Neurologique,* **126,** 161-178.

Lhermitte, J. (1942) De l'image corporelle. *Revue Neurologique,* **74,** 20-38.

Lhermitte, J. (1952) L'image corporelle en neurologie. *Schweizer Archiv fur neurologie and Psychiatrie,* **69,** 213-236.

Lhermitte, J. & Trelles, J.O. (1933) Sur l'apraxie pure constructive. *Encéphale,* **28,** 413-444.

Liepmann, H. & Maas, O. (1907) Fall von linksseifigen Agraphie und Apraxie bei rechtsseifigen Lahmung. *Journal fur Psychologie und Neurologie,* **10,** 214-227.

Lishman, W.A. (1971) Emotion, consciousness and will after brain bisection in man. *Cortex,* **7,** 181-192.

Lodge, A. (1966) Effects of facilitating, neutral and inhibiting instructions on perceptual tasks following brain damage. *Acta Psychologia,* **25,** 173-198.

Loeser, J.D. & Alvord, E.C. (1968a) Agenesis of the corpus callosum. *Brain,* **91,** 553-570.

Loeser, J.D. & Alvord, E.C. (1968b) Clinico-pathological correlations in agenesis of the corpus callosum. *Neurology,* **18,** 745-756.

Luria, A.R. (1961) *The Role of Speech in the Regulation of Normal and Abnormal Behaviour.* Oxford: Pergamon Press.

Luria, A.R. (1964) Factors and forms of aphasia. In *Ciba Foundation Symposium: Disorders of Language,* eds. de Reuck, A V.S. & O'Connor, M. London: Churchill.

Luria, A.R. (1965) Two kinds of motor perseveration in massive injury of the frontal lobes. *Brain,* **88,** 1-10.

Luria, A.R. (1966) *Higher Cortical Function in Man.* New York: Basic Books.

Luria, A.R. (1969) Frontal Lobe Syndromes. In *Handbook of Clinical Neurology,* eds. Vinken, P.J. & Bruyn, G.W. Vol. 2, Ch. 23. Amsterdam: North-Holland.

Luria, A.R. (1970a) The functional organization of the brain. *Scientific American,* **222,** 66-78.

Luria, A.R. (1970b) *Traumatic Aphasia.* The Hague: Mouton.

Luria, A.R. (1971) Memory disturbances in local brain lesions. *Neuropsychologia,* **9,** 367-376.

Luria, A.R. (1972) Aphasia reconsidered. *Cortex,* **8,** 34-40.

Luria, A.R. (1973a) Towards the mechanisms of naming disturbance. *Neuropsychologia,* **11,** 417-421.

Luria, A.R. (1973b) *The Working Brain.* London: Allen Lane, The Penguin Press.

Luria, A.R. & Homskaya, E.D. (1963) Le trouble du role régulateur de langage au cours des lésions du lobe frontal. *Neuropsychologia,* **1,** 9-26.

Luria, A.R. & Homskay, E.D. (1964) Disturbance in the regulative role of speech with frontal lobe lesions. In *The Frontal Granular Cortex and Behavior,* eds. Warren, J.M. & Akert, K. Ch. 17. New York: McGraw-Hill.

Luria, A.R., Homskaya, E.D., Blinkov, S.M. & Critchley, M. (1967) Impaired selectivity of mental processes in association with a lesion of the frontal lobe. *Neuropsychologia,* **5,** 105-117.

Luria, A.R. & Karasseva, T.A. (1968) Disturbances of auditory speech memory in focal lesions of the deep regions of the left temporal lobe. *Neuropsychologia,* **6,** 97-104.

Luria, A.R., Karpov, B.A. & Yarbuss, A.L. (1966) Disturbonces of active visual perception with lesions of the frontal lobes. *Cortex,* **2,** 202-212.

Luria, A.R., Pribram, K.H. & Homskaya, E.D. (1964) An experimental analysis of the behavioural disturbance produced by a left frontal arachnoidal endothelioma (meningioma). *Neuropsychologia,* **2,** 257-280.

Luria, A.R., Simernitskaya, E.G. & Tubylevich, B. (1970) The structure of psychological processes in relation to cerebral organization. *Neuropsychologia,* **8,** 13-20.

Luria, A.R., Sokolov, E.N. & Klimkovsky, M. (1967) Towards a neuro-dynamic analysis of memory disturbances with lesions of the left temporal lobe. *Neuropsychologia,* **5,** 1-12.

Luria, A.R. & Tsvetkova, L.D. (1964) The programming of constructive activity in local brain injuries. *Neuropsychologia,* **2,** 95-108.

Lynch, S. & Yarnell, P.R. (1973) Delayed forgetting after concussion. *American Journal of Psychology,* **86,** 643-645.

Mackie, J.B. & Beck, E.C. (1966) Relations among rigidity, intelligence, and perception in brain-damaged and normal individuals. *Journal of Nervous and Mental Disease,* **142,** 310-317.

Magoun, H.W. (1958) Early development of ideas relating the mind with the brain. In *Ciba Foundation Symposium. The Neurological Basis of Behaviour*, eds. Wolstenholme, G.E.W. & O'Connor, C.M. London: Churchill.

Maher, B.A. (1957) Personality, problem solving, and the Einstellung effect. *Journal of Abnormal and Social Psychology*, **54**, 70-74.

Malmo, R.B. (1948) Psychological aspects of frontal gyrectomy and frontal lobotomy in mental patients. *Research Publications, Association for Research in Nervous and Mental Disease*, **27**, 537-564.

Mandleberg, I.A. & Brooks, D.N. (1975) Cognitive recovery after severe head injury. 1. Serial testing on the Wechsler Adult Intelligence Scale. *Journal of Neurology, Neurosurgery, and Psychiatry*, **38**, 1121-1126.

Marie, P. & Béhague, P.(1919) Syndrome de désorientation dans l'espace consécutif aux plaies profondes du lobe frontal. *Revue Neurologique*, **26**, 1-14.

Marie, P., Bouttier, H. & van Bogaert, L. (1924) Sur un cas de tumeur préfrontale droite. Troubles de l'orientation dans l'espace. *Revue Neurologique*, **31**, 209-221.

Marquardsen, J. (1969) The natural history of acute cerebrovascular disease: a retrospective study of 769 patients. *Acta Neurologica Scandanavica, Supplement*, **38**, 1-192.

Maspes, P.E. (1948) Le syndrome experimental chez l'homme de la section du splenium du corps calleux. *Revue Neurologique*, **80**, 100-113.

Matarazzo, J.D.(1972) *Wechsler's Measurement and Appraisal of Adult Intelligence*. Fifth Edition. Baltimore: Williams and Wilkins.

Matthews, C.G., Shaw, D.J. & Kløve, H. (April 1965) Psychometric and adaptive ability comparisons in neurologic, and pseudo-neurologic subjects. Paper read at *Midwestern Psychological Association Meeting*, Chicago.

Matthews, C.G., Shaw, D.J. & Kløve, H. (1966) Psychological test performances in neurologic and "pseudo-neurologic" subjects. *Cortex*, **2**, 244-253.

Mayer-Gross, W. (1935) The question of visual impairment in constructional apraxia. *Proceedings of the Royal Society of Medicine*, **29**, 1396-1400.

McElwain, D.W. & Kearney, G.E. (1970) *The Queensland Test*. Melbourne: Australian Council for Educational Research.

McFie, J. (1960) Psychological testing in clinical neurology. *Journal of Nervous and Mental Disease*, **131**, 383-393

McFie, J. (1961) The effects of hemispherectomy on intellectual functioning in cases of infantile hemiplegia. *Journal of Neurology, Neurosurgery and Psychiatry*, **24**, 240-249.

McFie, J. (1969) The diagnostic significance of disorders of higher nervous activity. In *Handbook of Clinical Neurology*, eds. Vinken, P.J. & Bruyn, G.W. Vol. 4. Ch. 1. Amsterdam: North Holland.

McFie, J. (1972) Factors of the brain. *Bulletin of the British Psychological Society*, **25**, 11-14.

McFie, J. & Piercy, M.F. (1952a) Intellectual impairment with localized cerebral lesions. *Brain*, **75**, 292-311.

McFie, J. & Piercy, M.F. (1952b) The relation of laterality of lesions to performance on Weigl's Sorting Test. *Journal of Mental Science*, **98**, 299-305.

McFie, J., Piercy, M.F. & Zangwill, O.L. (1950) Visual spatial agnosia associated with lesions of the right cerebral hemisphere. *Brain*, **73**, 167-190.

McFie, J. & Thompson, J.A. (1972) Picture arrangement: A measure of frontal lobe function? *British Journal of Psychiatry*, **121**, 547-552.

McFie, J. & Zangwill, O.L. (1960) Visual-constructive disabilities associated with lesions of the left cerebral hemisphere. *Brain*, **83**, 243-260.

McHenry, L.C. (1969) *Garrison's History of Neurology*. Springfield, Illinois: Thomas.

McKenzie, K.G. (1938) Cited in Williams, D.J. & Scott, J.W. The functional response of the sympathetic nervous system of man following hemidecortication. *Journal of Neurology and Psychiatry*, 1939, **2**, 313-322.

McKenzie, K.G. & Kaczanowski, G. (1964) Prefrontal leucotomy. A five year controlled study. *Canadian Medical Journal*, **91**, 1193-1196.

McKeever, W.F. & Huling, M.D. (1971) Lateral dominance in tachistoscopic word recognition performances obtained with simultaneous bilateral output. *Neuropsychologia*, **9**, 15-20.

Meehl, P.E. (1954) *Clinical Versus Statistical Prediction*. Minneapolis: University of Minnesota Press.

Meehl, P.E. (1956a) Wanted—a good cook book. *American Psychologist*, **11**, 263-272.

Meehl, P.E. (1956b) When shall we use our heads instead of the formula. *American Psychologist*, **11**, 368.

Meehl, P.E. (1960 The cognitive activity of the clinician. *American Psychologist*, **15**, 19-27.

Meehl, P.E. (1961) Logic for the clinician. *Contemporary Psychology*, **6**, 389-391.

Meier, M.J. & French, L.A. (1966) Longitudinal assessment of intellectual functioning following unilateral temporal lobectomy. *Journal of Clinical Psychology*, **22**, 22-27.

Mensh, I.N., Schwartz, H.G., Matarazzo, R.R. & Matarazzo, J.D. (1952) Psychological functioning following cerebral hemispherectomy in man. *Archives of Neurology and Psychiatry*, **67**, 787-796.

Mettler, F.A. (ed.) (1949) *Selective Partial Ablation of the Frontal Cortex*. New York: Hoeber.

Mettler, F.A. (ed.) (1952) *Psychosurgical Problems*. New York; Blakiston.

Meyer, V. (1957) Critique of psychological approaches to brain damage. *Journal of Mental Science*, **103**, 80-109.

Meyer, V. (1959) Cognitive changes following temporal lobectomy for temporal lobe epilepsy. *Archives of Neurology and Psychiatry*, **81**, 299-309.

Meyer, V. & Falconer, M.A. (1960) Defects of learning ability with massive lesions of the temporal lobe. *Journal of Mental Science*, **106**, 472-477.

Meyer, V. & Jones, H.G. (1957) Patterns of cognitive test performances as functions of the lateral localization of cerebral abnormalities in the temporal lobe. *Journal of Mental Science*, **103**, 758-772.

Meyer, V. & Yates, A.J. (1955) Intellectual changes following temporal lobectomy for psychomotor epilepsy. *Journal of Neurology, Neurosurgery and Psychiatry*, **18**, 44-52.

Miller, E. (1971) On the nature of the memory disorder in presenile dementia. *Neuropsychologia*, **9**, 75-81.

Miller, E. (1972a) *Clinical Neuropsychology*. Harmondsworth, Middlesex: Penguin Books.

Miller, E. (1972b) Efficiency of coding and the short-term memory defect in presenile dementia. *Neuropsychologia*, **10**, 133-136.

Miller, E. (1973) Short-and long-term memory in patients with presenile dementia (Alzheimer's disease). *Psychological Medicine*, **3**, 221-224.

Milner, B. (1954) Intellectual function of the temporal lobes. *Psychological Bulletin*, **51**, 42-64.

Milner, B. (1958) Psychological defects produced by temporal lobe excision. *Research Publications, Association for Research in Nervous and Mental Disease*, **36**, 244-257.

Milner, B. (1959) The memory defect in bilateral hippocampal lesions. *Psychiatric Research Reports*, **11**, 43-58.

Milner, B. (1962) Laterality effects in audition. In *Interhemispheric Relations and Cerebral Dominance*, ed. Mouncastle, V.B. Ch. 9. Baltimore: Johns Hopkins Press.

Milner, B. (1963) Effects of different brain lesions on card sorting. *Archives of Neurology*, **9**, 90-100.

Milner, B. (1964) Some effects of frontal lobectomy in man. In *The Frontal Granular Cortex and Behaviour*, eds. Warren, J.M. & Akert, K. Ch. 15. New York: McGraw-Hill.

Milner, B. (1965) Visually-guided maze learning in man: effects of bilateral hippocampal, bilateral frontal, and unilateral cerebral lesions. *Neuropsychologia*, **3**, 317-338.

Milner, B. (1966) Amnesia following operations on the temporal lobes. In *Amnesia*, eds. Whitty, C.W.M. & Zangwill, O. London: Butterworth.

Milner, B (1967) Brain mechanisms suggested by studies of temporal lobes. In *Brain Mechanisms underlying Speech and language*. ed Darley, F.L. New York: Grune and Stratton.

Milner, B. (1968a) Disorders of memory after brain lesions in man. *Neuropsychologia*, **6**, 175-179.

Milner, B. (1968b) Visual recognition and recall after right temporal lobe excision in man. *Neuropsychologia*, **6**, 191-209.

Milner, B. (1970) Memory and the medial temporal regions of the brain. In *Biology of Memory*, eds. Pribram, K.H. & Broadbent, D.E. New York: Academic Press.

Milner, B. (1971) Interhemispheric difference in the localization of psychological processes in man. *British Medical Bulletin*, **27**, 272-277.

Milner, B. (1974) Hemispheric Specialization: Scope and Limits. In *The Neurosciences Third Study Program*, eds. Schmitt, F.O. & Worden, F.G. Ch. 8. Cambridge: Massachusetts, MIT Press.

Milner, B., Branch, C. & Rasmussen, T. (1962) Study of short term memory after intracarotid injection of sodium amytal. *Transactions of the American Neurological Association*, **87**, 224-226

Milner, B., Branch, C. & Rasmussen, T. (1964) Observations on cerebral dominance. In *Ciba Foundation Symptosium: Disorders of Language*, eds. de Reuck, A.V.S. & O'Connor, M. London: Churchill.

Milner, B., Branch, C. & Rasmussen, T. (1966) Evidence for bilateral speech representation in some non-right handers. *Transactions of the American Neurological Association*, **91**, 306-308.

Milner, B., Corkin, S. & Teuber, H.L. (1968) Further analysis of the hippocampal amnesic syndrome: 14-year follow-up study of H.M. *Neuropsychologia*, **6**, 215.

Milner, B. & Kimura, D. (April 1964) Dissociable visual learning defects after temporal lobectomy in man. Paper read at the 35th *Annual Meeting of the Eastern Psychological Association*, Philadelphia.

Milner, B. & Taylor, L.B. (April 1970) Somesthetic thresholds after commissural section in man. Paper presented at *American Academy of Neurology*, Miami.

Milner, B. & Taylor, L. (1972) Right-hemisphere superiority in tactile pattern-recognition after cerebral commissurotomy: Evidence for nonverbal memory. *Neuropsychologia*, **10**, 1-15.

Milner, B., Taylor, L. & Sperry, R.W. (1968) Lateralized suppression of dichotically-presented digits after commissural section in man. *Science*, **161**, 184-186.

Milner, B. & Teuber, H.L. (1968) Alteration of perception and memory in man: Reflections on methods. In *Analysis of Behavioral Change*, ed. Weiskrantz, L. Ch. 11. New York: Harper and Row.

Milner, P. (1970) *Physiological Psychology*. New York: Holt, Rinehart and Winston.

Mishkin, M. & Forgays, D.G. (1952) Word recognition as a function of retinal locus. *Journal of Experimental Psychology*, **43**, 43-48.

Mittler, P. (ed.) (1973) *The Psychological Assessment of Mental and Physical Handicaps*. London: Tavistock Publications.

Mohr, J.O., Leicester, J., Stoddard, L.T. & Sidman, M. (1971) Right hemianopia with memory and colour deficits in circumscribed left posterior cerebral artery territory infarction. *Neurology*, **21**, 1104-1113.

Moniz, E. (1954) How I succeeded in performing the prefrontal leucotomy. *Journal of Clinical and Experimental Psychopathology*, **15**, 373-379.

Moscovitch, M. (1973) Language and the cerebral hemispheres. In *Communication and Affect*, eds. Pliner, P., Krames, L. & Alloway, T. New York: Academic Press.

Mountcastle, V.B. (ed.) (1962) *Interhemispheric Relations and Cerebral Dominance*. Baltimore: Johns Hopkins Press.

Murphy, E.H. & Venables, P.H. (1970) Ear asymmetry in the threshold of fusion of two clicks: A signal detection analysis. *Quarterly Journal of Experimental Psychology*, **22**, 288-300.

Myers, R.E. (1955) Interocular transfer of pattern discrimination in cats following section of crossed optic fibres. *Journal of Comparative and Physiological Psychology*, **48**, 470-473.

Myers, R.E. (1956) Functions of corpus callosum in interocular transfer. *Brain*, **79**, 358-363.

Myers, R.E. (1959) Interhemispheric communication through the corpus callosum: Limitations under conditions of conflict. *Journal of Comparative and Physiological Psychology*, **52**, 6-9.

Myers, R.E. (1961) Corpus callosum and visual gnosis: In *Brain Mechanisms and Learning*, eds. Fessard, A., Gerard, R.W., Konorski, J. & Delafresnaye, J.F. Oxford: Blackwell Scientifiic Publications.

Myers, R.E. (1965) The neocortical commissures and interhemispheric transmission of information. In *Functions of the Corpus Callosum*, ed. Ettlinger, E.G. London: Churchill.

Nathanson, M., Bergman, P.S. & Gordon, G.G. (1952) Denial of illness. *Archives of Neurology and Psychiatry*, **68**, 380-387.

Nebes, R.D. (1971) Superiority of the minor hemisphere in commissurotomized man for the perception of part-whole relations. *Cortex*, **7**, 333-349.

Nebes, R.D. (1972) Dominance of the minor hemisphere in commissurotomized man on a test of figure unification. *Brain*, **95**, 633-638.

Nebes, R.D. (1973) Perception of spatial relationships by the right and left hemispheres in commissurotomized man. *Neuropsychologia*, **11**, 285-289.

Nebes, R.D. (1974a) Dominance of the minor hemisphere for the perception of part-whole relationships. In *Hemispheric Disconnection and Cerebral Function*, eds. Kinsbouse, M. & Lynn Smith, W. Ch. 7. Springfield, Illinois: Thomas.

Nebes, R.D. (1974b) Hemispheric specialization in commissurotomized man. *Psychological Bulletin*, **81**, 1-14.

Nehemkis, A.M. & Lewinsohn, P.M. (1972) Effects of left and right cerebral lesions of the naming process. *Perceptual and Motor Skills*, **35**, 787-798.

Netley, C. (1972) Dichotic listening performance of hemispherectomized patients. *Neuropsychologia*, **10**, 233-240.

New, P.F.J., Scott, W.R., Schnur, J.A., Davis, K.R. & Taveras, J.M. (1974) Computerized axial tomography with the EMI scanner. *Radiology*, **110**, 109-123.

Newcombe, F. (1969) *Missile Wounds of the Brain*. Oxford: Oxford University Press.

Nichols, I.C. & Hunt, J. McV. (1940) A case of partial bilateral frontal lobectomy: A psychopathological study. *American Journal of Psychiatry*, **96**, 1063-1087.

Neidermeyer, E. (1972) *The Generalized Epilepsies: A Clinical Electroencephalographic Study*. Springfield: Thomas.

Nielsen, J.M. (1937) Unilateral cerebral dominance as related to mind-blindness. Minimal lesion causing visual agnosia for objects. *Archives of Neurology and Psychiatry*, **38,** 108-115.

Nielsen, J.M. (1962) *Agnosia, Apraxia, Aphasia. Their value in Cerebral Localization.* New York: Harper.

Nielsen, J.M. & Friedman, A.P. (1942) The temporal isthmus and its clinical syndromes. *Bulletin of the Los Angeles Neurological Society*, **7,** 1-11.

Nuttin, J. & Greenwald, A.G. (1968) *Reward and Punusihment in Human Learning.* London: Academic Press.

Obrador, A.S. (1964) Cerebral localization and organization. In *Cerebral Localization and Organization*, eds. Schaltenbrand, G. & Woolsey, C.N. Madison: University of Wisconsin Press.

Orgass, B. & Poeck, K. (1966) Clinical validation of a new test for aphasia: An experimental study on the Token Test. *Cortex*, **2,** 222-243.

Orgass, B., Poeck, K., Kerschensteiner, M. & Hartje, W. (1972) Visuo-cognitive performances in patients with unilateral hemispheric lesions. *Zeitschrift fur Neurologue*, **202,** 177-195.

Oscar-Berman, M. (1973) Hypothesis testing and focusing behavior during concept formation by amnesic Korsakoff patients. *Neuropsychologia*, **11,** 191-198.

Osterrieth, P.A. (1944) Le test de copie d'une figure complexe. *Archives de Psychologie*, **30,** 206-353.

Oxbury, J.M., Campbell, D.C. & Oxbury, S.M. (1974) Unilateral spatial neglect and impairments of spatial analysis and visual perception. *Brain*, **97,** 551-465.

Oxbury, J.M. & Oxbury, S.M. (1969) Effects of lobectomy on the report of dichotically presented digits. *Cortex*, **5,** 1-4.

Paganini, A.E. & Zlotlow, M. (1960) Denial of lobotomy as a continuation of the defense mechanism of denial in schizophrenia. *Psychiatric Quarterly*, **34,** 260-268.

Pallis, C.A. (1955) Impaired identification for faces and places with agnosia for colours. *Journal of Neurology, Neurosurgery and Psychiatry*, **18,** 218-224.

Paillas, J.E., Cossa, P., Darcourt, G. & Naquet, R. (1965) Etude sur l'epilspsie occipital. Eighth International Congress of Neurology, Vienna. *Pathology of the Occipital Lobe*, Vol. 3, 193-196.

Papez, J.W. (1929) *Comparative Neurology.* New York: Crowell.

Papez, J. (1937) A proposed mechanism of emotion. *Archives of Neurology and Psychiatry*, **38,** 725-743.

Parker, J.W. (1957) The validity of some current tests for organicity. *Journal of Consulting Psychology*, **21,** 425-428.

Parker, N. (1969) Post-traumatic dementia. *Proceedings of the Australian Association of Neurology*, **6,** 39-44.

Parsons, A.O. & Huse, M.M. (1958) Impairment of flicker discrimination in brain-damaged patients. *Neurology*, **8,** 750-755.

Parsons, O.A. & Kemp, D.E. (1960) Intellectual functioning in temporal lobe epilepsy. *Journal of Consulting Psychology*, **24,** 408-414.

Parsons, O.A., Vega, A. & Burn, J. (1969) Differential psychological effects of lateralized brain damage. *Journal of Consulting and Clinical Psychology*, **33,** 551-557.

Paterson, A. & Zangwill, O.L. (1944) Disorders of visual space perception associated with lesions of the right cerebral hemisphere. *Brain*, **67,** 331-358.

Paterson, A. & Zangwill, O.L. (1945) A case of topographical disorientation associated with a unilateral cerebral lesion. *Brain*, **68,** 188-212.

Payne, R.W. (1957) Experimental method in clinical psychological practice. *Journal of Mental Science*, **103,** 189-196.

Penfield, W. (1938) The cerebral cortex in man. *Archives of Neurology and Psychiatry*, **40,** 417-442.

Penfield, W. (1954) Temporal lobe epilepsy. *British Journal of Surgery*, **41,** 337-343.

Penfield, W. (1958) *The Excitable Cortex in Conscious Man.* Liverpool: Liverpool University Press.

Penfield, W. & Evans, J. (1935) The frontal lobe in man: a clinical study of maximum removals. *Brain*, **58,** 115-133.

Penfield, W. & Jasper, H. (1954) *Epilepsy and the Functional Anatomy of the Human Brain*, 475-497, Boston: Little, Brown.

Penfield, W. & Milner, B. (1958) Memory deficit produced by bilateral lesions in the hippocampal zone. *Archives of Neurology and Psychiatry*, **79,** 475-497.

Penfield, W. & Perot, P. (1963) The brain's record of auditory and visual experience. *Brain*, **86,** 595-697.

Penfield, W. & Rasmussen, A.T. (1950) *The Cerebral Cortex of Man.* New York: Macmillan.

Penfield, W. & Roberts, L. (1959) *Speech and Brain Mechanisms.* Princeton, New Jersey: Princeton University Press.

Perez, F.I., Rivera, V.M., Meyer, J.S., Gay, J.R.A., Taylor, R.L. & Matthew, N.T. (1975) Analysis of intellectual and cognitive performance in patients with multi-infarct dementia, vertebrobasilar insufficiency with dementia, and Alzheimer's disease. *Journal of Neurology, Neurosurgery, and Psychiatry*, **38**, 533-540.

Perret, E. (1974) The left frontal lobe of man and the suppression of habitual responses in verbal categorical behaviour. *Neuropsychologia*, **12**, 323-330.

Peterson, L.R. & Peterson, M.J. (1959) Short-term retention of individual verbal items. *Journal of Experimental Psychology*, **58**, 193-198.

Petrie, A. (1949) Preliminary report of changes after prefrontal leucotomy. *Journal of Mental Science*, **95**, 449-455.

Petrie, Asenath. (1952a) *Personality* and *the Frontal Lobes*. London: Routledge Kegan Paul.

Petrie, A. (1952b) A comparison of the psychological effects of different types of operation on the frontal lobes. *Journal of Mental Science*, **98**, 326-329.

Petrovici, I.N. (1972) Schlafenlappen und apraxie. *Fortschritte der Neurologie und Psychiatrie*, **40**, 656-672.

Phelan, J.A. & Gustafson, C.W. (1968) Reversal and nonreversal shifts in acute brain-injured with injury diffusely organized. *Journal of Psychology*, **70**, 249-259.

Phelps, C. (1897) *Traumatic Injuries of the Brain and its Membranes*. New York: Appleton.

Piaget, J. (1969) *The Mechanisms of Perception*. London: Routledge and Kegan Paul.

Piercy, M.F. (1959) Testing for intellectual impairment—some comments on tests and testers. *Journal of Mental Science*, **105**, 489-495.

Piercy, M. (1964) The effects of cerebral lesions on intellectual function: A review of current research trends. *British Journal of Psychiatry*, **110**, 310-352.

Piercy, M., Hécaen, H. & Ajuriaguerra, J. de (1960) Constructional apraxia associated with unilateral cerebral lesions—left and right sided cases compared. *Brain*, **83**, 225-242.

Piercy, M.F. & Smyth, V. (1962) Right hemisphere dominance for certain non-verbal intellectual skills. *Brain*, **85**, 775-790.

Pikas, A. (1966) *Abstraction and Concept Formation*. Cambridge, Mass.: Harvard University Press.

Pillon, B. (1973) L'apport de la méthode des temps de réaction dans l'étude des performances des malades atteints de lésions cérébrales. *Année Psychologique*, **73**, 261-272.

Poeck, K. (July 1975) In editorial—On cerebral localization and dominance. *Bulletin of the International Neuropsychology Society*.

Poeck, K., Kerschensteiner, M., Hartje, W. & Orgass, B3 (1973) Impairment in visual recognition of geometric figures in patients with circumscribed retrorolandic brain lesions. *Neuropsychologia*, **11**, 311-317.

Poeck, K. & Orgass, B. (1966) Gerstmann's syndrome and aphasia. *Cortex*, **2**, 421-437.

Poeck, K. & Orgass, B. (1967) Uber Storungen der Rechts-links Orientierung. *Nervenarzt*, **38**, 285-291.

Pollack, F. (1938) Zur Pathologie Und Klinik der Orientierung, *Schweizer Archiv fur Neurologie und Psychiatrie*, **42**, 141-164.

Pollack, M. (1960) Effect of brain tumour on perception of hidden figures, sorting behavior and problem solving performances. *Dissertation Abstracts*, **20**, 3405-3406.

Pollack, M., Battersby, W.S. & Bender, M.B. (1957) Tachistoscopic identification of contour in patients with brain damage. *Journal of Comparative and Physiological Psychology*, **50**, 220-227.

Poppelreuter, W. (1917) *Die psychischen schadigungen durch kopfschuss im Kriege* 1914-1916. Leipzig: Voss.

Poppelreuter, W. (1923) Zur Psychologie und Pathologie der optischen Wahrnemung. *Zeitschrift fur die gesamte Neurologie und Psychiatrie*, **83**, 26-152.

Poppen, J.L. (1948) Prefrontal lobotomy: technique and general impression based on results in 470 patients subjected to this procedure. *Digest of Neurology and Psychiatry*, **17**, 403-408.

Porteus, S.D. (1950) *The Porteus Maze Test and Intelligence*. Palo Alto, California: Pacific.

Porteus, S.D. (1958) What do the Maze Tests measure? *Australian Journal of Psychology*, **10**, 245-256.

Porteus, S.D. (1959) Recent maze test studies. *British Journal of Medical Psychology*, **32**, 38-43.

Porteus, S.D. (1965) *Porteus Maze Test: Fifty Year's Application*. Palo Alto, California: Pacific.

Porteus, S.D. & Kepner, R. De M. (1944) Mental changes after bilateral prefrontal lobotomy. *Genetic Psychology Monographs*, **29**, 4.

Porteus, S.D. & Peters, H.N. (1947) Psychosurgery and test validity. *Journal of Abnormal and Social Psychology*, **42**, 473-475.

Post, F. (1975) Dementia, depression, and pseudodementia. In *Psychiatric Aspects of Neurological Disease*, eds. Benson, D.F. & Blumer, D. Ch. 6. New York: Grune and Stratton.

Pratt, R.T.C., Warrington, E.K. & Halliday, A.M. (1971) Unilateral ECT as a test for central dominance, with a strategy for treating left handers. *British Journal of Psychiatry*, **119**, 78-83.

Prisko, L.H. (1963) Short-term memory in focal cerebral damage. Unpublished doctoral dissertation. McGill University.

Ramier, A.M. & Hécaen, H. (1970) Role respectif des atteintes frontales et de la latéralisation lesionnelle dans les déficits de la "fluence verbal". *Revue Neurologique*, **123**, 17-22.

Rapaport, D., Gill, M. & Schafer, R. (1945) *Diagnostic Psychological Testing.* Vol. 1, Chicago: Year Book Co.

Raskin, N. & Ehrenberg, R. (1956) Senescence, senility and Alzheimer's disease. *American Journal of Psychiatry*, **113**, 133-136.

Ratcliff, G. & Newcombe, F. (1973) Spatial orientation in man: effects of left, right, and bilateral posterior lesions. *Journal of Neurology, Neurosurgery and Psychiatry*, **36**, 448-454.

Reed, H.B.C. & Reitan, R.M. (1963a) Intelligence test performances of brain-damaged subjects with lateralized motor deficits. *Journal of Consulting Psychology*, **27**, 102-106.

Reed, H.B.C. & Reitan, R.M. (1963b) A comparison of the effects of the normal ageing process with the effects of organic brain-damage on adaptive abilities. *Journal of Gerontology*, **18**, 177-179.

Reed, H.B.C. & Reitan, R.M. (1963c) Changes in abilities associated with the normal ageing process. *Journal of Gerontology*, **18**, 271-274.

Reitan, R.M. (1955a) Investigation of the validity of Halstead's measures of biological intelligence. *Archives of Neurology and Psychiatry*, **73**, 28-35.

Reitan, R.M. (1955b) Certain differential effects of left and right cerebral lesions in human adults. *Journal of Comparative and Physiological Psychology*, **48**, 474-477.

Reitan, R.M. (1958a) Qualitative versus quantitative changes following brain damage. *Journal of Psychology*, **46**, 339-346.

Reitan, R.M. (1959a) Impairment of abstraction ability in brain damage: Quantitative versus qualitative changes. *Journal of Psychology*, **48**, 97-102.

Reitan, R.M. (1962) The comparative psychological significance of ageing with and without organic brain damage. In *Social and Psychological Aspects of Ageing*, eds. Tibbits, C. & Donahue, W. New York: Columbia University Press.

Reitan, R.M. (1964) Psychological deficits resulting from cerebral lesions in man. In *The Frontal Granular Cortex and Behaviour*, eds. Warren, J.M. & Akert, K. Ch. 14. New York: McGraw Hill.

Reitan, R.M. (1966a) Problems and prospects in studying psychological correlates of brain lesions. *Cortex*, **2**, 127-154.

Reitan, R.M. (1966b) A research programme on the psychological effects of brain lesions in human beings. In *International Review of Research in Mental Retardation*, ed. Ellis, N.R. Vol. 1, New York: Academic Press.

Reitan, R.M. (1970) Sensorimotor functions, intelligence and cognition and emotional status in subjects with cerebral lesions. *Perceptual and Motor Skills*, **31**, 275-284.

Reitan, R.W. & Davison, L.A. (eds.) (1974) *Clinical Neuropsychology: Current Status and Applications.* New York: Wiley.

Rey, A. (1941) L'examen psychologique. *Archives de Psychologie*, **28**, 112-164.

Rey, A. (1959) *Le test de copie de figure complexe.* Paris: Editions centre de psychologie appliquée.

Ribot, T. (1904) *Les maladies de la mémoire.* Paris: Alcan.

Richardson, D.M. & Knights, R.M. (1970) A bibliography on dichotic listening. *Cortex*, **6**, 236-240.

Riddoch, G. (1935) Visual disorientation in homonymous half-fields. *Brain*, **58**, 376-382.

Rinnert, C. & Whitaker, H.A. (1973) Semantic confusions by aphasic patients. *Cortex*, **9**, 56-81.

Robin, A.A. (1958) A controlled study of the effects of leucotomy. *Journal of Neurology, Neurosurgery, and Psychiatry*, **21**, 262-269.

Robinson, M.F. & Freeman, W. (1954) *Psychosurgery and the Self.* New York; Grune and Stratton.

Rochford, G. (1971) A study of naming errors in dysphasic and in demented patients. *Neuropsychologia*, **9**, 437-443.

Rokeach, M. (1948) Generalized mental rigidity as a factor in ethnocentrism. *Journal of Abnormal and Social Psychology*, **43**, 259-278.

Romer, A.S. (1955) *The Vertebrate Body.* Second Edition. Philadelphia: Saunders.

Rose, F.C. & Symonds, C.P. (1960) Persistent memory defect following encephalitis. *Brain*, **83**, 195-212.

Rosen, H. (1971) A comparison of two scoring systems for the Memory-for-Designs Test. *Journal of Clinical Psychology*, **27**, 79-81.

Rosvold, H.E., Mirsky, A.F., Sarason, I., Bransome, E.D. & Beck, L.H. (1956) A Continuous Performance Test of brain damage. *Journal of Consulting Psychology*, **20**, 343-350.

Rosvold, H.E. & Mishkin, M. (1950) Evaluation of the effects of prefrontal lobotomy on intelligence. *Canadian Journal of Psychology*, **4**, 122-126.

Roth, M. & Myers, D.H. (1975) The diagnosis of dementia. *British Journal of Psychiatry. Special Publications No.* 9, 87-123.

Rowe, S.N. (1937) Mental changes following the removal of the right cerebral hemisphere for brain tumour. *American Journal of Psychiatry*, **94**, 605-614.

Rubino, C.A. (1970) Hemispheric lateralization of visual perception. *Cortex*, **6**, 102-130.

Russell, W. & Nathan, P. (1946) Traumatic amnesia. *Brain*, **69**, 280-300.

Russell, E.W., Neuringer, C. & Goldstein, G. (1970) *Assessment of Brain Damage: A neuropsychological key approach*. New York: Wiley.

Russell, J.R. & Reitan, R.M. (1955) Psychological abnormalities in agenesis of the corpus callosum. *Journal of Nervous and Mental Disease*, **121**, 205-214.

Russell, W.R. & Whitty, C.W.M. (1955) Studies in traumatic epilepsy. 3. Visual fits. *Journal of Neurology, Neurosurgery and Psychiatry*, **18**, 79-96.

Russo, M. & Vignolo, L.A. (1967) Visual figure-ground discrimination in patients with unilateral cerebral disease. *Cortex*, **3**, 113-127.

Rylander, G. (1939) Personality changes after operations on the frontal lobes: Clinical study of 32 cases. *Acta Psychiatrica et Neurologica*, Supplement 20, 5-81.

Rylander, G. (1943) Mental changes after excision of cerebral tissue. *Acta Psychiatrica et Neurologica*, Supplement 25.

Rylander, G. (1947) Psychological tests and personality analyses before and after frontal lobotomy. *Acta Psychiatrica et Neurologica*, Supplement 47, 383-398.

Salmon, J.H., Gonen, J.Y. & Brown, L. (1971) Ventriculoatrial shunt for hydrocephalus ex-vacuo. Psychological and clinical evaluation. *Disease of the Nervous System*, **32**, 299-307.

Samuels, I., Butters, N., Goodglass, H. & Brody, B.A. (1971) A comparison of subcortical and cortical damage on short-term visual and auditory memory. *Neuropsychologia*, **9**, 293-306.

Sanders, H.I. & Warrington, E.K. (1971) Memory for remote events in amnesic patients. *Brain*, **94**, 661-668.

Satz, P. (1966) Specific and non-specific effects of brain lesions in man. *Journal of Abnormal Psychology*, **71**, 65-70.

Satz, P., Aschenbach, K., Pattishall, E. & Fennell, E. (1965) Order of report, ear asymmetry, and handedness in dichotic listening. *Cortex*, **1**, 377-396.

Satz, P., Richard, W. & Daniels, A. (1967) The alteration of intellectual performance after lateralized brain injury. *Psychonomic Science*, **7**, 369-370.

Saul, R. & Sperry, R.W. (1968) Absence of commissurotomy symptoms with agenesis of the corpus callosum. *Neurology*, **18**, 307.

Schaie, K.W. (1955) A test of behavioral rigidity. *Journal of Abnormal and Social Psychology*, **51**, 604-610.

Schaie, K.W. (1958) Rigidity-flexibility and intelligence. *Psychological Monographs*, 72, No. 9, Whole No. 462.

Schein, J.D. (1962) Cross validation of the continuous performance test for brain damage. *Journal of Consulting Psychology*, **26**, 115-118.

Schmidt, H.E. (1961) An investigation into the relationship between Wechsler-Bellevue discrepancies and electroencephalographic results in terms of lateralization. Postgraduate dissertation for the Diploma in Abnormal Psychology, University of London.

Schmitt, F.O. & Worden, F.G. (eds.) (1974) *The Neurosciences Third Study Program*. Cambridge, Massachusetts: The MIT Press.

Schulhoff, C. & Goodglass, H. (1969) Dichotic listening: side of brain injury and cerebral dominance. *Neuropsychologia*, **7**, 149-160.

Scotti, G. & Spinnler, H. (1970) Colour imperception in unilateral hemisphere-damaged patients. *Journal of Neurology, Neurosurgery, and Psychiatry*, **33**, 22-28.

Scoville, W.B. & Correll, R.E. (1973) Memory and the temporal lobe. A review for clinicians. *Acta Neurochirurgica*, **28**, 251-258.

Scoville, W.B. & Milner, B. (1957) Loss of recent memory after bilateral hippocampal lesions. *Journal of Neurology, Neurosurgery and Psychiatry*, **20**, 11-21.

Semmes, J. (1965) A non-tactual factor in astereognosis. *Neuropsychologia*, **3**, 295-315.

Semmes, J. (1968) Hemispheric specialization: a possible clue to mechanism. *Neuropsychologia*, **6**, 11-26.

Semmes, J., Weinstein, S., Ghent, L. & Teuber, H.L. (1954) Performance on complex tactual tasks after brain injury to man: analyses by locus of lesion. *American Journal of Psychology*, **67**, 220-240.

Semmes, J., Weinstein, S., Ghent, L. & Teuber, H.L. (1955) Spatial orientation in man after cerebral injury—I: Analysis by locus of lesion. *Journal of Psychology*, **39**, 227-244.

Semmes, J., Weinstein, S., Ghent, L. & Teuber, H.L. (1960) *Somatosensory Changes after Penetrating Brain Wounds in man*. Cambridge, Mass.: Harvard University Press.

Semmes, J., Weinstein, S., Ghent, L. & Teuber, H.L. (1963) Correlates of impaired orientation in personal and extra-personal space. *Brain*, **86**, 747-772.

Serafetinides, E.A. (1966) Auditory recall and visual recognition following intracarotid amytal. *Cortex*, **2**, 367-372.

Serafetinides, E.A. & Falconer, M.A. (1962) Some observations on memory impairment after temporal lobectomy for epilepsy. *Journal of Neurology, Neurosurgery and Psychiatry*, **25**, 251-255.

Shallice, T. & Warrington, E.K. (1970) Independent functioning of verbal memory stores: a neuropsychological study. *Quarterly Journal of Experimental Psychology*, **22**, 261-273.

Shallice, T. & Warrington, E.K. (1974) The dissociation between short-term retention of meaningful sounds and verbal material. *Neuropsychologia*, **12**, 553-555.

Shalman, D.C. (1961) The diagnostic use of the McGill Picture Anomalies Test in temporal lobe epilepsy. *Journal of Neurology, Neurosurgery and Psychiatry*, **24**, 220-222.

Shankweiler, D. & Studdert-Kennedy, M. (1967) Identification of consonants and vowels presented to left and right ears. *Quarterly Journal of Experimental Psychology*, **19**, 59-63.

Shapiro, M.B. (1951) Experimental studies of a perceptual anomaly. I: Initial experiments. *Journal of Mental Science*, **97**, 90-100.

Shapiro, M.B. (1952) Experimental studies of a perceptual anomaly. II: Confirmatory and explanatory experiments. *Journal of Mental Science*, **98**, 605-617.

Shapiro, M.B. (1953) Experimental studies of a perceptual anomaly. III: The testing of an exploratory theory. *Journal of Mental Science*, **99**, 394-409.

Shapiro, M.B. (1973) Intensive assessment of the single case: an inductive deductive approach. In *The Psychological Assessment of Mental and Physical Handicaps*, ed. Mittler, P.E. Ch. 21. London: Tavistock Publications.

Shapiro, M.B., Brierley, J., Slater, P. & Beech, H.R. (1962) Experimental studies of a perceptual anomaly. VIII. A new explanation. *Journal of Mental Science*, **108**, 655-668.

Shaw, D.J. (1966) The reliability and validity of the Halstead Category Test. *Journal of Clinical Psychology*, **22**, 176-180.

Sherrington, C.S. (1951) *Man on His Nature*. Second Edition. Cambridge: Cambridge University Press.

Sherwood, M. & McNamee, H.B. (1967) Psychological study of the amnesic syndrome: Effects of interference on recall. *Cortex*, **4**, 359-371.

Shure, G.H. (1954) Intellectual loss following excision of cortical tissue. Unpublished doctoral dissertation, University of Chicago.

Shure, G.H. & Halstead, W.C. (1958) Cerebral localization of intellectual processes. *Psychological Monographs*, **72**, (12), Whole No. 465.

Sidman, M., Stoddard, L.T. & Mohr, J.P. (1968) Some additional quantitative observations of immediate memory in a patient with bilateral hippocampal lesions. *Neuropsychologia*, **6**, 245-254.

Siekert, R.G. & Millikan, C.H. (1955) Syndrome of intermittent inefficiency of the basilar arterial system. *Neurology*, **5**, 625-630.

Silverman, S.M., Bergman, P.S. & Bender, M.B. (1961) The dynamics of transient cerebral blindness. Report of nine episodes following vertebral angiography. *Archives of Neurology*, **4**, 333-348.

Simmel, M.L. & Counts, S. (1957) Some stable response determinants of perception, thinking and learning: A study based on the analysis of a single test. *Genetic Psychology Monographs*, **56**, 3-157.

Simpson, C.D. & Vega, A. (1971) Unilateral brain damage and patterns of age-corrected WAIS subtest scores. *Journal of Clinical Psychology*, **27**, 204-208.

Simpson, J.A. (1969) The clinical neurology of temporal lobe disorders. In Current problems in neuropsychiatry: Schizophrenia, epilepsy, the temporal lobe, ed. Herrington, R.N. *British Journal of Psychiatry*, Special Publication No. 4, 42-48.

Slaby, A.E. & Wyatt, R.J. (1973) *Dementia in the Presenium*. Springfield, Illinois: Thomas.

Smith, A. (1962a) Ambiguities in concepts and studies of "brain damage" and "organicity". *Journal of Nervous and Mental Disease*, **135**, 311-326.

Smith, A. (1962b) Psychodiagnosis of patients with brain tumours. *Journal of Nervous and Mental Disease*, **135**, 513-533.

Smith, A. (1966a) Certain hypothesized hemispheric differences in language and visual functions in human adults. *Cortex*, **2**, 109-126.

Smith, A. (1965) Verbal and nonverbal test performances of patients with "acute" lateralized brain lesions (tumours). *Journal of Nervous and Mental Disease*, **141**, 517-523.

Smith, A. (1966b) Intellectual functions in patients with lateralized frontal tumours. *Journal of Neurology, Neurosurgery and Psychiatry*, **29**, 52-59.

Smith, A. (1966c) Speech and other functions after left (dominant) hemispherectomy. *Journal of Neurology, Neurosurgery and Psychiatry*, **29**, 467-471.

Smith, A. (1967) Nondominant hemispherectomy: Neuropsychological implications for human brain functions. *Proceedings of the 75th Annual Convention, American Psychological Association*.

Smith, A. (1969) Nondominant hemispherectomy. *Neurology*, **19**, 442-445.

Smith, A. (1973) *Symbol Digit Modalities Test*. Los Angeles: Western Psychological Services.

Smith, A. (April 1974) Diaschisis and neuropsychology. *The Bulletin of the International Neuropsychology Society*, 2-3.

Smith, A. (1975) Neuropsychological testing in neurological disorders. In *Advances in Neurology*, ed. Friedlander, W.J. Vol. 7. New York: Raven Press.

Smith, A. & Burklund, C.W. (1966) Dominant hemispherectomy: Preliminary report on neuropsychological sequelae. *Science*, **153**, 1280-1282.

Smith, A. & Kinder, E.F. (1959) Changes in psychological test performances of brain-operated schizoprenics after eight years. *Science*, **129**, 149-150.

Smith, A. & Sugar, O. (1975) Development of above normal language and intelligence 21 years after left hemispherectomy. *Neurology*, **25**, 813-818.

Smith, E. (1974) Influence of site of impact on cognitive impairment persisting long after severe closed head injury. *Journal of Neurology, Neurosurgery, and Psychiatry*, **37**, 719-726.

Smith, K.U. & Akelaitis, A.J. (1942) Studies of the corpus callosum. I. Laterality in behavior and bilateral motor organization in man before and after section of the corpus callosum. *Archives of Neurology and Psychiatry*, **47**, 519-543. Chicago.

Sokal, R.R. & Sneath, P.H. (1963) *Principles of Numerical Taxonomy*. San Francisco: Freeman.

Solomon, P. & Patch, V.D. (1974) *Handbook of Psychiatry*. Third Edition. Los Altos, California: Lange Medical Publications.

Solursh, L.P., Margulies, A.I., Ashem, B. & Stasiak, E.A. (1965) The relationship of agenesis of the corpus callosum to perception and learning. *Journal of Nervous and Mental Disease*, **141**, 180-189.

Sparks, R. & Geschwind, N. (1968) Dichotic listening in man after section of the neocortical commissures. *Cortex*, **4**, 3-16.

Sparks, R., Goodglass, H. & Nickel, B. (1970) Ipsilateral versus contralateral extinction in dichotic listening from hemisphere lesions. *Cortex*, **6**, 249-260.

Spellacy, F.J. & Spreen, O. (1969) A short form of the Token Test. *Cortex*, **5**, 390-397.

Sperry, R.W. (1961) Cerebral organization and behaviour. *Science*, **133**, 1749-1757.

Sperry, R.W. (1964) The great cerebral commissure. *Scientific American*, **210**, 42-52.

Sperry, R.W., Gazzaniga, M.S. & Bogen, J.E. (1969) Interhemispheric relationships: the neocortical commissures; syndromes of hemispheric disconnection. In *Handbook of Clinical Neurology*, eds. Vinken, P.J. & Bruyn, G.W. Vol. 4, Ch. 14. Amsterdam: North-Holland.

Spinnler, H. (1971) Deficit in associating figures and colours in brain damaged patients. *Brain Research*, **31**, 370-371.

Spreen, O. & Benton, A.L. (1969) *Neurosensory Centre Comprehensive Examination for Aphasia*. Canada: Neuropsychology Laboratory, University of Victoria.

Squire, L.R. (1974) Recent memory as affected by aging. *Neuropsychologia*, **12**, 429-435.

Squire, L.R. (1975) A stable impairment in remote memory following electroconvulsive therapy. *Neuropsychologia*, **13**, 51-58.

Starr, A. & Phillips, L. (1970) Verbal and motor memory in the amnestic syndrome. *Neuropsychologia*, **8**, 75-88.

Stepien, L. & Sierpinski, S. (1964) Impairment of recent memory after temporal lesions in man. *Neuropsychologia*, **2**, 291-303.

Strauss, H. (1924) Uber konstruktive apraxie. *Monatsschrift fur Psychiatrie und Neurologie*, **63**, 739-748.

Strom-Olsen, R. & Carlisle, S. (1971) Bi-Frontal Stereotactic Tractotomy. *British Journal of Psychiatry*, **118**, 141-154.

Stroop, J.R. (1935) Studies of interference in serial verbal reactions. *Journal of Experimental Psychology*, **18**, 643-662.

Strub, R.L. & Gardner, H. (1974) The repetition defect in conduction aphasia: Mnestic or linguistic? *Brain and Language*, **1**, 241-255.

Subirana, A. (1958) The prognosis in aphasia in relation to cerebral dominance and handedness. *Brain*, **81**, 415-425.

Subirana, A. (1969) Handedness and cerebral dominance. In *Handbook of Clinical Neurology*, eds. Vinken, P.J. & Bruyn, G.W. Vol. 4, Ch. 13. Amsterdam: North-Holland Publishing Company.

Sunderland, S. (1940) The distribution of commissural fibres in the corpus callosum of the macaque monkey. *Journal of Neurology and Psychiatry*, **3**, 9-18.

Sweet, W.H. (1973) Treatment of medically intractable mental disease by limited frontal leucotomy-justifiable? *New England Journal of Medicine*, **289**, 1117-1125.

Sweet, W.H., Talland, G.A. & Ervin, F.R. (1959) Loss of recent memory following section of fornix. *Transactions of the American Neurological Association*, **84**, 76-82.

Swisher, L.P. & Sarno, M.T. (1969) Token Test scores of three matched patient groups: left brain-damaged with aphasia; right brain-damaged without aphasia; non-brain-damaged. *Cortex*, **5**, 264-273.

Sykes, M.K. & Tredgold, R.F. (1964) Restricted orbital undercutting. *British Journal of Psychiatry*, **110**, 609-640.

Talland, G. (1965) *Deranged Memory*. New York: Academic Press.

Talland, G.A., Sweet, W.H. & Ballantine, H.T. (1967) Amnesic syndrome with anterior communicating artery aneurism. *Journal of Nervous and Mental Disorders*, **145**, 179-192.

Talland, G.A. & Waugh, N.C. (1969) *The Pathology of Memory* New York: Academic Press.

Tallent, N. (1963) *Clinical Psychological Consultation*. Englewood Cliffs, New Jersey: Prentice-Hall Inc.

Taylor, A. & Warrington, E.K. (1971) Visual agnosia: A single case report. *Cortex*, **7**, 152-161.

Taylor, A.M. & Warrington, E.K. (1973) Visual discrimination in patients with localized cerebral lesions. *Cortex*, **9**, 82-93.

Teng, E.L. & Sperry, R.W. (1973) Interhemispheric interaction during simultaneous bilateral presentation of letters or digits in commissurotomized patients. *Neuropsychologia*, **11**, 131-140.

Terrace, H. (1959) The effects of retinal locus and attention on the perception of words. *Journal of Experimental Psychology*, **58**, 382-385.

Terzian, H. (1958) Observations on the Clinical Symptomatology of Bilateral Partial or Total Removal of the Temporal Lobes in Man. In *Temporal lobe epilepsy*, eds. Baldwin, M. & Bailey, P. Springfield, Illinois: Thomas.

Teuber, H.L. (1950) Neuropsychology. In *Recent Advances in Diagnostic Psychological Testing*, ed. Harrower, M.R. Ch. 3. Springfield, Illinois: Thomas.

Teuber, H.L. (1955) Physiological psychology. *Annual Review of Psychology*, **6**, 267-296.

Teuber, H.L. (1959) Some alterations in behavior after cerebral lesions in man. In *Evolution of Nervous Control from Primitive Organisms to Man*, ed. Bass, A.D. Washington: American Association for the Advancement of Science.

Teuber, H.L. (1960) The premorbid personality and reaction to brain damage. *American Journal of Orthopsychiatry*, **30**, 322-329.

Teuber, H.L. (1964a) The riddle of frontal lobe function in man. In *The Frontal Granular Cortex and Behavior*, eds. Warren, J.M. & Akert, K. Ch. 20. New York: McGraw Hill.

Teuber, H.L. (1975) Recovery of function after brain injury in man. *Ciba Foundation Symposium* 34 (new series) 159-190. Amsterdam: Elsevier.

Teuber, H.L., Battersby, W.S. & Bender, M.B. (1949) Changes in visual searching performance following cerebral lesions. *American Journal of Physiology*, Vol. 159, 592 (Abs.)

Teuber, H.L., Battersby, W.S. & Bender, M.B. (1951) Performance of complex visual tasks after cerebral lesions. *Journal of Nervous and Mental Disease*, **114**, 413-429.

Teuber, H.L., Battersby, W.H. & Bender, M.B. (1960) *Visual field Defects after Penetrating Missile Wounds of the Brain*. Cambridge, Massachusetts: Harvard University Press.

Teuber, H.L. & Liebert, R.S. (1958) Specific and general effects of brain injury in man; evidence of both from a single task. *Archives of Neurology and Psychiatry*, **80**, 403-407.

Teuber, H.L. & Mishkin, M. (1954) Judgement of visual and postural vertical after brain injury. *Journal of Psychology*, **38**, 161-175.

Teuber, H.L. & Rudel, R.G. (1962) Behaviour after cerebral lesions in children and adults. *Developmental Medicine and Child Neurology*, **4**, 3-20.

Teuber, H.L. & Weinstein, S. (1954) Performance on a formboard task after penetrating brain injury. *Journal of Psychology*, **38**, 177-190.

Teuber, H.L. & Weinstein, S. (1956) Ability to discover hidden figures after cerebral lesions. *Archives of Neurology and Psychiatry*, **76**, 369-379.

Teuber, H.L. & Weinstein, S. (1958) Equipotentiality versus cortical localization. *Science*, **127**, 241-242.

Thurstone, L.L. & Jeffrey, T.E.(1956) Closure Flexibility Test. (Concealed Figures). Chicago: Industrial Relations Center.

Tooth, G.C. & Newton, Mary P. (1961) *Leucotomy in England and Wales*, 1942-1954. London:

Tow, P.M. (1955) *Personality Changes Following Frontal Leucotomy*. London: Oxford University Press.

Trescher, J.H. & Ford, F.R. (1937) Colloid cyst of the third ventricle. *Archives of Neurology and Psychiatry*, **37**, 959-973.

Trevarthen, C.B. (1969) Cerebral midline relations reflected in split-brain studies of the higher integrative functions. Paper presented at XIX International Congress of Psychology, London.

Trevarthen, C. (1974a) Analysis of cerebral activities that generate and regulate consciousness in commissurotomy patients. In *Hemispheric Function in the Human Brain*, eds. Diamond, S.J. & Beaumont, J.G. Ch. 9. London: Paul Elek (Scientific Books).

Trevarthen, C. (1974b) Functional relations of disconnected hemispheres with the brain stem and with each other: monkey and man. In *Hemisphere Disconnection and Cerebral Function*, eds. Kinsbourne, M. & Lynn Smith, W. Ch. 10. Springfield, Illinois: Thomas.

Tureen, R.G., Schwartz, M.L. & Dennerll, R.D. (1968) The Halstead-Reitan Neuropsychological Battery in brain damaged, normal and epileptic subjects. *Perceptual and Motor Skills*, **27**, 439-442.

Tzavaras, A. & Hécaen, H. (1970) Colour vision disturbances in subjects with unilateral cortical lesions. *Brain Research*, **24**, 546-547.

Tzavaras, A., Hécaen, H. & Le Bras, H. (1970) The problem of specificity of deficit of human face recognition in unilateral hemispheric lesions. *Neuropsychologia*, **8**, 403-416.

Tzavaras, A., Hécaen, H. & Le Bras, H. (1971) Disorders of color vision after unilateral cortical lesions. *Revue Neurologique*, **124**, 396-402.

Tzavaras, A., Merienne, L. & Masure, M.C. (1973) Prosopagnosie, amnésie et troubles du langage par lesion temporale gauche chez un sujet gaucher. *Encephale*, **62**, 382-394.

Tzavaras, A. & Tzavaras, H. (1975) Cited as personal communication by Howes & Boller.

Van Wagenen, W.P. & Herren, R.Y. (1940) Surgical division of commissural pathways in the corpus callosum; relation to spread of an epileptic attack. *Archives of Neurology and Psychiatry*, **44**, 740-759.

Vega, A. & Parsons, O.A.(1967) Cross-validation of the Halstead-Reitan tests for brain damage. *Journal of Consulting Psychology*, **31**, 619-625.

Victor, M., Angevine, J.B., Mancall, E.L. & Fisher, C.M. (1961) Memory loss with lesions of the hippocampal formation. Report of a case with some remarks on the anatomical basis of memory. *Archives of Neurology*, **5**, 244-263.

Victor, M. & Yakovlev, P.I. (1955) S.S. Korsakoff's psychic disorder in conjunction with peripheral neuritis. A translation of Korsakoff's original article with brief comments on the author and his contribution to clinical medicine. *Neurology*, **5**, 394-406.

Vignolo, L.A. (1969) Auditory agnosia: A review and report of recent evidence. In *Contributions to Clinical Neuropsychology*, ed. Benton, A.L. Ch. 7. Chicago: Aldine.

Vinken, P.J. & Bruyn, G.W. (1969) *Handbook of Clinical Neurology*. Amsterdam: New Holland.

Volpe, A. & Kastenbaum, R. (1967) Beer and TLC. *American Journal of Nursing*, **67**, 100-103.

Von Monakow, C. (1911) Localization of brain functions. *Journal fur Psychologie und Neurologie*, **17**, 185.

Vosburg, R. (1962) Lobotomy in Western Pennsylvania: looking back over ten years. *American Journal of Psychiatry*, **119**, 503-510.

Wada, J. (1949) A new method for the determination of the side of cerebral speech dominance. A preliminary report on the intracarotid injection of sodium amytal in man. *Igaku to Siebutsugaku*, **14**, 221-222.

Walsh, E.G. (1964) *Physiology of the Nervous System*. Second Edition. London: Longmans.

Walsh, F.B. & Hoyt, W.F. (1969) The visual sensory system: anatomy, physiology, and topographic diagnosis. In *Handbook of Clinical Neurology*, eds. Vinken, P.J. & Bruyn, G.W. Vol. 2, Ch. 19. Amsterdam: New Holland.

Walsh, K.W. (1960) Surgical modification of the personality. Unpublished Master's thesis, University of Melbourne.

Walsh, K.W. (1976) Neuropsychological aspects of modified leucotomy. In *Neurosurgical Treatment in Psychiatry, Pain and Epilepsy*, ed. Sweet, W.H. Ch. 11. Baltimore: University Park Press.

Warren, J.M. & Akert, K. (1964) *The Frontal Granular Cortex and Behavior*. New York: McGraw-Hill.

Warrington, E.K. (1962) The completion of visual forms across hemianopic field defects. *Journal of Neurology, Neurosurgery and Psychiatry*, **25**, 208-217.

Warrington, E. (1969) Constructional apraxia. In *Handbook of Clinical Neurology*, eds. Vinken, P.J. & Bruyn, G.W. Vol. 4, Ch. 4. Amsterdam: New Holland.

Warrington, E.K. (1971) Neurological Disorders of memory. *British Medical Bulletin*, No. 3, 243-247.

Warrington, E.K. (1973) Neurological deficits. In *The Psychological Assessment of Mental and Physical Handicaps*, Ch. 9. London: Tavistock Publications.

Warrington, E.K. & Baddeley, A.D. (1974) Amnesia and memory for visual location. *Neuropsychologia*, **12**, 257-263.

Warrington, E.K. & James, M. (1967a) An experimental investigation of facial recognition in patients with cerebral lesions. *Cortex*, **3**, 317-326.

Warrington, E.K. & James, M. (1967b) Tachistoscopic number estimation in patients with unilateral cerebral lesions. *Journal of Neurology, Neurosurgery and Psychiatry*, **30**, 468-474.

Warrington, E.K., James, M. & Kinsbourne, M. (1966) Drawing disability in relation to laterality of cerebral lesion. *Brain*, **89**, 53-82.

Warrington, E.K., Logue, V. & Pratt, R.T.C. (1971) The anatomical localization of selective impairment of auditory short-term memory. *Neuropsychologia*, **9**, 377-387.

Warrington, E.K. & Rabin, P. (1970) Perceptual matching in patients with cerebral lesions. *Neuropsychologia*, **8**, 475-487.

Warrington, E.K. & Rabin, P. (1971a) A preliminary investigation between visual perception and visual memory. *Cortex*, **6**, 87-96.

Warrington, E.K. & Rabin, P. (1971b) Visual span of apprehension in patients with unilateral cerebral lesions. *Quarterly Journal of Experimental Psychology*, **23**, 423-431.

Warrington, E.K. & Sanders, H.I. (1971) The fate of old memories. *Quarterly Journal of Experimental Psychology*, **23**, 432-442.

Warrington, E.K. & Shallice, T. (1969) The selective impairment of auditory verbal short-term memory. *Brain*, **92**, 885-896.

Warrington, E.K. & Shallice, T. (1972) Neuropsychological evidence of visual storage in short-term memory tasks. *Quarterly Journal of Experimental Psychology*, **24**, 30-40.

Warrington, E.K. & Silberstein, M. (1970) A questionnaire technique for investigating very long-term memory. *Quarterly Journal of Experimental Psychology*, **22**, 508-512.

Warrington, E.K. & Taylor, A.M. (1973) The contribution of the right parietal lobe to object recognition. *Cortex*, **9**, 152-164.

Warrington, E.K. & Weiskrantz, L. (1968) A study of learning and retention in amnesic patients. *Neuropsychologia*, **6**, 283-292.

Warrington, E.K. & Weiskrantz, L. (1972) An analysis of short-term and long-term memory defects in man. In *The Physiological Basis of Memory*, ed. Deutsch, J.A. New York: Academic Press.

Warrington, E.K. & Weiskrantz. L. (1974) The effect of prior learning on subsequent retention in amnesic patients. *Neuropsychologia*, **12**, 419-428.

Watson, R.T., Heilman, K.M., Cauthen, J.C. & King, F.A. (1973) Neglect following cingulectomy. *Neurology*, **23**, 1003-1007.

Watson, R.T., Heilman, K.M., Miller, B.D. & King, F.A. (1973) Neglect following mesencephalic reticular formation lesions (Abstract). *Neurology*, **23**, 395.

Watson, C.G., Thomas, R.W., Anderson, D. & Felling, J. (1968) Differentiation of organics from schizophrenics at two chronicity levels by use of the Reitan-Halstead organic test battery. *Journal of Consulting and Clinical Psychology*, **32**, 679-684.

Wechsler, D. (1944) *The Measurement of Adult Intelligence*. Third Edition. Baltimore: Williams and Wilkins.

Wechsler, D. (1958) *The Measurement and Appraisal of Adult Intelligence*. Fourth Edition. New York: Williams and Wilkins.

Weigl, E. (1941) On the psychology of the so-called process of abstraction. *Journal of Abnormal and Social Psychology*, **36**, 3-33.

Weingartner, H. (1968) Verbal learning in patients with temporal lobe lesions. *Journal of Verbal Learning and Verbal Behavior*, **7**, 520-526.

Weinstein, S. (1965) Deficits concomitant with aphasia or lesions of either cerebral hemisphere. *Cortex*, **1**, 154-169.

Weinstein, S., Semmes, J., Ghent, L. & Teuber, H.L. (1956) Spatial orientation in man after cerebral injury. II. Analysis according to concomitant defects. *Journal of Psychology*, **42**, 249-263.

Weinstein, S. & Sersen, E.A. (1961) Tactual sensitivity as a function of handedness and laterality. *Journal of Comparative and Physiological Psychology*, **54**, 665-669.

Weinstein, S. & Teuber, H.L. (1957) The role of pre-injury education and intellectual loss after brain injury. *Journal of Comparative and Physiological Psychology*, **50**, 535-539.

Weinstein, S. & Teuber, H.L. (1957) Effects of penetrating brain injury on intelligence test scores. *Science*, **125**, 1036-1037.

Weinstein, S., Teuber, H.L., Ghent, L. & Semmes, J. (1955) Complex visual test performance after penetrating brain injury in man. *American Psychologist*, **10**, 408.

Weiskrantz, L. (1968) Some traps and pontifications. In *Analysis of Behavioural Change*, ed. Weiskrantz, L. Ch. 15. New York: Harper and Row.

Weiskrantz, L. (ed.) (1968) *Analysis of Behavioural Change*. New York: Harper and Row.

Weiskrantz, L. & Warrington, E.K. (1970a) A study of forgetting in amnesic patients. *Neuropsychologia*, **8**, 281-288.

Weiskrantz, L. & Warrington, E.K. (1970b) Verbal learning and retention by amnesic patients using partial information. *Psychonomic Science*, **20**, 210-211.

Wells, C.E. (1971) *Dementia*. Philadelphia: Davis.

Werner, H. (1946) The concept of rigidity: A critical evaluation. *Psychological Review*, **53**, 43-52.

Wheeler, L. (1963) Predictions of brain damage from an aphasia screening test: an application of discriminant functions and a comparison with a non-linear method of analysis. *Perceptual and Motor Skills*, **17**, 63-80.

Wheeler, L. & Reitan, R.M. (1963) Discriminant functions applied to the problem of predicting cerebral damage from behavioral tests: a cross validation study. *Perceptual and Motor Skills*, **16**, 681-701.

Wheeler, L., Burke, C.J. & Reitan, R.M. (1963) An application of discriminant functions to the problem of predicting brain-damage using behavioral variables. *Perceptual and Motor Skills*, **16**, 417-440.

Whitaker, H.A. (1971) *On the Representation of Language in the Human Brain*. Edmonton, Canada: Linguistic Research Inc.

White, M.J. (1969) Laterality differences in perception: a review. *Psychological Bulletin*, **72**, 387-405.

White, M.J. (1972) Hemispheric asymmetries in tachistoscopic information-processing. *British Journal of Psychology*, **63**, 497-508.

Whitty, C.W.M. & Lewin, W. (1960) A Korsakoff syndrome in the post-cingulectomy confusional state. *Brain*, **83**, 648-653.

Whitty, C.W.M. & Lishman, W.A. (1966) Amnesia in cerebral disease. In *Amnesia*, eds. Whitty, C.W.M. & Zangwill, O. New York: Appleton-Century-Crofts.

Whitty, C.W.M. & Newcombe, F. (1965) Disabilities associated with lesions in the posterior parietal region of the nondominant hemisphere. *Neuropsychologia*, **3**, 175-186.

Whitty, C.W.M. & Zangwill, O.L. (eds.) (1966) *Amnesia*. London: Butterworth.

Wickelgren, W.A. (1968) Sparing of short-term memory in an amnesic patient: Implications for strength theory of memory. *Neuropsychologia*, **6**, 235-244.

Wilkins, R.H. (1965) *Neurosurgical Classics*. New York: Johnson Reprint Corporation.

Williams, D. (1956) The structure of emotions reflected in epileptic experiences. *Brain*, **79**, 28-67.

Williams, D. (1969) Temporal lobe syndromes. In *Handbook of Neurology*, eds. Vinken, P.J. & Bruyn, G.W. Vol. 2, Ch. 22. Amsterdam: North-Holland.

Williams, D. & Gassel, M.M. (1962) Visual function in patients with homonymous hemianopia. Part I: The visual fields. *Brain*, **85**, 175-250.

Williams, M. (1965) *Mental Testing in Clinical Practice*. London: Pergamon.

Williams, M. (1970) *Brain Damage and the Mind*. Harmondsworth, Middlesex: Penguin.

Williams, M. (1973) Geriatric patients. In *The Psychological Assessment of Mental and Physical Handicaps*, ed. Mittler, P. Ch. 11. London: Tavistock Publications.

Wilson, P.J.E. (1970) Cerebral hemispherectomy for infantile hemiplegia. *Brain*, **93**, 147-180.

Wittenborn, J.R. & Holzberg, J.D. (1951) The Wechsler-Bellevue and descriptive diagnosis. *Journal of Consulting Psychology*, **15**, 325-329.

Wolff, H.G. (1962) Discussion of Teuber's paper. In *Interhemispheric Relations and Cerebral Dominance*, ed. Mountcastle, V.B. Baltimore: Johns Hopkins Press.

Woods, R.T. & Piercy, M. (1974) A similarity between amnesic memory and amnesic forgetting. *Neuropsychologia*, **12**, 437-445.

Woodworth, R.S. & Schlosberg, H. (1954) *Experimental Psychology*. Third Edition. London: Methuen.

Woollam, D.H.M. (1958) Concepts of the brain and its functions in classical antiquity. In *The History and Philosophy of Knowledge of the Brain and its Functions*, ed. Poynter, F.N.L. Oxford: Blackwell.

Worster-Drought, C. (1931) Mental symptoms associated with tumours of the frontal lobes. *Proceedings of the Royal Society of Medicine*, **24**, 1007.

Wright, M.K. (1959) *Fibre Systems of the Brain and Spinal Cord*. Second Edition. Johannesburg: Witwatersrand University Press.

Wyke, M. (1966) Postural arm-drift associated with brain lesions in man. *Archives of Neurology*, **15**, 329-334.

Wyke, M. & Holgate, D. (1973) Colour-naming defects in dysphasic patients. A qualitative analysis. *Neuropsychologia*, **11**, 451-461.

Yarcorzynski, G.K., Boshes, B. & Davis, L. (1948) Psychological changes produced by frontal lobotomy. *Research Publications, Associated for Research in Nervous and Mental Disease*, **27**, 642-657.

Yamadori, A. & Albert, M.L. (1973) Word category aphasia. *Cortex*, **9**, 112-125.

Yates, A. (1954) The validity of some psychological tests of brain damage. *Psychological Bulletin*, **51**, 359-380.

Yates, A.J. (1966) Psychological deficit. *Annual Review of Psychology*, **17**, 111-144.

Zaidel, D. & Sperry, R.W. (1974) Memory impairment after commissurotomy in man. *Brain*, **97**, 263-272.

Zangwill, O. (1943) Clinical tests of memory impairment. *Proceedings of the Royal Society of Medicine*, **36**, 576-580.

Zangwill, O.L. (1946) Some qualitative observations on verbal memory in cases of cerebral lesions. *British Journal of Psychology*, **37**, 8-19.

Zangwill, O. (1960) *Cerebral Dominance and its Relation to Psychological Function*. Springfield, Illinois: Thomas.

Zangwill, O.L. (1961) Asymmetry of Cerebral Hemisphere Function. In *Scientific Aspects of Neurology*, ed. Garland, H. London: Livingstone.

Zangwill, O. (1966a) The amnesic syndrome. In *Amnesia*, eds. Whitty, C.W.M. & Zangwill, O. London: Butterworths.

Zangwill, O. (1966b) Psychological deficits associated with frontal lobe lesions. *International Journal of Neurology*, **5**, 395.

Zangwill, O.L. (1969) Intellectual status in aphasia. In *Handbook of Clinical Neurology*, eds. Vinken, P.J. & Bruyn, G.W. Ch. 6. Amsterdam: North-Holland.

Zangwill, O.L. (June 1972) Communication. *XVIIth International Neuropsychological Symposium*. Aix-en-Provence.

Zimmerman, I.L., Woo-sam, J.M. & Glasser, A.J. (1973) *The Clinical Interpretation of the Wechsler Adult Intelligence Scale*. New York: Grune and Stratton.

Zollinger, R. (1935) Removal of left cerebral hemisphere: report of a case. *Archives of Neurology and Psychiatry*, **34**, 1055-1064.

Zulch, K.J. (1971) Some basic patterns of the collateral circulation of the cerebral arteries. In *Cerebral Circulation and Stroke*, ed. Zulch, K.J. New York: Springer-Verlag.

Zurif, E.B. & Bryden, M.P. (1969) Familial handedness and left-right difference in auditory and visual perception. *Neuropsychologia*, **7**, 179-187.

Zurif, E.B. & Ramier, A.M. (1972) Some effects of unilateral brain damage on the presentation of dichotically presented phoneme sequence and digits. *Neuropsychologia*, **10**, 103-110.

Index